DEATH COMES TO THE MAIDEN

DEATH COMES TO THE MAIDEN

Sex and Execution 1431–1933

Camille Naish

London and New York

First published in 1991
by Routledge
11 New Fetter Lane, London EC4P 4EE

Simultaneously published in the USA and Canada
by Routledge
a division of Routledge, Chapman and Hall Inc.
29 West 35th Street, New York, NY 10001

© 1991 Camille Naish
set in 10/12pt Garamond by
Selectmove
Printed and bound in Great Britain by
TJ Press (Padstow) Ltd, Padstow, Cornwall

All rights reserved. No part of this book may be reprinted or
reproduced or utilized in any form or by any electronic,
mechanical, or other means, now known or hereafter
invented, including photocopying and recording, or in any
information storage or retrieval system, without permission in
writing from the publishers.

British Library Cataloguing in Publication Data
Naish, Camille
Death comes to the maiden: Sex and execution, 1431–1933.
1. Women: Capital punishment. History
I. Title
364.66

Library of Congress Cataloging in Publication Data
Naish, Camille
Death comes to the maiden: sex and execution, 1431–1933/Camille Naish.
p. cm.
Includes bibliographical references and index.
1. Executions and executioners-History. 2. Women prisoners-History. I. Title.
HV8551.N35 1991
364.6'6'082-dc20
91–2438
CIP
ISBN 0 415 05585 7

To my parents, Ruth and Michael Naish

Go on, o go on past me!
Go on, you rough scythe-man!
I am still young, go, dear man,
Go on, and do not touch me.
     (Matthias Claudias, *Death and the Maiden*)

The Queen turned crimson with fury, and, after glaring at her for a moment like a wild beast, screamed 'Off with her head! Off –!'

 'Nonsense!' said Alice, very loudly and decidedly, and the Queen was silent.
     (Lewis Carroll, *Alice's Adventures in Wonderland*)

    Torture of every kind
    may await me;
    I scorn torment and pain.
    (Mozart/Bretzner, *Die Entführung aus dem Serail*)

CONTENTS

List of illustrations viii
Preface ix

INTRODUCTION 1

1 BURIALS AND BURNINGS 7

2 BEHEADING 37

3 HANGING 80

4 DAME GUILLOTINE 103
   'Tis crime and not the scaffold: Charlotte Corday, Marie Antoinette 110
   Citizen bluestockings: Olympe de Gouges, Manon Roland 132
   The sleep of innocence, or wives, whores and parricide 157

5 THE ART OF IMMOLATION 185
   Tragedy, Romance: Antigone and Joan 185
   Romantic madness 211
   Sisterhood and sacrifice 223

CONCLUSION 243

Notes 252
Bibliography 257
Index 263

ILLUSTRATIONS

between pages 36 and 37
1 Joan of Arc at the stake. (Fifteenth-century manuscript; Bibliothèque Nationale)
2 Thomas Artur de Lally-Tollendal, beheaded in May 1766. (Anonymous etching; Bibliothèque Nationale)
3 Robespierre as executioner, showing a guillotine and the victim strapped to the *bascule*. (Anonymous etching; Bibliothèque Nationale)
4 Portrait of Charlotte Corday above a drawing of her arrest, with Marat dying in his bath. (Duplessis-Bertaux; Bibliothèque Nationale)
5 Olympe de Gouges. (Imaginary portrait; Bibliothèque Nationale)
6 A couple being drowned on the Loire. (Thermidorian engraving; Bibliothèque Nationale)
7 Execution of Madame Elisabeth, May 1794. (Anonymous German print; Bibliothèque Nationale)

PREFACE

This book would not have been written but for two students. The first was enrolled in a third-year French course at the University of Wisconsin in the fall of 1980; the class was asked to prepare oral presentations on something typically French. While everyone else spoke of Camembert, the Eiffel Tower, Monet or General de Gaulle, this young woman did a highly original presentation on the Sanson family, executioners in Paris and Versailles from 1688 to 1847. Fascinated, I promptly devoured what books the library contained on the subject, which I thought might make an interesting play.

The second student had come from Paris to study violin at the University of Tulsa. In the spring of 1982 he suffered a collapsed lung after sunbathing. The doctors had to open his chest and insert a tube to re-inflate the cavity – a procedure repeated four times, without a general anaesthetic. It was thought necessary to keep the patient conscious, and also to inform him of what was going on; however, in the horror of the moment he did not always understand. Thus a translator was needed. Having what are sometimes termed 'language skills', I was present for three of the four operations, holding the young man's hands and translating his howls of pain. This experience of civilised barbarity was something of a jolt. Banal though it must be to say it reminded me of the Sansons and their horrendous duties, that is nonetheless what happened. I began finding out more about these intriguing executioners, intending to write their biography. Struck by their evident dislike for what they did – and particularly the dismay they felt at executing women – I subsequently decided this would be a better topic: guillotined women, and their *bourreaux*. While many individual biographies existed of famous executed females, such as Charlotte Corday, or Marie Antoinette, I was not aware of any book that put them all together and compared their deaths; nor of one that attempted, while so doing, to consider the lives of the men who beheaded them. The stories of the executed women are being published first under the title *Death Comes to the Maiden*; the history of the Sanson family is scheduled for a second volume.

Since beheading was not the only means of giving death, the study began to grow in other directions, including burning, burial alive and hanging. Reading the lives of the protagonists, I was struck by the extent to which fiction entered their biographies, as if no absolute means existed for determining parts of the historical truth; reading the literary treatments of their lives, I was struck by details of execution which reflected historical fact. In consequence my approach to novels and dramas dealing with executed women is more historical than is customary in present academic trends, while the approach to those women's lives is frankly narrative: horizontal threads, suddenly cut through. The civil rights aspect of the question seemed particularly important with regard to the beheadings of the French Revolution, and Olympe de Gouges' insistence that women who were fully punishable by law should also enjoy full legal status. The state's right to punish private individuals in the first place had been laid down by Rousseau in his *Social Contract*: 'Since every wrongdoer attacks the society's law, he becomes by his deed a rebel and a traitor to the country; by violating its law, he ceases to be a member of it.' Trial and judgement 'are the proof that he has broken the social treaty and is in consequence no longer a member of the state'. But what to think of a contract which omitted to consult half its citizens?

The choice of chapters included in *Death Comes to the Maiden* reflects not only my own idiosyncrasies but the material available in libraries. A grant from the University of Tulsa enabled me to pursue research on the Sanson family in the Bibliothèque Nationale and the Archives Nationales of France; the University of Tulsa library was also relatively well equipped with books on religious persecution. The library of St John's College in Santa Fe graciously allowed me borrowing privileges, including access to a bequest of books about the French Revolution. Given the enormity of the general topic, however, it seemed physically impossible to broach certain of its aspects: women put to death under the Third Reich, executions in the former Communist countries or any portion of the East.

In the course of carrying out research from the plains of Oklahoma and the Sangre de Cristo mountains I incurred many debts of gratitude. Dr Germaine Greer was kind enough to encourage the project at an early stage, when it concerned the Sanson family. Nell Gotkovsky and Daniel Odier extended hospitality and help in Paris, as did Brigitte Bell, Dr Michèle Jacquet and Henry Gronnier. Harold Peterson of the Minneapolis Institute of Art patiently listened to queries about illustrations. Numerous other friends offered practical assistance or suggestions: of those then in Tulsa I am particularly indebted to Susan Hastings, Charlotte Stewart, Sabra Martin and Jan Donley. In Santa Fe I am grateful to Pat Pritchard and Ellen Bayard O'Neill; to Alice Davis of the Santa Fe Public Library, and Florence Goulesque, James Benefiel and Tracy Kimball of the St John's College Library. At Routledge I would like particularly to thank Andrew

Wheatcroft, Penny Wheeler, Margaret Deith, Julia Moffat and Hilary Moor; I am also indebted to Brian and Jean Hopkins and Michael Turner. Then, too, words of encouragement from Germaine Brée, Célia Bertin, Annie Le Brun, Radovan Ivsic, Ida Gotkovsky, Anne Martin and James Robinson have been much appreciated. Nor would I wish to conclude without mentioning the late Mrs June Ortiz, of Santa Fe, whose courage, elegance and warmth will not be forgotten.

Four people in particular gave help and encouragement without which the book would certainly not have been completed. It is impossible adequately to thank Nell Gotkovsky for her unfailingly generous support. A former student of history from Harvard, Dr Leslie Choquette, provided answers to endless questions and read early chapters in a most felicitous reversal of the student–teacher relationship. Finally my parents, who fed and housed me and put up with the inconvenience of having a member of the family perpetually glued to a computer. To all of these, vast gratitude is due.

Santa Fe, 1990

INTRODUCTION

Jean Genet once wrote that the only man to stand out in modern society is the man condemned to death. It is indeed hard to think of an event more dramatic than a public execution, of a moment when the social order and an individual's destiny conflict more acutely – an extreme instance of the principle by which small boys are caned in class. In France, since 1792, death by execution has almost always meant the guillotine, and in that nation's literature a small, distinguished band of heroes has made its way to the great knife: Stendhal's Sorel, Camus' Meursault, Genet's Notre-Dame-des-Fleurs, their demises dignified in varying degrees by irony and an implicit rupture with society. 'The only man', wrote Genet, and indeed, his own novels, which are based on real events, focus on the destinies of miscreant, decapitated males. But what of heroines? Were any women singled out by history or literature for destinies exceptional? And, to add a word to the Red Queen's celebrated utterance, who cut off their heads?

The guillotine itself has always been endowed with female attributes, even though it was invented by men and operated by them almost exclusively. Until the Revolution, the practice was to decapitate condemned persons with a sword, if they were noble, or to hang them, if they were not. In cases of regicide, the victim was tortured with hot pincers, then quartered by four horses, or however many were necessary, before being tossed into expectant flames. As late as 1750 people could be burnt at the stake for incest, sorcery or sodomy; until about 1787 violent robbers were broken on the wheel, their mangled bodies left to die. All this took place in public, could last several hours and, besides being a spectacle, was thought to deter the onlookers from crime. When Revolution came, torture was abolished, and a simple form of punishment proposed for all: 'Everyone condemned to death shall have his head cut off'. Designed therefore as an egalitarian, humane measure, the guillotine descended from a series of primitive decapitation machines that included the sixteenth-century Scottish 'Maiden'. Rapidly baptised anew for the doctor who invented it, Louis Guillotin, it became known, among other things, as 'Guillotine's daughter', or 'The Widow'. It may in that linguistic sense be regarded as the principal female agent in the ongoing spectacle of public execution, a spectacle that lasted well into the present century.

This is not to say that women were not victims. History, indeed, has been most generous in its bequest of women who 'stand out'. The axe, the sword, the guillotine claimed several British queens, medieval saints, and women from all walks of life who figured in the French Revolution. That is without mentioning the many women condemned to other, less rapid forms of death. The more illustrious die on in theatre or the pages of grand opera: Schiller's *Maria Stuart*, Verdi's *Giovanna d'Arco*, Donizetti's *Anna Bolena*, Poulenc's *Dialogues des Carmélites*. Others have become the subject of literary biographies, such as Stefan Zweig's *Marie Antoinette*, while still others are the focus of sociological studies by recent American feminists, such as Ann Jones' *Women Who Kill*. Many seem simply to have collided with superior religious or political forces, and got the worst of the collision; others had committed actual crimes. Curiously, French fiction of the nineteenth and twentieth centuries – pedigree French fiction, as studied by Ivy League undergraduates – has not produced a guillotined heroine of note; while everybody knows the name of Manon Roland, there is no female equivalent of Julien Sorel. Bearing in mind that crime, indeed murder, is a prerequisite for Genet's distinguished condemned men, it would seem to be Genet himself who provides the closest approximation to the heroine of note in his play *Les Bonnes* (*The Maids*), a work thought to have been inspired by the real-life drama of the Papin sisters, who murdered their employers on the plush red carpet of their bourgeois stairs.

There was, of course, a heroine of fiction, one of the most celebrated ever, but she is chiefly remembered for her ability to avoid execution, rather than endure it. She was the wife of the sultan Schariar, a spectacularly magnificent ruler of Persia, and her story provides the frame for an exotic collection of tales thought to have been elaborated in sixteenth-century Egypt. It also provides an excellent example of a woman who, through her superior wisdom and imagination, gets the better of an unjust law she had no part in framing. At the beginning of the story, Schariar's younger brother Schazenan reluctantly informs his omnipotent sibling that his own wife has recently loved another man 'better than himself', and that maddened with rage and grief he has smitten off the heads of the offending pair; not only that, but he has also seen Schariar's wife 'in secret conversation' with another man. Schariar flies into an even more excessive fury and sentences his queen and her accomplice to immediate death. In order to forestall any such future calamity he then binds himself by solemn vow to take a new bride every night, and command her to be strangled in the morning. This course of action proves disastrous to Schariar's city, whose quota of young maidens rapidly declines; everywhere the laments of unhappy parents rend the air, and subjects who formerly praised their ruler for his wisdom and munificence now heap invectives on his head.

INTRODUCTION

In these discouraging circumstances Scheherazade, the elder daughter of the grand vizier, makes a most astonishing request: she asks her father if she may have the honour of becoming the sultan's next bride. Appalled, the grand vizier – a kindly man, obliged to carry out the sultan's revolting orders at risk of his own head – makes every attempt to discourage her, even going so far as to tell her the story of the Ox and the Ass, wherein the Ass recklessly exposes his person to destruction. But Scheherazade, who possesses vast beauty, 'a degree of courage beyond her sex', and an enormous memory besides, remains undeterred and simply reiterates her purpose: she is convinced she can put a stop to the sultan's cruel behaviour, thus rendering great service to her country. Her stratagem is simple, although it might not work in cultures where the word is honoured less: as a last favour, she obtains permission for her younger sister Dinarzade to sleep at the foot of the royal couch during the wedding night. Next morning Dinarzade wakes before dawn and begs Scheherazade to relate 'one of [her] delightful stories', this being the last time, alas, that anyone will hear her. With the sultan's consent, Scheherazade begins to tell the story of the Merchant and the Genie, breaking off just at the point where the Genie is about to lift his sabre to cut off the Merchant's head. Schariar is most curious to learn the outcome, but is himself obliged to spend the rest of the day in prayers and in council. He thus delays the execution for a second night, permitting Scheherazade to complete the tale. One thousand and one nights later, we read that Schariar's 'temper was softened and his prejudices removed'; convinced at last of the merit, wisdom and great courage of his wife, the sultan freely repeals his self-imposed law and declares Scheherazade the deliverer of those many damsels he had vowed to sacrifice to his 'unjust resentment'.

It is easy to take the story of Scheherazade as an illustration of the irrational cruelty of men, or the impotent and inferior state of women in classical Araby, which, being remote in both time and geography from current western ways, can be more easily condemned as barbaric and absurd. Again, the story is often referred to disparagingly as a paradigm for feminine wiles. And yet this elegant narrative far transcends this species of interpretation. At its highest level, it becomes a parable for civilised creativity: storytelling is literally a matter of life and death, without which both the individual and society would plunge towards disaster. Scheherazade's resourcefulness saves not only the young damsels, but by extension the city, which would otherwise soon lose all marriageable girls and with them, the possibility of babies and a future. Through love and courage she frees the sultan from a morbid eroticism and his obsessive fears of infidelity; her imagination and ingenuity redeem a disastrous abuse of power and restore the country to more balanced government.

The opening of the *Thousand and One Nights* is interesting from both the psychological and legal points of view. For one thing, it casts doubts on the efficacy of capital punishment. Execution is clearly the penalty for adultery, since both brothers' wives suffer it; yet the prospect of having one's head lopped off by one's husband does not seem very effective as a deterrent here. Nor do the absolute prerogatives of power enjoyed by Schariar stand up particularly well against intelligent obedience. Scheherazade undermines them by her very deference, asking the sultan's permission before she begins her tale, falling to the floor to embrace his feet when he 'forgives' her at the story's end. Indeed, it is not clear whether he forgives her for having thwarted his self-binding vow, or for being a woman and his wife, and therefore doomed to die. In either case, the sultana's voluntary submission to the unjust law eventually erodes it.

Unfortunately, and in less literary plights, not all women have wrought such felicitous effect upon the law as Scheherazade. In western societies of every type in almost every era numbers of women have mounted the scaffold in ultimate obeissance to laws they have sometimes violated but seldom, until the present time, have had the possibility to make. The exceptional periods of time – late nineteenth- and early twentieth-century France, nineteenth-century America – when women were scarcely executed at all do not reflect an increased legal power or social standing. Nor do they reflect a female skill in telling stories. It was rather that the legal system was obeying, in an inverted and probably unmeditated form, a new logic that concerned women's rights.

It was in September 1791 that a French *femme de lettres* firmly linked the question of women's rights with that of capital punishment: 'Women have the right to take their places on the scaffold, they must also have the right to take their seats in government.' So read Article 10 of her *Declaration of the Rights of Woman*, a critical response to the better-known but, she felt, lop-sided *Declaration of the Rights of Man*. She was to illustrate her elegant, ironic logic two years later when in November 1793 the One and Indivisible French Republic sentenced her to have her head cut off for penning federalist opinions. It was a curious way of taking her seriously. For some years Olympe de Gouges had addressed her literary talents to a variety of social issues – the abolition of slavery, women's rights, urban hygiene and assistance to the poor – had, in her own words, 'flooded France with useful projects'. The response had not been positive; when one of her letters was read aloud in the all-male National Assembly, somebody called for the floodgates to be shut. In another letter, addressed to patriotic women, she enquired: 'My fellow women citizens, is it not time we had a revolution too?' Political journalists and legislators alike had generally giggled, had failed to realise she was forging a new view of women as useful citizens who might help govern the new France. They would have preferred it had she knitted trousers for the *sans-culottes*. Olympe de Gouges, who had hoped that revolutionary change would better the legal status of women, had received only the right to mount the scaffold. Nonetheless, in cutting off her head, the National Assembly proved that she was not ridiculous, or

INTRODUCTION

mad, as had occasionally been stated; on the contrary, there was something in her writing to be feared.

The feminists of revolutionary France were not the only persons hoping that the current paroxysm of social change would bring about improvement of their state. A most singular category of men, the public executioners, had thought that the advent of a new régime would transform that peculiar disdain in which society held them. Here one may remark without the shadow of a scholarly qualm that execution was a profession dominated by males; if women were entitled to be victims, the actual executioners were almost always men. In 1746 a lone Frenchwoman, Marguerite Le Paistour, obtained the public post of *bourreau* in Lyon, but only by posing as a man. Denounced to the authorities after a tenure of two years she was thrown into prison, remaining there until she could be safely married off to a young footman. Once or twice, in fairly remote provinces, male executioners received assistance from intrepid female aides – their wives. But for the most part, and for hundreds of years, the post of Master of the High Works in France's major cities was held by men from ten or so dynastic families, members of an abominable and reverse élite that had developed as a consequence of social prejudice: anyone who had ever been a *bourreau*, even a temporary one, could never hope to find another job, nor could he aspire to marry any woman not herself the daughter of a colleague. In this way the dreadful dynasties developed, passing on the title from father to son or son-in-law. The best-known recipients of this peculiar distinction were the Sanson family, who operated in Paris and Versailles from 1688 to 1847; the diary kept by Charles-Henri Sanson, executioner of Paris during the Terror, provides details of the deaths of many illustrious female victims, including Charlotte Corday and the Queen.

Several passages in the Sanson diary suggest that professional executioners did not particularly like having to kill women. Called upon to guillotine an 18-year-old seamstress who looked as young and fragile as a child, the same Charles-Henri was overcome with dizziness and had to leave the scaffold in his nephew's charge. On another occasion his aides were completely demoralised by having to execute a cartload of distraught women, and protested that 'the guillotine was being dishonoured'. This chivalrous repugnance later spread through the Cours d'Assizes; while women were regularly condemned to death in the late nineteenth and early twentieth centuries, in fact they were almost always reprieved. A roughly contemporaneous reluctance to execute women in the United States has been explained by recent American feminists as evidence of women's almost non-existent social status at that time; to compensate for legal inegality the men who were women's judges, prosecutors, jurors adopted a 'protective' stance, frequently acquitting women who, in modern retrospect, seem guilty. In France the egalitarian practices of earlier centuries were ultimately reinstated by the collaborationist government of Marshal Pétain, which guillotined five women, including an abortionist from Cherbourg.

This temporary preservation of execution as an exclusively male domain – a thing too necessary and revolting to be inflicted on or endured by half the population – apparently did not strike legislators as being intolerably illogical, or as being rather a back-handed sort of compliment to men. Proper equality would have involved either equal rights and equal punishment for men and women, or else abolition. However, arguments against the death penalty tend rather to develop from general humanitarian principles, and less from the putative equality of women.

Chivalry, indeed, would seem to have been the nineteenth-century's solution to the problems posed to the authorities by 'female' executions. For one thing it avoided the embarrassments of public execution. Throughout preceding centuries the hanging or beheading of a woman almost invariably had attracted thousand of spectators, not all of whom were drawn by edifying thoughts of being deterred from crime. In cases of hanging, the difficulty could partly be resolved by covering the victim's neck and face; but in decapitation, whether by axe, guillotine or sword, a bare neck was essential. The sometimes unseemly curiosity manifested by the crowd tended in consequence to offset the high moral tone of the proceedings. But more importantly, chivalry enabled society to observe a version of that logic set forth in 1791 by Olympe de Gouges, a logic echoed later in the United States by American feminists such as Elizabeth Cady Stanton, and by sympathetic males such as Wendell Phillips, who bluntly declared 'You have granted that woman may be hung; therefore you must grant that woman may vote'. In not executing women, the judiciary body was able to sidestep these irritating formulations: if women did not receive equal punishment under law, perhaps they need not be assured of equal rights. This position at least offered philosophical consistency. The problem was, it did not make for a very consistent administering of justice – nor did it content American feminists. 'A citizen cannot be said to have a right to life', they argued, 'who may be deprived of it for the violation of laws to which she has never consented – who is denied the right of trial by her peers – who has no voice in the election of judges who are to decide her fate.'[1] These words were spoken in 1860. In France, the universal suffrage recommended by Olympe de Gouges was not granted until well into the twentieth century; in the United States, fully equal protection under law still does not obtain, when the Equal Rights Amendment is routinely defeated in the diverse states. Two centuries beyond the storming of the infamous Bastille we are still in a position to reflect that, of the two rights mentioned by Olympe de Gouges, society has generally hesitated less in granting women the first right than the second.

1
BURIALS AND BURNINGS
Modesty, chivalry and heresy

I'll be hung, drawn and quartered but I won't, Mr Goldstein, I won't be viewed in the nude.
        (Sung by Julia Migenes-Johnson on the Johnny Carson Show)

Before 1449, women were not hanged, at least not in France; public decency required that their legs not dangle naked from the gibbet for those below to see. Therefore it was found more suitable to bury them alive. In 1448 a gypsy woman quoted the ancient 'law of her race' and asked to be hanged, a favour that was granted, but, as a Parisian observer noted, with her skirt tied round her knees.[1] Quaint though the incident must doubtless seem, it is one example among countless many of the effects of modesty in female, medieval execution.

Impeccable in precedent, the practice of burial alive harked back to Roman law: it had been the punishment for vestal virgins who broke their vows of chastity. The crime was deemed serious, because the tasks performed by vestal virgins were among the most important in Roman religion. They tended the sacred fire of Vesta, virgin goddess of the hearth, whose perpetually burning flame was thought to have been brought to Rome by Aeneas, founder of the city. The six Roman *Vestales* were chosen from patrician families while still little girls, and not allowed to marry. They served for thirty years, after which they were allowed to return to normal life – an opportunity which most declined, preferring the honours and restrictions of their state. But if a vestal broke her vows, she was stripped of her insignia, dressed like a corpse and conducted on a funeral bier to the Campus Sceleratus, or Wicked Field, where she was buried, still alive. A symbolic aspect may have attached to this fate: unfaithful to the sacred fire, consumed by private fires of love, the vestal was ritually extinguished in the earth, her shame all covered up with soil. Burial alive certainly acquired symbolic connotations among the Germanic tribes during the Dark Ages: according to both Grimm and Michelet, the Ditmars had the right to bury unmarried pregnant girls beneath the ice, advised and assisted by friends of the family, so that 'the flames of concupiscence would be quenched beneath this frigid bed'.² Similarly, the Burgundians drowned adulterous wives in the marshes 'to conceal their lewdness'.³

By 1270 and the Establishments of Saint-Louis, women convicted of helping to steal their feudal lord's horse were condemned to be buried alive. The reason for the death penalty was that feudal lords often relied upon their mounts to gallop out of danger, and so the horse came to be considered as part of the said lord's body. Jules Loiseleur, who records these facts, adds that 'this explains the severity of certain customs with regard to women accomplices of such thefts'. The man who had committed them was simply condemned to be hanged and drawn on a *claie*. In fifteenth-century France, burial alive was frequently the punishment for women who received and hid stolen goods. The victim was quite literally buried at the foot of the scaffold where male criminals were hanged. In the reign of Louis XI this fate befell Perrette Mauger, convicted of both theft and concealment. Having vainly appealed against her sentence, Perrette declared herself pregnant and was examined by 'ventrieres' and 'matrosnes', who 'reported to Justice' that she was not with child. Immediately after the report was made Perrette was 'dispatched to be executed in the fields before the gibbet, by Henry Cousin, executor of high justice in the said city of Paris' (Loiseleur, p. 139).

Burial alive could also be the penalty for religious misdeeds, as Michelet makes clear in his *Guerres de religion*. When, in 1540, inflamed with holy zeal, Charles V left Spain to crush the Protestant revolt in Flanders, the Flemish clergy apparently told him that Spanish laws were far too mild, that new and dreadful ones would have to be invented. The edict of that year accordingly forbade public assembly, public speaking, singing or writing, on pain of death. Failure to denounce those who did assemble, speak or sing also resulted in death: the men were burned, the women buried. As Michelet explains:

> The burning of a woman offered a spectacle not only horrifying, but horribly indecent, which northern modesty could never have endured. This can be seen in the execution of Jeanne d'Arc. The first flame to rise consumed the clothes, revealing poor trembling nakedness.

'Therefore', Michelet concludes, 'women were buried out of decency'.⁴ Northern modesty must have been a rather localised phenomenon, however, as the same century would witness the executions of thousands, by some accounts hundreds of thousands, of women burned at the stake in the Teutonic states; executed, like Jeanne d'Arc, for crimes of heresy and sorcery. But in Flanders in the 1540s they were buried alive:

> one, named Antoinette, from a family of magistrates; the other was the wife of an apothecary in Orchies. Marguerite Boulard, wife of a rich *bourgeois*, was also buried, on the feast of All Souls. Then,

in Douai, Matthinette du Buisset, the wife of a clerk; in Tournai, Marion, a tailor's wife; in Mons, another Marion, a barber's wife, and later, a lady called Vauldrue Carlyer, from the same town, for not having denounced her son, who had been reading the Holy Scriptures.

Michelet describes the process: a coffin with no cover was placed in a ditch. The victim was restrained by three iron bars, across the stomach, head and feet. The executioner would charitably strangle her, after which earth was thrown into the coffin. This was the method used for Marion the tailor's wife, executed at Tournai in 1545. There existed a second means, employed to dispatch the second Marion, the barber's wife, in 1549: here the victim was not strangled, but simply covered over with earth. The second Marion could not bear the thought of having soil thrown on her face, and asked for a handkerchief to cover it, which was provided by the executioner. He then jumped onto the pile of earth and trampled on her stomach, until she 'happily gave up the ghost unto her Lord'.

Curiously, a similar concern for public decency had quite the opposite effect in England, where women convicted of both petty and high treason were burnt at the stake. Indeed, the medieval concept of modesty begins rather to resemble Kant's notion of the sublime: it assumes a different national hue in England, Spain, Germany and France. By petty treason was understood the murder of a husband. Whereas men found guilty of high treason – offences against the state – were hanged, drawn and quartered, women's anatomy rendered them unsuitable for such a fate: 'For as decency due to the sex forbids the exposing and publicly mangling their bodies', writes one apologist of the flames, 'their sentence is, to be drawn to the gallows, and there to be burnt alive'.[5] The last instance of due decency in face of high treason occurred in 1685, when Elizabeth Gaunt was found guilty of assisting in the escape of a Mr Burton, himself implicated in the Rye House plot. Mr Burton responded by testifying against Ms Gaunt, who was then condemned. While she was actually being burned a thunderstorm developed, causing spectators to interpret the sudden downpour as a sign of divine displeasure at her unjust end.

The English custom of burning women who had killed a spouse, or other male, is reflected in courtly literature of the early Middle Ages. In the anonymous thirteenth-century French *Romans de Claris et Laris*, the Arthurian knight Sagramors comes upon a great throng of people about to burn a lady. Sagramors learns that she is charged with murdering her husband: she awoke one morning to find him dead beside her in the bed. The husband was both well born and well bred, and is much lamented by his vassals and his brother, who charges the widow with the crime. Steadfastly denying the accusation she declares herself willing to be defended in single combat by a champion. No gentleman having stepped forward, the widow is on the point of being hurled into the flames when Sagramors proposes riding off with her: 'Make me a present of the lady, and I shall take her to my lands, for she seems sensible and brave to me; it would be a pity if you burn her'.[6] The brother furiously refuses and insists upon the duel. A long and complicated fight ensues, in which Sir Sagramors kills the irate brother and thereby frees the lady of all blame. A comparable situation occurs in the *Perceval* of Chrétien de Troyes, when Arthur's nephew Gawain frees another lady menaced with the stake, this time for allegedly disposing of her brother during the night. Medievalists have indicated a resemblance between these incidents and a passage from Caesar's *De Bello Gallico*, referring to the Roman practice in such cases:

> when the father of a family, born in a more than commonly distinguished rank, has died, his relations assemble, and if the circumstances of his death are suspicious, hold an investigation upon the wives in the manner adopted toward slaves; and if proof be obtained, put them to severe torture and kill them.
>
> (Riedel, p. 85)

It is likely that the historical punishment of burning inflicted in such investigations did derive from Roman law; but the knightly conventions obtaining in the literary passages – the challenge, followed by the duel on the accused woman's behalf – owe more to the Accusatorial procedures of the Germanic tribes, which coexisted with the Roman law until about the seventh century, and then combined with them until the early Middle Ages.

The single combat, by which a champion preserves the honour of high-born ladies in Romance, thus corresponded to an actual practice. As its name implies, Accusatorial Law required that the suspected person be openly accused by his or her accuser; then the accuser had to be ready to make good his charge in single combat, before a jury of both parties' peers. The facts of the case were aired in public, established by the depositions of witnesses and 'co-adjurors', who took an oath affirming the truthful character of the person on whose behalf they swore. Strict rules governed the admissibility of witnesses, women and priests being disqualified because they could not defend their testimony by force of arms. Torture was seldom if ever applied, although the accused might be subjected to the 'ordeals' of fire and water (the accused would either retrieve an object with his hand from a boiling cauldron, or else carry a red-hot iron bar a prescribed number of paces; sealed bandages were then applied, and if the wounds had healed three days later, the accused was freed). A woman accused of serious crimes – murder, *lèse-majesté*, adultery – could be defended by a champion, as in the passage from *Claris et Laris*. A nineteenth-century reworking of this convention is found in Wagner's *Lohengrin*, wherein the white knight of the title is brought by a swan to the banks of the river Scheldt; there he defends the heroine, Elsa von Brabant, unjustly accused of murdering her brother.

In literature of chivalry the judicial duel provides an elegant, idealised solution to the problem of force: God, and the nobler knight's greater courage, generally make sure that right equals might. In history, this was not always so. A class of professional champions arose, provoking resentment when innocence visibly did not prevail; the judicial duel became unpopular, too, on account of the lack of real redress it could provide. Rare in any case are factual instances of women rescued from the flames by charging knights; can one think of even one? By the time of Saint-Louis the practice was discredited. Moreover, from the twelfth and thirteenth centuries on the annals of execution lay increasing emphasis on a species of misdeed from which not even knights were safe: the crime of heresy, or 'bougrerie', sometimes known as 'vauderie', thought likely to offend the majesty of God. At the same time the open, confrontational forms of Accusatorial Law were gradually replaced by the more sinister and secretive procedures of Inquisitorial Law, which owed more to Roman custom than to the whimsical habits of the Franks.

In France as in England, heretical offences were judged by ecclesiastical, not civil courts, although the secular authorities would carry out the actual sentence. As the Establishments of Saint-Louis ordained, 'If anyone is suspected of *bougrerie*, lay justice must arrest him and send him to the bishop, the which being proven, must burn him therefor, all his furnishings then going to the baron' (Loiseleur, p. 141). Yet ecclesiastical power was actually to some extent curtailed under the Establishments, which resisted the invasion of the temporal by the episcopate. The role of the Church was limited to gathering evidence, determining the facts, pronouncing sentence and applying the ecclesiastical penalties, which never involved violence: 'Ecclesia abhorret a sanguine'; the Church abhorred bloodshed. The power of the Holy Inquisition was greatly augmented after its investigation of the Albigensian heresy, in the twelfth century, and that increase of power accompanied the increasing domination of the forms of law which took its name. Under Inquisitorial procedure, the accused might be arrested on mere suspicion or denunciation, and interrogated without knowing who his accusers were, or of what he stood accused. He was denied legal counsel, much less 'co-adjurors'. In this state of ignorance the accused would be interrogated and encouraged to 'confess'. To assist him to this end, torture might be and was frequently applied. The influence of Roman practice is apparent in the definition of the crime (Rome assimilated *lèse-majesté* with sacrilege; the Church saw heresy as *lèse-majesté* against God); the penalty (Rome punished *lèse-majesté* by beheading noble culprits, and by burning common ones); and in the application of torture (Rome routinely tortured slaves in the investigation of a case, and eventually freemen as well).

DEATH COMES TO THE MAIDEN

As might be supposed from its resemblance to an English word, the term 'bougrerie' – deriving from the French for Bulgars – denoted not only heresy and sorcery, but sodomy as well. This curious etymological honour had been bestowed upon the Bulgars because, at the time of the division of the Holy Roman Empire, they had chosen to be faithful to the Christianity of the East. Although akin to English 'buggery', 'bougrerie' had rather a broad application in the Middle Ages. Its meaning could also extend to carnal knowledge of Jewish and Turkish women – pagan women generally. Committing sex with pagans was deemed not only heretical but bestial, for pagan women were considered beasts. In 1222 a deacon was burned in Oxford for 'embracing' Judaism; he had wished to marry a Jewess, and had converted to her faith. Indeed, 'many who lived with Jewesses were sentenced to death for having committed an unnatural offence' (Pritchard, p. 9).

The primary senses of 'bougrerie', however, were heresy and homosexuality, two practices linked closely in the medieval mind.[7] While no records apparently exist of women being burned as 'bougres' in the homoerotic sense, the punishment was often meted out to men, the most spectacular instance being the persecution of the Knights Templar in 1305–14. Founded in 1118 as a monastic-military order to protect poor pilgrims visiting the Holy Land, the Templars had grown from an original force of nine knights into a complex body of four different ranks, some 20,000 strong, wealthy beyond imagination, having enormous privilege and power, protected by the Popes. Not surprisingly, such earthly standing begot jealousy, in both the ordinary clergy and the temporal monarchs. Immensely popular at its inception and bound by rigorous Cistercian vows, the order eventually acquired a reputation for arrogance, intemperance and luxury. Its secret rites were rumoured to be Gnostic, Dualist, heretical, obscene – these, at least, were some of the charges levelled against them, when Philip II of France succeeded in forcing a reticent Pope Clement IV to take action. In 1307, following a Papal Bull, the Inquisition asked for civil aid; as many Templars as could be found in France were seized and thrown into prison, where the desired confessions were obtained through torture and the miscreants burned. In their heyday the Templars are said to have embodied 'the two absorbing passions of the Middle Ages, religious fervour and chivalry'. The manner of their downfall reflects a third, no less absorbing interest: a fascination for proscribed sexuality, which surfaces repeatedly in witch trials of the later Middle Ages and the Renaissance, even into the seventeenth century.

'More, perhaps, than any other military figure in history, she forces us to think.' So comments Vita Sackville-West, concluding her 1935 biography *Saint Joan of Arc*. She might have added, more than any other figure executed in that age her career reflects the abiding medieval preoccupations with modesty, chivalry and heresy. In G. B. Shaw's terse summary,

BURIALS AND BURNINGS

Joan of Arc, a village girl from the Vosges, was born about 1412; burnt for heresy, witchcraft and sorcery in 1431; rehabilitated after a fashion in 1456; designated venerable in 1904; declared Blessed in 1908; and finally canonised in 1920; she is the most notable Warrior Saint in the Christian calendar, and the queerest fish among the eccentric worthies of the Middle Ages.[8]

Even Jean Genet, asked by *Playboy* in 1964 if any women had ever 'interested' him, listed Jeanne among the four who had (the three others were Marie Antoinette, Marie Curie and Saint Teresa of Avila). Certainly Jeanne's military achievements, her capture, trial and death have been the subject of numerous dramatic interpretations: in *Henry VI Part One* the patriotic Shakespeare presents her as an astute strategist, first valiant in arms, whose characterisation rapidly degenerates into that of witch and bawd. Schiller creates a Romanticised Jeanne who dies on the battlefield, the fact of her burning being apparently too awful to portray. Voltaire writes mock epic combats wherein Jeanne rides a flying donkey or, taken unaware in the nude, defends the Dauphin's mistress with her sword. Dreyer depicts an ascetic, cinematic saint, discreetly crumpling in the flames with vestments intact; Shaw, a practical country girl. A 1989 issue of *Vogue* reproduces a painting of Jeanne in full armour, illustrating an article about androgyny. Despite many posthumous likenesses, Jeanne actually left no credible contemporary portrait of herself, a distinction she would share with the Marquis de Sade.

Her rather belated canonisation in 1920 gave rise to fresh debates about Jeanne's innocence or guilt. Shaw, in the preface to *Saint Joan* (1923) describes her as an unusually sensible and imaginative girl, possessed of great purity; he also sees her as a premature Protestant martyr of overweening spiritual presumption and 'superbity'. Several subsequent writers, historians of witchcraft, have found her spiritually unorthodox: she claimed to be the direct recipient of divine aid, without recourse to the interpretation of the Church; had she not seen visions and heard voices? Had she not worn male attire, even armour, immodest in a woman? At her trial, as Charles Williams remarks, she refused, most alarmingly, to say the Lord's Prayer, 'unless it be in confession', which was denied her. In later centuries this refusal would have been tantamount to a confession of witchery. As if all this were not damning enough, at the beginning of each session of the court she refused to tell the whole truth absolutely, on the grounds that God did not permit it. In her anthropological study *The Witch Cult in Western Europe* Margaret Murray goes further, being at pains to argue that Jeanne, Jehanne or Joan was indeed a witch, a salient god-figure in a surviving pagan cult that ritually murdered its gods – or, if it could not slaughter them directly, caused them to be murdered by judicial means – every ten or so years, other salient victims in this cult having been, she suggests, Gilles de Rais and William Rufus. Miss Murray also points to the importance that attached in Jeanne's trial to her wearing of male breeches – without, however, totally explaining how this indicates Jeanne was a witch: 'It is impossible to say why so much stress was laid on her attire, as in itself it has never been a capital crime for a woman to appear as a man'.[9]

The wonder, according to such lines of thought, is not so much that Jeanne was ultimately condemned as 'idolator, heretic, apostate and relapsed', but rather that the Church went to such subsequent pains to rehabilitate her. Most curiously, in the eyes of Charles Williams, the Church organised its rehabilitation hearings a mere twelve years after the hanging and burning of one of her closest associates. For in 1440 the immensely rich, cultivated, handsome Gilles de Rais – Marshal of France, friend, admirer and chosen champion in battle of the Maid – had been condemned by an ecclesiastical court after confessing to the buggery and murder of eight hundred little boys. Williams even speculates that Gilles himself suffered some form of mental collapse after Jeanne's death, having previously become enamoured of her androgynous beauty: she was seventeen when he met her, virginal, in armour, and wielding a sword. He was her designated protector, chosen by the Dauphin himself, and after one brief year he lost her. He was not present when she was captured; yet after her death he devoted his enormous wealth to mounting a vast pageant, a continuing theatrical depiction of her life in which he himself played Gilles de Rais. Williams seems quite seriously to imply that Gilles' subsequent experiments in satanism, alchemy and paederasty were influenced by his obsession with the Maid. If guilt by association had carried any weight, as it would in later centuries, Jeanne's rehabilitation trial would surely have gone ill.

It is curious to find such speculation as to witchcraft and androgyny in books written at about the same time as the down-to-earth approaches of G. B. Shaw and Vita Sackville-West. Of Jeanne's physical attractiveness, Shaw baldly comments that 'all the men who alluded to the matter declared most emphatically that she was unattractive sexually to a degree that seemed to them miraculous'. Vita Sackville-West presumes her to have been a 'strong, healthy, plain and sturdy girl', probably dark and sunburned, with thickish thighs and black hair cropped short like a boy's; she adds that when Robert de Baudricourt suggested turning her over to the pleasure of his soldiers there were 'some who would have tried; but as soon as they saw her, they were chilled, and inclination left them' (Sackville-West, p. 7). True, the androgynous explanation might possibly account for this reaction in the soldiers, but Sackville-West suggests a subtler cause: 'such inward beauty of expression as Jeanne may, and surely must, have possessed, was not of a nature to rouse the concupiscence of men-at-arms.' As for Gilles de Rais, Sackville-West simply lists him among the captains who escorted Jeanne at Orléans and Reims; information is of the barest, limited to one small footnote, 'Gilles de Rais, of infamous memory'. This immensely detailed study does not even mention the Dauphin choosing Gilles to act as champion.

BURIALS AND BURNINGS

Proceedings for Jeanne's rehabilitation trial were actually initiated by her mother. A woman of determined character, she had moved from Domremy to Orléans in 1440 and then, in 1450 and in failing health, begun the appeal which prodded the Pope into ordering a re-examination. Her husband, Jacques d'Arc, had died in 1431, apparently of grief at his daughter's execution. Both Jeanne's parents were persons of unassailable respectability, honest, poor, devout, hard-working and severe. Their second daughter and fourth child, the future Maid of Orleans, was born on 6 January 1412. Her childhood, harsh and uncomfortable, was spent helping her parents with domestic tasks, occasionally watching the sheep. When she was twelve, she had her first encounter with her voices:

> I was in my thirteenth year when God sent a voice to guide me. At first, I was very much frightened. The voice came towards the hour of noon, in summer, in my father's garden. I had fasted the preceding day. I heard the voice on my right hand, in the direction of the church. I seldom hear it without seeing a light. That light always appears on the side from which I hear the voice.

The voice, she eventually decided, belonged to Saint Michael; later on she thought she heard and saw Saint Catherine and Saint Margaret. Slowly, they prepared her for her task: she was to trust God, come to the aid of the King of France, wear male clothes and lead an army. For five whole years she kept this to herself, even after her father started having dreams in which his daughter went away with soldiers. Much distressed, he instructed her brothers that if this ever came to pass they were to drown her. By May 1428 the voices had grown more insistent. Jeanne persuaded her cousin Durand Lassois to escort her to Vaucouleurs – the nearest military town held in the name of the Dauphin. The visit was abortive: Baudricourt, the governor, told Lassois to take her home and give her a good spanking. A year later, without confiding in anyone, she once again set out to visit Lassois' wife near Vaucouleurs, and this time succeeded in persuading Baudricourt and the citizens of that town to equip her with a horse, a page's suit, and an escort to set out for the Dauphin's court at Chinon.

The situation of France in 1429 was complex and discouraging. An infant English King, Henry VI, pretended to its throne and was recognised as King of France and England. The Dauphin Charles was excluded from succession and rumoured illegitimate. English troops held much of France and had besieged Orléans. The French themselves were bitterly divided between the Burgundians, who sided with England, and the Armagnac party, who opposed them. The Dauphin lacked all military ambition and cut a rather frivolous, bored and pitiful figure. He was hiding amid his courtiers when Jeanne strode into the Great Hall at Chinon, recognised him, curtsied in her page's pants and bluntly informed him she had been sent by God to get him crowned at Reims; not only that, but she was to lift the siege of Orléans.

For all her bluntness and clairvoyance – 'Make the most of me', she told Charles, 'for I shall last but a year' – matters did not proceed as fast as Jeanne hoped. First, Mesdames de Trèves and de Gaucourt were deputed to find out what sex she was. Then she was taken to be examined by the Faculty of Theology at Poitiers, where a Carmelite professor asked her, in his heavy Limousin accent, what language her voices spoke: 'A better one than yours', she replied. Did she believe in God? 'Yes, and better than you.' Back in the Loire valley, the Queen of Sicily was put in charge of an examination to determine whether or not she was a virgin – an important point, since, if virginal, she could have had no dealings with the Devil. Having been found satisfactory in all respects she was provided with a household – two pages, two heralds, servants, and her own confessor. Jean d'Aulon was assigned to her service, and her brother Pierre came from Domremy to join her. She was given splendid clothes, a suit of armour, banners and another horse. Her sword was brought from the church of Saint Catherine at Fierbois where, as her voices had revealed, and to general astonishment, it lay buried behind the altar. She was allowed to write to the English:

> Jhesus Maria. King of England, and you, Duke of Bedford, calling yourself Regent of France . . . deliver the keys of all the good towns you have taken and violated in France to the Maid who has been sent by God the King of Heaven.

And then, escorted by the greatest captains in France, she was permitted to proceed, with an army and supplies, to Orléans.

Jeanne was never in command of this force, although she behaved with it quite arrogantly – dismissing all its women, making the soldiers attend confession, and forbidding them to swear. She argued with its leaders (La Hire, Dunois, Xaintrailles, Sainte-Sévère, Gilles de Rais), who were wont to hold councils of war without her; Jeanne would arrive, guess that they were keeping something from her, and furiously demand to know their real intent. Unpropitious as this sounds, she nonetheless entered Orléans on 29 April 1429 to the boundless jubilation of its citizens; in the ensuing days the French army succeeded in retaking several English forts and *bastilles*. On 7 May Jeanne raised the siege by storming the *Tourelles*, the forts which held the bridge across the Loire; the captains had opposed this, but Jeanne and the people of Orléans overrode them. Did that make her a 'great military genius', as Marshal Foch would later claim? Sackville-West thinks not, for instead of following up her advantage Jeanne allowed the English to retreat on Meung: it was a Sunday. Sending for a portable altar, which was set up on the field, she caused two masses to be said in front of the whole army. The incident was typical of her religious attitude to war. Jeanne never struck a blow with the sword of Saint Catherine, although she personally carried her white standard wherever the fight was thickest. She wept on seeing wounded men, and cradled the heads of dying English soldiers while encouraging them to confess their sins. Shaw has termed her 'the first French practitioner of Napoleonic realism in warfare', but anything more different from the attitude of Napoleon would be hard to conceive: Napoleon who said, 'I grew up on a battlefield and when one has done that one cares little for the lives of a million men'. Like a white knight of the Grail, Jeanne felt that fighting was a holy matter: every soul in an army must be commended to God.

Further successes followed. Jeanne retook Jargeau on the Loire, the bridge at Meung, Beaugency, then scored a major victory at Patay, where Sir John Talbot was captured and between 2,000 and 4,000 Englishmen were taken prisoner or killed; as was her wont, Jeanne wept for them. Then, finally, she managed to persuade the recalcitrant Charles to march on Reims and be crowned. The coronation was the height of Jeanne's glory. She stood at the King's right, in full armour, standard in hand. Her cousin Durand Lassois came to watch, as did her father; he was treated with high honour, and lodged at the town's expense.

Perhaps this meeting with Jacques d'Arc emotionally exhausted Jeanne. Far from throwing her into the Meuse, he pardoned her unceremonious departure from home; perhaps this unexpected mildness took away her strength. She even confessed to the Archbishop of Reims that she would gladly return to Domremy to help her family with the sheep. For whatever reason, the second phase of her career was less successful than the first. She would no longer, after Reims, overcome all theoretical and concrete obstacles by force of personality. Nor was she much helped by Charles, who negotiated peace with the Anglo-Burgundians, thereby wasting her recently acquired tactical advantage; also, he foiled her attack on Paris, actually ordering the destruction of an invasion bridge built by Jeanne and the Duc d'Alençon. In despair Jeanne abandoned her armour in the cathedral at Saint-Denis. The army was disbanded for lack of money, and she spent the next few months of her short life captive at Charles' court – an occupation for which she was singularly unsuited.

Allowed to take up arms again in October, she was, for the first time, named co-commander of the army with d'Albret. In March she campaigned around Compiègne, which was threatened by the Duke of Burgundy. Warned by the voices that she would soon be captured, Jeanne struggled on courageously but without her former inspiration. She was taken in May, in a field near Compiègne, her small force suddenly outnumbered by a larger body of the Anglo-Burgundians; Jeanne's soldiers turned and fled. Standing her ground, she fought to cover their retreat, but no sooner were her men back inside the city than the governor, de Flavy, ordered the drawbridge to be raised. Jeanne was cut off, almost alone, d'Aulon and his brother and her own brother Pierre still with her. Finally an archer of Jean de Luxembourg pulled her from her horse, and it was over.

The Burgundians exulted. The Duke himself hastened to visit his prestigious captive. Put in the care of three women relatives of Jean de Luxembourg, Jeanne was treated kindly for a while; an aunt even begged her nephew on her knees, for honour's sake, not to sell Jeanne to the English. But Jean de Luxembourg was poor, and bound to obey the British crown; at the same time the University of Paris was demanding that Jeanne be handed over to an ecclesiastical court and tried for idolatry and other related sins. Charles, who could have ransomed her, did absolutely nothing to obtain her release; nor did the French captains mount any sort of rescue attack. After an abortive attempt at escape (she leapt from a high tower) Jeanne was taken to Rouen to face the ecclesiastical court of Pierre Cauchon, Bishop of Beauvais. Finished were the days of respectful treatment. Kept in chains and in a common cell, she was mocked by five English soldiers who watched her day and night and tried repeatedly to rape her. She was examined for virginity again, this time by the Duchess of Bedford. Whereas G. B. Shaw insists repeatedly that the subsequent trial was impartial – far more impartial than a prisoner held in similar circumstances would receive in a secular court today – Vita Sackville-West stresses from the outset its disastrous lack of balance. Cauchon was an ambitious churchman who had sided with the English; if he and his all-male court of six bishops, one cardinal, seven doctors of medicine, thirty-two doctors and sixteen bachelors of theology did not find her guilty, the English were more than ready to drown her in the Seine. Jeanne was tried with 'all the impressive apparatus of ceremony, learning and scholasticism that the Holy Catholic Church, the Court of the Inquisition and the University of Paris between them could command, but in essence the trial was a pre-ordained and tragic farce' (Sackville-West, p. 274).

The trial lasted, in its various phases, from 9 January to the end of May, 1431. In it, Jeanne's entire life was passed in review. Her examiners darted from one topic to another, evidently hoping she would grow confused and contradict herself. But certain recurrent issues emerge from the apparently chaotic mass of interrogation: her preference for male clothes and refusal to abandon them; her reluctance to recognise the supreme authority of the Catholic Church as far as her own actions were concerned; and, above all, her voices. Dealing with the questions, Jeanne showed a mixture of grace, evasiveness and obstinacy. She showed reticence when asked about her visions, either because the subject seemed too sacred to be broached, or because she found to her dismay that the saints' images were less precise than she had thought; sometimes she would refuse to answer awkward questions, sometimes promise a delayed reply. Or again, she would refer to her examination at Poitiers, claiming already to have answered what they asked. A number of her answers were most spirited:

Q. Does Saint Margaret speak English?
A. Why should she speak English, as she is not on the English side?
Q. What did Saint Michael look like when he appeared to you?
A. I did not see any crown, and I know nothing about his garments.
Q. Was he naked?
A. Do you think our Lord has nothing to dress him in?

Once, she caught the court recorder in an error and threatened to box his ears. As Sackville-West remarks, her answers were often so simple that no one could believe them. Her skill at avoiding potential traps could verge on the sublime:

Q. Do you believe yourself to be in a state of grace?
A. If I am not, may God put me there; if I am, may he keep me in it.

Most endearingly, she evinces an utter unconcern with presenting herself in a light that might save her life. Pestered on the problematical matter of her lack of submission to the Church, she would say only that she believed the Pope and Church appointed to guard the Christian faith and punish its transgressors, 'but so far as her own actions are concerned, she will submit herself only to the Church in Heaven'.

As to the vexed question of her clothes, Jeanne herself said it was a small thing, one of the smallest things. Her judges disagreed, quoting Saint Paul and Deuteronomy: 'The woman shall not wear that which pertaineth unto a man, neither shall a man put on a woman's garment; for all that do so are abomination unto the Lord thy God.' Jeanne agreed to wear a woman's dress if they would guarantee her Mass, which was denied her; the examiners promised, but the promise was not kept. Later she pointed out that she could better defend herself against the guards if she wore pants, and that the question would never have arisen if they had put her in a Church prison with women to observe her. But, she admitted, 'It is true that at Arras and Beaurevoir I was admonished to adopt feminine clothes; I refused, and still refuse. As for the other avocations of women, there are plenty of other women to perform them.'

Inexorable as it was the trial had interruptions. Jeanne twice fell ill, so that sessions were conducted in her cell, the prisoner still in chains. By 27 March they had returned to the main hall of Rouen Castle, and were deliberating whether to read her the seventy articles of accusation or simply declare her excommunicate without more ado. Exhorted to renounce her visions and return to the Church, Jeanne refused. On 8 May she was led to the Great Tower to be shown the instruments of torture; still, she did not recant. 'Even if you were to tear my limbs asunder and drive my soul out of my body, I could not speak otherwise; and if I did say anything, I should say afterwards that you had forced me to it.' Cauchon concluded her soul would draw little profit from the torture, and sent her back to her cell. Delegates were dispatched to the University of Paris, to expound the entire case. On 19 May they returned to express the University's view that the Maid's poison had infected Christian sheep throughout the western world. Unanimously, the assembled tribunal then concurred: if the prisoner persisted in refusing to retract, she must be condemned as heretic, sorceress, schismatic and apostate.

On 24 May an enormous crowd – citizens of Rouen, English lords and soldiers, theologians from the trial, the executioner and his cart – gathered in the walled cemetery to hear the formal exhortation: 'The branch cannot bear fruit of itself, except it abide in the vine'. Midway through this discourse the exhorter called Charles of France a heretic; Jeanne protested loudly, and was told to shut up. Again she was asked to submit to the Church, and again she refused. As Cauchon was reading the sentence the astonishing occurred: Jeanne gave in to fear for the only time in her short and startling life, interrupting him, agreeing to defer to the Church in all matters. She signed a shortened version of her abjuration with an 0 – she could neither write nor read – and was led back to her cell, to the great fury of the English, who wished she had been burned.

Incarcerated again, Jeanne meekly allowed them to shave her head (removing the shame of her boyish crop) and actually put on a dress. But by 27 May word was brought to Cauchon that she had been seen in male clothes. The bishop immediately dispatched two of the judges to bring her back to reason, but their path was blocked by the English. Jeanne gave two accounts of what had happened: in the first, she had worn the dress for three days, during which time her boy's clothes were kept in the cell in a sack. One morning she awoke and wished to go to the latrines, but the soldiers took away the dress and threw her old clothes on the bed. Jeanne argued with them until noon, when she reluctantly gave in; the dress was not returned. But the account she gave Cauchon when he came to conduct a personal enquiry on 28 May bears the stamp of her customary arrogant pronouncements:

> I took it of my own free will. . . . I prefer to dress as a man, than to dress as a woman. . . . I resumed it because you did not keep your word to me, that I should go to Mass and receive my Saviour, and that I should be taken out of irons.

Cauchon enquired whether she had heard her voices since the abjuration; she said yes, that they told her God forgave her for the recantation, that in saving her life she was damning her soul. The clerk inscribed these words, wrote 'fatal response' in Latin in the margin. Without this 'responsa mortifera', it might well appear that the future national saint of France had forfeited her life for male attire.

On 30 May Jeanne was given Communion, which she received with many tears, and led out to be burned. She was afraid of fire, declaring she would 'rather be beheaded seven times'. In the marketplace a crowd of some ten thousand had assembled. In a spirit of forgiveness she knelt and prayed aloud, until many wept; several of the judges left, unable to bear what was to come. Contrary to custom no lay sentence was pronounced; English soldiers simply seized her and led her to the stake, which was very high. Brothers Ladvenu, Massieu and de la Pierre went with her, holding up a cross for her to see. At first she called loudly on the saints and on Jesus; finally her head sank forward in the rising flames. To prevent all possible rumour of her having escaped the executioner was ordered to part the fire. Jeanne's dead and naked body was revealed, its clothes burnt to soot:

> and she was seen naked by all the people, and all the secrets which may or must exist in woman, to dispell the doubts of the populace. And when they had seen her as much as they wanted, dead and bound to the stake, the executioner rekindled the fire beneath her poor body, which was soon entirely burned, and flesh and bones reduced to ash.
> (Sackville-West, p. 325)

Later on that day the executioner called on Ladvenu, most upset: he had burned a saint, he said, and was damned. Unable to reduce her heart to ashes he had thrown her remains into the Seine.

Was Jeanne d'Arc inspired by God? Most of her interpreters make some sporting effort to explain this thorny point. For Shaw, Joan's voices were actually the unconscious projection of her inspired common sense, an aspect of genius that drives such superior minds as those of Socrates, Luther and Swedenborg. Andrew Lang, her Scottish biographer, delicately ascribes them to the onset of puberty. In a radio play, *The Trial of Joan of Arc in 1431*, Bertolt Brecht suggests Joan's inner voice was really her awareness of the voice of the people. Vita Sackville-West, though not herself religious, bravely declares belief in a 'mysterious central originating force' with which certain persons are more in touch than others, Jeanne being one of those who are. If it is Jeanne's fate and her achievement to be perpetually reassessed in terms of the spiritual and intellectual fashions of each era, the New Age of the declining twentieth century might well define her as clairvoyant, telepathic, and subject to extra-terrestrial visitation: a sort of military Shirley MacLaine. Or, it could consider her as a knight, which was, after all, her chosen profession. 'In the thirteenth century', writes psychiatrist Thomas Szasz,

> the symbol of nobility is the knight-in-armour, and of depravity, the black witch; benevolent motivation is chivalrous, malevolent is satanic. This imagery embodies and expresses the sexocidal hatred of woman; the knight, the symbol of good, is male; the witch, the symbol of evil, is female ... social reality is portrayed as if it were a dream in which symbols signified their opposites.
> (Szasz, p. 118)

Small wonder that the fifteenth century, which was to witness an accelerated witch-hunt, confused the sexual opposites and, impelled by politics, set fire to its purest knight. As symbols go, her funeral pyre does not compare badly with the heap of bloodied metal into which collapsed the whole of King Arthur's court in their legendary battle on a western plain, its noble fellowship of knights reduced to Sir Bedevere and a sword for not having better dealt with the jealousy, passion and ambition in its midst. She was captured in arms, holding off a greater force to cover a retreat, as had Roland, as would Bayard. At the very least it must be said that in her better days, she inspirited an army, and in her very worst, she died true to herself.

The penalty of fire, which claimed Jeanne and so many witches, black and white, can only be described as frightful. In the centre of a public square was set a stake, about seven or eight feet high, sometimes caked with plaster. All around it bundles of wood were placed, with added layers of logs, more bundles, and bales of straw; a small circular space, about the size of a human being, was left around the central pole. In its external form the pyre looked like a cube, about two metres square. A narrow corridor was left above the lower stratum, permitting access to the stake: through this the executioner would lead the condemned. Attached to the stake at neck, feet and waist, the victim stood upon the lower layer of logs. Sometimes he or she was bound by iron chains; sometimes trapped inside an iron cage, buried in the faggots. Only the head and shoulders were left visible. Having firmly bound the victim, the executioner and his assistants closed off the corridor with further logs and straw and set fire to the whole thing.

That was the regular operation. According to a few rather optimistic versions, the victims were often dressed in nightshirts soaked in sulphur, the fumes of which were thought to choke them dead. Other accounts describe an iron arrow on a spring, aimed at the victim's heart, and which the executioner released no sooner than the flames were lit. A more reliable form of mercy was provided by the *retentum*, a secret clause in the sentence instructing the executioner to strangle the victim privily by means of a fine cord, before the burning began. That many victims were indeed burned alive, and conscious, is certain. The pyre of Jeanne d'Arc was built unusually high, so that the numerous spectators cramming the marketplace of Rouen could get a look; thus, the executioner was unable to strangle her beforehand. From the descriptions in Foxe's *Acts and Monuments* of fifteenth- and sixteenth-century religious persecutions in England it is apparent that those burned were quite heroically conscious. Bishop Hooper, for one, feeling that his execution could be speeded up, called out 'More wood! More wood, good people'. Referring to Foxe, Helen C. White quotes several instances of conscious female martyrs:

> Especially did God give the weaker sex [and in the world of Foxe there was nothing conventional in that phrase] supernatural strength for their trial. Mistress Joyce Lewis consulted her friends for advice as to 'how

she might behave herself, that her death might be most glorious to the name of god, comfortable to his people, and also most discomfortable to the enemies of god'. It was reported that Cicely Ormes stood in the flame at Norwich and died as if she felt no pain.[10]

Dr White adds that 'the most atrocious circumstance, the throwing back into the fire of a babe born in the fire, seems to have horrified authority'; clearly, the unfortunate mother had been conscious. Nor was this mere casual cruelty; the torture had been carefully thought out to cause a maximum of pain. In cases of witchcraft and heresy the judges believed it was their duty to burn an erring body, the better to conserve, in the next world, its soul.

The role of the Holy Inquisition in such cases was complex, and varied according to the different countries. Its participation in a trial depended rather on the delicate relationship between witchcraft and heresy. In Spain, where witches were frequently defined as mentally deluded, there was a greater interest in heresy; few witches were burned, because the Inquisition was far too busy setting fire to Jews. In France, the dealings of that body were dealt rather a blow when a large number of persons accused of sorcery and heresy in Arras appealed to the Parliament of Paris. This Parliament actually caused some of them to be freed by force from prison; in 1491, after a trial lasting thirty years, it forbade the tortures which had been applied in the case. In 1490 an Ordonnance of Charles VIII removed competence in magic and sorcery from ecclesiastical hands; the Inquisition took notice, however, when a heresy was involved in a sorcerer's dealings with demons. It would be especially active along the Franco-German border, a circumstance which the Reverend Montague Summers – a leading historian of witchcraft, a man of vast erudition, no mean turn of phrase, and curiously Inquisitorial views – attributes to the Reformation. This, he says, brought unusual stresses to the Catholic Church, and is largely to be blamed for the explosion of witch-trials in sixteenth-century Germany.

> The Lutheran princes fostered the spread of the new doctrines, interpreting them as they pleased.... A horror of sorcery and witchcraft filled every heart. Unrest and disquietude scorched the land like a fierce flame, vague ill-defined shadowy fear, drove the people to a frenzy of cruel prosecution.[11]

Thus the spread of Protestantism fostered an atmosphere of tension and fear.

The total number of witches actually consigned to the flames is hard to assess. According to American feminist Barbara Ehrenreich, 'Many writers have estimated the total number killed to have been in the millions'. One must hope her over-generous, for she goes on to add that 'women made up some 85% of those executed – old women, young women, and children'.[12] John Laurence Pritchard observes that 'from the fifteenth to the beginnings of the eighteenth century some thousands of wretched witches were burnt, and all on their own confession, a confession usually obtained by torture'. In his *Salem Witchcraft*, W. F. Poole estimates the death toll of witches in Europe at 200,000 during the sixteenth and seventeenth centuries. As to the specific districts, numerous women were burned in the late sixteenth century in Biscaye and Lorraine: Michelet quotes a judge in Nancy who claimed to have burned 800 sorceresses in a mere sixteen years. 'My justice is so good', declared this worthy, 'that last year, sixteen killed themselves in order to escape my grasp.'[13] More alarming still are the figures for sixteenth-century Germany recorded by Montague Summers in his *Geography of Witchcraft*: 'In the year 1586 the diocese of Trier was so scoured and purged of sorcerers and witches that in two villages only two women were left alive' (Summers, *Geography*, p. 489).

Was there in fact a systematic persecution of women, especially of the peasant class, as Barbara Ehrenreich contends? According to the rationalist Henry Charles Lea the persecution of witches, at least in France, was not directed chiefly against women until the late fifteenth century. Referring to 'an extensive witch persecution in Dauphiné commencing about 1425 and extending from Lyon to Grenoble and thence through the Durance valley to Briançon and Argentière', Mr Lea cites the case of Pierre Vallin who spontaneously confessed in 1438 that '63 years before he had given himself to the devil, body and soul'. Interrogated, Vallin accused his accomplices – three men, one woman – all of whom were dead; threatened with torture, he thought of three more men and two more women. The majority of the accused, Lea notes, were men – 'not, as subsequently, women, whose later preponderance may perhaps be ascribed to the *Malleus*'.[14] A similar opinion is expressed in Hansen's *Zauberwahn*, to which Lea frequently refers: 'Hansen points out how the *Malleus Maleficarum* attributes witchcraft chiefly to women and justifies this by exaggerating the customary monkish abuse of the sex.' What Lea terms the 'then widespread abuse of women by theological preachers' was apparently 'one of the factors in extending the witchcraft craze, from which men rarely suffered and which they were ready to ascribe to the other sex' (Lea, vol. I, p. 337).

What was this *Malleus*, this 'hammer of witches', described as a remarkable intellectual achievement even in the present century? First published at Cologne in 1489, it was composed by two Dominican Inquisitors, Henry Kramer and James Sprenger, to whom Pope Innocent VIII had recently granted fresh, extraordinary powers. In Montague Summers' remarkable translation the *Malleus* is prefaced by Innocent VIII's famous Bull of 1484, *Summis desiderantes affectibus*, in which the Pontiff writes of certain 'heretical pravities' which have caused him bitter grief:

> It has indeed lately come to Our ears ... that many persons of both sexes, unmindful of their own salvation and straying from the Catholic Faith ... have abandoned themselves to devils, incubi and succubi, and

by their incantations, spells, conjurations, and other accursed charms and crafts, enormities and horrid conjurations, have slain infants yet in the mother's womb, as also the offspring of cattle, have blasted the produce of the earth, the grapes of the vine, the fruits of trees ... vineyards, orchards, meadows, pastureland, corn, wheat, and all other cereals; these wretches furthermore afflict and torment men and women, beasts of burthen, hard-beasts, as well as animals of other kinds, with terrible and piteous pains and sore diseases, both internal and external; they hinder men from performing the sexual act and women from conceiving, whence husbands cannot know their wives nor wives receive their husbands; over and above this they blasphemously renounce that Faith which is theirs by the sacrament of Baptism, and at the instigation of the Enemy of Mankind they do not shrink from committing and perpetrating the foulest abominations and filthiest excesses, to the deadly peril of their own souls.[15]

Comprehensive as this list of foul abominations seems to be, it is far outdone by the *Malleus* itself, which provides detailed instruction as to how to proceed in actual trials: how to arrest, examine, interrogate and torture the accused; how to judge and punish them. Moreover, it far exceeds the Bull in its misogyny. Innocent VIII places equal blame on 'persons of both sexes' and shows a fatherly concern for their victims – men and women equally, but also animals, fruit-trees, corn: nature itself is threatened and outraged in the satanical calamity. On the other hand the *Malleus*, which addresses all the same disasters – sterility, impotence, abortion, sexual commerce with succubi and incubi, black magic, incantations – manages to place a great portion of the blame upon the sexuality of women.

An essential element in the Faustian pact of witchcraft was copulation with demon spirits, if not with Satan himself. So thoroughly do Fathers Kramer and Sprenger deal with this question that Charles Williams, writing in the mid-twentieth century, was led to comment that the *Malleus* is

long, carefully detailed, and (allowing for its hypotheses and its particular appreciation of evidence) extremely scientific.... It refers continually to certain first principles which, its authors supposed, would be accepted by any clear and educated mind.... Nothing less like the common notion of the self-indulgence of half-mad sexual perverts can be imagined. They deal with sex, of course, as any examination of a great part of human life must, but there is no sign that they were particularly interested in sex.

(Williams, p. 123)

Be that as it may, several sections of the *Malleus* specifically condemn women, and in the most erotic terms. In one chapter, entitled 'Concerning witches who copulate with devils: Why is it that women are chiefly addicted to Evil Superstitions?' the authors propose to 'chiefly examine women', and first, 'why this kind of perfidy is to be found more in so fragile a sex than in man ... secondly, ... which sort of women are found to be given to superstition and witchcraft; and thirdly, ... midwives who surpass all others in wickedness'. To establish beyond doubt the perversity of women they cite St John Chrysostom, *Ecclesiasticus*, Cicero and Seneca. Good, chaste, Christian women are praised, but on the other hand 'in many vituperations that we read against women, the word woman is used to mean lust of the flesh. As it is said: I have found a woman more bitter than death, and a good woman subject to carnal lust.' Not only are women more lustful than men,

> they are more credulous ... naturally more impressionable, and more ready to receive the influence of a disembodied spirit ... they have slippery tongues, and are unable to conceal from their fellow-women those things which by evil arts they know; and, since they are weak, they find an easy and secret manner of vindicating themselves by witchcraft.
>
> (Sprenger and Kramer, pp. 41–5)

From which the friars conclude: 'All witchcraft comes from carnal lust, which is in women insatiable.'

Nor do the two Dominicans shrink from describing how women 'infect with witchcraft the venereal act and the conception of the womb'; insatiable in lust, women are also scourges of fecundity. First,

> by inclining the minds of men to inordinate passion; second, by obstructing their generative force; third, by removing the members accommodated to that act; fourth, by changing men into beasts by their magic art; fifth, by destroying the generative force in women; sixth, by procuring abortion; seventh, by offering children to devils, besides other animals and fruits of the earth with which they work much harm.

Further chapters discuss such interesting topics as 'How in Modern Times Witches perform the Carnal Act with Incubus Devils, and how they are Multiplied by this Means', and 'Whether Incubi and Succubi Commit this Act visibly on the part of the Witch, or on the part of Bystanders'. (Charles Williams retrospectively applies this latter question to the trial of Jeanne d'Arc, when she was asked about her visions in terms that suggest a succubus or incubus was present in the judges' minds: How did she know whether they were male or female? Was there any heat in them?) Of visibility the two Inquisitors observe that 'in all the cases of which we had knowledge, the devil has always operated in a form visible to the witch; for there is no need for him to approach her invisibly, because of the pact'. The bystanders, however, were less privileged, and did not get to glimpse the Devil; all they saw was 'the witches themselves ... lying on their backs in the fields or the woods, naked up to the very navel', busily agitating their lower bodies and their legs and thighs; from this it was 'apparent' that, 'all invisibly to the bystanders, they have been copulating with Incubus devils' (Sprenger and Kramer, p. 114). Of all this, and more, Montague Summers – in 1928 – is led to conclude that 'Even those to whom in a later day the pages of this encyclopaedic manual seem most fantastic, most unreal', will be bound to acknowledge the 'profundity of the exposition, the tireless care and exactest pains with which a subject wellnigh infinite is pursued and clearly tracked in all its ramifications and subtlest intricacies'. Some, he goes on, 'may not grant its premises, some may not approve, but surely no man can scorn or contemn so zealous an earnestness, so serious and grave a labour' (Summers, *Geography*, p. 479).

Perhaps not, were it not for the thousands of women arrested, tortured and burned on the basis of this profound exposition and this zealous earnestness; were it not for a certain inconsistency obtaining even in the logic of torture itself, of tortures recommended by this 'encyclopaedic manual'. For the Inquisitors apparently never thought to doubt the veracity of the confessions extracted from these weak, feeble-minded, impressionable creatures, liars by nature, credulous and deceptive; confessions made without the benefit of legal counsel, made by women incessantly badgered by questions while in extremities of pain: the two friars seem never to have doubted for a second that confessions made were true. Nor did silence help the woman who resisted; it was simply assumed that she had literally demonic strength.

In the administration of torture, interrogators of presumed witches appear generally to have been devoid of that delicacy of feeling that caused women to be buried alive rather than hanged, and burned alive rather than quartered. Women accused of heresy and sorcery were subjected to the normal forms of the *question* both *ordinaire* and *extraordinaire*: the boot, which crushed the shins and ankles; the ingestion of several quarts of water, which distended the stomach while arms and legs were stretched with rope; and the *strappado* or estrapade, which dislocated the body almost as badly as did quartering. True, in France at least, it was recommended in the case of nuns that 'the tortures employed should not be too indecent or too severe for the fragility of the sex'. For women who were not nuns the usual horrors were in force. Some tortures were, in a sense, non-violent: in Italy, it was found particularly effective to deprive the prisoner of sleep for periods of up to forty hours: the more knowledgeable authorities found this second to none in clouding the victim's intellect and breaking his or her will, without apparent damage to the body. This torture was also used successfully in England, but without the limitation on time. Other tortures seemed designed specifically to humiliate the victim sexually. Such was the 'question' by *chevalet*, in which the victim, with feet attached to heavy weights, was made to sit astride a sharp and pointed metal horse. Again, Henry Charles Lea reports that female witches were often placed on red-hot stools. Thus on 29 April 1462 at Chamonix, Inquisitorial justice records that

> as Perronette, widow of Michel de Ochiis, had prostituted herself to the demon and to men *contra naturam* and had eaten children at the synagogue [i.e. the sabbat] and committed other unspeakable crimes, she was to be firmly tied aloft to the stake and made to sit naked for three minutes on a red-hot iron before burning
> (Lea, Witchcraft, p. 236)

– Perronette having previously been tortured, and having confessed.

Scarcely better was the practice of 'pricking', used in Britain and France to discover the insensitive spot of skin that was the 'devil's mark', deemed an invariable proof of the satanic bargain. There were even professional 'prickers', called in as experts in the trials to thrust long pins into the accused until some result was obtained, positive or negative. At the prosecution of Janet Barker in Edinburgh 1643, it was recorded that 'she had the usual mark on her left shoulder, which enabled James Scober, a skillful pricker of witches, to find her out by putting a large pin into it, which she never felt'. As Lea further relates, a witch pricker named Kincaid 'used to strip his victims, bind them hand and foot, and then thrust his pins into every part of their bodies until, exhausted and rendered speechless, they failed to scream, when he would triumphantly proclaim that he had found the witchmark'. In *Magistrats et sorciers* Robert Mandrou quotes a case occurring in 1624 near Vesoul when a pricker actually lost his needle in a woman's buttock: 'in the buttock muscles of the right side, into which mark entered the said needle so entirely that one could in no way withdraw it'.[16] Stripped, prodded, and pricked, the witch would then be shaved all over and searched in her secret parts for the elusive talisman, a piece of paper or charm supposedly provided by the Devil to give her strength during the tortures that still lay ahead.

The confessions obtained by these appalling methods were needed not simply to establish guilt and to implicate other wretches, but to establish heresy, thinly divided as it was from sorcery and magic. As Charles Williams explains:

> One point on which the distinction could be made was this: was there, in the sorcery, any attribution of power to the Devil as such? It was orthodox belief everywhere that the Devil could only do what God permitted. Any assumption that he had power in himself was heretical. The distinction, if a sacrifice had been offered to the Devil, depended on the witch's confession in regard to that abstract point. If the witch meant only a repudiation of God in her inmost soul, if she was, so to speak, perverse and irrational, then she was not heretical. But if she believed that she repudiated God in favour of another power, if she was, so to speak, rationalist and dualist, then she was heretical.
> (Williams, p. 89)

Quite possibly the Christian tendency to characterise Satan as commanding the services of fallen angels and powers inferior only to those of God enhanced him in some unhappy women's eyes. In 1493 Jehanneta Relesce of Freiburg in Switzerland confessed under torture; her husband, she declared, used to beat her continually, so that in the end she went to a rock in a forest and

> called on God or the devil to help her. A dark man appeared and promised relief. She kissed his posteriors and gave him three hairs of her head. She goes to the Sabbat Wednesdays and Fridays of every week – those who fail to do so are soundly beaten by the devil. They eat unbaptized children, having no power over the baptized. She names her accomplices. A number are burned.
>
> (Lea, 1929, p. 256)

While Jehanneta may have seriously believed in her 'dark man', one cannot help but suspect that the interrogators themselves consciously or unconsciously suggested the material for most confessions. Lea actually qualifies the recurrent aberrations of confession – having sex with demons, eating unbaptised babies, kissing the Devil's rump, flying to the Sabbath on a broomstick – as creations of the scholastic Inquisition. Quoting Hansen's exhaustive study of secular court records, Lea observes that these conceptions as to the power of demons found in the abstract scholastic definitions and 'brought to life in the trials for heresy' – intercourse with incubi, etc. – are 'nowhere to be found in the secular trials prior to 1400'. These 'creations of scholasticism' occur exclusively in the heresy processes of the Inquisition (ibid., p. 245). Secular cases, Hansen found, were concerned only to determine whether an individual had used the love-potions, wax figurines and poisons found in traditional sorcery. In other words, the exotic sexual confessions characteristic of witches tried by the Inquisition occur *only* in those trials.

Frequent among the 'creations of scholasticism' was the accusation of killing and eating unbaptised babies at the sabbath. The high infant mortality rate – together with their evident facility of access to the babies – made midwives particularly vulnerable to this charge: as the *Malleus* put it, 'No-one does more harm to the catholic faith than midwives, For when they do not kill children, then, as if for some other purpose, they take them out of the room and, raising them up in the air, offer them to devils' (*Malleus*, p. 66). If the baby survived being born, the midwife, who could not then actually be charged with killing it, might still encounter difficulties, simply for having helped the birth. In the view of Margaret Murray, many English midwives were actually highly skilled; some could even perform Caesarean sections 'with complete success' for mother and child. But they were also credited with 'being able to relieve the "natural and kindly" pains of travail by casting those pains on an animal, or still worse on the patient's husband; no wonder that every man's hand was against them'.[17] Barbara Ehrenreich takes a glowing view of witches' powers, saying modern pharmacology owes much to their herbal remedies:

> They used ergot for the pain of labor at a time when the Church held that pain in labor was the Lord's just punishment for Eve's original sin. Ergot derivatives are the principal drugs used today to hasten labor and aid in the recovery from childbirth. Belladonna – still used today as an anti-spasmodic – was used by the witch-healers to inhibit uterine contractions when miscarriage threatened. Digitalis, still an important drug in treating heart ailments, is said to have been discovered by an English witch.
>
> (Ehrenreich and English, p. 12)

Michelet, who attributes the discovery of herbal healing to a sort of mythological original woman, 'la femme', indicates in *La Sorcière* that medieval witches used belladonna to prevent convulsions during childbirth.

Midwives and witches, then, did not simply risk a charge of infanticide, or casting pains on men: they might also be accused of doing good. Whether they were considered white or black witches depended rather on whether the patients lived or died; but from a legal point of view it made little difference. In the words of Williams Perkins, uttered in 1608,

> By witches we understand not only those who kill and torment, but ... all good witches, which do no hurt but good, which do not spoil and destroy, but save and deliver. ... It were a thousand times better for the land if all Witches, but especially the blessing witch, might suffer death.[18]

How to explain this violence against healers? Perkins himself reasons that the witch is bad in any case because she denies God and gets her power from Satan; but she is more dangerous if she does good, because that makes her popular. The very etymology of the words *witch* (thought to derive from Old English *witan*, to know) or the French *sage-femme*, 'wise woman', suggests part of the problem: the witch was one who *knew*. Knowledge which healed without visible recourse to God could not be approved of by the Church, which held that man was powerless to effect change without divine assistance. Whether change effected without God was bad or good, it was ascribed to Satan, to whose disastrous influence all heathendom had been assigned.

More recent writers, such as Margaret Murray, have suggested that witches posed a professional threat to doctors, 'who recognised in witches their most dangerous rivals in the economic field'. Religion and medical science, she thinks, 'united against the witches, and when the law could no longer be enforced against them, they were vilified in every way that human tongue or pen could invent'. Her thoughts would be echoed several decades later by Ehrenreich and English, who argue that witch-healers were practical and empirical in approach, with remedies tested through many years of

BURIALS AND BURNINGS

direct contact with their patients; not being allowed to enter universities, they had learned by experience. Male doctors, on the other hand, tended to have degrees in theology and theoretical medicine, which relied greatly on the theory of humours, and taught them to write prayers on the jaws of persons suffering from toothache. Since, in the *Malleus Maleficarum*, only accredited doctors could decide whether an illness was caused by witchcraft or by nature, Ehrenreich and English conclude: 'In the witch-hunts, the Church explicitly legitimized the doctors' professionalism, denouncing non-professional healing as equivalent to heresy' (Ehrenreich and English, p. 17).

A more conservative view is taken by Muriel Joy Hughes in her 1943 study, *Women Healers in Medieval Life and Literature*. Ms Hughes, who is one of Ehrenreich's sources, shows a greater respect for the medical establishment than either Murray or Ehrenreich, admitting that women empirics, healers and 'old wives' frequently evinced an 'abysmal ignorance' of the principles of medicine; too often, they tended to rely on amulets and incantations, formulas and charms. According to Hughes' copious, multilingual researches, the fault was not entirely theirs, since women were barred from most European universities; Florence and Naples seem to have admitted one or two, but Oxford and Cambridge most definitely did not. Even so, many women practitioners had studied with doctors who did possess degrees; others, such as the *barbières*, had been taught by their licensed barber-husbands. Of the various categories of female practitioner recognised in medieval French – lady *médecines*, *chirurgiennes* and barbers, *guarisseuses* and 'old wives', midwives and *ventrières* – the most likely to incur suspicion of witchcraft seem indeed to have been the healers and old wives, who concocted their own remedies, and the midwives who, according to Hughes, fell back on charms and incantations when things did not go well. Influenced by the school of Salerno, midwifery had known a period of brilliance in eleventh-century Italy, but showed 'signs of regression' in the late Middle Ages, being utterly unregulated. While *Women Healers* recognises the success of many herbal remedies, its point of view is relatively pro-medical:

> With a natural bent for healing, the wise women earned their living through the application of a number of secret remedies. Since their medicine represented at best a combination of some good herbal cures and a large number of superstitions, the physicians who discriminated between magic and science *were obliged* to condemn them and classify them as witches and sorceresses.[19]

This disadvantage of the pro-medical viewpoint is that it takes little account of the elaborate misogyny informing the ecclesiastical prosecutors behind the said 'physicians who discriminated;' the witch trials appear as an almost genteel phenomenon, having as their aim the purification of medicine.

Given the momentum acquired by witch trials in the fifteenth and sixteenth centuries, the wonder of the matter was, not so much how they ever started, but that they ever stopped. By the mid-eighteenth century the Biblical injunction 'Thou shalt not suffer a witch to live' was giving way, as a guiding dictum, to the laconic, sceptical formulations of the rationalist philosophers: '*Sorcery*. Shameful magical or ridiculous operation, stupidly attributed by superstition to the invocation and power of demons', as the *Encyclopédie* put it. Or, in Voltaire's words, 'We have already said that more than one hundred thousand sorceresses were put to death in Europe. Philosophy alone finally cured men of this appalling folly and taught the judges not to burn fools' (*Dictionnaire philosophique*). How did this transformation come about?

Ironically, the medical profession itself was instrumental in the change of attitude. In 1562 Johann Weyer, physician to Duke William of Cleves, published in Basle a treatise in which he recognised the influence of Satan and his works, but drew a distinction between Satan's 'wicked magicians' and the unfortunate female witches whose wild imaginings Satan had provoked; such witches, he declared, were particularly susceptible to these delusions on account of their 'melancholy humour' and 'doting old age'. The actual infirmities were better treated by physicians than by priests; as for copulation with the Devil, Weyer simply laughed at it. Not only that, he termed the prosecutors 'tyrants, sanguinary judges, butchers, torturers and ferocious robbers, who have thrown out humanity and do not know mercy'. His treatise was translated into French and German in 1567 and provoked much debate, culminating in the 500-page reply of the French judge Jean Bodin, the famous *Démanomanie des sorciers*. In this vitriolic volume Bodin implied that Weyer, 'that petty Rhenish doctor', was Satan's agent on earth and contended that women's humour was contrary to melancholy; how, moreover, could women 'confess to having had copulation with the devils if it was not true?' – Weyer having argued, like Montaigne, that confession must contain what is humanly possible.

Although Weyer's book had been placed on the *Index Librorum Prohibitorum*, a number of other doctors were subsequently to voice similar opinions, ascribing diabolical possession to mere natural phenomena. Among them was Philippe Gavars, who in 1574 diagnosed melancholia in one Perrine Sauceron of Blois; Perrine claimed that the Devil had told her to kill her husband and four children and 'undo herself'. Perrine was duly sent back to Blois to be a good girl and obey her husband, equipped with a letter full of medical instructions. In 1589 Pierre Pigray, physician to Henri III, was asked by the Paris Parliament to examine fourteen persons accused of witchcraft at Tours. Pigray and four other doctors concluded that the accused were poor things with a depraved imagination who did not even have the fatal *punctum diabolicum*; the case was dismissed. In 1599 Marescot examined Marthe Brossier for diabolical possession in Paris, and pronounced himself unconvinced. Then too there were the interventions of the various French

BURIALS AND BURNINGS

Parliaments, as narrated by Robert Mandrou in his *Magistrats et sorciers*. In 1570 the Parliament of Dijon returned two unusual verdicts, unusual in that the condemned were not burned, but that the local clergy were berated for not having taken better care of their flock. In the seventeenth century, and especially around 1639–40, the Paris Parliament enforced François I's edict of 1539, referring all cases involving torture or the death sentence to its own scrutiny, and guaranteeing, in cases involving sorcery, the right to appeal. By 1670–82, when the King's minister Colbert succeeded in reforming the codification of the law, the word 'sorcery' had practically disappeared from the Ordonnances.

Objections to the witch trials were heard in other countries besides France. In 1631 Friedrich von Spee, a German Jesuit who had formerly assisted the Inquisition, published his *Cautio Criminalis* or *Precautions for Prosecutors*. Father von Spee had previously acted as confessor to hundreds of witches burned at the stake, and lived to regret it; his *Cautio* frankly criticises the methods by which criminal confessions were obtained:

> If she confesses, [the accused's] guilt is clear: she is executed.... If she does not confess, the torture is repeated.... The most robust who have thus suffered have affirmed to me that no crime can be imagined which they would not at once confess to, if it would bring ever so little relief.
>
> (Szasz, pp. 30–1)

Father von Spee's book is said to have influenced the Prince-Elector of Mainz (1647–73), one of the first to check the prosecution of witches in Germany. In 1656 the English physician Thomas Ady declared that the confessions of witches were either obtained by fraud, or else invented by the Inquisitors. He further criticised the mania for finding *marks* upon the culprit: 'Very few people in the world are without privy marks upon their bodies, as moles or stains, even such as witchmongers call the devil's privy marks.' In other words, a growing medical criticism of the *premise* (that the accused were diabolically possessed) let to a reassessment of their *condition* (witches suffered from an excess of the melancholy humour), and, at the same time, of legal and religious procedure: witches were better cured by doctors than by priests; tests such as pricking were scientifically unreliable.

Of still greater consequence in discouraging the prosecution of sorcery were the three great 'scandalous' trials of the early seventeenth century. What Mandrou does not emphasise in these particular miscarriages of justice is that their victims were not women, but men – indeed, priests – accused by women of good family: Louis Gaufridy, in Marseille; Urbain Grandier, in Loudun; and, at the Convent of Louviers in Normandy, Picard and Boullé. In the first two cases, respected if not totally chaste priests were accused of seducing the nuns in their care and concluding bargains with the Devil; as a result, other nuns were thought contaminated by 'possession'. In Louviers, Mathurin Picard, though dead for some years, was posthumously charged with having fathered several infants at the convent and offered them to be roasted at the sabbath; the accusation was also levelled at his curate, Thomas Boullé, who was still alive, though not for long. Gaufridy was burned in April, 1611; Grandier in August 1634. Picard's body was exhumed and subsequently burned in August 1647; Boullé suffered the same fate. Four executed men, one of whom was previously dead: what so distinguished their trials and condemnations from those of the countless farm-girls who preceded them? For one thing, Gaufridy and Grandier were both educated men, capable of reasoning with their judges; both firmly denied the charges, and managed to emerge unscathed from the first phases of investigation. Grandier never confessed; Gaufridy held out for months, and even after torture never implicated anybody else. Even Boullé, who was regarded as something of a churl, denied the charge of sorcery, although he admitted to unchastity. Doubts crept in when one of the girls accusing Gaufridy acknowledged intermittently that the charges were unfounded, that he was really a good priest; in the Loudun case, it was clear that the brilliant Urbain Grandier had made many political enemies, some of whom were active in his prosecution. In addition, Jeanne des Anges and several other possessed women of Loudun went on being possessed, with sensational public exorcisms, long after the execution of the man whose death they had demanded as essential to their cure. A further factor, according to Mandrou, was the scene of 'scandal': all three trials took place in major cities, as opposed to rural villages, involved persons of at least a bourgeois standing, and provoked much pamphleteering and discussion among the clergy, as also among the sophisticated but astonished townsfolk. Once doubt and debate had reached the cities it became harder to prosecute cases of possession in the countryside. Medical objections, therefore, Parliamentary and ministerial interventions, together with the manifestly inappropriate and widely debated condemnations of respected priests eventually brought about the emergence of radically different cultural 'structures', in which God and the Devil were less involved in the everyday affairs of men.

Was it better, then, to be hysterical, or burned? From being victims of the Devil, the women who accused these priests came subsequently to be regarded as deluded, melancholic creatures subject to uterine disorder, inclined to Hell and death. Brave and relatively rational as they were, the efforts of sixteenth- and seventeenth-century doctors to regard witches and possessed women as constitutionally subject to melancholy and 'suffocations or furies of the womb' appear to anticipate the nineteenth-century view of women as frail hysterical beings who know not what they do. In the findings of feminist sociologist Ann Jones, the view of insanity held in late nineteenth-century America presupposed both an underlying, predisposing factor and a sudden, precipitating cause; in 1867 an international congress listed among such factors and causes intemperance, venereal excess, onanism, pregnancy, lactation, menstrual period, critical age, and puberty. As Ann Jones comments, 'the only inescapable one for man is puberty; but *every* phase in the life cycle of woman is listed as *both* a predisposing condition and a precipitating cause. Almost naturally insane, a woman might easily be a natural criminal.'[20] In fact several women who had actually killed their philandering seducers were 'chivalrously' acquitted in the 1870s, their feminine infirmities having been stretched into the insanity defence. It thus comes as no surprise to find turn-of-the-century biographers of Jeanne d'Arc accounting for her voices in terms of such wisdom: in the words of Andrew Lang, Jeanne was 'at a critical age, when, as I understand, female children are occasionally subject to illusions'. In the opinion of C. Maclaurin, on the other hand, Jeanne's puberty never arrived at all, giving rise to a 'well-marked repression of the sex complex' in which divine apparitions were substituted for menstruation.[21]

The view of witchcraft taken by contemporary psychiatry does not greatly differ. As Thomas Szasz remarks, Freud essentially replaced the demonological definition with a psychoanalytical one, referring to the theory of a splitting up of consciousness: 'in our eyes, the demons are bad and reprehensible wishes, derivatives of instinctual drives that have been repudiated and repressed.' Szasz finds fault with Alexander and Selesnick and their 1966 pronouncement that

> A witch relieved her guilt by confessing her sexual fantasies in open court; at the same time, she achieved some erotic gratification by dwelling on all the details before her male accusers. These severely emotionally disturbed women were particularly susceptible to the suggestion that they harbored demons and devils and would confess to cohabiting with evil spirits.
>
> (Szasz, p. 78)

Such remarks, Szasz declares, are immoral because they completely ignore the tortures used to extract these gratifying confessions; a problem with the psychoanalytical theory of witchcraft generally is that it considers the witches only as it finds them, defined by their tormentors, entirely excluding 'the possibility that the phenomena in question – called witchcraft during the Renaissance, and mental illness today – are actually created through the social interaction of oppressor and oppressed'. The more active assessment of witches as being agents of the Devil, willing partners in an infamous, indecent bond is gradually replaced by the more passive view of severely deluded women; from having been heretics and healers, women become merely infirm. Szasz, who acknowledges white witches as the 'mothers' of the healing arts, expresses this transformation in the bluntest possible term: 'Man (the Masculine Physician) robs Woman (the White Witch) of her discovery: he declares her mad, and himself the enlightened healer' (Szasz, p. 92). At the same time, the disadvantages of having been pursued as a witch persist. In the words of Ehrenreich and English: 'The witch-hunts left a lasting effect: an aspect of the female has ever since been associated with the witch, and an aura of contamination has remained – especially around the midwife and other women healers.'

In view of Szasz's arguments one might well wonder what psychiatric studies of the Dominican Inquisitors would yield – or for that matter, of the Reverend Montague Summers, whose brain gives no evidence of the changed 'structures' of which Mandrou speaks, and who writes with perfect seriousness of Gaufridy's supposed Black Masses:

> Upon one occasion a dog who had been led in to devour the consecrated Species, stretched out his paws in adoration before God's Body and bowed his head, nor could kicks and blows compel him to stir. Several broke in floods of tears and began to bewail their sins, after which it was decreed that in future the Host should be defiled and trodden under foot, but that no dogs should be admitted.
>
> (Summers, *Geography*, p. 411)

One might wonder – but for the immediate risk of falling into the same error as the neuropathological or psychoanalytical theories of female witchery which fail to consider the psychology of their tormentors. It would be, in a sense, Manichean psychiatry, defining evil, prejudice or illness elsewhere, always outside the self, always arising in the opposite sect or sex, just as Renaissance persecutions of witches and heretics seem to evince a recurring tendency on the part of humanity to split itself into two, attributing forbidden and repressed wishes to the wicked and external Other: woman, heretic or Jew.

1 Joan of Arc at the stake, shown in feminine attire. (Fifteenth-century manuscript; Bibliothèque Nationale)

2 Thomas Artur de Lally-Tollendal, beheaded in May 1766. An example of a male decapitation under the *ancien régime*. Note the posture of the victim, shirt torn back to reveal his neck. (Anonymous etching; Bibliothèque Nationale)

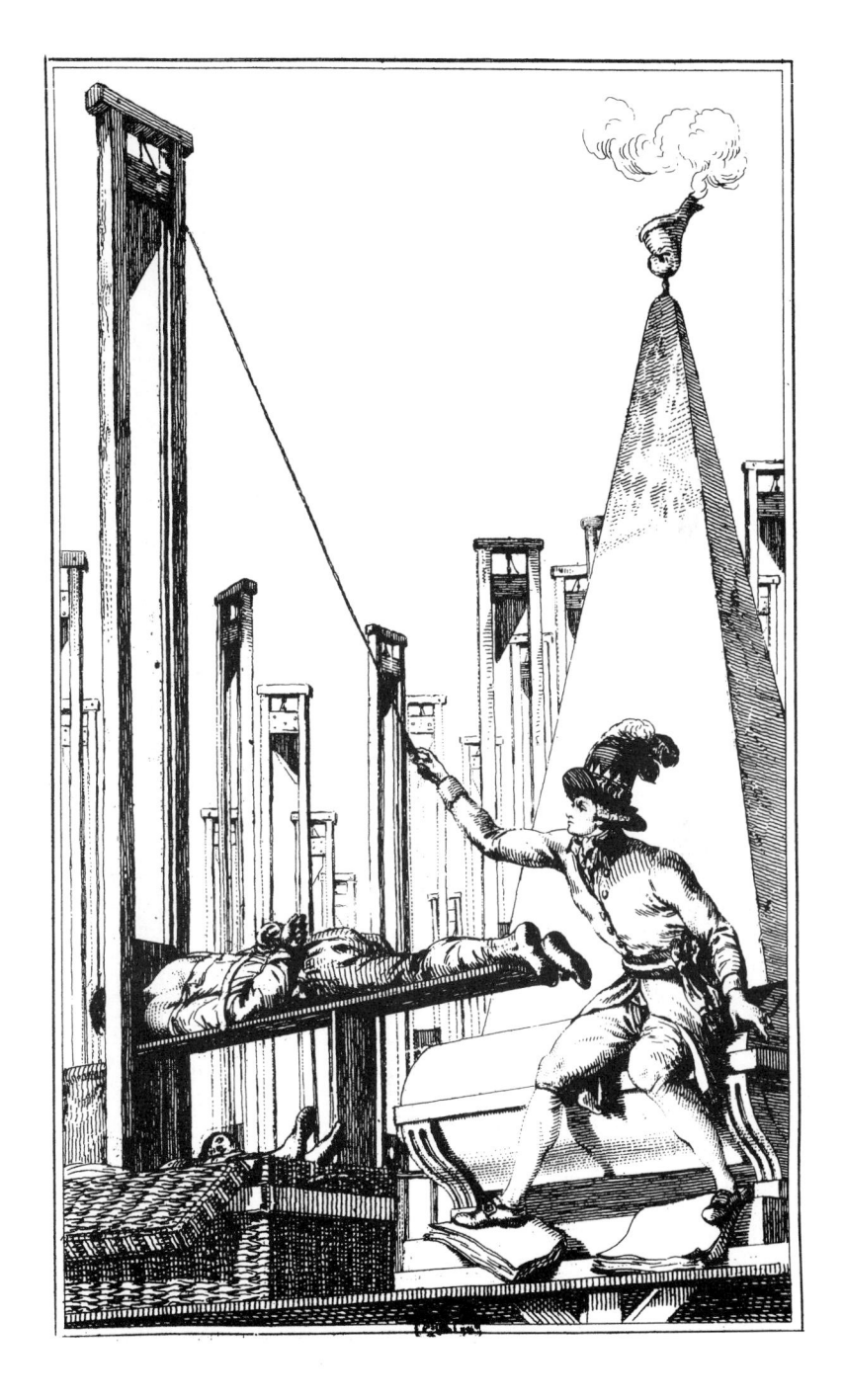

3 Unable to find any more executioners, Robespierre does the job himself. Shows the general features of the guillotine, and the position of the victim strapped to the *bascule*. (Anonymous etching; Bibliothèque Nationale)

4 Charlotte Corday; Duplessis-Bertaux. Underneath the portrait can be seen a rather inaccurate depiction of Charlotte's arrest, with Marat dying in his bath and Charlotte seated calmly beside the body as soldiers rush in. (Duplessis-Bertaux; Bibliothèque Nationale)

5 Olympe de Gouges. (Imaginary portrait; Bibliothèque Nationale)

6 Revolutionary marriage on the Loire. At Nantes men and women were allegedly stripped naked and tied together before being drowned. The sans-culotte appears to be stealing the victims' clothes. (Thermidorian engraving; Bibliothèque Nationale)

7 Execution of Madame Elisabeth, May 1794. This German print incorrectly shows the guillotine blade as round. (Anonymous; Bibliothèque Nationale)

2

BEHEADING
Nobility, martyrdom, matrimony

> Meekly, steadfastly,
> I will endure all pain and torment.
> Then order, command,
> Bluster, roar and rage!
> In the end, death will set me free.
> (*Die Entführung aus dem Serail*, Act II)

The greater efficiency of beheading is evident from early times. Accounts of the executions of the pioneer Christian saints indicate the sword was resorted to in Rome and most parts of its empire, when every other means had failed ignominiously. One such source is the thirteenth-century *Legenda Aurea* of Jacobus de Varagine, which enthusiastically records the deaths of at least twelve female saints, among them Lucy, Margaret, Juliana, Agnes and Euphemia. As the *Legenda* is devotional, rather than scholarly, in nature, its accounts may raise some rational eyebrows; nonetheless they are valuable indicators of the association of nobility with martyrdom and beheading.

To be exact, not all of the twelve were actually beheaded. In several cases a sword is thrust through the throat, terminating both the saint's heroic and miraculous resistance to execution, and the embarrassment of the authorities. In AD 310 Saint Lucy, a noblewoman of Syracuse, is threatened with life in a brothel by the Roman consul Paschasius. But the Holy Ghost makes her so infinitely heavy that she cannot be moved, even by one thousand men and yokes of oxen. The consul has a fire built on the spot and drenches her in pitch, resin and boiling oil, but Lucy continues to profess Christ until the consul's friends, seeing him grow furious, plunge a sword into her throat. The same sort of thing happens in AD 309 to Saint Agnes who, aged thirteen, has the misfortune to be glimpsed on her way home from school by the son of the Roman prefect. Immediately smitten with love the boy tries to marry her, but she refuses. The prefect tells her she must either sacrifice to Vesta, with the other virgins of that goddess, or be locked up with the prostitutes. Unimpressed, Agnes again refuses, is stripped of all her clothes and led naked to a 'house of debauch'. But God causes her hair to grow very long, covering her nakedness; moreover, an angel awaits her in the place of shame, proffering a tunic of most dazzling white. The prefect's son arrives with all his friends and invites them to take pleasure of her, but the friends are terrified and run away. An obligingly subservient devil throttles the prefect's son 'because he had not honoured God'. The prefect comes in tears to see Agnes, and at his request she prays; the young man is restored, and praises God. At this, the heathen priests cry witchcraft, arousing the populace. The prefect is inclined to release Agnes, but dare not. Sadly, he leaves her with his lieutenant, Aspasius. This latter causes Agnes to be thrown into a raging fire, but the flames divide, consuming not Agnes, but the pagans. Aspasius causes a dagger to be thrust into her throat, 'and in this manner her heavenly spouse claims her for his bride, having decked her with the crown of martyrdom'.[1]

The essential structure of martyrdoms in the *Legenda Aurea* has already emerged: the chaste Christian female, beloved by a Roman, is made to suffer all manner of erotically tinged torments while the pagan continues to lust after her. So it is in accounts of actual decapitations, such as that of Juliana. Betrothed to Eulogius, prefect of Nicodemia, Juliana refuses to receive him carnally unless he embraces the Christian faith. Irritated by this obdurate chastity her father has her stripped and beaten, but to no avail. An enterprising fiancé, Eulogius also has her beaten with rods, then hung up by the hair while molten lead is poured upon her scalp. Juliana is clapped into prison, where a devil visits her and orders her to sacrifice to Roman gods, but Juliana seizes him and beats him with her chains until he begs for mercy. Ordered forth by Eulogius she drags this very physical devil the full length of the marketplace and throws him down a privy. The prefect then has Juliana stretched and broken on a wheel until the marrow spurts; but an angel makes her whole. Seeing this, all persons present – about 500 men, with 130 women – believe in Christ, and suffer martyrdom by beheading. Undeterred, Eulogius has his bride plunged into molten lead; but the metal suddenly cools, becoming 'as a lukewarm bath'. This is finally too much for the prefect. Cursing his own gods for being impotent against this frail woman, he orders her to be beheaded too. Apparently this last move is successful, for the saint 'goes bravely to her death'.

Similar tribulations befall Saint Margaret, of whom the prefect Olybius becomes enamoured when she is aged 15 and guarding sheep. Olybius does his utmost to persuade her to renounce Christianity, having her racked and beaten, first with rods, then with sharp instruments that cut her to the bone. Rebuking those 'evil counsellors' who sympathetically bemoan the loss of her beauty, Margaret roundly declares that 'this torture of my flesh is the salvation of my soul', calling the prefect a 'ravening and shameless dog'. As for Olybius, he is unable to watch the 'outpouring of blood', and hides his face in his mantle. He has Margaret cast into prison where she, like Juliana, is tempted by a devil. Margaret easily defeats the fiend and is ready for the next day's torments. This time she is stripped of her garments and burned

BEHEADING

with lighted torches. 'To increase pain by varying her sufferings' the prefect has her plunged into a tub of water; but instantly the earth shakes, the tub breaks, and Margaret steps forth unscathed before the multitude. Witnessing this, 5,000 persons are converted, and suffer decollation for professing Christ. The narrator does not explain how so many people come to be beheaded when the prefect is having such difficulty dispatching one; but the lesson of decapitation is not lost on Olybius who, 'fearing still other conversions', orders Margaret to have her head cut off as rapidly as possible. Before dying Margaret manages to obtain of heaven that any woman in labour who calls upon her name shall give birth without harm to the child.

The deaths of other saintly women are no less spectacular: wild beasts will not touch them, flames part in their presence, molten lead is as a pleasant balm. On the other hand, the sword almost never fails. The one occasion when it is not totally effective is the martyrdom of Saint Cecilia. Called before the inevitable prefect – Almachius, this time – Cecilia refuses to give up her faith and insults him. 'Exceeding wroth' at her words, Almachius first orders her to be boiled in her bath. When that fails he has her beheaded, still sitting in the tub. The executioner strikes three times without severing the head; since the law decrees that 'a fourth blow could not be given', he has to leave her, wet and nearly dead. Cecilia lingers on three days and gives all her possessions to the poor. Finally, she dies. Confronted with the detail of the three failed blows – and fortified in demon doubt by accounts of bungled executions in a later age – one begins to wonder whether the inefficient torments of these martyrdoms do not derive more from human error than divine intervention; but perhaps that is the same thing. But even allowing for the hagiographer's understandable zeal, decapitation was clearly the most reliable means of dispatching women who had God on their side.

It was also the most noble. Of twelve martyred female saints in the *Legenda*, eight were put to death by sword. Of these, five are described as being of noble birth, and two are daughters of pagan high priests. The eighth martyr, Juliana, is betrothed to a prefect and thus presumably of equal rank. Another saint, Euphemia, actually reminds her persecutors that she is daughter to a senator, and should therefore have been executed before the other martyrs in her group. In other words, the decapitated martyrs had received a death appropriate to their rank, for execution by axe or by sword was a privilege of patricians, and was not considered shameful by the Romans. This contrasts with accounts in the *Ecclesiastical History* of Eusebius, whose martyrs are often from the lower classes: possibly the most heroic is Blandina, a slave, who endures every form of torture, is roasted on a heated chair and resists wild beasts (they will not touch her) before being tossed to death by a bull. But by the time Jacobus was writing, decapitation by sword was the privileged means; thus it would seem that this bishop of Genoa combined Roman patrician practice with the aristocratic forms of his own time. (Noble birth, incidentally, was a characteristic of the *Legenda*'s saints generally: of those four not killed by the sword, three are put to death by some form of fire, and one is killed by arrows; all but one are described as hailing from patrician families. Even the non-martyred saints found in Jacobus' charming mini-biographies are largely noble. Mary Magdalene, who is one of them, was 'born of parents who were of noble station, and came of royal lineage'. She owned the town of Magdala, while her brother Lazarus owned portions of Jerusalem. To be fair to Jacobus, two more saints had been prostitutes, another was the daughter of Saint Peter, and Marina and Pelagia dressed as men and lived as monks.)

Apart from illustrating the superior efficiency of the sword, Jacobus' *Legenda* demonstrates the veneration in which female chastity was held, both at the time of the martyrdoms and in the thirteenth century. One might describe chastity as the bright side of a female coin whose dark reverse was a satanic predisposition to lewdness. Thanks to their epic resistance to pagan lust these sorely tried women were apparently viewed by the Church Fathers as being on a par with the male saints who suffered similar torments. Then again, Christianity provided access to bodily and spiritual dignity for former prostitutes. As Helen C. White has pointed out, many of the women Jacobus describes lived highly original lives – dressing up as monks, refusing to get married, making fools of Roman prefects. If one has lived in the American Bible Belt one may not necessarily associate Christianity with female freedom; nevertheless, Jacobus' martyred saints evidently found chastity a means of assuring their own physical and spiritual independence and integrity. Athletes of God, as Helen White terms them, they were 'ordinary' women who found the courage to hold physical pain as nothing if it bought freedom of the soul.

The noble status granted to beheading in the Middle Ages and thereafter derived no doubt to some extent from Roman precedent; but perhaps from even earlier times. Besides being a tool, the axe – the alternative weapon to the sword in Roman beheadings – was a symbol of patriarchal authority in certain cultures; Robert Claiborne in *The Roots of English* records that men were often buried with their battle-axes. But there may also have been strictly practical considerations. To kneel and hold perfectly still while the headsman whirled his heavy sword, gathering momentum, undoubtedly required the sort of superior self-control normally attributed to French aristocrats of the *ancien régime* – and even aristocrats would sometimes move. Reproached in July 1766 for his bungled decapitation of Lally-Tollendal, Marshal of France, Charles-Henri Sanson replied: 'It was not my fault, Monsieur. He moved', the first blow having slashed the Marshal's jaw. The man uttering this rebuke was the Chevalier de la Barre, a young man of 18 condemned to have his own tongue and head cut off for singing blasphemous songs. The amputation of the tongue was

BEHEADING

done in sham, leaving the Chevalier able to issue a challenge: if he himself guaranteed to stand upright and not waver, Sanson must promise to sever his head with but a single stroke. The executioner agreed, and it is said that both men kept their word.

But before the elegantly disdainful beheadings of the eighteenth century another cluster of decapitations occurred. It is a curious paradox of the English Renaissance that the very class of women whose position might seem to afford them, for once, some possibility of influencing the course of law would count among its most illustrious victims. Queenship was a high-risk occupation: two wives beheaded out of Henry's six; Lady Jane Grey, who ruled for slightly more than a week; and then the Queen of Scots. To have been royal, and female, was precisely their political misfortune. Yet males of the time were not necessarily safer: many aristocratic families counted it almost an honour to have at least one drawn and quartered or beheaded male ancestor. To die on charge of treason was a means of rendering service to the state, with its not always moral political necessities. What was different in the case of queens was the extent to which their predicament was caused by matrimony. For, unlike the Christian saints who chose martyrdom to avoid wedlock, the four Queens may be said to have died in consequence of the particular marriages they made. And far from being executed for their chastity, three of the four were doomed by charges of adultery.

The man directly responsible for two of these deaths had been described, at the age of 23, as 'the best-looking royal person in Christendom'. He was also the most learned, the most liberal, and probably the most athletic. He excelled at tennis and dancing, and was addicted to lavish formal entertainments in which the court became a chivalrous allegory and he himself fought single combats in emulation of the heroes of Romance. He played the lute, organ and other keyboard instruments, and could have made a living as a professional musician, had he not been King; two of his motets – 'O Lord the maker of all things' and 'Quam pulchra es' – are still performed. Fascinated by theology, he wrote a critical reply to Luther that earned him the title of Defender of the Faith. A friend to humanists and scholars, he was surrounded with the best minds of his time; he was, in short, the ideal Renaissance prince. To cap it all he was married to the bride of his dreams, Catherine of Aragon, a woman six years his senior but possessed of beauty, charm and vast erudition. Yet by middle age he was divorcing and beheading and generally on his way to becoming, in another of the Reverend Summers' slightly memorable phrases, the 'fat and syphillitic monster who terrorised England'. Whatever had gone wrong?

The most poetic account is that provided by Edith Sitwell in her *Fanfare for Elizabeth*. For Sitwell, the story of Anne, Henry and their child Elizabeth was a gigantic tragedy, a Sophoclean drama of an escape from an imagined or pretended incest cursed by heaven: the tale was of bloodshed and of huge lusts of the flesh and spirit; of man's desire for spiritual freedom; and of a great Queen who sacrificed her heart and life on the altar of her country.[2]

The drama of which Sitwell speaks had developed from Henry's consuming obsession to produce a son and heir. By the time he was 32 – the age at which he met Anne Boleyn – Henry was disappointed in Catherine's failure to provide him with a male heir; disappointed in the numerous miscarriages that thickened her once pretty form. Production of a son was essential, both to prolong the Tudor dynasty and to preserve England from foreign domination: the obstacles were his infertile marriage and the spiritual allegiance Christian princes owed to Rome. The catalysts of the great tragedy were Henry's conscience, and his love for Anne Boleyn.

As Anne's biographer Nora Lofts remarks, though no one can be certain of the date of birth of Anne Boleyn, everybody knows the hour and place of her death. The first public mention of the infant Anne occurs in 1514; aged about 9, she accompanied Henry's sister Mary Tudor on her marriage trip to France. Mary had been betrothed as part of a peace treaty to Louis XII, an older man with stinking teeth. When Louis died, shortly afterwards, Mary married the man of her choice, Charles Brandon, and returned to England. Initially furious that she had married without consulting him – a marriageable princess was a tool in foreign policy – Henry later forgave them both and made Charles Duke of Suffolk. Precocious and bilingual, Anne Boleyn remained in France until 1522, entering first the household of Claude, Queen to Francis I, then that of Marguerite de Navarre. In 1522 war broke out between the two countries – less than two years after the French and English kings had met in splendour and extravagance at Calais in the Field of the Cloth of Gold, exchanging promises of peace amid an array of spurious palaces and gold-encrusted tents suddenly toppled by a violent, unexpected storm.

The Anne who came from France in 1522 was known for two things: her grace, which owed much to Marguerite de Navarre, and her neck, which was unusually long and slender – as slender as the monarch's was beginning to be thick. She joined the court of Catherine which, though pious, was not dull, for Catherine enjoyed modest gambling, cards, and the company of elegant young people. It is not known exactly when Henry first fell in love with the new lady-in-waiting, but Neville Williams records that in March 1522 she was one of five beautiful maidens rescued by the King in an allegorical pageant, in which Henry played the allegorical part of Ardent Desire. Quite soon the young and highly eligible Harry Percy, heir to the earldom of Northumberland, fell in love with Anne, and she with him; preliminary vows were exchanged. But Cardinal Wolsey intervened, which suggests to

BEHEADING

Nora Lofts that Henry already wanted Anne for himself. The junior Percy nonetheless proved so stubborn that his father had to be sent for, to threaten him with disinheritance; finally he was married off to Mary Talbot, in a match Lofts deems disastrous.

As a result of this thwarted romance Anne lost her place at court and returned to Hever Castle, home of the Boleyns, in frustration and disgrace. When Henry VIII visited the castle unexpectedly in October 1523, Anne's father Thomas ordered her to go to bed and stay there until the King had left. But Henry came again. He was now 32, accustomed to the high competence of his faithful, ruthless Cardinal Wolsey; accustomed, in short, to getting his own way. Production of a son was well on its way to becoming that grandiose obsession that might invite comparison with Captain Pequod's quest for the white whale, or Frankenstein's pursuit of his monster across the frozen wastes of the North Pole, had it occurred in literature, or some more natural setting than an English four-poster bed. Anne Boleyn was of childbearing age, witty and aloof – a combination that proved irresistible. Henry would later say she had bewitched him, a theory to which Nora Lofts adds more than passing credence. Anne had a mole on her neck, and a rudimentary sixth finger; both appendages were thought signs of witchcraft. She also possessed an 'unusually devoted' wolfhound who bore the satanic name of Urian, and might have passed for a familiar; but most telling in Loft's eyes was the King's sudden disenchantment; when free of the 'spell', he passed almost into hatred, very fast.

Before that sexual peripeteia, however, Anne stubbornly refused, from 1523 to 1532, to become Henry's mistress unless he also married her; she would be Queen, or nothing. To her sardonic arrogance the King responded with ever more devotion. Lofts even suggests he saw himself as an armoured knight protecting her virtue, when that virtue was in fact protected by the more reliable safeguard of Anne's implacable ambition. Henry began to think of obtaining a divorce. More exactly, he set about proving he had never been married at all. Catherine had been his brother's bride. The King was troubled, he said, by a text of Leviticus, which said a man should not wed his deceased brother's wife, at risk of being childless. Was it not God's judgement upon him that all his male children by his wife had been stillborn?

The task of arranging the divorce fell to Cardinal Wolsey. Not least among the difficulties he faced was the situation of Pope Clement, whose assent was required: Imperial forces had recently mutinied, imprisoning Clement in the Castel Sant'Angelo. Himself a papal legate, Wolsey had thought to take control of things in Clement's absence and negotiate the assent of fellow cardinals. That plan failed, leaving philosophical obstacles. Henry's marriage to Catherine had already required a papal dispensation, on account of Leviticus; permitting a divorce would have obliged the Pope to declare his predecessor's judgement null and void. Besides, Clement rather believed in papal dispensations, having needed one himself: born illegitimate, he had needed a dispensation of legitimacy in order to be Pope. To cope with this embarrassment he dispatched a very old man, the cardinal Campeggio, to judge the case in England. Campeggio had to be carried every inch of the way on a litter, which burdensome journey took three months. Once arrived, the cardinal told Henry that the Pope was willing to recognise his marriage to Catherine! His next suggestion was for her to enter a nunnery. Henry was pleased, but Catherine, whose genuine piety would not stoop to so political an end, flatly refused. There was nothing for it but to proceed with a 'trial' of the King's marriage. The outcome was indecisive and Wolsey, having failed to obtain this much-desired annulment, fell into disgrace.

To console Anne for the delay – it was now 1532 – Henry granted her a great honour, one never before bestowed upon a woman: she was created lady Marquess of Pembroke, and thus ennobled in her own right. That same year, now a wealthy landowner, she was presented to Francis I, with whom Henry was currently at peace. Shortly thereafter, in Nora Loft's chronology, she granted the King the honour of her bed. By January 1533 she was pregnant. Things did not look wholly black for Henry's plan: in 1531 he had dismissed Catherine from court, stripping her of all her jewels; Anne had been given apartments of her own. In 1532 the death of Warham, Archbishop of Canterbury, had left Henry the possibility of finding a prelate more amenable to his divorce. He therefore married Anne privately early in 1533, permitting her a splendid coronation that May. He also did his best to screen her from unwelcome news, such as Clement's threat to excommunicate him if he did not repudiate her. Above all, preparations were made for the birth of a son, obligingly predicted by the royal astrologers.

The eagerly awaited boy, however, was a girl, delivered on 7 September 1533, the future Elizabeth. Henry took it well: 'She will have brothers', he declared, too proud to recognise defeat. With the Act of Supremacy, Henry took measures to bolster up Elizabeth's legitimacy, and that of future progeny; England's national sovereignty was pronounced in 1533 with the Act Restraining Appeals to Rome. These measures met with some resistance. The Carthusian monks refused to recognise the Acts, and were sentenced to be hanged, drawn, quartered and disembowelled alive. More damaging still, Bishop Fisher and Sir Thomas More also refused, and had to be beheaded, in 1534. Henry was not pleased, in Loft's analysis, at ridding himself of his best friend, and bitterly complained to his Queen that because of her 'the honestest man in my kingdom is dead'. Then, in January 1536, Catherine died. Anne was pregnant at the time, but by now Henry was in love with Jane Seymour, plain, past 30, but sweet of disposition – unlike Anne, whose jealousy and arrogance increasingly displeased the King. Henry celebrated Catherine's demise by ordering a joust, in which he himself took part. It proved disastrous: he was knocked unconscious and unhorsed, incurring a leg wound which never properly healed. The Duke of Norfolk, Anne's less than pleasant uncle, brutally informed her that Henry was dead. A few days later Anne miscarried – of a boy.

Furious, Henry told her she would get no more sons by him. Anne had been safe while Catherine was alive, since Henry could scarcely get rid of her for fear of having to remarry his first wife; but now he was in love with Jane. How to be rid of Anne? He could not face another tedious divorce; he could not really accuse her of heresy, given that she was the direct cause of the English Reformation, though not precisely Protestant; therefore she must die. She must be accused of treason. And since in a queen – as in the Middle Ages of Romance – adultery was treason, Anne must be accused of adultery.

At this point it is necessary to interrupt the narrative to cast doubt on all that has just been said – all that pertains to the chronology of Anne and Henry's romance, and the motives behind the royal divorce. In her recent, complex study *The Rise and Fall of Anne Boleyn*, Retha Warnicke insists at length on Henry's religious development and the importance of his *Assertio Septem Sacramentorum* – the anti-Lutheran reply begun in 1518, at a time when Catherine was pregnant for the final time. Publication in several editions and translations of this work had turned Henry into a recognised authority on religious matters – not least in his own mind, wherein he pondered the increasingly desperate question of Catherine's stillborn children. In Warnicke's view, Henry's doubts about the validity of his marriage were quite genuine, and had set in long before he met Anne. Then again, he had the all too real worry of the English succession. He had several times met Margaret, the Habsburg regent of the Netherlands, and seen what a woman ruler could achieve; but there was no such precedent in England, even for capable women like Margaret Beaufort, his own grandmother. The best he could hope for was that his daughter Mary would marry Charles of Spain and rule England under his authority. But then Charles married Isabella of Portugal, and Henry had no son; in 1526 he recognised Mary as his heir, thus admitting he expected no further children by the ageing Catherine. Divorce began to seem a rational solution, both to his personal guilt and to the problems of succession.

To support this argument – that Henry was disposed to a divorce before he fell in love with Anne – Warnicke demolishes the chronology, advanced by Lofts and others, according to which Henry's passion for Anne dated from 1523. Henry, she suggests, did not actually even dance with Anne until 25 May 1527; and when he did, it was not Anne's arrogantly ambitious chastity but rather her grace and poise that so attracted him. For Anne had been accustomed from her earliest years to life at court; her education had been superb; and she had been exposed from childhood to the best possible role models. Thanks to an invitation from Margaret, the Habsburg archduchess, Anne had been educated in the Netherlands with Margaret's four wards; thus, her first formative influences had taken place at the court of Malines, a centre of humanist poets and painters. It was only subsequently that Mary Tudor sent for her to come to France. She had been well trained in the rigorously pious court of Queen Claude, then exposed to further humanist and artistic influences when attending Marguerite Queen of Navarre, author of the *Heptameron* and *Miroir de l'âme pécheresse*. 'Anne's charm arose primarily from the deep-seated confidence with which she was able to handle herself in courtly surroundings. She was the perfect woman courtier.'[3] Graceful, elegantly dressed, Anne spoke excellent French, danced well, sang, played the lute, did beautiful embroidery and may even have written a masque and composed music. Small wonder that Henry was delighted with her, because she had been educated to delight: nor was it surprising, in Warnicke's view, that she should be delighted with Henry, who was still being described by the Venetian Ambassador as 'a perfect model of manly beauty'.

Warnicke further takes issue with prevailing explanations for Anne's downfall. Professor E. W. Ives, for example, argues that Thomas Cromwell, Wolsey's replacement as Chancellor, allied himself with the Aragonese faction at court and plotted to effect Anne's ruin, together with that of her five alleged partners in adultery. Nora Lofts implies that Anne herself was responsible for her misfortunes, having always behaved with a high-handedness unsuitable for her station and ultimately irritating to Henry; when she complained about his taking a mistress he roughly told her to put up with it, as her 'betters' – that is to say, Catherine – had done. In Retha Warnicke's opinion these two types of approach rely too heavily on the correspondence of the Imperial Ambassador, Eustace Chapuys, who readily confused fact both with gossip overheard at court and speculations of his own; moreover, he was heavily biased in favour of Catherine, to the point of refusing even to converse with Anne. Warnicke therefore strikes out with a bold postulation of her own. Rejecting much of what Chapuys relates about the deteriorating relationship of Anne and Henry (that is, between the birth of Elizabeth and Anne's final pregnancy), Warnicke decides to take seriously Chapuys' claims that many of Anne's contemporaries viewed her as a witch. Maintaining that Henry remained fond of Anne until her final pregnancy, she argues that the precipitating cause of his sudden change of attitude, as of Anne's subsequent trial, was that the baby boy of whom the Queen so tragically miscarried had been born deformed.

Naturally this is impossible to prove. Reports of the foetus indicate only that it was a boy, apparently conceived fifteen or sixteen weeks before, and that it was born dead. To support her contention, Warnicke reminds the reader that in the sixteenth century witchcraft was associated with sodomy, lechery, incest, the birth of stillborn or dead babies, and impotence in men – all factors in Anne's trial. For, 'despising her marriage' and 'entertaining malice against the King', the Queen was accused of charming 'divers of the

King's daily and familiar servants' into yielding to her 'vile provocations'. These 'daily and familiar servants' were Mark Smeaton, Anne's musician; her own brother, Lord George Rochford; Sir Henry Norris, Master of the King's Horse; Sir Richard Page; Sir Francis Weston; and William Brereton. The clumsiness with which the charges were drawn up – alleging adultery at a moment when she was known to be with the King – is taken most seriously by Warnicke, who reminds us that witches were thought capable of being in several places at once.

A further interesting point in this argument is that all of the men accused were libertines, hence liable in the public mind to commit everything from incest to sodomy. The most important of them was Rochford, who 'was to be given responsibility for her last pregnancy'; Rochford and Smeaton, she speculates, may have been buggers. This, too, is hard to prove, since a crime too abominable to be mentioned at the time of its committing is hard to trace four centuries later; but the essential point to retain is that Henry would be very anxious to disavow a child born deformed, hence sought to blame the disaster on some credible scapegoat. Another charge levelled at Rochford was that he had giggled at reports of Henry's impotency. This accusation was so offensive to Henry's dignity that the question was put to Rochford on a bit of paper, to which he was supposed to answer yes or no; but in a fit of defiant frivolity the viscount read the dreadful charge aloud for all to hear, thereby sealing his own doom. The other four men were sentenced to the block; George, for his impious levity, was sentenced to be hanged, drawn and quartered, and disembowelled alive.

One should not conclude from this that Warnicke believes Anne to have actually been a witch. Taking issue with the prevailing view of Anne as a seductress whose religious views were shallow, Warnicke stresses on the contrary her pious education, her preference for reading the Bible in translation, her protection of religious reformers and her good works to the poor. Warnicke's brilliance is to make her argument plausible by referring to the very images of Anne she undercuts. One has only to read Edith Sitwell, evoking Anne in the simple act of going down a stair, to see the power of demonic imagery:

> A few steps more; and a barbarous refulgence fell upon her face, and one could see that she was a place of torment, – not a woman at all; but an infernal region, a Pandemonium of the Princes of Darkness and the Powers and Principalities of the Air.
>
> (Sitwell, p. 18)

If Anne's contemporaries had entertained such visions, it would surely have been easy for them to condemn the mother of a stillborn son. The main objection to Warnicke's approach is that it involves venturing so far along the tightrope of speculation; however, such speculation as she does advance is always within the context of sixteenth-century opinions on the subject.

Anne herself alludes to some unspoken motive in her trial, for when she was condemned she said to her judges, who were led by her uncle, the Duke of Norfolk: 'I think you know well the reason why you have condemned me to be other than that which led you to this judgement. My only sin against the King has been my jealousy and lack of humility.' She was prepared to die; her only regret was that 'men who were innocent and loyal to the King' must die because of her. Many, including the Lord Mayor of London, thought her innocent. Learning of her arrest the new Archbishop of Canterbury, Thomas Cranmer, had written with a sort of schizophrenic courage to the King, expressing his good opinion of her while tactfully recognising that the King must have reasons for his act. None of this helped her. Even Harry Percy had voted 'guilty' with all the other lords; then he fainted, and was carried out. Anne was told she might be burned: 'Thou shalt be burned here within the Tower of London on the Green, else to have thy head smitten off as the King's pleasure shall be further known.'

Fortunately for Anne and George the King's pleasure stopped at mere decapitation, a possible reason for this mildness being that Cranmer held a secret court, in which it was determined that Anne had never been lawfully married to Henry at all: he had bedded her younger sister Mary Boleyn, while she had once been engaged to Harry Percy. Apparently no one pointed out that if Anne had never been married she could not logically have committed treason through adultery. Nonetheless Henry's conscience was now greatly relieved; Lofts suggests that Cranmer was sent privily to persuade Anne of Elizabeth's illegitimacy, which being done, she was spared the stake. Her four supposed lovers were beheaded first. Pronounced guilty, they could not proclaim their innocence as this was considered a special form of treason implying criticism of the law, leading to the confiscation of their property and disinheritance of their heirs. Thus, they all made brief remarks, curt to the point of ambiguity, that they 'deserved the death'. Anne's own execution was put off for two days, during which the nervous strain of waiting – to say nothing of the 'pent-up shock and disbelief', as Warnicke observes – seems to have made her slightly mad. Kingston, Master of the Tower, tried to comfort her: there would be no pain. 'I have heard say that the executioner is very good. And I have a little neck', she replied. And then putting her hand to her 'lytel neck', she laughed heartily.

Anne was sent to the block on 19 May 1536. Always elegant, she wore a dark damask dress with a white collar, which she removed herself. Her famous black hair was coiled on top of her head, beneath a small black velvet hood sewn with pearls. Nora Lofts declares she sent a message to the King so scathing, so distinctly hers in its sardonic arrogance that no one dared deliver it:

BEHEADING

Commend me to his Majesty and tell him that he hath ever been constant in his career of advancing me; from a private gentlewoman he hath made me a Marchioness; from a Marchioness a Queen, and now that hath left no higher degree of honour he gives my innocency the crown of martyrdom.

As a special act of mercy, a swordsman had been sent for from Saint-Omer in France; the neck was severed with a single blow. Shortly thereafter Cranmer issued a special dispensation permitting the monarch to remarry. Henry, dressed all in royal mourning white, was betrothed to Jane Seymour the next day, and wedded ten days later.

In a sense the downfall of Anne Boleyn illustrates the persistence of medieval stereotypes, as if the unhappy Queen, suspected, at the very least in Henry's jokes, of witchcraft, was also betrayed by the superficial chivalry of Henry's reign: one thinks of the allegorical pageants, the jousts, the Field of the Cloth of Gold. Could this chivalrous vision of his own court have yielded the inverse image of the adulterous Queen, years later when it came to framing charges? For Anne suffered in reality the fate almost met in literature by Guinevere, Halis and Yseult, had they not been rescued by their Lancelots and Tristans at the point of a sword. The only one of the five men to admit to the adultery was Smeaton, her personal musician, thus a sort of troubadour, arrested on Sunday 1 May 1536 and tortured into a confession; Henry was at a tournament at Greenwich when this news was brought. All unknowing, Anne dropped her handkerchief from a balcony into the hand of Sir Henry Norris, the King's Master of Horse, the sign, in Romance, of the favour of a lady. Henry promised freedom if Norris would confess, but Norris had his own ideas of chivalry. Convinced of the Queen's innocence, he offered to defend it in single combat with the King, or any other possible accuser. The privilege was denied, and Norris and the other suspects were taken to the Tower.

A more potent factor in Henry's changed feelings with regard to Anne was probably religion. He had gone to great, irrevocable lengths to impose her as Queen; those unwilling to recognise his Acts had been killed as traitors. The effects of these deeds – particularly the execution of Sir Thomas More – on a once-scrupulous conscience must have been devastating. Then there was the threat of excommunication, which would compound the damage, for as Edith Sitwell remarks, once this had been braved, there was nothing to restrain him. Anne's own achievement in all this was not unremarkable. She is regarded as the direct cause of the English Reformation, of the schism which enabled England to break free of the spiritual domination of Rome. And in giving birth to Elizabeth she mothered the most leonine of Henry's progeny, the celibate Queen under whom England would enjoy decades of stability. That the example of her mother's calamitous marriage probably contributed to Elizabeth's own refusal to wed was not the least of the ironies attendant on the tale.

Henry's remaining wives all faced their separate risks. On 12 October 1537, Jane Seymour bore him the desired male heir, Edward, but died herself as a result. Henry's fourth marriage – to the suitably Protestant but hopelessly unattractive Anne of Cleves – was never consummated, a disaster which cost Cromwell, who arranged it, his own head. A disappointed Henry soon displayed a more than paternal interest in one of Anne's young maids of honour, Catherine Howard. At about the same time he grew troubled in his conscience that Anne was pre-contracted to the Duke of Lorraine. Anne sensibly agreed to a divorce. Mad with gratitude, Henry granted her precedence over all other ladies of the realm, save his own Queen and daughters, together with a pension of five hundred pounds a year. The Duke of Cleves, Anne's brother, could not admit to the invalidity of Henry's marriage, but privately observed that he was 'glad his sister had fared no worse'.

But Catherine Howard would fare worse. Gay, frivolous, quick-tempered, she has been described as the most beautiful of Henry's Queens. She was also what we would today term an abused child. Her father, Edmund Howard, had been a younger son, lacking wealth and position; he had married a rich widow, who died when Catherine was not thirteen. She was taken into the house of her step-grandmother, the Dowager Duchess of Norfolk; the influential Duke found her a place in Anne of Cleves' attendance. She was 20 when the by now bloated and repulsive monarch married her on 28 July 1541.

What Henry did not know was that the Duchess had largely abandoned her to the care of waiting-women. Through them she met Henry Manox, a musician. This Manox took advantage of the child and 'was in the habit of indulging ... in an unspeakably lewd and frightful conduct which cannot be described here', as Edith Sitwell puts it; 'and this he did in full view of the waiting-women'. Then, when Catherine was fifteen, she was raped by Francis Dereham, a young pensioner in the household. The friendless Catherine seems to have forgiven Dereham, who gave her little presents and considered her his bride. All this was known to Mary Lassels, one of the Norfolk housewomen, and to her brother John. Perhaps fearing blackmail, Catherine employed several of her companions in shame when she set up house as Queen. Among these were Joan Bulmer, a former bedfellow; Dereham, who became her secretary; and Manox. Lady Rochford, widow of the beheaded George, was named lady-in-waiting. For a while things went relatively well. Henry adored Catherine, and spoiled her like a child. The young Queen was kept busy with seemingly endless dances and formal entertainments: Anne of Cleves visited them, bearing gifts, and danced into the night with Catherine while Henry went to bed. But during the summer progress Henry fell ill with an ulcerated leg – a complication from a fall, sustained during a joust in the days of Anne Boleyn. Revels and presents ceased, and Catherine grew bored. Before long Thomas Cranmer was able to acquaint the King with flirtatious details from his new bride's past. These had been supplied by the Lassels, and hearing them, Cranmer had turned pale.

In the ensuing inquiry Dereham tried to take the blame upon himself, claiming that he and Catherine had been betrothed. This argument seemed likely to satisfy Henry, given recent precedent; but Catherine denied it. More damning was the implication of Thomas Culpeper, one of Henry's grooms. To him Catherine had written: 'Master Culpeper, I heartily recommend me unto you, praying you to send me word how you do. I heard you were sick, and never longed so much for anything as to see you. It makes my heart die to think I cannot always be in your company.' Put to the torture Culpeper denied actual adultery, but admitted to a mutual inclination. Had Catherine hoped that Culpeper would sire a child, explicable as Henry's? Whatever the case, Cranmer's inquiry revealed lax standards of behaviour in her household. At first Henry found this hard to believe, then flew into a rage. An hysterical Catherine was sent to Syon House with a reduced attendance, and stripped of all her jewels. After two months she was taken to the Tower. Uncle to Catherine as he had been to Anne Boleyn, the Duke of Norfolk now wrote a cringing letter to Henry expressing shame at his degenerate kin's behaviour. By siding with her accusers he managed to retain his position at the Treasury, though with some loss of prestige. For her part Catherine begged the lords of the council to implore the King 'not to impute her crime to her whole kindred or family'. She was executed on 18 February 1542, after expressing remorse for her treatment of the King – astonishingly, the only person who had ever shown her kindness.

In 1543 Henry married Catherine Parr, an educated, pious woman who dealt kindly and rationally with her royal stepchildren: under her benevolent scholasticism, Mary returned honourably to court, while Edward and Elizabeth pursued their all-consuming and precocious studies. Yet even the impeccable domestic comportment of Catherine Parr contained an almost fatal flaw: she discussed points of religion with her spouse. Bishop Gardiner and Chancellor Wriothesley found this to be dangerous and a writ was drawn up, condemning her on changes of heresy. Catherine got wind of this and burst into opportune and wifely tears, which Henry overheard. He sent his personal physician to her and a reconciliation was effected. Catherine then professed herself unfit to hold personal views on religion: the wisdom of her husband was her anchor under God. When Henry remained peeved – 'You have become a doctor, Kate, to instruct us, as we take it, and not to be instructed or directed by us' – Catherine had the presence of mind to answer that she only argued to distract him from the pain of his ulcerated leg, and to learn from him what true doctrine was. 'And is it even so, sweetheart, and tended your arguments to no worse end?' When Wriothesley arrived with a posse of forty men to arrest her he found the royal couple seated in the garden; Henry rose, and roared at him: 'Blockhead! Imbecile!'

The outcome could have been disastrous for Catherine, for Chancellor Wriothesly is said to have racked and tortured with his own hands the lay woman preacher Anne Askew, who may, according to some speculations, have been a waiting-woman to the Queen. Married against her will to a Catholic she did not love, Anne Askew had become a Protestant and may have tried to obtain a divorce. According to feminist scholar Betty Travitzky, Anne Askew did not accept Henry's opinions about transubstantiation, and as Henry did not accept divorce on grounds of cruelty or desertion, her preachings were something of a threat. In Wriothesley's interrogation 'the questioners broached the names of many of Catherine Parr's associates close to Anne Askew, though she refused to incriminate any'.[4] As Anne herself put it,

> Then they ded put me on the racke, bycause I confessed no ladyes nor gentyllwomen to be of my opinion, and theron they kept me a longe tyme. And because I laye styll and ded not crye, my lorde Chauncellour and mastre Ryche, toke paynes to racke me their own handes, tyll I was nigh dead.

Among the matters discussed at her first examination was the question of female preachers:

> Then the Byshoppes chauncellor rebuked me, & sayd, that I was moche to blame for utterynge the scriptures. For S. Paule (he sayd) forbode women to speake or to talke of the worde of God. I answered hym, that I knewe Paules meaning so well as he, whych is, i Corinthiorum xiiii, that a woman ought not to speake in the congregacyon by the waye of teachynge. And then I asked hym, how manye women he had seane, go into the pulpett and preache, he sayde, he never sawe non. Then I sayd, he ought to find no faute in poore women, except they had offended the lawe.[5]

Anne Askew was burned for heresy on 16 July 1546.

If Anne Boleyn was arrogant, Catherine of Aragon obdurate, and Catherine Howard scatterbrained and indiscreet, Lady Jane Grey, dutiful and pliant, exemplified the destiny of one who kissed the rod of parental authority too sweetly and too well. Like Catherine Parr, Jane was religious and scholarly; like Catherine Howard, she was subject to abuse as a child. Born the same day as Edward, Jane Seymour's son, Jane had been named after the Queen. Her own parents were Frances Brandon – the elder daughter of Mary Tudor and Charles Brandon – and Lord Henry Grey, Marquis of Dorset. This meant Jane was great-niece to Henry VIII and theoretically in line for the throne. From this stemmed all her troubles.

Because they were ambitious, Jane's parents insisted on her receiving the best possible education: it was useful at court. The example of Margaret Beaufort, Henry VIII's learned grandmother, had made female erudition eminently respectable; though scarcely studious, Frances Brandon had taken lessons in her youth with Catherine Parr. It was also desirable to have the right religion. Prince Edward and Princess Elizabeth were being brought up Protestant, and therefore Jane, with her royal blood, had to be a Protestant too. At a tender age Jane accordingly studied Latin, Greek and French, then rhetoric, grammar, philosophy, science, mathematics and scripture, besides music and dance. Her tutor was John Aylmer, who took up residence in her parents' home in Leicestershire. Jane's sympathetic biographer Mary Luke maintains that Jane was beaten by her parents – sternly reprimanded on every possible occasion, pinched and struck and harshly boxed about the ears, especially by her mother; apparently, the Greys were annoyed that Jane was not a boy, which might have given her some realistic claim upon the throne. Aylmer was much distressed, because his tiny charge was already inordinately shy, besides being quiet and respectful in the extreme. Yet this unpleasant background may have helped her to become a good scholar. Greek and Latin provided respite from the hunt, which was Frances Brandon Grey's preferred occupation: Mary Luke paints a picture of her roaming about the Leicestershire countryside, free to maim and slaughter to her heart's content. In another century and state, Frances Grey might well have joined the National Rifle Association.

When Jane Grey was ten she was sent into the royal household to live at Whitehall with Edward, Mary and Elizabeth. John Aylmer was given leave of absence, while Jane studied with Elizabeth and her tutor William Gridal. She also played with Edward, who was exactly the same age. Catherine Parr and Henry were both kind to Jane, who slowly grew more confident. But scarcely a year had passed in this relatively civilised manner when Henry died, and the children were sent away.

Henry's will had been designed to avoid creating factions. He left the throne to Edward, followed by Mary and Elizabeth. Should they for any reason not inherit, the crown would pass to the descendants of his sister – that is, Jane Grey and her younger sisters. Henry expressly refrained from naming a Protector, hoping that the Privy Council would help Edward with unanimous decisions; but the Council did not heed his wish. Within a year it appointed the new King's uncle, Edward Seymour, to the post of Lord Protector. The problem with this arrangement was that Edward had a younger brother, Thomas, who, although Lord Admiral, was afflicted with the rivalry of siblings, and discontented with his less powerful lot. Having quickly married the freshly widowed Catherine Parr, Thomas also conceived a plan to marry Edward to Jane Grey, to this end paying Jane's father £2,000 for her wardship. Jane went to live with the Seymours in Chelsea, remaining Thomas' ward even after Catherine Parr died in childbirth in 1548; but the following year the Lord Admiral's presumption ended in disaster. On the night of 19 January 1549 he tried to gain admittance to the royal apartments. Edward had bolted the door, and placed his little dog outside; the animal barked, and Thomas shot the dog. The incident did not look well, and to make matters worse the Lord Admiral was found to have secretly debased the coinage. Thomas was executed for treason on 20 March. His execution was bloody, like that of Margaret Pole, the Plantagenet Countess of Salisbury whom Henry VIII had tried for treason in 1539. Both Thomas and the Countess refused to co-operate with the headsman, who had to get their heads 'as best he might', throwing them to the ground and hacking away with mighty blows. One could say they were the aristocratic exceptions who confirmed the rule of sang-froid at the block.

After the execution of her guardian Jane returned to Leicestershire, where her parents were most disappointed to see her. Two unexpected events brought further unwelcome change. Edward Seymour himself fell from grace and was beheaded; then, in 1551, the dukedom of Suffolk passed to Henry Grey, Jane's father. Jane meanwhile had been peacefully acquiring a reputation as a scholar and a Protestant, having begun a learned correspondence with Swiss and German theologians, disciples of Ulrich Zwingli. Now the destruction of the Seymour brothers left her vulnerable to the ambitions of the new Lord Protector, John Dudley, Earl of Northumberland. In 1553 King Edward fell seriously ill; his 'Progress' exhausted him, and also he missed his two beheaded uncles. Realising the boy might die, Northumberland decided to marry Jane to his own youngest son, Guildford Dudley.

Pale and nervous, Jane refused. Mary Luke writes that she loathed the upstart Dudleys, particularly Guildford, who was spoiled, handsome and conceited. But the Duchess her mother intervened, slapping Jane until she consented, Dudley having promised she need not cohabit with his son.

The Lord Protector's next move was to persuade the dying Edward that Mary might be dangerous: she was partly Spanish, and a Catholic, and would probably marry a foreigner. Elizabeth, too, might marry a foreign prince and similarly threaten England's future. The ideal course would be to give the throne to Jane, who was English and safely wedded to a Dudley. At the same time he decided that the marriage should be consummated: better still, Jane should be pregnant. Against the protests of the Duchess of Suffolk, who wanted Jane to leave *her* home as Queen, Lady Jane Grey was taken to the Dudley house and put to bed with Guildford. Nothing – according to Mary Luke, who seems extraordinarily privy to the secrets of their bedchamber – had prepared the learned little girl for the duties of matrimony. Guildford told his shocked bride she was lucky that he did not beat her, a logic which Jane recognised, having been beaten so often by her parents. After a week, however, the strain on her health was apparent even to the Dudleys. She was permitted to go to Thomas Seymour's former home at Chelsea, where she fell ill.

Three days after Edward's death, Jane was summoned to Syon House. The Great Hall slowly filled with nobles, including Jane's parents; many knelt before her. Northumberland explained Edward's aversion to Catholicism, and everyone looked hopefully at Jane who, in stunned amazement, fainted. When she came to she had wit enough to murmur that she sought not the crown, and it 'pleaseth her not'. Dudley and Jane's parents glared at her and said it was her duty to obey, the word 'obey' being a shrewd choice. Jane struggled to her knees and asked all present to pray for her; God would assist her in this right and duty. Her parents nodded approvingly and Jane was allowed to go to her room. She was told she would be taken to the Tower until her coronation.

Once in the Tower, the reluctant monarch's unqueenly behaviour continued to cause pain. First she refused to wear the crown jewels when they were brought by the aged Marquis of Winchester. This was dismissed as a female whim. Then she refused to make Guildford Dudley King; only an Act of Parliament could do that, she declared. This put Guildford and his parents in a furious temper. Jane fell ill again and was put to bed by her servant, Mrs Ellen. Then she made the one real decision of her reign; it turned out to be fatal. The Privy Council had proposed sending Henry Grey to do battle with Henry VIII's daughter Mary, who appeared inconveniently disposed to fight for her crown. Jane burst into tears and asked that her father be allowed to remain at her side. Much to her surprise, they agreed, and Dudley was dispatched instead. The decision was a bad one, because Dudley was the one man who could keep the Privy Council in order. No sooner had he set forth than the Privy Lords betrayed him, proclaiming Mary Queen and ordering Henry Grey to tell Jane to give up the throne, which she did most willingly. Dudley surrendered, trusting to Mary's pardon. Jane's father and Dudley's sons and brothers were indeed pardoned; but Dudley himself was not. He was sentenced to be hanged, drawn and quartered, mitigated later to beheading. At the last moment he was converted to Catholicism by Bishop Stephen Gardiner, much to the Londoners' disgust.

Jane, who had written a disarmingly straightforward letter to Mary, was now kept in the Tower, Mary having decided she was safer there than at home. Guildford was incarcerated elsewhere in the Tower and not allowed to see her, probably to Jane's relief. Unfortunately Mary's advisers were appalled at this leniency and pressed for Jane's death. Jane and Guildford were brought to a speedy trial at which the Duke of Norfolk once again presided. There was no defence, no cross-examination, just the indictment and a quick deliberation. Jane was sentenced to be burnt alive or beheaded, 'as the Queen shall please'. Hoping for a pardon she wrote to both Mary and her father, receiving no reply. More than a month passed. Finally Jane learned that, mindless of her plight, Henry Grey had taken up arms in the

Wyatt rebellion – a folly which meant certain death for Jane. As soon as the rebellion ended she and Guildford were told to prepare for the beheading. Then the execution was delayed for two days to give Feckenham, a Catholic priest, time to convert her. Jane resisted magisterially, as if all the learning of her early years had schooled her for this moment. The subject of the Sacrament was raised; was it indeed Christ's flesh? 'Doth he not say it is his body?' asked the priest. 'I grant it, he saith so, and so he saith "I am the vine, I am the door . . ." but he is never the more for that, the vine or the door.' Christ was alive, Jane continued, when he said this, and meant his words to be symbolic. Feckenham, a kindly man who had tried to obtain mercy for several less important prisoners, eventually gave up.

In all this Guildford Dudley, kept apart from his reluctant wife, was most distressed to learn that Jane would not walk with him to Tower Hill for their beheading; she was to be executed within, on account of her rank. Guildford therefore wrote to Mary for permission to see Jane, which was granted; but Jane, in a kindly worded note, refused. On Monday 12 February Guildford was led out, elegant as ever in black velvet. Having declined Feckenham's offers of assistance he was attended by Sir Anthony Browne, Master of the Horse and a friend of his dead father; Guildford sobbed, and Browne held his hand all the way to the scaffold. Many in the crowd wept too, displeased at the slaughter of these children. Guildford's bisected body was flung hastily into an uncovered cart which then passed beneath the window where Jane and Mrs Ellen stood: both women saw it. When the officials of the Tower came for Jane she burst into tears, and spent the next hour praying for a return of her self-control. No one hurried her. Towards eleven o'clock she emerged on the arm of Sir John Bridges to the sound of beating drums. Two hundred yeomen of the guard stood ready to escort her. She turned to Feckenham, thanking him for his attentions, although they had tried her 'more than death' could frighten her; together they intoned the Miserere, she in English, he in Latin. Touched by his evident distress she kissed him on the cheek – probably the most spontaneous act ever recorded of her.

One of the reasons why decapitation was considered less demeaning than other forms of execution was that it enabled the victim to die without being touched by the headsman. When the executioner, dressed all in red, stepped forward to help her disrobe Jane therefore pushed him away. She then had to stand shivering in her undergarment for five minutes, awaiting the possible reprieve: none arrived. Finally she tied a handkerchief across her eyes, but then could not see the block. Groping vainly in the chilly air she called out 'Where is it?' while all present stood transfixed in shock. Eventually someone mounted the scaffold and guided her hands, at which Jane signalled she was ready, murmuring 'Lord, into thy hands I commend my spirit'. The head fell, but the drama did not end. Since the nearby Tower church, St Peter's-ad-Vincula, was now Catholic, Jane, a heretic, could not be buried there. Feckenham rushed to get the necessary permission from either Mary or the Archbishop of York, Thomas Cranmer being in prison. Jane's body lay exposed for at least four hours and was seen by François de Noailles, brother of the French Ambassador; he was 'amazed at the quantity of blood that had poured out of so small a corpse'. She was eventually buried without any religious service near two beheaded Queens, Protector Somerset and her husband, Guildford Dudley.

As presented by novelist Mary Luke, Jane's execution was thus a direct consequence of her royal birth and the ambitions of her parents and her in-laws. Clearly she was guilty, having mounted the throne in evident violation of the line of succession; equally clearly, the law made itself absurd in condemning her. Her ardent Protestantism and the obvious unfairness of her death almost make of her a martyr, an impression compounded by her resistance to the well-intentioned Feckenham; dutiful and chaste, she begins to resemble an early Christian saint, except that the saints described by Jacobus would probably not have submitted to the embraces of a Dudley. Her reign, which lasted for nine days, is unremarkable as history. Jane's scholarship, however, has attracted increased attention from feminists, who see her as one of the better products of humanist reform in education. Her grasp of reformed doctrine promised exceptionally well; her learning, had she lived, would probably have contributed to that slight improvement in the attitude towards women which took place in the reign of her classmate Elizabeth.

The life and death of Mary Stuart have been subject to innumerable interpretations, literary, operatic and historical. Controversy has raged over questions of her character: Was she guilty of adultery and complicity to murder? Did she conspire against the person of Elizabeth? In general the gradations of colour in the answers provided depend rather on whether the individual historian is Protestant or Catholic, the Protestants tending to vilify, the Catholics to absolve. Despite this flow of ink the mystery of Mary remains largely unresolved; as Betty Travitzky remarks, she may have 'remained a puzzle because she could not actually be cut to fit the martyr's or the villain's role'.[6] This puzzle does not prevent Travitzky from giving Mary's career possibly its most succinct appraisal ever: 'Mary Stuart (1542–1587) was imprisoned, dethroned, and eventually executed because she had aspired to self-realisation through both power and sexuality.' From these reassuring words, penned by a scholar who puts Mary in the context of 'Renaissance Englishwomen writers', Mary emerges strangely modernised, a woman ahead of her time who wanted thrones and sex like any other Renaissance prince but who found she 'could not order her married life with the same freedom as men'. Whether one reads Mary as a villain or a martyr, matrimony appears as the signal problem of her reign.

Born, then, in 1542, the year in which Catherine Howard was beheaded for 'misconduct', Mary Stuart was the daughter of Mary of Guise and James I of Scotland. A brave, generous-hearted man worn out by battles with the English, James died shortly after his daughter's birth, having paused in his agony long enough to sigh at the news. In the words of Antonia Fraser, 'The position of a country with a child heiress at its head was widely regarded as disastrous in the sixteenth century'.[7] Or in the words of grouchy Protestant John Knox, 'all men lamented' that the realm was left without a male to succeed, the fear being that a girl would marry a foreign prince in order to produce an heir, and thus subject her country to another power. (Interestingly, John Dudley had used this argument in reverse to put Lady Jane Grey on the throne.) Henry VIII had hoped that Mary would marry Edward, but religious differences, and Henry's own brutal incursions into Scotland, soon made this impossible. At the age of nine months Mary was solemnly crowned in the chapel at Stirling Castle; in 1548, aged 6, she was betrothed to Francis, son of the French King, on condition that France respect Scotland's sovereignty while defending it militarily. That same year she was taken from her mother and sent into France to be educated.

Despite this tearful parting, the years Mary spent in France were probably her happiest. The French court adored her; Henri II termed her 'my daughter, the Queen of Scotland' and gave her precedence over his own little girls. In addition to French, which soon became her favourite tongue, Mary learnt Italian, Spanish and some Greek; when she was 12, Brantôme heard her addressing the court in Latin on the desirability of women receiving a liberal education. She soon knew how to draw, dance, ride and play the lute; Ronsard and du Bellay taught her the metric mysteries of verse. Sometimes, to the great amusement of the court, she would dress up in Scottish national costume – not elegant plaids, but bearskins draped about her person. At the age of 12 she was given her own household, and lessons in politics from her mighty Guise uncles. At 15 she wedded the sickly Dauphin Francis in the cathedral of Notre-Dame, her affectionate young spouse being only fourteen at the time. Two years later Henri II was killed at a joust and Mary Stuart became Queen of France. Her mother having meanwhile been named Regent of Scotland, Guise power was at its height.

Perhaps too much prestige had come too soon: Queen to two countries, Mary claimed the English succession in 1558 when Mary Tudor died. Citing her own impeccable Catholic descent from Henry VII she thus raised the spectre of Elizabeth's illegitimacy by virtue of Henry VIII's divorce – a most unwise move on Mary's part, which would prove a constant worry to the Tudor Queen and her advisers, though Mary seems never adequately to have realised that fact. Then in 1559 Francis died of an ear infection, when not yet 17. Mary, to whom so much had been given without her lifting a finger, now lost her precedence at court: the dominant female in France was suddenly Catherine de' Medici. A subservient role did not suit the young dowager – although the image of Mary in white mourning, advancing down the paths at Fontainebleau, did inspire an elegiac poem from Ronsard:

> ... pensive, et baignant votre sein
> Du beau cristal de vos larmes roulées,
> Triste marchiez par les longues allées
> Du grand jardin de ce royal château
> Qui prend son nom de la source d'une eau.
>   Tous les chemins blanchissaient sous vos voiles ...[8]

In 1561 she decided to return to Scotland, where public opinion was turning in her favour. She left France in great sadness on 14 August, accompanied by four inseparable female companions – all called Mary – plaintively repeating 'Farewell, France! Farewell! I fear I shall never see you more'.

Great difficulties awaited her: a windswept land of poor roads and worse communication, a nobility decimated by battles with the English but rarely missing an opportunity to feud. National consciousness was lacking, and tastes were generally vulgar. As one ambassador put it, Scotland was 'the arse of the world'. Nonetheless Mary was most tactful, and her beauty and dignity endeared her to the people. She was tolerant of Protestants, despite being baited on every possible occasion by the Puritanical, misogynistic Knox who in 1558 had written his *First Blast of the Trumpet against the Monstrous Regiment of Women*. In fairness to Knox, he did not just disapprove of Catholic Queens: for woman to rule at all was a 'subversion of good order, of all equity and justice', a thing contrary to God and repugnant to all Nature. He could never understand why this misogyny infuriated Elizabeth, by this time Queen of England; the fact that she was managing so well, he told her, was proof that God, for once, had willed it. Curiously, in view of Knox's strictures, Mary's behaviour did not strike everyone as womanly: the Pope, for one, said she had a 'man's soul in a woman's body'. Embellishing on what he may have meant, Stefan Zweig remarks in 1934 that Mary was 'a mistress of the arts of chivalry, dextrous in archery and pall-mall, an ardent lover of fowling and the chase', wont to ride forth of a morning with a falcon on her wrist, much to the delight of the people of Edinburgh.

Before long this princely Stuart had set up court in the French style. Surrounding herself with volumes of Erasmus, Ariosto, Rabelais and Ronsard she caused verses to be read, music and masques to be performed to the light of flickering candles. In one such masque, *The Purpose*, Mary herself appeared as a young man, clad in black silk breeches, while her French poet Chastelard wore a woman's gown. This was not the sort of thing to be approved of by John Knox, who railed against musicians and flatterers, 'these corrupters of youth'; princes would do better to listen to wise old men. In fact Mary was soon obliged to listen to her advisers, because Chastelard mistook her frank informal charm for romantic encouragement, and hid one night in her bedchamber. He was discovered, and since Mary's reputation was at stake it was decided to behead him, in full view of the Queen.

DEATH COMES TO THE MAIDEN

This incident marked the beginnings of Mary's troubles. For three years she had occupied the throne quite ably while her Protestant half-brother Moray administered the kingdom; now she was advised to take a spouse, to discourage gossip. Several suitors were deemed eligible, but the choice eventually narrowed to Lord Henry Darnley and Robert Dudley, Earl of Leicester. Whereas Darnley was reasonably well-born, Mary was shocked by the suit of Robert Dudley, whom Elizabeth favoured for the match; Dudley had not a drop of royal blood and to her mind was a traitor, having sided with his father and the Greys against Mary Tudor. But Mary was much taken with Lord Darnley, a handsome, well-dressed young man with long and splendid legs. She insisted on marrying him despite violent opposition, and without Elizabeth's approval.

The marriage could not have been more catastrophic. Darnley soon appeared increasingly vain, arrogant, insolent and ambitious, until even Mary was jolted from infatuation. He had no interest in the practical responsibilities of government, but sulkily demanded the crown matrimonial of Scotland, which had been granted Mary's first husband Francis. In 1566 a group of scheming lords succeeded in persuading him that Mary was having an affair with David Riccio, her devoted but unprepossessing secretary. They also promised they would put him on the throne if he complied with their requests. The result of this plot was that Darnley burst into the Queen's apartments with armed nobles who held loaded pistols to her stomach – she was then six months pregnant with the future James II – dragged forth Riccio, who was clinging to her skirts, and stabbed him some fifty or sixty times. Mary was then imprisoned in her rooms by the conspirators, who intended to keep her closeted until the child was born while they themselves held power with Darnley. But Mary had no difficulty in persuading Darnley that these lords were unreliable, and together they succeeded in escaping to Dunbar – a six-hour ride. This escape demonstrates Mary's courage, will, and ability to manipulate Darnley when she put her mind to it. Loyal supporters flocked to her side and from Dunbar she marched on Edinburgh with 8,000 men.

It is in the events which follow next that the interpretive battle is most bloodily joined between the different camps of Marian biographers. After giving birth to her son James, Mary suffered a virtual nervous breakdown, apparently a reaction to the physical strains of recent months and her appalling marriage. The ambitious but hitherto loyal Earl of Bothwell now contrived to have Darnley murdered, an event which threw Mary further into shock, disaffected though she was. This left her vulnerable to Bothwell's next ploy: to abduct the Queen, imprison her at Dunbar, and ravish her, leaving her with no honourable alternative but marriage to himself. This, at least, is how Antonia Fraser sees it. Stefan Zweig, on the other hand, thinks that Mary fell violently in love with Bothwell between the birth of James and the death of Darnley; that this unexpected, thwarted passion was the cause of her depression; that she plotted with Bothwell to lure Darnley to his doom.

BEHEADING

Zweig, whose eminently romantic approach is antithetical to the careful scholarship of Fraser, bases his assumptions largely on the evidence of a series of 'Casket' letters and sonnets ostensibly written by Mary to Bothwell while in the thrall of lust. The authenticity of these poems was angrily questioned in their own time by Ronsard and Brantôme, who found them too crude to be of Mary's composition; Antonia Fraser considers the entire contents of the casket unreliable because the originals were lost, thereby precluding an analysis of the handwriting. Betty Travitzky does not hesitate to include the sonnets in her Renaissance anthology, on grounds of 'the obvious emotion of the poet'. One begins

> For him what countless tears I must have shed:
> First, when he made himself my body's lord
> Before he had my heart . . .
> (Travitzky, p. 196)

Apparently this was a reference to the rape, of which Zweig remarks 'He took her by storm or violated her. Who, at such moments, can distinguish between the two?' Overwhelmed by this indistinction, Mary had to face the fact that she was technically a criminal. Had she not recently signed an edict declaring adultery a capital offence? Having committed this crime, she could only save herself by further criminal offences that would clear the path to marrying Bothwell; 'She therefore stumbled onward, bondmaid of her passion, unwitting and yet all the time cruelly aware, towards the abyss of her deed' (Zweig, p. 187).

Whatever one may think of Zweig's analysis of Mary's rape – it was not, he says, 'premeditated' on either side, but was definitely an act 'devoid of spiritual tone' – the fact remains that Bothwell divorced his wife and married Mary on 15 May 1567. As G. B. Harrison records in *The Letters of Queen Elizabeth I*, this was 'too much for the Scottish lords', who revolted. It was also too much for Elizabeth, who had already written to Mary in February of that year expressing astonishment at the 'horrible and abominable' murder of her cousin Darnley, advising Mary to avenge him fully, and not 'look through your fingers' at those who had done her that pleasure, 'as most people say'; now Elizabeth addressed her in even sterner terms: 'Madam, to be plain with you', she disapproved of Mary's haste to marry a subject who 'besides other notorious lacks, public fame has charged with the murder of your late husband'. Then Mary and Bothwell lost their battle with the lords, and Mary was imprisoned in the castle of Lochleven, Bothwell remaining at large to ride all over Scotland, trying to enlist support for their party.

Mary's health in Lochleven was exceptionally poor: a total nervous collapse, complicated by a miscarriage, in which she lost much blood. During this period she was compelled to sign letters of resignation in favour of her thirteen-month-old son. After ten and a half months she managed to escape from the watery fortress with the aid of her gaoler's kin, the dashing George and Willy Douglas. Supporters once more flocked to her cause but were defeated by the Earl of Moray at the decisive battle of Longside. Obliged to take refuge in the castles of the Lords Herries and Maxwell, who were loyal Catholics, Mary found she had two rational alternatives: to flee to France, where as Dowager Queen she had castles of her own, and certain inalienable rights; or to weather the storm in Scotland, until things improved.

She chose instead to flee to England, thereby setting the stage for the fatal political duel with her sister Queen. Vainly, Mary's loyal lords had advised her not to trust Elizabeth, whose territories she now entered without any guarantee of welcome. Obsessed with the curious hope that Elizabeth would name her as her successor, confident of her ability to charm her English cousin, should they ever meet, Mary seems not to have anticipated what problems would be posed by her stay on English soil: Catholic, marriageable, and a viable heir to the English throne, she would inevitably become the focus of plots involving English Catholics — as Elizabeth had been the focus of plots involving discontented Protestants, when Mary Tudor had been Queen. Then, too, there was the matter of Darnley, still fuelling the criticisms of Mary Stuart's enemies.

Elizabeth, to whom it fell to deal with these problems, actually intended to restore Mary to her throne, but was prevented from so doing by insuperable complications. Soon, however, the accuracy of the loyal lords' dire warnings became only too apparent. Mary was in effect put on trial *in absentia* at the Conference of York, an investigation of her part in Darnley's murder and of her marriage to the principal suspect. From the political standpoint it actually did not matter whether Mary was guilty or not; the important thing was to have an excuse for 'detaining' her and preventing her return to Catholic France. Even so the conference ended inconclusively. The matter was taken up in Westminster; here again, production of the famous 'Casket' letters notwithstanding, a most ambivalent verdict of 'not proven' was returned. In Scotland the Earl of Moray was permitted to continue as regent, while Mary was to remain incarcerated in a succession of more or less draughty English country homes and castles until 'liberated' by her execution at Fotheringay in 1586.

There followed the inevitable series of plots involving Mary's marriageability and claim to the throne. In one of the most serious she was betrothed to the Duke of Norfolk, to whom she wrote affectionately; the Duke was subsequently executed for high treason although Elizabeth — aghast at having to sign the warrant for a noble of such rank, and a relative to boot — put off the beheading for as long as was feasible. But the real catastrophe for Mary was the Babington Conspiracy of 1586. Here Elizabeth's Secretary of State Walsingham succeeded in implicating the Scottish Queen in two separate conspiracies: to assassinate Elizabeth, and to remove Mary from her prison and set her on the English throne, both plots involving the assistance of a foreign power. To this end, Walsingham set up a provocative line of correspondence between Mary and the French Embassy. Unfortunately Mary's responses to the conspiratorial missives passed through Walsingham's office on their way. When Mary's own letters were not sufficiently incriminating, Antonia Fraser adds, Walsingham forged a postscript. In consequence Sir Anthony Babington and friends were arrested and condemned to the full displeasure of the law concerning traitors. With Elizabeth's assent they were hanged, cut down while still alive, disembowelled in sight of each other and the watching public, deprived of their 'privities', then quartered.

Mary's behaviour at her own trial was most dignified. Denied both counsel and witnesses for the defence she insisted she could be tried by her 'peers' alone – which meant Elizabeth. Although she steadfastly proclaimed her ignorance of any plot to kill the Queen, Mary's conduct before, during and after the trial made it clear she considered herself destined to be a Catholic martyr. The advantage of this attitude was that it assured her the respect of history and forced Elizabeth into the less attractive role of executioner – a circumstance of which the English Queen was well aware. Hesitating to sign the dread warrant Elizabeth observed that 'we princes stand . . . upon a stage, exposed to the prying glances of the world'. She would probably have preferred some loyal minion to have murdered Mary, relieving her of the responsibility; but Mary's gaoler honourably refused.

Finally obtaining the warrant, Elizabeth's secretaries contacted the executioner, one Bull, paid him ten pounds and smuggled him into Fotheringay, where Mary was imprisoned. On the evening of 7 February 1586, Mary was informed the execution would take place at eight o'clock next morning without the benefit of her chaplain. She spent her last evening making little packets of her personal effects and the little money she still had: these were to be given to her servants. Throughout the night the sound of hammering could be heard as the scaffold was erected in Fotheringay's Great Hall.

Next morning the Sheriff of Nottingham entered and found Mary at prayer. She was, Zweig writes, 'ready, as a Christian woman, to accept the afflictions imposed on her by God's will, and perhaps welcomed her martyrdom gladly as the last triumph He might vouchsafe her in this life'. Determined to die a great death, she had given careful thought to her attire. Thus, when she entered the Great Hall of Fotheringay, attended by six of her servants, she was dressed in state: a robe of black velvet, stamped with gold, and shoes of Spanish leather. To minimise the effect of the blood she wore, underneath, a petticoat and camisole of crimson velvet: the liturgical colour of martyrs in the Catholic Church. 'Never', continues the admiring Zweig, 'had a woman condemned to death made herself ready for execution with such artistry and dignity'. But Zweig, who has earlier described the death of the poet Chastelard as 'a ballad', is full of horror for the actual block:

> On no-one (however much the books and reports may lie about the matter) can the execution of a human being produce a romantic or touching impression. Always death by the executioner's axe must be a horrible spectacle of slaughter. The first blow fell away, striking the back of the head instead of severing the neck. A hollow groan escaped from the mouth of the victim. At the second stroke, the axe sank deep into the neck, and the blood spurted out copiously.
>
> (Zweig, p. 352)

Mary's head was only severed at the third stroke, after which Bull lifted it and showed it to those present – about 300 people having assembled in the hall. This gave rise to a further gruesome detail: the wig fell off, causing the head to drop and roll across the scaffold. For quarter of an hour the lips 'continued to twitch convulsively'. When the headsmen came to strip the body it was found that a small Skye terrier had slipped into the hall, unobserved beneath the endless petticoats, staying close to Mary whose corpse it now refused to leave. The little dog was taken out and washed, but pined away and died.

Informed of the deed Elizabeth, in whose honour Mary's head had been detached, now flew into a rage and railed against the treacherous minions who had acted on the signed warrant instead of leaving it safely buried in some bureaucratic pile. Her second secretary Davison was tried in the Star Chamber and imprisoned in the Tower. Undoubtedly a part of her grief was political: she had no wish to stand on history's platform with her honour besmirched, the first monarch to execute another regnant sovereign – and a 'sister' Queen at that. But there was also an emotional element deriving from the traumas of her childhood. In the sleepless nights that ensued Elizabeth must have recalled the death of her own mother – and the deaths, natural or violent, of three of her stepmothers. In Edith Sitwell's words,

> Soon, when she was old enough to speak, she would ask, 'Has the Queen my mother gone away?' But this would not be yet, for there were still three months between this time and the day of her mother's beheading – and then Elizabeth would not be three years old. 'Where is she? At Hampton Court?' Silence. Then Death would come again. Her stepmother, Queen Jane, would vanish, and could not be found in the great staterooms or the unoccupied rooms of the Palace. 'The Queen's grace is dead.' 'Why did she die?' 'She died when the Prince's grace was born.' Then that later stepmother, the lewd, sly, pitiable little ghost Katherine Howard, who came back to haunt the King from the tomb of her cousin, Elizabeth's mother – she too would vanish. 'Why has she gone away?' 'The King's grace is angered against her. She is dead.' '*Dead*?' 'Yes, the King's grace has had her put to death because she was wicked.'
>
> (Sitwell, p. 32)

For Sitwell, the fates of these mothers – coming, as they did, at the most impressionable moments of her childhood – were to affect Elizabeth's whole life: 'They were to affect her sexually, laying the chill of death on her hot blood, in the midst of passion; they were to instill moments of cold fear into the blood of this lion-brave creature.' Thus does a great poet indicate the psychological element in that avoidance of matrimony which preserved the autonomy of both Elizabeth and her country. The beheading of Mary, with its inevitable reminder of previous decapitations, would have revived the traumatic spectres of death, passion and virginity.

If Sitwell's point seems reasonable it is not the explanation always adopted by poets in comparisons of the two Queens' personalities – comparisons not usually to Elizabeth's advantage. Staging, in his tragedy *Marie Stuart*, a personal confrontation which never actually took place, Schiller stresses Mary's warmth of heart at the expense of Elizabeth's calculating 'virtue'. This is more or less the line followed by Stefan Zweig, who early stresses the differences in the two Queens' approaches to statecraft: 'What Elizabeth looked upon as a carefully thought-out game of chess, a diplomatic issue demanding the utmost intellectual exertion, was for Mary a delightful entertainment, an enhancement of joy in life, a chivalric tourney.' The same distinction obtained in love; Mary, though initially reticent – 'markedly strait-laced', in Fraser's view – eventually turned into a complete woman, whereas Elizabeth did not. But far from providing a psychological explanation, as Sitwell discreetly does, for this difference, Zweig plunges into lurid biological speculation. 'The reason for this was a physiological one: she was not "like other women." ... Not voluntarily, as she pretended, but perforce, did she remain a "virgin queen."' Whatever does Zweig mean? Did Elizabeth not have parts? That is certainly the impression conveyed, and it is prevalent enough to be discussed by Retha Warnicke. 'When Anne miscarried her fetus in 1536, the rumors circulated ... that it was her "defective constitution" that had prevented her from delivering live male sons' (Warnicke, p. 240). From early in Elizabeth's reign, 'gossip maintained that there was something wrong with her anatomy', rendering her incapable of giving birth. Although medical examinations showed her to be normal, Elizabeth's 'personal fear about her fertility' may have been subconsciously influenced by gossip that her mother was a witch.

While Warnicke's remarks at least have some basis in reality, the effect of Zweig's wild postulations is to undercut the rationality of Elizabeth's choice. For, as Antonia Fraser states, 'The consort was ... the perennial problem of the female ruler in this century: it is significant that the one queen who emerged in the eyes of the people as never having made a mistaken match was Queen Elizabeth' (Fraser, p. 211).

With some difficulty Mary had obtained permission for several of her women to attend her at the block, having first had to promise that they would not weep. Comforted by Mary to the last, they had helped remove her outer garments, preserving her from some of the attentions of the headsmen. The same concern with propriety at the scaffold is seen in accounts of the death of Beatrice Cenci, an Italian noblewoman beheaded by the *mannaia* in 1599:

> mounting the scaffold she stepped quickly across the plank, placed her neck beneath the *mannaja*, and took up her position so well she managed to avoid being touched by the *bourreau*. Her quick movements prevented the public from catching sight of her shoulders and breast when the taffeta veil was removed. But the blow was slow to be given, because a complication arose.[9]

This account goes on to explain that the 'complication' resulted from the spiritual concern of Pope Clement VIII, who had unjustly condemned her, and knew it. Thus, when Beatrice settled on the block, a cannon was fired from the nearby Castel Sant'Angelo to warn the Pope. The Holy Father, who had been praying at Monte Cavallo while awaiting this signal, was then able to give her papal absolution *in articolo mortis*. While this was going on, Beatrice had to wait.

The instrument about to claim her head was a primitive version of the guillotine, a cousin of the Scottish 'Maiden' used to behead Mary's unwelcome suitor Chastelard. It was described by a traveller to Italy in 1730:

> In the middle [of the scaffold] was placed a great block, of the height to allow the criminal, when kneeling, to lay his head on it between a kind of gibbet which supported a hatchet one foot deep and one and a half wide.... The hatchet was loaded with a hundred pounds weight of lead, and was suspended by a rope made fast to the gibbet.... The executioner had nothing to do but cut the cord that held up the hatchet, which, descending with violence, severed the head.[10]

So effective was this means of execution that the hatchet buried itself in the block to a depth of two inches, thereby forestalling the sort of bungling suffered by Mary Stuart. The victim Stendhal describes was to be martyred in another sense: the victim of paternal rape, she had committed patricide. All appeals were rejected by the Pope, who knew her father to have been a rich man and looked forward to confiscating the Cencis' enormous wealth. The atrocity visited upon Beatrice was widely credited; thus, while Mary Stuart came to be regarded as martyred *for* papal authority, Beatrice was seen as martyred *by* it.

For years, indeed centuries, this was Beatrice's legend, as reflected in Shelley's tragedy *The Cenci* of 1819. A remarkable deconstruction of the prevailing belief was undertaken in 1925 by Corrado Ricci, who disputes the incestuous rape while nonetheless affirming the appalling circumstances of

BEHEADING

Beatrice Cenci's life – circumstances which place her in the select category of abused, aristocratic and executed girls. The first part of Ricci's tale is devoted more to the energetic turpitude of Francesco Cenci than to his daughter; but that provides a picture both of what Beatrice was up against, and of the workings of papal justice.

Count Francesco Cenci was born in 1549, the son of Cristoforo Cenci and his second consort Beatrice Arias. At the tender age of twelve and a half he inherited the vast fortune – 422,580 scudi – and numerous properties – Torrenova, Testa di Lepre, Falcognano, Capo di Bove, Casaletto, the castles of Assergi, Pescommaggiore and Filetto – acquired by his self-serving father. The favoured boy was of a violent disposition; already, at the age of 11, he had set upon another child and beaten him about the head. Perceiving him precocious in violence and lust his tutor, Francesco Santacroce, set about remedying or at least domestically containing the second penchant by marrying him in 1563 to his daughter Ersilia, then aged 13. Children did not result from this union until 1567, when a son was born, Cristoforo, who died. Ersilia gave birth to eleven more little Cenci before dying in childbed in 1584. Of these, seven lived: Giacomo (born 1568), Cristoforo II (1572), Antonina (1573), Rocco (1576), Beatrice (1577), Bernardo (1581), and Paolo (1583). Ersilia's death was unfortunate for Francesco in that married life had always gone relatively smoothly: 'knowing him from infancy, [she] had made no opposition to his tendencies and had suffered him to commit every sort of violence and infidelity'.[11]

Examples of his violence are not wanting. He lay in wait for and attacked his cousin, Cesare, with a sword; he beat his servants and gave them insufficient food. It was said he hanged a vassal on the gallows; numerous peasants complained to the Pope, in documents since gnawed by mice, but whose narrative is reconstructible. In 1570 he underwent his first trial for sodomy and was saved by the intercession of the Cardinals Farnese and Santacroce. It is not known whether he paid a fine on that occasion, but money was certainly an expedient he resorted to in other lawsuits, always with success. In 1572 he was again imprisoned 'for unnatural vice', and liberated for a fine of 50,000 scudi. In 1587 he took a mistress, Maria di Spoleto, a tall, hairy-faced woman with whom he proceeded to have 'intimate and reprehensible relations'. Maria, too, he beat: he beat her with broomsticks, belts, and once about the eyebrows with a spoon. That same year Sixtus V was elected to the papacy. The new Pontiff was no respecter of persons and determined to re-divert into the papal revenues much that had been appropriated by Cristoforo Cenci senior. An action was brought against Francesco, who saw resistance was vain, and paid a fine of 25,000 scudi, 'for no other purpose than to be never again molested'. A few months later, Sixtus died.

In November 1593 Francesco married Lucrezia Petroni, a widow, who was possibly induced to take this step by promises to aid her daughters. Scarcely were the nuptials celebrated than Francesco found himself on trial again for sodomy. The witnesses were numerous and graphic, including stable-boys, a one-eyed youth who called him *buggerone*, and Maria di Spoleto, who declared herself coerced by beatings into doing things she did not want. Francesco denied all, but eventually confessed. He bought himself out of the situation with 100,000 scudi. His treatment differs markedly from that accorded a group of fifteen sodomites tried several years later: 'They had no gold to pay into the state coffers; two were burned and eleven condemned to various penalties.' As for Francesco, he returned from prison in 1594 tormented by a skin disease. To relieve the irritation he made his coachman scrape him with a towel, from head to foot, and then he made Beatrice scrape him, even to his thighs and private parts.

While Beatrice and the coachman were thus employed Francesco railed against his sons. His boys had always hated him, and he, it seems, them. As children he had left them unprovided for, roaming through the streets in rags; they had reciprocated with a series of lawsuits. Now, itching in his bed, he accused them of having intrigued against him – with some reason, since Giacomo may actually have denounced his father. For their part the young men accused him of dishonouring the house with moral turpitude, of wasting the family fortune, and of refusing them sufficient money for their needs – all of which was true. In the end a court order obliged him to pay 100 scudi a month to Giacomo, who had a family, and 80 scudi a month to Rocco and Cristoforo. This drain on his finances did not last for long, because Rocco and Cristoforo were soon killed – Rocco in a fight over another man's wife, Cristoforo in a duel. At the end of 1594 Francesco's daughter Antonia married, costing him a further 20,000 scudi in dowry. Francesco was broke: Beatrice must not be married at such a price – must not be married at all. To forestall this possibility he decided to withdraw from Rome, sequestering his women in the mountain fortress of La Petrella, which rose, behind the village of that name, on a forbidding cliff.

One of Francesco's first deeds on arriving at La Petrella was to make advances to Curzio, Lucrezia's son by her previous marriage. Rebuffed, he struck Lucrezia across the face with a spur, then beat her till she fell. Curzio rode hastily back to Rome, where he informed his companions that, his stepfather having 'attempted sodomy', he himself had 'run away'. Next Francesco absented himself for about a year, leaving Beatrice and Lucrezia to roam about the castle; when he returned, he had them confined. In a sense, he buried them alive, walling up their windows and locking them inside a four-room suite, with food pushed through the door. Light filtered in through the tops of windows; to see the outside world, they had to climb up on a chair. Francesco rode off to Rome again, where he recruited two female servants. He sent them to La Petrella under false pretences and kept them there by threats: Olimpio, the *castellano*, had been instructed to throw them from the cliff if they rebelled.

BEHEADING

The four women lived in this manner for about a year and a half. As Ricci casually observes, it was a tendency of the time to shut up women, to prevent other men from getting near them. But Cenci's stratagem backfired. Beatrice, who had a proud and energetic mind, grew desperate. She wrote letters to her brother Giacomo, imploring him to try to see her married, or send her to a convent; one letter passed through several hands and was shown, perhaps with kind intentions, to Francesco. Mad with rage he rode back to La Petrella and chastised her with a bull-whip. Having observed with dire understatement to Lucrezia, 'I mean to make Signor Francesco repent of these blows he has given me!', Beatrice began to plot revenge.

The two main instruments of vengeance were close at hand: Marzio Catalano, who worked in the castle, and Olimpio, the overseer, who fell in love with her. Beatrice was 20; she had, as Ricci puts it, 'the mad blood of Francesco Cenci' flowing in her veins. Olimpio was 'an unusually handsome man', and Beatrice's life was dreadful. By means of money, she induced Marzio to participate in her revenge; and by means of love, Olimpio. A Shelley scholar, K. N. Cameron, asserts that Beatrice had an illegitimate child by Olimpio, and that discovery of this fact was probably 'what led to Cenci's ill-treatment of his daughter'. Yet from Ricci's account it is clear that the affair with Olimpio was not the cause, but the consequence, of her incarceration; moreover, although Beatrice's intimacies were promptly known by several at the castle, mention is not made of Cenci making any such 'discovery'. In any event, Beatrice's plottings did not immediately take effect, for Francesco had time to commit further foul deeds. He still made Lucrezia and Beatrice scrape him to the belly, and now caused Beatrice to sleep in the same room with himself and her stepmother. He ordered his chamber-pot set near the fire in front of them in winter, then made the women carry out his turds. And according to the seventeenth- or eighteenth-century sources used by Shelley he set about debauching Beatrice, who was now grown up, and 'exceedingly beautiful'. In Cameron's words, 'Presumably he raped her, because at this point Mary Shelley in her copy supplied a series of asterisks with the note: "The details here are horrible, and unfit for publication."'[12]

This incest, while recognised by Shelley and almost everybody else who treats of the story, is hotly contested by Corrado Ricci. Reconstructing the later evidence of witnesses he finds only one moment when the deed could possibly have taken place, and that rather quickly: one evening Lucrezia entered one of the female servants' rooms and threw herself on the bed in great agitation, while Francesco remained closeted 'for a short time' with Beatrice.

Possible or not, the alleged rape was part of the defence when Beatrice was tried for murder in 1599. For after several unsuccessful attempts to put Francesco away by poison, or by having him fall into the hands of bandits, Beatrice had finally bullied Olimpio into staving in his skull with a hammer. She herself had put opium in Francesco's wine; stunned, the Count had gone to bed, with Lucrezia lying gently beside him. Then Marzio and Olimpio had wavered, Olimpio being seized with a coughing fit. Spurred on by Beatrice, Marzio and Olimpio eventually went into Francesco's room and quickly beat him to death. Their next step was to demolish the Count's balcony, to seem as if their master had fallen through a hole. Meanwhile a great quantity of blood poured into the sheets, which Lucrezia tore up and stuffed into a privy: 'her wits benumbed by terror, she filled the entire house with evidences of the crime'. Olimpio and Marzio clothed Cenci's body and laboriously threw it down the hillside. They left the castle, and Beatrice began to call for help.

In the ensuing days a number of suspicious circumstances began to be noticed. Francesco's body bore strange pointed wounds, not likely to be caused by falling from a balcony; the damage to the balcony itself did not correspond to that which might precipitate a fall. Again, Olimpio had shown unseemly haste in bullying the priests to get the body buried. These, and other matters, caused much discussion in the village, so that when Giacomo and Bernardo came to fetch the women back to Rome it was openly said that Beatrice and Lucrezia had somehow brought about Francesco Cenci's death. Olimpio's behaviour in Rome did not help; he practically blackmailed the Cenci, took frequent liberties with Beatrice, and dined with the family – conduct unheard of in a servant. One evening Beatrice did not appear at dinner, and Ricci speculates that she was otherwise engaged in giving birth to Olimpio's child.

An investigation of the crime was launched, and then a proclamation issued, naming Olimpio, Marzio and their wives, together with Beatrice and Lucrezia, Giacomo and Bernardo, as co-conspirators in Cenci's death. Marzio, who had fled, was recaptured, imprisoned, interrogated and ultimately tortured, at which point he confessed, incriminating Beatrice. The three Cenci – Giacomo, Lucrezia and Beatrice – persisted in denying everything, Beatrice with great resolve; Lucrezia with inept lies and contradictions; Giacomo with some incipient attempt to disculpate himself at the expense of the women. The situation was still not entirely compromising, however, because as long as the Cenci denied all it was their word against Marzio's. Realising the danger posed to the family by Olimpio, who had also fled, a certain Monsignore Guerra, their cousin, resolutely planned his murder. After this was carried out the Monsignore also disappeared; additional witnesses were interrogated and tortured, and Lucrezia herself was put to the rack. She soon confessed to everything. It had been Beatrice's idea, she said, to kill Francesco; Beatrice could not stand the ill-treatment. Giacomo, Lucrezia and Bernardo were then hoisted on the *strappado* in Beatrice's presence; still she denied. But when hoisted up herself she immediately declared her willingness to tell the truth – not, Ricci thinks, from any lack of courage, but because she realised that the burden of evidence was now too overwhelming to resist.

BEHEADING

It was widely reported, after Beatrice's confession, that she had borne, for nine hours and with the utmost constancy, the torture of the *veglia* – a particularly excruciating torment in which the sufferer was stripped naked, shaved, and suspended by an apparatus of taut ropes and pulleys, in such a way that his rump just touched a tripod; on that tripod a sharp stone was set, causing unspeakable muscular spasms whenever the victim's tense buttocks came into contact with it. But Beatrice and Lucrezia were merely racked, fully dressed, and Beatrice for no great length of time. The more extreme account was simply a part of the embellishment of Beatrice now entered upon by popular imagining. For Beatrice would be a martyr; she would be the Roman virgin, heartbreakingly innocent and devastatingly beautiful, a victim of iniquity both papal and paternal. The affair with Olimpio was ignored. On the other hand the 'paternal outrage' was apparently known to and believed by the public, who demanded papal clemency. It was openly speculated that if Clement VIII sought the destruction of the Cenci with such moral vigour, it was principally to confiscate what remained of their wealth. But any possibility of pardon was obviated by a sudden spate of crimes, all committed by high-born young men attacking relatives who blocked their inheritance; the murderers were naturally said to be 'imitating the Cenci'.

Thus Clement could show no mercy, even had he wished. Francesco was described in the papal sentence as a 'most wretched father' and an 'unhappy husband' – the authorities apparently forgetting that they had thrice pursued him for sodomy, fined him all his wealth, prosecuted him for violence on numerous occasions, and forced him to feed his sons. The judgement was not popular. Lucrezia and Beatrice would have their heads cut off; Giacomo, be quartered. The younger brother Bernardo was spared on account of his age (14) and because the defence had shown him as a half-wit; his punishment was simply to watch the execution of his kin.

On the night of 10 September 1599, the Cenci were therefore wakened at about midnight by Brothers from the Company of St John the Beheaded. Bearing torches, their faces hidden by black hoods, these 'Comforters' had as their special mission to fortify the condemned during their final night. Invariably, they would accompany the victim to the scaffold and remain there to the last. Then they would retrieve the body and bury it, at their own expense. The device of this humane company was the head of John the Baptist, on a salver.

At about 9.30 on 11 September, suitably humbled and forgiving and repentant, Giacomo and Bernardo were borne in carts through Rome. Giacomo was bound and stripped to the waist; during the journey the flesh and tendons of his chest and shoulders were torn with hot pincers. He bore this, Ricci says, with 'heroic fortitude'. Bernardo sat in another cart, his head covered in a cloth. After several miles the gruesome procession halted and Lucrezia and Beatrice emerged from their prison. In the record the Comforters made of the event they walked unbound, wearing 'mourning garments'. A great throng of people followed this cortège, through the finest and most populous streets of Rome; women wept, and men muttered. The calm behaviour of Beatrice was much admired; she walked without faltering towards the place of execution, which was set up on the left bank of the Tiber, before the Ponte Sant'Angelo. Bridges and balconies were thick and black with people; many spectators fell into the Tiber and several were drowned. As many as five or six hundred people fainted in the sun.

The quartet of Cenci was led into a chapel to hear Mass. Then Lucrezia was borne to the scaffold, pale and tottering, by the Brothers of St John the Beheaded. She was in a faint, unconscious, when the axe descended. Beatrice went up lightly and quickly and laid her head down on the block; it was severed with one blow, eliciting a loud wail from the crowd. Watching on the scaffold, Bernardo fainted for the second time and had to be assisted by the Comforters. Their next task was to help the mangled Giacomo to stand; he took advantage of the moment to proclaim Bernardo's innocence. His head was crushed by a mallet on the block, his throat cut, his body sliced into four quarters and hung on hooks about the scaffold. Bernardo was taken back to the Tordinona prison where, in spite of the clemency, he languished for years. Surrounded by torches the bodies of his kin were displayed until far into the night; flowers had been brought by young girls, covering the head of Beatrice. All of Rome was present at her funeral as confraternities and monks, commoners, noblemen and tourists wound in a vast procession up the Via del Gianocolo, following the body to the church of San Pietro in Montorio. Such was the outpouring of sorrow, a saint might have died.

In fact Beatrice, although beheaded, did not suffer nearly so atrocious a punishment as Giacomo, the greater severity of whose tortures was probably due to his sex. For in Italy as in England, modesty apparently forbade the quartering of female bodies on the scaffold. The multiple penalties exacted on the body of her brother – as if killing him several times – recall the many pains inflicted on the Babington conspirators, guilty of the only slightly more heinous crime of attempted regicide. If anything, considering that patricide was an offence to natural order and to God, Beatrice got off lightly. That she was thereafter considered something of a martyr illustrates the tendency to whitewash the memory of beheaded noblewomen: in a polarising activity inclined either to whitewash or sexually to vilify them, she was at the clean end of the scale. Beatrice nonetheless departs from the pattern in that her problems did not spring from matrimony; had she been allowed to marry, as she begged her brother, her destiny might well have proved less disastrous.

The grand period of female beheading did not end with Beatrice Cenci. An equally celebrated French patricide, the Marquise de Brinvilliers, would terminate her days in the Place de Grève in Paris in 1676 after a criminal career that defies all posthumous attempts at whitewashing. Even so, the privileges due her class appear in the fact of her decapitation, for the crimes she had committed would have qualified a less aristocratic being for burning at the least.

'Notorious for her gallantries and crimes', Marie-Madeleine d'Aubray, daughter of the municipal lieutenant of Paris, was born in 1630 into one of the most prominent families in France. After a childhood her biographers deem astonishingly lacking in moral and religious instruction she grew into an intelligent young woman, proud, passionate, attractive and vain. In 1651 she was married to the Marquis de Brinvilliers, a spendthrift. Their union was noted for the infidelities of both its partners, but it is her hopelessly prodigal husband who appears the more indiscreet. Nonetheless the marriage endured quite stably until 1659, when the Marquis met a young adventurer from Gascony, Captain Gaudin de Sainte-Croix. It has been cynically suggested that Brinvilliers thrust this brilliant, gorgeous friend in the direction of his wife, wishing to spend more time himself with a certain Mlle Dufay. The resulting *ménage à trois*, or possibly *à quatre*, continued happily until the rash extravagance of man and wife began seriously to dissipate a hitherto vast fortune. Sainte-Croix then advised the Marquise to obtain a legal separation of her wealth from that of her husband – a manoeuvre which would have resulted in his own enrichment, had it been successful; instead, it simply enraged the d'Aubray family. The two elder brothers first reproached their sister for the scandal she was causing. Marie-Madeleine took no heed. Concerned that his daughter was consorting with a low-born Gascon knave who might reduce her to penury, Dreux d'Aubray then asked Marie-Madeleine to break off the liaison. Her answer was to laugh in his face.

Her laughter was not wise, for the municipal lieutenant next turned to the King, obtaining a dread *lettre de cachet* – one of the most detested privileges of the *ancien régime*. As Louis XVI's ill-fated lawyer Malesherbes would write in 1789, *lettres de cachet* were 'graces accorded by the king' to protect families from the dishonour to which some errant member might otherwise expose them. Fathers frequently requested them, and the resulting summary incarceration of offspring, or near-offspring, was a mark of royal grace. It was not even necessary for the child to have done something criminal; suspicion that he might do was enough. Dreux d'Aubray chose to have the order served on Sainte-Croix while the Gascon was riding in a coach with the Marquise. A sizeable crowd witnessed the arrest, and Mme de Brinvilliers took this as a public humiliation she was never to forgive.

Sainte-Croix was held in the Bastille for six weeks in the spring of 1663. There he met a mysterious Italian known as Exili or Eggidi, a professional poisoner rumoured to be in the employ of persons as diverse as Queen Christina of Sweden and a niece of Innocent X. Exili took a liking to Sainte-Croix and taught him something of his skill, which Sainte-Croix passed on to the Marquise as soon as he was freed. Charitably, Mme de Brinvilliers took to visiting the Paris hospitals, bestowing wine and biscuits on the unsuspecting patients, many of whom died in agony. Curiously for the medical profession, no one seems to have found this odd. Back in her *hôtel* in the Marais she seems even to have experimented on her servants, feeding them doped gooseberries and ham. In 1666 her father invited her to his country house in Picardy, where he had been in poor health for several months. After Marie-Madeleine's arrival his condition worsened rapidly and he returned to Paris, to die.

The money willed to the Marquise was soon squandered in excesses; once again, she found herself in need of cash. In 1670 one of Sainte-Croix' loyal servants entered the service of her brothers and poisoned them in turn. All went well, the Marquise inheriting fresh funds – although one sister-in-law did grow rather suspicious. Emboldened by so much success, Mme de Brinvilliers reportedly tried to poison her husband, failing because an antidote was supplied to the latter by Sainte-Croix, who did not wish to marry the Marquise.

In 1672 the *ménage*'s happiness was unexpectedly shattered when Sainte-Croix – by this time married himself – suddenly died, apparently from breathing in the toxic fumes of a potion he was heating. His widow found a sealed casket containing letters of a compromising nature, including an extraordinary letter of confession from Mme de Brinvilliers. She summoned the authorities. The servant called La Chaussée was arrested, tortured and put to death. Perhaps respectful of her sex and station the police dawdled, allowing Mme de Brinvilliers to flee first to England, then to a convent in Liège. Here she was captured by a diligent policeman named Desgrez, who disguised himself as a gallant young priest and charmed the Marquise with his amiable behaviour. He brought her back to Paris, there to face the usual horrors of trial, torture, imprisonment and death. The penalty for poisoning was still the stake; because she was noble, Mme de Brinvilliers was merely to be decapitated, after which her corpse would be thrown into the flames. But first she must undergo torture and the *amende honorable*, or public penance for her crimes.

So great a scandal involving so prominent a social figure could not fail to provoke gossip. For months the arrest, trial and impending execution were the talk of the town, as Mme de Sévigné's letters make quite clear. Although the Marquise – who had converted to Christianity during her trial – had sworn on Holy Scriptures to make a full confession, she was nonetheless subjected to the Ordinary and Extraordinary Torture. The Marquise was undressed and extended on a trestle, her wrists and ankles pulled by ropes; thus suspended, she was shown eight jars of water. At this she smiled and uttered her last witticism: 'Do you wish to drown me? I am so small a person, you can scarcely mean to make me swallow so much water.'[13] Swallow it she had to, without adding anything to her previous evidence, except to say that toads were used in brewing the poisons, and the only antidote was milk. After this contribution to science she was untied, laid on a mattress, and fed eggs. Here her confessor found her, exhausted by six hours of interrogation and several hours of torture; having with great difficulty persuaded this proud woman to repent the Abbé Pirot was much distressed to find that following the 'Question' it was almost impossible to direct her mind to matters of religion. Nor was the long day over. At six in the evening she was placed naked in a nightshirt and led to Notre-Dame, where many brilliant former friends had come to see her public shame, among them several great ladies themselves rumoured to be poisoners. The Abbé attemped to console her and together they entered the cart, a conveyance so small that the priest was hit across the face when the headsman whipped up the horses. To Marie-Madeleine's distress Desgrez, the enterprising officer responsible for her arrest, was now riding in the escort. The executioner obligingly tried to block him from view, whereupon the Abbé told her this humiliation was necessary for her soul. Mme de Brinvilliers accordingly asked pardon of Desgrez, mounted the scaffold bravely, and prayed until smitten by the broadsword, after which her body was thrown into the flames.

Next day Mme de Sévigné wittily informed her daughter that the Marquise, being burned, had passed into the air they breathed; she herself had witnessed the scene from the bridge by Notre-Dame, with the d'Escars maid. 'Never was there seen such a crowd, nor Paris so attentive and emotional; and ask me what we saw, for all I caught sight of was a paper hat' – the conical hat worn by the penitent in the *amende honorable*. Scornful of the Abbé Birot's claims that the Marquise died like a saint, Mme de Sévigné felt, on the contrary, that the penalty had not been hard enough: 'it's not possible that she could be in Heaven; her infamous soul is surely separated from the others'. The beheading was 'a trifle in comparison with the eight months she spent murdering her father, accepting his affection and his kindness, to which she responded with a doubly potent dose'.[14] But Mme de Sévigné's judgement would be far exceeded by that of the nineteenth-century criminologist Cesare Lombroso, who uses her appalling example to demonstrate that female criminals are crueller than male ones. Having observed that even normal women 'have many traits in common with children, that their moral sense is deficient; that they are revengeful, jealous, inclined to vengeance of a refined cruelty', Lombroso states that these defects are neutralised most of the time by 'piety, maternity, want of passion, sexual coldness, by weakness and an underdeveloped intelligence'. But when a 'morbid activity of the psychological centres intensifies the bad qualities of women', terrible things occur. When, in place of piety and maternity are found

> strong passions and intensely erotic tendencies, much muscular strength and a superior intelligence for the conception and execution of evil, it is clear that the innocuous semi-criminal present in the normal woman must be transformed into a born criminal more terrible than any man.[15]

Among such women Lombroso includes the Marquise de Brinvilliers. Certainly her specific example is not pleasant; however, Lombroso's period jargon extends beyond it to a pseudo-scientific denunciation of the entire sex.

If Mme de Brinvilliers killed to inherit, family fortune, in a sense, brought about the doom of Mme Tiquet, France's second best known female decapitee. Angélique Carlier was a wealthy heiress who had married one Claude Tiquet, a counsellor in the Paris Parliament. Early in their union Tiquet confessed that the fortune he had claimed to possess did not in fact exist, but that he intended to maintain his social position by means of his wife's dowry. Besides being elderly and broke, Tiquet soon proved to be jealous, strict and morose. Angélique, who was witty, charming and ravishingly beautiful, presently conceived a passion for the inevitable captain in the guards, Count Gilbert Galmyn de Montgeorges. Becoming suspicious, Tiquet took to round-the-clock surveillance of his wife; in retaliation Angélique turned his creditors against him and sought a legal separation of her own possessions. Not to be outdone Tiquet obtained a *lettre de cachet*, empowering him to imprison her at will on the grounds of her conspicuous misconduct. Angélique managed to retrieve and burn this document, whereupon her husband tried to get another one. Failing in this second attempt he decided to imprison her at home, employing to this end some large, ferocious servants, one of whom soon fell in love with her. Angélique was tiring of her tyrannical spouse and seems to have welcomed this development, seeing therein the means of getting rid of Tiquet; apparently she did not realise that the ridding would put her for ever at the servant's mercy. Moura, the enormous porter in question, procured some assassins and organised an ambush. Tiquet was attacked and wounded, on the evening of 8 April 1699, while returning to his house in the rue des Saints-Pères. The attack was not fatal. Still alive and kicking Tiquet was able to suggest the arrest of Moura who promptly denounced Angélique. Servant and mistress were condemned, Moura to be hanged, Angélique to have her head cut off.

At the same time the court confiscated all of Mme Tiquet's money, thereby ruining her spouse. Tiquet hastened to Versailles to beg for Angélique's life. Mercy was not forthcoming, but Tiquet did succeed in having her fortune made over to himself. In addition his colleagues in Parliament granted him another 20,000 livres in damages.

Angélique was to have been executed on 18 June, but this was a religious feast, so the event had to be postponed. The holy nature of the day did not prevent her from being put to the Question; she provided the desired confession, previously withheld, at the second *pinte*. The nineteenth of June dawned hot and stormy. Angélique had reached the scaffold when a sudden violent downpour further delayed the beheading. The crowd stood stoically in place at first, then scattered in all directions – into doorways, beneath porches, under trees – while the executioner himself hid underneath the scaffold. Windows in the town hall, where numbers of Angélique's former friends had managed to find seats, were hastily closed; Angélique and Moura were left standing in the deluge. Finally a soldier guarding them seized the black cloth provided by Angélique's family to cover her remains, and threw it on her shoulders. With something of the wit of Mme de Brinvilliers, Angélique remarked upon her extraordinary circumstance: alive, yet covered with her mortuary sheet. After about thirty minutes the torrent ceased. Carlier, the *bourreau* from nearby Pontoise, then managed to hang Moura. The sky still being favourable he turned to help Angélique from the cart, for which courtesy she kissed his hand. Unnerved by this gesture, by the unexpected delay, and possibly by her beauty, Carlier forgot to cut her soaking wet hair. The omission was disastrous. Calm and more beautiful than ever, Angélique laid her head upon the block; a lock of hair slipped down. The headsman missed his stroke, making only a slight cut at the base of the neck. After four more blows, haggard, trembling, and spattered with blood he succeeded in detaching the head, which he was then too horrified to show the people. A soldier held it up and the spectators rushed forwards to catch a glimpse of Angélique's still dazzling features; many were crushed to death in the process.

Informed of this mishap the King reacted very ill that so many members of his court had gone to see the spectacle. Conspicuously absent from the scene was Captain Galmyn de Montgeorges, who seems to disappear from the story at the time of Angélique's arrest; but in this execution, as in that of Mme de Brinvilliers, one notices the readiness of former acquaintances of the accused to attend the beheading – clearly among the more interesting social events of the season. Yet such attendance could be dangerous, as the drownings and faintings at the Cenci execution and the tramplings at the Tiquet decapitation show; the semi-private beheadings of the British Queens, within the confines of their prison, were decorous by comparison. And while the sex and high rank of the victims preserved them from the extremities of torture undergone by men, it may have exposed them to another hazard: the incompetence of the headsmen, periodically unnerved at having to kill women.

Mme de Brinvilliers and Angélique Tiquet were not the only women to lose their heads in France. Another female beheading was recorded in 1710; and in the reign of Louis XIV an elderly couple, the Comte and Comtesse Pé de Louësmes, were condemned to have their heads cut off after an act of armed insubordination in their castle. They were saved from this sentence by the intervention of the King's mistress, Mme du Barry. By this time most condemned women were executed by hanging, a less bloody but more painful death; the disparity in the punishment undergone by noblemen and poor was one of the factors in the invention of the guillotine in 1792. Revolution would prescribe the same manner of death for all, abolishing the confiscation of victims' property and punishing only the victim: henceforth shame would not fall on a condemned person's family.

In England the last persons to be decapitated were male: the Earls of Kilmarnock and Balmerino in 1746, and Lord Lovat in 1747 – although beheading for treason remained theoretically possible until 1814. The practice enjoyed a brisk posterity in other European countries, being employed in Holland in the eighteenth and early nineteenth centuries; in Denmark, where the sword was thought more honourable than the axe; and in Sweden, where the axe held sway. Swedish beheadings were carried out inside the prison in the presence of certain public officials and twelve representatives of the commune where the crime had taken place. In cases involving women the scaffold was set on fire at all four corners, and the body cremated accordingly.

Decapitation remained the preferred method of execution in Germany until the twentieth century; the axe was used in Prussia, the guillotine in Saxony. An engraving in Pritchard's *A History of Capital Punishment* shows the execution of a woman in Ratisbon in 1782. The victim is seen kneeling on a cushion with her throat placed on the block, hands tied firmly behind her; a basket has been set before her, and an aide is pulling on her hair, presumably to make sure that the head lands in the basket. The executioner is masked, in shirtsleeves with a waistcoat, raising high a long-bladed axe. The event appears to be taking place privily inside a prison, although Pritchard elsewhere declares that German decapitation remained public until 1851. No doubt scenes like the Ratisbon beheading were what the French *procureur-syndic* Roederer had in mind in 1792; writing to the Secretary of the Academy of Surgeons he recommended the German habit of beheading women 'without regard to rank'. Further instances of female beheading recorded by Pritchard occurred in 1893 and 1914. The former case involved a Frau Zillman, who had murdered her husband after being brutally ill-treated. According to newspaper accounts of the scene Frau Zillman's dress was cut at the neck down to the shoulder and her hair tied in a knot. At 8 o'clock two warders came and found her prostrate in her cell; they raised her up and helped her to the block. Wordlessly she removed her shawl, and was dead three minutes after eight. More active in their resistance were two murderesses beheaded in 1914, Pauline Zimmer and Marie Kubatza; both manacled, they had to be held in place in order for the executioner to carry out his task.

German decapitation did not end with Zimmer and Kubatza. In *The Rise and Fall of the Third Reich* William Shirer mentions that Goering hoped to reinstate the practice. Either he succeeded or decollation had never been discontinued, for in her *Berlin Diaries 1940–1945* Princess Marie Vassiltchikov describes the fate of friends who had plotted to kill Hitler. 'As there were no gallows in Germany', her editor writes, '(*the usual way of execution being beheading*) ordinary meat hooks had been fixed to an iron rail set in the ceiling of the execution cell.'[16] Presumably this 'usual way' extended to women as well as men, although the princess mentions only male executions in this incident, which involved strangulation by piano wire. Other tortures revived by the Nazis included thumbscrews and the medieval rack.

The men who invented the guillotine in France in 1792 were far from imagining such regressive applications of capital punishment; one of the truly humane advances of the French Revolution was to do away with torture. This did not mean its social retributions were devoid of irony. It is a strange outcome to the Age of Reason that the Revolution it engendered chose, as its preferred means of punishment, to amputate the member wherein reason was thought to reside. Then again, in certain periods of revolutionary atheism a favourite activity was to guillotine the statues of saints. Thus did a chapter in the history of beheading go full circle, from noble martyrdom that founded a religion to egalitarian destruction of the symbols of that faith.

3

HANGING
From dangling virgins to illicit sex

> I know that I hung
> in the windy tree
> for nine full nights.
> Wounded by the spear
> consecrated to Odin
> an offering to myself
> on the tree
> whose roots are unknown.
> (Song from the Havamal, c.900–1050)

La hache au noble, la hart au vilain.   (Old French proverb)

Both hanging and beheading are ancient enough to have symbolic aspects. 'Strange pagan rites were at the bottom of certain forms of execution', writes Carl Riedel of thirteenth-century custom: 'beheading was associated with the god of lightning, death by the wheel with the sun-god, drowning with the water-demons, and hanging with the wind-god'.[1] Reasons are not hard to imagine: a flash of steel on the neck might be compared to lightning, a body swinging from a rope is homage to the breezes, while a cartwheel with its spokes suggests the sun and its rays. In Nordic countries hanging may even have originated as a sacrifice to Odin, Wagner's Wotan, who sacrificed himself on the World Ash in order to gain wisdom. The connection between spritual knowledge and suspension is recalled in the image of the Hanged Man, the twelfth card in the major arcana of the Tarot: a young man hangs upside-down, suspended by one ankle from a wooden gibbet or a tree. His hands are tied behind his back, and his face shows an expression of calm detachment, even bliss. Historians of the Tarot – a card game of mysterious origins, established in Italy and northern Europe by the late fourteenth century – find the image among the strangest, with no apparent precedent in orthodox Christian symbolism; they compare 'Lo Impichato' not only to the sacrifice of Odin but to Sumerian rites and the death of Dionysus in Orphic cults. In terms of Jungian psychology the image represents a turning point in life. Whereas the first half of one's existence is concerned with developing the conscious mind and stabilising the ego with regard to the outer world, the second half reverses the process as one seeks to establish links with the inner self. The inverted position of the Hanged Man symbolises this reversal of values and aims; the knot by which he hangs represents the supporting knot of faith; and the tree symbolises the mother as the source of all sustenance. Thus the card of 'Le Pendu' is interpreted as a trial of courage and faith in which one learns to reconcile the conscious and unconscious halves of self.

In classical antiquity hanging was considered a disgraceful death, not suitable for those of noble birth. Men and women whose honour had been stained were expected to fall privily upon a sword – even when the misdeed was scarcely of their choosing. Thus, in Sophocles' *Ajax*, the hero discovers he has killed a herd of sheep instead of Trojan soldiers; shamed and ridiculous, he embeds his sword in sand and rushes at the blade. Raped by Sextus Tarquinius, the Roman matron Lucretia first exhorts her husband to avenge her, then stabs herself to death. When public execution was found necessary, to be beheaded or cut down by sword or axe was less demeaning than all other forms of punishment – a preference probably due in the part to the military connotations of those weapons. Even so, the antique repugnance for the rope is hard to understand. Why was hanging shameful to the ancient world?

A possible semiotic answer is provided in a special issue of *Poetics Today* entitled 'The Female Body in Western Culture'. Here Eva Cantarella tells how Diogenes the Cynic, 'while strolling among the olive groves, saw several hanged maidens swinging from the branches of a tree', and reportedly exclaimed 'If only all trees bore such fruit!' This incident is related in Diogenes Laertius' *Lives of the Philosophers*. Greek literature contains further examples of this phenomenon – 'dangling virgins', in Cantarella's phrase – in which maidens 'frightened by a menace' escape by collectively suspending themselves from walnut trees (they were thought to be reborn as walnuts). The menace in question was probably rape. That hanging was normally associated with the death of women, Cantarella argues, is apparent from the use of the word *brochos* – a 'mortal noose' – to designate the instrument of death in the suicide of Epicaste (Jocasta in the Homeric poems). The *brochos* reappears in a Rhodian legend told by Pausanias: exiled in Sparta after the death of Menelaus, Helen of Troy seeks help from her friend Polixe. But Polixe, who had lost her husband in the Trojan war, now exacts revenge, sending slaves disguised as Furies to hang Helen with the *brochos*. The 'mortal noose' is also the instrument chosen by Ulysses when he hangs those of Penelope's maidservants who have not been loyal to him. As proof that the connection of women and hanging continues into Roman times, Eva Cantarella goes on to quote the fourth-century writer Pacetus, who grumbles about the 'unjust infamy' of suffering the 'death of women'; men, he declares, should kill themselves with swords. From these remarks one might deduce that hanging was inherited by medieval man as a demeaning punishment because it derived from the ancient death of women and also because it was inflicted from without and involved an intermediary.

Not only was hanging feminine and shameful, but it was erotic too. The sexual connotations of suspension can be seen in Greek art. Eva Cantarella mentions a girl depicted on a swing, being pushed by a satyr: 'The symbolic value of the rite is easily perceived: swings are connected with sexual intercourse.' In swinging and hanging alike a rite of passage is implied: in both activities a person must die symbolically in order to pass into a further stage. Girls pushed by the satyr could emerge from that rite as childbearing women; inversely, girls who escaped from rape by hanging would pass into death. Then again, the traditional identification of women with the earth made it appropriate to kill women by hanging. 'It is difficult to imagine a better way to symbolise the death of a woman than by separating her from the earth', concludes Cantarella.

Identifications, of course, vary with cultures: the modest northern Europeans chose to execute women by burying them in that same earth. In the sin-conscious Middle Ages women were seldom hanged, leaving one to wonder how they came to be separated from a form of execution traditionally, in the Greek world, theirs. One is left to postulate the Protean influence of Christian pudency again; post-Christian authorities who suspected the erotic implications of swinging on a rope would scarcely have approved. An incident in Boccaccio's *Concerning Famous Women* in which a dutiful daughter saves her incarcerated mother from starvation by feeding her in prison indicates that the gaoler had first intended strangling his victim in her cell. Possibly female hanging passed through some intermediary, private phase of cellular strangulation before becoming public. It is interesting that the woman hanged in Paris in 1449 was a gypsy – that is, a woman of different race and religion, who may not have been thought worthy of modesty. Commenting on the singularity of that event the memoirs of the executioner of Paris remark that 'Oncques plus ne fut vu au royaume de France', never was such a thing seen in France. Once re-established, however, the practice remained in force until the Revolution.

The basic procedures of hanging differed little between sexes. As most authorities explain it the criminal, with hands tied behind his back, was first conveyed in a cart to the place of execution, or gallows. This consisted of two uprights with a horizontal beam, against which leaned a ladder. The hangman would attach three ropes around the victim's neck: two of these, known as *tortouses*, were draped across the horizontal. The executioner then clambered backwards up the ladder, dragging the victim behind him by means of the *tortouses*. A priest ascended after, facing forwards, encouraging the victim. Once the confessor had safely climbed back down, the executioner pulled on the third rope, known as the *jet*, and simultaneously kicked the victim off the ladder. As the slip knots on the two *tortouses* began to choke the victim, the hangman would mount his or her shoulders, or stand on his tied hands, and kick him in the stomach. Death thus resulted more from strangulation than from a broken neck, as would later be the case. Small wonder that beheading was considered less painful and disgraceful; after this treatment the faces of the victims were blackened and convulsed, quite unlike the bliss of the Hanged Man in the *Tarocchi*. But there, of course, besides being upside-down, the hanging is symbolic.

The *Memoirs* of the Paris executioner, whence these particulars are drawn, also state that in England the custom was to use a horse and cart. When everything was ready the hangman covered the victim's face in a bonnet and waited for the signal; as soon as this was given he whipped up the horse, the cart moved onwards and the victim remained. After hanging for an hour – from a single rope – the body was cut down and, in the case of murderers, given over to whatever school of anatomy had previously purchased it.

With such arrangements much could and did go wrong. In 1749 the *prieur* Charles-François Fleur, condemned to death for reasons not recorded, 'grew very agitated and did not want to die', so that the *bourreau* was obliged to upbraid him for his cowardice: 'Come, Monsieur le Curé, be a little brave.'[2] Even so, the *prieur* managed to wedge his legs in the rungs of the ladder, so firmly that his feet could scarcely be dislodged. Fleur was 'at last' executed, dying without 'the slightest sign of repentance' for his unspecified misdeed. In 1743 Guillaume Aubin, a receiver of stolen goods – that crime for which women had formerly been buried alive – was convinced that the rope would decapitate him and offered such resistance that the executioner was forced to suspend him by the waist. (Aubin's misgivings were not totally unfounded, since even when hanging had been reduced to a fine art in nineteenth-century England someone was decapitated when the hangman miscalculated his celebrated 'drop'.) At the execution of Jean Masson in 1751 the rope broke – twice – when Masson was kicked into the void; the executioners set about strangling him where he had fallen. Outraged by this incompetent display the normally unsympathetic crowd roared in no uncertain terms for mercy, and had to be subdued by bayonets. Masson was carried to the scaffold and hanged for 'the third time, although dead', the authorities being ever punctilious about carrying out the letter of the sentence.

It cannot be said that women were hanged more efficiently. In January 1765 Marie Groison, pretty, plump and with 'exceedingly much bosom', was hanged for theft in Paris. The executioner, Charles-Henri Sanson, 'made her suffer greatly because he managed the execution very badly'. Ten years before, when he was just 18, the same young man had been called upon to hang Marie-Catherine Lescombat, a well-known beauty credited with the invention of fashionable walks – and also with being an accomplice in the murder of her husband. Perhaps emotionally disturbed at having to dispatch a woman, Charles-Henri 'handled this execution rather badly and had to make four or five attempts'.[3] Yet the Lescombat fate illustrates one curious advantage: women were sent out to be hanged with neck and face concealed in a cloth. Mumblings of discontent were heard when Mme Lescombat was glimpsed in a cowl. It was rumoured that the wrong woman had been hanged, and what was more annoying, Mme Lescombat's good looks were hidden from the public view.

Except in the case of the gypsy woman whose skirt was strapped to her legs it is not recorded how justice dealt with the problem of crowds staring at the lower extremities. Stare, however, it seems they did. If fiction could attest to fact, one might advance a text by Marguerite Yourcenar – meticulous and indefatigable researcher that she was – who recreates the atmosphere of seventeenth-century Holland in a short novel entitled *Un homme obscur*. The protagonist's wife, Saraï, is hanged for stealing money from a sea-captain she had previously seduced. Her husband Nathanael afterwards has the misfortune to overhear an account of her death. A man whom Nathanael mentally compares to a pig tells his girl-friend:

> 'She was singing as she climbed the ladder.'
> 'What, you mean, hymns?'
> 'Oh no, musicians' songs. And when she got to the top, she pushed away the man in red, the one whose name brings bad luck . . . Bit harder and he'd have come clattering down off the ladder. And then suddenly she jumped, all by herself. The rope made her do a few fancy circles in the air, and everybody in the square knew that she had pretty legs.'
> 'Just legs?'
> 'Pity. I couldn't see any more, on account of her petticoats.'[4]

Nathanael, who is crossing the Zuider Zee on a particularly tranquil day when he hears this, goes to the ship's rail, and vomits.

Both in the Age of Reason and before, the crimes deemed worthy of this acrobatic penalty were numerous and varied. In France hanging gradually replaced burning at the stake as the punishment for sorcery. Montague Summers relates that in 1618 the Provost of Loudinières 'hanged eight wretches who were found guilty of attending the Sabbat and adoring Satan there'. In addition the archives of Rouen, Orléans, Bordeaux and 'other great cities' contain vast lists of trials and condemnations, 'whilst in their proportion the smaller towns and even villages are no whit behind in their holocausts and hangings'. Hanging had always been the preferred punishment for witches in England, though drowning was common, and burning if the case was tinged with treason, since it was often felt that witchcraft had been used in attempts against the sovereign. Although officially dominated by Protestantism from 1559, England was by no means immune to superstition and the prosecutions it engendered: a law established in 1563 during the reign of Elizabeth enacted that any who 'shall use, practice, or exercise any Witchecrafte, Enchantment, Charme or Sorcerie, whereby any person shall happen to be killed or destroyed ... shall suffer paynes of Deathe as a Felon or Felons'.[5] When Mary Stuart's son James acceded to the English throne in 1602 the Elizabethan statute was thought to be too mild, differing but little from laws prohibiting murder. The Stuart King passed a new, more comprehensive statute which included the conjuration of evil spirits for any intent or purpose whatsoever. Montague Summers records the execution of some fifty witches under James, many of them hanged and most of them women.

Possibly the most serious persecution of English witches occurred during the Civil War. In Summers' view the notorious trials of the 1640s are largely to be blamed on Puritanism: after the outbreak of rebellion in 1642, 'there was, as might have been expected when England fell gradually into the hands of gloomy and grossly superstitious fanatics as cruel as Calvin and as very knaves as Knox, a hideous epidemic of blind and bloody persecution'. Summers, the defender of the Holy Inquisition, is now found deploring the narrow-minded zeal of Puritan Matthew Hopkins, a minister's son from Suffolk, and responsible for several scores of executions between 1644 and 1646. John Gaule criticised Hopkins' proceedings in his *Select Cases of Conscience Touching Witches and Witchcrafts* of 1646, after which date little is heard of the churchman's son. According to some accounts he perished peacefully of consumption; according to others, he was himself put to the water-ordeal as a witch, and thereby drowned, leaving Summers to conclude of the Puritan fiends that 'The brute instincts of primitive man are but insecurely disguised under the cloak of religious principle, and a garnish of Gospel texts may satisfy the canter but only serve more deeply to offend the impartial judge.'

Hanging was also the punishment meted out to witches in Puritan New England, apparently by much the same means as in France: Marion Starkey's *The Devil in Massachusetts* mentions an oak tree and a ladder in connection with the sentences. Nor were the gender-biased prosecutions carried out in England in the 1640s without effect. True, the colonial communities frequently resorted to the milder penalties of banishment or mere incarceration; but despite the relative leniency shown by this new society in dealing with an ancient offence, the patterns of accusation and prosecution are still sexist. As Carol F. Karlsen records in a recent demographic study, *The Devil in the Shape of a Woman*, 'At least 344 persons were accused of witchcraft in New England between 1620 and 1725. Of the 342 who can be identified by sex, 267 (78%) were female.'[6] Of the remaining seventy-five suspected males almost half were husbands, sons or friends of female witches – contaminated, as it were, by women. The same holds true for actual convictions. Between 1647 and 1663, in the first phase of New England's witch-fear, seventy-nine persons were accused of witchcraft. 'Sixty-one of the seventy-nine people accused were female, as were thirteen of the fifteen who were convicted and executed. Nine of the nineteen men accused, and both of the men who were hanged, were married to women who were witches.' At all times, Karlsen concludes, women were more likely to be accused than men, and far more women were convicted.

These patterns link New England with the mother country. Referring to the several hundred executions of 1644-6 Karlsen points out that 'More than ninety percent of these English witches were women'. Although New England witches were less poor than their English counterparts – many of the American suspects were from the middle or upper class – colonial witchcraft was apparently 'rooted in the towns and villages of England'. The strongest link, Karlsen says, was that the witches were mostly women. This fact was 'never made explicit' in the young colonial culture; nonetheless, it was so.

What was it, in this new, Puritanical view of things, that proved as detrimental to the female sex as late medieval theology? The execution of Anne Hibbens in 1656 provides several clues. Though not actually prosecuted until neighbours formally accused her of supernatural activities, Mrs Hibbens had been excommunicated from her Boston church some sixteen years before her trial for witchcraft. The reasons given were the 'obstinate challenge' she posed to religious, secular, and familial authority, and her 'evil influence over other church members'. In other words, Anne Hibbens had a mind of her own. She suffered for it almost as much as did Anne Askew, a century before. Karlsen discerns two main sources of alarm in New England witch-fear: the damage that witches might wreak upon their neighbours and their neighbours' property, and the covenant with Satan, which might result in the destruction of Puritan churches. Women who expressed religious dissent were thus the objects of peculiar suspicion, since their independent thinking was one possible disguise for the diabolic pact. As examples, Karlsen cites the cases of Anne Hutchinson and her two friends and supporters, Jane Hawkins and Mary Dyer. Anne Hutchinson was a lay healer who had assumed the additional role of spiritual leader in her community, a fact which 'was not tolerable nor comely in the sight of God, nor fitting for your sex'; she was excommunicated from the Boston church in 1638. Jane Hawkins, also a lay healer and midwife, was rumoured to be a witch; John Winthrop, then Governor of Massachusetts, wrote that she was 'known to give young women oil of mandrakes and other stuff' to cause conception. When Mary Dyer gave birth to a stillborn child and Hutchinson's own last pregnancy ended in a miscarriage it was assumed by Winthrop and others that God was punishing them for their 'misshapen' religious views. Hutchinson and Hawkins were subsequently banished from the Commonwealth, while their friend Mary Dyer was hanged as a Quaker activist in 1660.

In this connection Karlsen seems to find the Puritans far more reactionary than the English Quakers of the 1640s, who openly claimed the right to spiritual leadership, advocating a lay ministry based on 'inner light', and following the principle of the priesthood of all believers; if God revealed his word to all, then women could teach it too. This seemed blasphemous to the New England Puritans. When the first female Quaker preachers, Ann Austen and Mary Fisher, arrived in Boston Harbour in 1656 their reception was of the chilliest: they were stripped naked on the ship and searched for marks of devil worship. After being imprisoned for five weeks they were ejected from the colony.

In other respects the accusations levelled against New England witches were reminiscent of the European charges: they were thought to damage children, animals and crops, obstruct reproduction, cause miscarriages or deformed births, even to provoke spontaneous abortions in themselves. Even the European courts' fascination with supernatural eroticism resurfaced, though greatly more restrained. In Hartford, Connecticut in 1662, Ann Cole, though pious, was taken with strange fits, and spoke with voices not her own. Her demonic conversations were duly written down and then read back to her by clergymen. It was true, she admitted: the Devil had made 'frequent use of her body with much seeming delight'. Another modern commentator, Chadwick Hansen, explains this possession in the psychiatric manner denounced by Thomas Szasz: 'What is involved is apparently an erotic fit, in which the woman actually goes through the motions of copulation and achieves an orgasm; similar fits have been observed in mental patients of the twentieth century.'[7]

To contemporaries of the Salem trials a connection existed between lechery and sorcery. Cotton Mather, who had been a medical student before becoming a minister, wrote in his *Wonders of the Visible World* that 'a lewd and naughty kind of life' was a 'probable' sign of witchcraft. Oddly enough Cotton and his father Increase would attempt to calm one girl, ostensibly possessed by the Devil, by stroking her nude breast and stomach in a ritual laying-on of hands. Odder still, the girl seemed to enjoy it.

Attempting no medical diagnosis of the witches, but confining herself rather to an analysis of the social conditions in which accusations of witchcraft tend to occur, Carol Karlsen observes that instances of lewd behaviour in women – particularly in older women – may have fostered accusations. It was widely feared that witches would influence the women they drew into their covens, and make them adulterous. Witches, Karlsen says, were thought to afflict men in ways that suggest an obsessive fear of their erotic power. Numerous male witnesses in trials would testify that witches entered their bedchambers at night and physically oppressed them as though with a great weight, sitting on their stomachs, lying on them and thus depriving them of sleep. When Mary Webster was acquitted of witchcraft in Hadley in 1688 some young men of the town dragged her from her house, hanged her till she was nearly dead, then rolled her in the snow and left her buried in it. Cotton Mather later exonerated them because they 'were at their wits' end', and because the man she had reportedly afflicted felt better while she was being attacked. Mary Webster's crimes? She had been accused of causing the man's breast to swell 'like a Womans', and of having 'wounded or burned' his sexual parts.

Witch-fear in New England reached its height in the celebrated Salem trials. It all began innocently enough: two little girls, the nine-year-old daughter and eleven-year-old niece of the Reverend Samuel Parris, tried gazing at a home-made crystal ball. Tradition has it they were aided by one Tituba, a Carib slave-woman brought by Parris from Barbados. Together with some other little girls, on long winter evenings

> when dusk had fallen and all was snow and bitter cold outside in the blackness, this young coterie used to invite Tituba into the room, and huddled round the blazing logs they would listen hour after hour to her grim tales of Indian wizardry, barbaric rites, and human sacrifice in the heart of the pathless forest where the hideous drone of the drums drowned the despairing cries of victims tortured and mangled before the monstrous bulk of some grinning shark-fanged god. She spoke of ju-ju sorceries, of warlocks, who by means of dancing, chants and invocations were able to cast withering spells upon their enemies.
> (Summers, *Geography*, p. 290)

So at least believes Montague Summers, who declares Tituba a thoroughly ignorant person, though well-versed in voodoo. Less romantically, Chadwick Hansen and Carol Karlsen explain that the little girls were looking at egg-white, poured into a glass, to find 'what trade their sweet harts should be of'. The image they beheld – a spectre in the shape of a coffin – was apparently so much more frightful than anything conceived of in a future spouse that the little girls fell ill. Their fits, deemed symptomatic of diabolical possession, spread rapidly among other young females of the community. After a month or two, three witches had been named: Tituba, Sarah Osborne and Sarah Good. Tituba, who obligingly confessed to everything, declared that still other witches were at large. Then one of the afflicted children named as her tormentor Martha Corey, a respectable if sarcastic matron of Salem Town. In the succeeding rashes of accusations the possessed girls were invested by public credulity practically with prosecuting powers, and fourteen women and five men were convicted and hanged. The second group of executions, carried out on 19 July 1692, included three of the five men: George Jacobs, John Proctor and George Burroughs. John Proctor was married to Elizabeth Proctor, a mild and Christian woman imprisoned on the evidence of hysterical possession; Proctor succeeded in saving her by getting her with child, which meant she could not be executed before giving birth. Burroughs was the former pastor of Salem Village and George Jacobs a sceptic sufficiently reckless and brave to term one of the afflicted girls a 'witch bitch'. All in this second group died with such firm assurances of innocence that doubts began to be entertained as to their guilt. A fourth man, Giles Corey, husband of the executed Martha, resorted to the highly original ploy of refusing to plead; as in English law, a defendant who refused to plead could not be tried, and Giles seems to have thought his goods could not be confiscated. He could, however, be pressed to death, so elderly Giles Corey was stripped down to his drawers and crushed with weights in a futile attempt to secure the inheritance of his children. The only words he deigned to pronounce during this ordeal constituted a defiant call for 'more weights'.

By the end of that summer the accusations were becoming quite preposterous. Margaret Phipps, wife of the Governor of Massachusetts, was now named; so was Mrs Margaret Thatcher, widow of a clergyman and mother-in-law to one of the principal judges in the witch-trials. Mrs Increase Mather was rumoured to have been accused after her ecclesiastical spouse had read the manuscript of his celebrated *Cases of Conscience* to a group of Boston clergymen. Although Puritans preferred to reach unanimous decisions on fundamental matters, their radical Protestantism did recognise that a free and unforced conscience made consensus impossible in certain cases – 'cases of conscience', as they were known. Appealing to this radical belief, Increase Mather indicated that anyone could be falsely accused of witchcraft: even Luther had been. 'It were better', Mather argued, 'that ten suspected witches should escape than that one innocent person should be condemned.' Not only that, but some of the 'tests' engaged in by the courts – seeing whether the accused could witch someone into a fit, for example – did themselves constitute a kind of preliminary witchcraft. According to Chadwick Hansen the New England clergy had long recommended caution and restraint in witch trials; it was the juries and magistrates who erred on the side of enthusiasm – unlike the magistrates in France who, in Robert Mandrou's thesis, came to form a more 'enlightened' class. This is also the impression to be received from Marion Starkey's *The Devil in Massachusetts*, where courts were held in credulous thrall by the impious antics of the possessed children.

Mather's slender volume is often credited with halting the New England witch trials, but it seems that other factors were involved. Only at the height of the Salem outbreak, reports Karlsen, did the authorities relinquish to any significant degree their belief that witches must be women. The fact that several men – and prominent women – were actually convicted and executed may have fostered growing public doubts about the proceedings; when those accused were mainly poor women of Salem, no one appeared seriously troubled. Again, women living alone – single, widowed or divorced – were particularly vulnerable to accusation, unlike married women, whose husbands could, and did, protect their wives with petitions and lawsuits charging slander. Tracing the decline of the New England prosecutions Chadwick Hansen and Marion Starkey both refer to a man who threatened to sue his wife's accusers for one thousand pounds, bringing the said accusers to their senses as only money could. Sometimes the mere existence of a spouse seems to have preserved women reputed to be witches, but not formally accused until their husbands died. As Karlsen further indicates,

> In the eyes of the community, the woman alone in early New England was an aberration: the fundamental female role of procreation was at best irrelevant to her.... Moreover, women alone no longer performed – perhaps never had performed – the other main functions of women in New England society: they were not the 'helpmeets' to men Puritans thought they should be.
>
> (Karlsen, p. 75)

If not actually lewd, women alone were liable to be viewed as solitary subverters of the helpmeet ethic, with potentially fatal consequences.

Karlsen's statistical studies reveal two other categories of women at risk: older women, and women likely to inherit property. Almost 40 per cent of older women accused of witchcraft in New England were subsequently brought to trial, and well over half of those tried were convicted. This point is not especially remarkable, for almost all commentators on witchcraft at some point refer to the potential witch as an old hag. More startling is Karlsen's treatment of statistics pertaining to inheritance. Under English Common Law, which still affected Massachusetts, married women had no right to own property. Upon her marriage, 'the very being or legal existence of a woman is suspended', as William Blackstone declared. In the Puritan colonies, where widows rarely inherited more than their dowry portion, some men did try to make more substantial provisions for their wives and daughters. Karlsen discovers that women who stood to benefit from an inheritance were often suspected and accused. An example is middle-class Martha Allen of Andover, who had married Thomas Carrier, an impecunious servant, returning to Andover in the 1680s destitute and with several children to support. The township actually gave the Carriers some land, but viewed them ever after with dislike and distrust. In 1690 Martha and several of her progeny caught smallpox. When her father and both brothers died of the disease, it began to be rumoured that Martha was a witch. She was formally accused after a confessing witch from Andover charged her with murdering all her male relatives, who would otherwise have inherited the Allen wealth. Martha Carrier was condemned to death and hanged on 19 August 1692. In Karlsen's chilling statistics, 'women from families without male heirs made up 64 percent of the families prosecuted; 76 percent of those who were found guilty, and 89 percent of those who were executed'. The implication is that such women were vulnerable because their mere existence threatened to disrupt the orderly transfer of property from male to male; it challenged 'prescribed gender arrangements'.

As Marion Starkey affirms, the New England witch hunts were by no means the most excessive in their genre. In Massachusetts only twenty witches were executed, 'a microscopic number compared to the tens of thousands who had been put to death in Europe and England' in the late Middle Ages, to say nothing of the 'millions who have died in the species of witch-hunts peculiar to our own rational, scientific times'. Yet this very numerical modesty is one of its attractions; the episodes are manageable in a way that 'catastrophes involving astronomical figures are not'. Indeed, Marion Starkey's principal achievement is probably to have created memorable portraits of the individual protagonists: Rebecca Nurse, for example, a gentle Christian grandmother executed mainly because, through deafness, she misheard a crucial question; or Margaret Jacobs, a young woman with the courage to retract a confession of witchcraft she had made to save herself from hanging. Margaret was not executed, but kept incarcerated even after the hysteria abated, for want of funds to pay her prison bill. Both were victims of a climate of opinion that did not change until prominent and powerful citizens began to react in the name of common sense. It was to Massachusetts' credit, Starkey feels, that it emerged from its delusion without intervention from outside; moreover, the colony would later have the intellectual honesty to apologise to families of victims hanged during the hunt.

Back in the Old World women could be hanged for far less subversive crimes than preaching the Gospel or becoming modest heiresses. On 28 April 1762 a servant girl, Marie-Jeanne Houillon, was hanged in Paris for the theft of an embroidered napkin. The case was not unusual, since from the early Middle Ages any servant caught stealing from his master could be sent to the gallows. 'Shame on him who takes from his master and who depends on him for bread and wine; he may be hanged, for this is treason of a kind', as the Establishments of Saint-Louis explained in 1270. Since eighteenth-century servants often went unpaid, though housed and fed by their employers, thefts were not uncommon. In 1728 a chambermaid who had been in the service of M de Mouy for more than eighteen years was hanged for petty theft. In 1755 Marie-Thérèse Brière, another domestic thief, died most incorrectly with her face uncovered; in addition, she did not wait for the executioner to push her but jumped from the ladder on her own initiative. Nine years later, despite the pleadings of her parish priest, a dumb and mentally retarded servant, Elisabeth Gommery, was executed for stealing a napkin and a towel. Evidently the severity of the punishment did not deter the judges from prescribing it, any more than it deterred the servants from their pitiful crimes.

Nor did the prospect of hanging seem to deter people from committing the numerous types of sexual crimes listed as capital. Of the numerous 'motifs d'inculpation' listed by the lawyer Guy du Rousseau de Lacombe, about half were 'crimes of luxury' or sexual offences. These included fornication, seduction of a minor, adultery, bigamy, polygamy, procuring of prostitutes, incest, homosexuality, rape and abduction. Most unjust from the male point of view were laws against seduction, or 'fornication with a free person of honest conduct, and not a prostitute'. Certain forms of seduction entailed the hanging of the man involved: fornication between a gaoler and his female prisoner, between a teacher and his female student, or a servant and his master's daughter – even if the latter had initiated the deed. In these instances even a consenting female was apparently considered at the mercy of the man, who had abused his position.

The idea of seduction as a trust betrayed would seem to have a medieval ancestry. German nobles who took advantage of a young girl placed in their care could lose their fiefs, if she was willing; their lives, if she was not. The ethic of the Old French Romances explicitly reproved forcible seduction. In *Claris et Laris* Sir Gawain berates Mordred for attempting to force a damsel: 'Brother, a gentleman of great rank truly commits too great an outrage who forces a woman ... it is a very great misprision and cruelty and treason, for a woman cannot defend herself' (Riedel, p. 65). A story told on the fifth day of Boccaccio's *Decameron* (c.1350) recounts the plight of Teodoro, a young boy taken by Genoese pirates and sold as a slave. Brought up kindly enough by Messer Amerigo, a nobleman of Trapani, he falls in love with his master's daughter Violante and gets her with child. Realising this will cost him his life, he decides to flee; Violante begs him to remain. Unfortunately Messer Amerigo catches his daughter in the act of giving birth to a son. Brandishing his sword he compels Violante to reveal her lover's name; Teodoro is then put to the torture and condemned to be hanged. But on the way to the gallows he is recognised by his own father, an ambassador for the King of Armenia. Being a man of great rank – and on his way to see the Pope – the ambassador succeeds in freeing his son and arranging a marriage between the young couple. As frequently occurs in the *Decameron*, Teodoro's tale presents an act of transgression that is later rectified by a happy conjunction of reason and nature. The earlier case involving Gawain and Mordred is more reflective of feudal honour, harking back to the accusatorial system of justice: the significant words are 'for a woman cannot defend herself', recalling the reasons by which women and priests were disqualified as witnesses.

Rather than condemning thirteenth-century seducers to death, as did the secular authorities, the Church had insisted that a man who had ravished a maiden should marry her. Unfortunately the prescription was not always sweetened by the mutual love found in Boccaccio. In eighteenth-century France, Brittany in particular was likely to condemn seducers to matrimony. Penal historian Roger Anchel recounts how young men were frequently obliged to wed the dishonoured girl, or else die: if they consented, the couples were led swiftly to the church, the grooms with feet in chains. One such fellow, apparently a nobleman, persisted in expressing a preference for decapitation rather than forced matrimony, and was only persuaded with great difficulty that wedlock would be preferable to death. He covered his face with a hat at the ceremony, to avoid looking at his bride, and his marriage-vows consisted of these words: 'Yes, since the court so wishes, and since I am constrained.'[8] This obligatory conjugation was stopped by royal decree in 1730, none too soon according to Anchel, and replaced by payment of damages.

In the absence of divorce, matrimony could sometimes lead to murder. Men guilty of 'uxoricide' were often broken on the wheel; male or female spouses who used poison could be burned alive. Poisoning was popular with women, Anchel says, since it compensated for lack of physical strength. But wives there were who resorted to more ingenious means. Louise Billet, wife of grape-grower Jean Laurent in Givors, attached her sickly husband to his bed with ropes, telling him the surgeon had so instructed her in order to stop blood from rushing to his head. She also tied a handkerchief about his throat, with two thin cords inside. When she began to tighten the cords her husband realised something was amiss and struggled from the bed; he ran into the neighbour's house in his nightshirt and bonnet, with ropes round his neck. Next day he died. Unable to decide which was responsible – his illness, his doctor, or his wife – the authorities resolved the dilemma by hanging the wife.

Whereas eighteenth-century rape and seduction laws seem unjustly repressive of the sexuality of Frenchmen, the very nature of certain other statutes victimised women: abortion, concealment of birth or pregnancy, abandoning a new-born child, and infanticide. The prohibition against abortion can be traced to Christian Rome. Before Christian times, the practice had been legal, and even in the second century AD the jurist Papinian held that before birth the 'fruit' was not a human being. This doctrine was borrowed from the stoic philosophers, who held the seed to be a substance so dependent on the mother as to have no life of its own. A former pagan turned Montanist heretic, Tertullian (AD 160–c.230) was one of the first to view abortion as a crime, describing it as an 'anticipated' homicide: 'Homo est qui futurus, et fructus jam in semine est.' The 1270 Establishments of Saint-Louis prohibited abortion, but in a manner that seemed to value the mother almost more than the child: ill-treatment of a pregnant woman, such as might cause her to abort or die, was punishable by hanging. By the French classical period the emphasis had shifted: anyone who procured or performed an abortion for a woman or a girl could be sentenced to death. A woman who paid money for an abortion, or who performed the deed upon herself, could be hanged. The law against concealment of pregnancy – which in effect deprived women of all sexual privacy – was intended to forestall the possibility of abortion or infanticide, for a registered embryo or baby could scarcely be done away with in secret. More important even than the preservation of the child seems to have been the religious reason behind the concealment law: a child aborted, or abandoned at birth, would die unbaptised.

Still enforced in the Englightenment, these provisions of the Ordonnance of 1670 reflected a society that manufactured laws requiring unmarried pregnant women to bear babies, while in no way modifying its chronic moral disapproval of their state. This injustice was recognised by Voltaire. In a letter of 1754 he seeks protection for an unmarried mother because, as he puts it, 'Men are sufficiently barbarous to punish by death a girl whose fault was to hide a tiny mass of flesh from the miseries of life'. Voltaire returns to the subject in 1766 in his famous commentary on the *Traité des délits et des peines* of Cesare Beccaria, recently translated into French by the Abbé Morellet (or 'Mords-les', 'Bite them' as Voltaire affectionately called him). In the opening pages of the commentary Voltaire evokes a similar case. Having just read Beccaria's book,

> I was deluded enough to think that this work would soften the barbarism remaining in the jurisprudence of so many nations; I was hoping for some reform in the human species, when I was told that an eighteen year-old girl had just been hanged in one of the provinces. She was beautiful and shapely, with useful talents, and from an honest family.[9]

And what had this girl done? She was 'guilty of having allowed herself to become pregnant; and more so, of having abandoned her fruit'. Fleeing from her parents' home the girl had been overcome by labour pains, and given birth alone beside a fountain. Overcome with shame she had returned home and concealed her condition, leaving the infant exposed; next day, it was found dead. The mother was discovered, tried and hanged. The first of her errors, Voltaire maintains, should have entitled her to the protection of the law, obliging the baby's father to repair the harm he had done; the second was admittedly more criminal. But 'Because a child dies, is it absolutely necessary to put to death its mother?' Better by far to establish houses where children left exposed could be raised; for proper jurisprudence makes laws which prevent catastrophes, rather than being content simply to punish them.

Voltaire does not trace the history of infanticide to ancient Rome. If he had, he might have pointed out that the early Christian emperors showed more responsibility and consistency in dealing with unwanted children than did European legislators some fifteen centuries later: if laws decreed that babies must be born, the state would make some show of looking after them. Constantine had cribs placed in churches for abandoned babies to be put in, and ordered clothes to be found for parents otherwise too poor to keep their offspring. Not until the time of Valentinian I, however, were laws created to prohibit infanticide and child exposition. Strangely, this edict of AD 374 would probably not so much have curtailed female freedom – already minimal – as it diminished the general autonomy of Roman households, particularly of their male heads. Roman husbands had hitherto held power of life and death over their wives and children; suddenly, this power was invested in the state.

Ironically, that eighteenth-century society which morally condemned women for having illegitimate babies – and condemned them to death for concealing the pregnancy – could also grant a stay of execution to a woman who was pregnant. The aim of this provision was to save the 'innocent' child; but it could theoretically have permitted a woman guilty of infanticide later to prolong her life by getting pregnant while in prison. Once the infant was born, the mother would of course be hanged. Such was the fate – respite followed by death – that befell Marie-Catherine Lescombat, whom Charles-Henri Sanson hanged so ineptly in 1755. Initially arrested in July 1753, Mme Lescombat had kept Paris on tenterhooks for almost two years with news of her affairs. First of all, her husband – a debauched, drunken, extravagant, brutal, jealous sort of man – had been run through with a sword in the rue des Fossoyeurs. The murderer, who claimed to be acting in self-defence, was found to be one Jean-Louis Demougeot, Marie-Catherine's lover. Marie-Catherine was immediately presumed to have assisted him, and thrown into gaol. But she was pregnant, and in the absence of all formal proof was provisionally set free, giving birth in November 1753. Demougeot, who had not confessed to murder, was sentenced to be hanged. An appeal only made things worse, for he was then condemned to be broken on the wheel. Having endured the customary pre-execution torture of the boot without avowing any guilt, Demougeot was pressed by his confessor at the scaffold and decided to relieve his conscience by implicating his mistress. He was executed on 8 January 1755. The next day his beloved was sentenced to be hanged; but being pregnant once again she was granted a second stay, producing the necessary child a few weeks later. The execution was rescheduled for 5 March, in front of today's Hôtel de Ville. When the moment came Marie-Catherine declared herself pregnant a third time. This was not impossible, since prison visits were allowed; a respite of four months was granted, during which Marie-Catherine was transferred to a less liberal institution. Extracted from her cell by the lieutenant-general she was examined by four doctors, who declared her without child. The execution could no longer be delayed. As an event, it was eagerly awaited; a large crowd jammed the towers of Notre-Dame, voicing discontent when her by this time legendary beauty was veiled from its gaze.

France was not the only country to prohibit sexual crimes. The religious basis for such interdiction appears in a Swedish ordinance of 1563:

> henceforth the following crimes shall not be punished by fine or imprisonment, to wit, blasphemy, treason, assassination, open adultery, incest, rape, sodomy and other similar crimes, for as much as Almighty God has himself decreed, and nature and reason agree that those who commit such crimes should not escape death. Further, too, divers scourges such as plague and famine come to punish men for their sins to such an extent that it often happens that a whole country is devastated and suffers for the crime of one man.
>
> (Pritchard, p. 16)

In 1681, a further Swedish statute decreed that women suspected of killing their illegitimate children should be condemned to death on mere presumptive evidence. The deliberately harsh punishment was thought to be preventive: the crime was 'becoming frequent', and the 'anger of God' must be averted at all costs. Mothers who were definitely known to have murdered their illegitimate babies were put 'inflexibly' to death. By virtue of the Swedish Code of 1734, adultery, abortion, sodomy and infanticide remained capital crimes, along with some sixty-four other offences. Offenders were not hanged, as in France, but decapitated.

It was in 1626 that concealing the death of a bastard child became a capital offence in England. The law seems to have remained in force for at least two centuries, since a late nineteenth-century encyclopaedia records that if a 'child is found dead, and its mother has concealed her pregnancy, the legal presumption is that she has murdered it. The burden of proving that it was born dead or died from natural causes is thrown on her.'[10] Of actual infanticide, the same source remarks that this 'well-known crime' of modern times follows generally on 'illicit intercourse', and that 'motives of shame' lead the unhappy mothers to criminal abortion, concealment or infanticide, for which the charge was murder. As this succinct entry understatedly concludes, 'it was often difficult to prove a complete birth'.

Once born, the child itself was not immune to law. The concern with preserving infant life from the ravages of justice seems only to have extended to the age of 7. A child below that age was deemed incapable of crime. Between 7 and 14, the infant culprit was considered capable, on proof it knew that it was doing wrong. In 1831 a boy of 9 was hanged at Chelmsford for having set fire to a house. In 1808, Michael Hamond, aged 7, and his sister, aged 11, were hanged at Lynn for felony. A century before 'it was no uncommon thing for children under the age of ten years to be hanged, and on one occasion ten of them were strung up together, as a warning to men and a spectacle for the angels', to quote Pritchard's laconic words. Fourteen was quite fatal: in 1794, Elizabeth Marsh, who was 15, was executed in Dorchester for the murder of her grandfather. As in the case of elderly witches, the operative legal maxim seems to have been that malice is equivalent to age.

In colonial America the unhappy status of a bastard baby gave rise to contradictory laws. Bastardy was considered shameful, for both the infant and the mother. Many young couples were severely whipped on the presumptive evidence of a seven-month baby. During the seventeenth century a servant who gave birth to a bastard would be publicly whipped, then bound to her master for an additional year or two – apparently without wages. This arrangement proved so advantageous to the masters that many raped their servants, to get them pregnant. Virginia law soon had to be changed. A woman impregnated by her employer was henceforth sold to someone else. At the same time, the marriage of indentured servants was expressly forbidden, so that legal childbearing was practically denied them. As for suspicions of infanticide, the Massachusetts General Court of 1692 applied to England for approval of a law making concealment of a bastard's death a capital offence. According to the resultant statute,

> If any Woman be Delivered of any Issue of her Body, Male or Female, which if it were born Alive, should by Law be a Bastard; and that they endeavour privately . . . so to conceal the Death thereof, that it may not come to light, whether it were Born Alive or not, but be concealed: In every such case the Mother so Offending, shall suffer Death, as in case of Murder.[11]

As in the English law, the burden of proving that the baby was born dead was cast upon the mother. Even before this enactment women had been hanged for child-murder – Mary Martin, for example, executed in Boston in 1646. Left to fend for herself at the age of 22 when her father returned to England, Mary Martin had gone into service in the house of Mr Mitton. Although himself married, Mr Mitton set about seducing Mary, who subsequently left his employ, only to discover she was pregnant. She gave birth alone in the middle of the night; then, overcome with shame, killed the child. Its body was soon discovered, and Mary condemned to death. Apparently New World hangmen were no better than the Old: the execution was bungled, so that instead of dying, Mary Martin 'hung in space', and asked them boldly what they meant to do. Then, according to John Winthrop's *Journal*, someone stepped up, and turned the knot backwards, whereupon Mary soon expired.

The eighteenth century provides abundant examples of women condemned for infanticide. Alice Clifton was a 16-year-old slave who had been raped in an alley by a white man, one 'Fat' Shaffer. Her owners, John and Mary Bartholomew, testified that she had received serious injuries while pregnant; two doctors added that her baby was born dead. Nonetheless, Alice had concealed the birth, prejudicing the Philadelphia court of 1787 to condemn her to death. The sentence was later repealed, but not all women were so fortunate. In *Women Who Kill* Ann Jones lists twenty or thirty by name, hanged for child-murder between 1632 and 1787. One black woman, a former slave, said she killed her child because 'she thought it would be happier out of the world than in it, where its mother had a hard lot, and it would have the same'. As in France, the reason for this mortal penalty was largely religious. Murdering an unbaptised infant was tantamount to murdering its soul, for the unbaptised could not enter heaven. But, as Ann Jones declares, mothers guilty of infanticide had committed more than murder: they in effect mocked God. They violated laws of nature and of men and, in so doing, scorned the authority of patriarchal leaders who upheld the laws of God. Furthermore, they asserted, 'symbolically at least', that a woman 'should not be punished for her sexuality, that she is entitled to some measure of control of her own body. Such statements challenge civil and divine authority most of all. In a patriarchal society, they are revolutionary' (Jones, p. 48).

In America, as in Europe, the execution of women who were pregnant was readily postponed – assuming that the embryo met certain conditions. If the foetus was sufficiently developed to be thought alive, the mother was granted a stay. If not, she was executed. Hanged in Massachusetts in 1778 for the murder of her husband, Bathsheba Spooner had vainly 'pleaded her belly'. Some years before he fled to Nova Scotia on the eve of revolution, Bathsheba's father, a leading citizen of the state, had married her to a rich but unattractive merchant, Joshua Spooner. Tiring of her clod-like spouse, Bathsheba – who was spirited, well educated and beautiful – enlisted the services of two passing British soldiers, who eventually agreed to beat Spooner to death and push him down a well. His widow then paid them from his money box. The crime being discovered, the soldiers and Bathsheba were condemned to death, whereupon the men burst into tears and blamed the lewd woman who had led them astray. Bathsheba remained calm, but did request a stay of execution on the grounds that she was pregnant with a lawfully conceived child. A panel of two male midwives and twelve matrons was appointed to examine her, their task being to determine if the child was 'quick' – that is, developed enough for the Church to recognise it as a living being. Most curiously, the point of quickening was set at thirty to forty days for a girl foetus, and eighty to ninety for a boy. Unfortunately for Bathsheba Spooner, the panel of midwives and matrons declared that not only was the child unquick, but she was not with child at all. Bathsheba calmly requested an autopsy and went quietly to the gallows, carried on a chaise and 'bowing graciously to old acquaintances who came to see her hanged'; she was by this time so weak she had to crawl up to the scaffold. The body was cut down and examined, whereupon Bathsheba was found to be carrying a five-month male baby. This case can only compare unfavourably with the comic-opera postponements of the notorious Mme Lescombat, whose judges had at least the prudence – necessary, given the stringent laws against infanticide – to vouchsafe her a delay.

The hanging of Bathsheba Spooner so traumatised the Massachusetts conscience that more than fifty years elapsed before a jury dared convict another woman. By the time it did, the alternative possibility of prison had been introduced. As Ann Jones stresses, women were almost never executed in nineteenth-century America. She postulates that they were hanged in previous centuries because pioneer women were so scarce, and hence a valued commodity; their rarity ensured them a primitive and paradoxical equality, which meant, equality of punishment. But in the nineteenth century women became more numerous, and gentrification set in; women were taken less seriously.

No longer a responsible individual, possessed of civil rights and accountable legally and morally for her offenses and her soul, 'the female' became a nonentity, a mere appendage of the father or husband whose name she bore, a name that had to be protected at all costs. The lady had arrived.

(Jones, p. 65)

Since this primitive equality accorded American women of the seventeenth and eighteenth centuries does not wholly tally with the picture of inheritance rights painted by Carol Karlsen in her study of the witch trials, one must suppose Ann Jones refers to an equality of function, rather than of legal rights. On the other hand the nineteenth-century decline in female hanging parallels a similar diminution of female guillotining in France, where late Romantic sensibility was having an effect. In England, too, female execution declined, although it by no means ceased. Thomas Hardy, who was born in 1840, saw a woman hanged while he was still a child. Pritchard cites a contemporary record of the hanging of Elizabeth Brown, executed at Dorchester in 1856 for the murder of her husband. Arrangements for erecting gallows varied from prison to prison, and in this case the scaffold was at some considerable distance from the condemned cell:

> The prison van was in readiness at the gaol door to convey the culprit to the place of execution but she preferred walking. . . . On arriving at the place of execution she walked with firmness up the first flight of eleven steps. The pinioning being completed, the culprit, in company with the executioner (Calcraft) then proceeded up the next flight of stairs, nineteen in number, to the platform, and, still walking with a firm step, crossed the platform to the next flight, which led to the gallows.
>
> (Pritchard, p. 52)

By this time it had been realised that the sufferings of the 'culprit' were greatly reduced by a prompt snapping of the second cervical vertebra, which caused immediate and fatal injury to the medulla oblongata. From about 1760 variations in the length of the prisoner's fall were introduced, leading to the invention of the famous 'drop' – whence the great height of the gallows at the Dorchester prison.

Fictional treatments of female hanging occur in George Eliot's *Adam Bede* of 1859 and Hardy's *Tess of the d'Urbervilles* (1891). The heroine of *Adam Bede* is Dinah, a comely, grey-eyed Methodist 'preaching woman' whose virtuous and sisterly deeds include accompanying another young woman in the cart to the gibbet. Hetty Sorel, the condemned woman, is an extremely pretty and somewhat foolish country girl loved by Adam Bede. Instead of marrying him she has been seduced by Arthur Donnithorne, the local squire, who subsequently disappears to Ireland with his regiment. When she finds that she is pregnant, Hetty leaves home, runs out of money, gives birth among strangers and subsequently abandons the child, half-burying it beneath a tree. Unable to purge her memory of its cries – Eliot evidently does not wish her to seem a totally unnatural mother – she returns to the spot, only to find the baby has died. Hetty is arrested and tried for infanticide. Obstinately, she refuses even to admit that she gave birth; but in the face of overwhelming evidence is condemned to be hanged by the neck until dead.

Forsaken by all except the faithful Adam, deeply wounded but forgiving in his love, Hetty is visited in prison by Dinah. Admirable lay parson that she is, Dinah succeeds in getting her to confess and repent, staying with the despairing victim until the last possible moment. Laden with the two young women the 'fatal cart' cleaves its way through the 'waiting watching multitude . . . towards the hideous symbol of a deliberately-inflicted sudden death'. Praying steadfastly as Hetty clings to her – 'the only visible sign of love and pity' in this horrid scene – Dinah does not even know that they have reached the fatal spot when the cart stops and a loud hideous shriek, 'like a vast yell of demons' rends the air. But this is no exultant yell of cruelty; it is the crowd's excitement at the appearance of a horseman madly galloping. The man is Arthur Donnithorne, 'carrying in his hand a hard-won release from death'.[12]

Thanks to this timely intervention Hetty is resentenced to 'transportation'. Arthur is smitten in his conscience and Dinah gets to marry dark, strong, brave, honest Adam Bede. They are not married at once, for Adam does not realise he loves Dinah and has to be prompted by his mother; then Dinah worries that her deep love for Adam will distract her from God's work. But the upright Adam is unusually sensitive to what is due to women. Already, when informed of Hetty's crime, he has protested '"Is *he* to go free, while they lay all the punishment on her . . . so weak and young?"' A man such as Adam will not fail Dinah. '"But suppose,"' he says shyly to his brother, testing out the ground before proposing, '"suppose there was a man as 'ud let her do just the same and not interfere with her . . ."' – in other words, let her go on preaching. So it proves to be. Dinah marries, becomes a mother and continues in her work until female preaching is forbidden, not by Adam but by the Methodist Conference.

Seduction and a capital sentence constitute the fate of another innocent country girl, Hardy's Tess Durbeyfield. A distant, rustic cousin of the arrogant Alec d'Urberville, Tess is taken up by Alec and subjected to rape – so it seems – in a chapter celebrated for its reticence: upon this 'beautiful feminine tissue, sensitive as gossamer, and practically blank as snow as yet' there is traced 'such a coarse pattern as it was doomed to receive'. Reading Hardy when he was 13, the critic Albert Guérard was told by a Frenchwoman that he could not hope to understand this scene, and should put down the book. Having replied that American children were precocious in these matters he reread the novel ten or fifteen years later and was 'by no means so confident'; the 'seeming rape of Tess was in fact a seduction'. Considered a device to enable Hardy to elude the censors, this reticence distinguishes the description of the death that Tess eventually suffers. For, recovering from her experiences with Alec, Tess marries Angel Clare, the idealistic and freethinking son of a clergyman. Unfortunately Angel has more knowledge of ideas than of reality; discovering his wife is not a virgin he priggishly deserts her. Time passes. In remote Brazil, whither he has fled, Angel is exposed to more broad-minded influences and comes to repent of his hasty conduct, but too late. He returns to Wessex, only to find that circumstances have forced Tess back to Alec. Realising Alec has shattered her every hope of happiness, Tess kills him with a carving-knife and runs after her husband. In a chapter ironically entitled 'Fulfilment' the couple enjoy a fugitive idyll in an empty house before fleeing onto Salisbury Plain. Here Tess lies down on one of the stone slabs where Druids once gave sacrifices to the sun, and goes to sleep. She is still asleep when the posse comes for her:

> 'What is it, Angel?' she said, starting up. 'Have they come for me?'
> 'Yes, dearest,' he said, 'they have come.'
> 'It is as it should be,' she murmured ... 'This happiness could not have lasted ... I have had enough, and now I shall not live for you to despise me.'[13]

Hardy avoids direct presentation of the execution as he has avoided the seeming rape; but the scene is no less effective for this vast ellipsis. The child of nature, the good, self-sacrificing Tess is hanged in Winchester prison as Clare and Tess's younger sister Liza-Lu ascend the road that rises from the city, their heads bowed like those of Giotto's Two Apostles. At the stroke of eight they turn and fix their eyes on an ugly flat-topped octagonal tower: 'A few minutes after the hour had struck something moved slowly up the flag, and extended itself upon the breeze. It was a black flag.'

Thus Hetty, whose execution was supposed to take place in about 1800, would have died outside the prison; that later heroine Tess dies within it. It is a small point, but the distinction between these two fictional scenes parallels the changed attitude to public execution that was occurring throughout Europe. From the end of the eighteenth century through the early twentieth the penal aesthetic of France, for example, was gradually transformed as execution went from being a public spectacle to a more private matter that took place inside prison; as for the actual sentences, incarceration became a viable alternative to death. In Michel Foucault's words, 'Punishment passed from being an art of unbearable sensations to an economy of suspended rights'.[14] The focus of the punitive process was no longer the culprit's body but his soul which, it was hoped, might be reformed. A modern enough idea, one thinks, and one which liberals still occasionally voice. But it was not to reach us without violent jolts. Scarcely had it begun than this gradual transformation, already discernible in the reforms that followed Beccaria's book, would be subject to the rudest shock of all: Revolution.

4

DAME GUILLOTINE

For our fathers, Revolution is the greatest thing created by the genius of an Assembly. . . . For our mothers, Revolution is a guillotine.
(Victor Hugo, 1820)

Revolution is that which goes full circle. It is also the Utopian obsession of the modern age: the founding myth of liberty for states which have already had one, the dreamed-of instrument of change for those which have not. Revolutions of the left or right, peaceful revolutions, revolutions salved with blood: all are to some extent beholden to the experiment conducted by the French in 1789. 'The French Revolution', observes R.R. Palmer in 1947, '. . . was the great turning point of modern civilisation'.[1] Or as Simon Schama declares in his epic *Citizens* of 1989, 'At the core of revolutionary social truths was an axiom, shared by liberals, socialists and for that matter nostalgic Christian royalists alike, that the Revolution had indeed been the crucible of modernity' – the event which shaped the modern social world for good or ill.[2]

The first female figure of consequence to emerge from this 'crucible of modernity' was neither liberal nor royalist, though certainly egalitarian. This figure was not, in fact, a person at all, although soon charged with enforcing the edicts of transformation. Undeniably modern in invention it derived from both improved technology and the humane promptings of the Enlightenment. It could not have been conceived without a philosophical repudiation of the penal horrors of the old régime, and it developed directly from the debates on civil rights held by the first revolutionary legislators. This figure was the guillotine.

Among the concerns the new Constituent Assembly set about addressing on its formation in 1789 were demands for law reform. A simpler legal code was called for, providing moderate, equal penalties for all, abolishing seigneurial privilege, torture and the detested *lettres de cachet*. These demands were answered in Lafayette's *Declaration of the Rights of Man*, certain articles of which suppressed arbitrary imprisonment, arbitrary penalties and useless cruelty. First proposed by Lafayette on 11 July 1789 and accepted by the King in November, the document bore some relation to the American Bill of Rights, while the legal views informing it in turn reflected the opinions of the liberal philosophers. Not only had Beccaria's *Trattato dei Delitti e delle Pene* moved Voltaire to write a Commentary, it had greatly influenced legal thinking throughout Europe. Convinced that it was better to prevent than to punish crime, Beccaria had rejected torture and even argued against the death penalty, which in his opinion contradicted its own moral logic as to the sanctity of human life. The cogent comments of this melancholy and aristocratic man influenced the reforms of both Leopold of Tuscany and Catherine of Russia; Austria abolished capital punishment in 1787, as did the Margrave of Bade. In France Voltaire, who had not hitherto favoured abolition, suddenly embraced it. Penal reform became a fashionable topic of prestigious essays, with prizes competed for by a generation of aspiring revolutionaries, among them the future Jacobins Robespierre and Marat; other theoreticians included the future Girondins Brissot, Servan and Dufriche-Valazé.

On 14 July 1789 took place that most famous of revolutionary events, the storming of the Bastille, symbolic stronghold of privilege and repository – it was thought – of the unfortunate victims of *lettres de cachet*. That only seven such victims were freed in the storming did not dampen philanthropic fervour. A wave of humanitarian feeling swept through the Assembly, where in the general enthusiasm for rapid and egalitarian punishment a certain Dr Guillotin spoke of a decapitation machine: 'Messieurs, with my machine I can whisk off your heads in the twinkling of an eyelid. You won't feel a thing.' The text of this astounding speech, delivered in December 1789, was promptly lost; but according to newspaper reports it did conclude with words to that effect. Guillotin's remarks were met with gales of mirth. When the Assembly had recovered its sobriety it set about considering the six articles of criminal reform also mentioned in the doctor's oration. The sixth of these proved difficult: Guillotin had proposed the same penalty – decapitation – for every sort of crime. This equitable proposition seemed scandalously mild to some, and two of the six articles were promptly adjourned. The subject of legally inflicted death would not be raised again for eighteen months; meanwhile, the punishment was hanging.

On 30 May 1791 Maximilien Robespierre took the podium to suggest that the death penalty be eliminated altogether: it was, he said, unjust, and useless in deterring crime. His proposal was not adopted. Rather, a report rapidly commissioned from the deputy Le Peletier de Saint-Fargeau declared simply that 'Everyone condemned to death shall have his head cut off'. This time the Assembly voted in the measure on that very day, 3 June. Declining further responsibility in the matter, this democratic body then entrusted the task of carrying out the necessary operation to Charles-Henri Sanson, *bourreau* of Paris.

Sanson responded with a laconic memorandum in which he explained the infelicitous possibilities inherent in decapitation as effected by a sword.

DAME GUILLOTINE

The executioner must be skilful, he declared, and the victim courageous; otherwise 'dangerous scenes' might result. Was this an allusion to nobiliary *sang-froid*? Did Sanson envisage a society which, purged of aristocrats, would no longer be capable of mustering the stoic virtues necessary for public decollation? As a matter of arithmetic it evidently flashed through his mind that, if all men were beheaded equally, the number of beheadings must certainly increase. For with each execution the sword needed beating out and sharpening anew. 'If there were several condemned persons to execute at once, sufficient swords would thus be needed in readiness.' One sword per decapitee; Sanson himself had only two, provided by the pre-revolutionary Parliament at a cost of 600 livres each. And then, even when everything went well, decapitation was so extremely bloody that in any multiple proceeding those waiting to be served would either collapse in feebleness, or else put up a fight. It was indispensable, he concluded, to find some means of immobilising the condemned, in order to carry out 'with certainty' the Assembly's humane wishes.

Having thus consulted an expert in the field the Assembly found itself obliged to reconsider Guillotin's hilarious machine and asked Dr Antoine Louis, secretary of the Academy of Surgeons, to design it. Dr Louis produced a memoir of his own, agreeing with Sanson's conclusions and mentioning among other things the greater virtuosity of German executioners, who were able to practise on women, the latter being always executed that way, no matter what their rank. He also pointed out the inconveniences of a vertically operating knife, recommending instead an oblique action which would operate by invariable, mechanical means: such a machine would be easy to design and build. Reassured, the Assembly instructed the Minister of Public Contributions to have the necessary item made and uniformly used throughout the Republic. The resulting apparatus immobilised the victim on a horizontal plank, and dropped a weighted, diagonally slanted knife upon his neck, the knife being set in descent by means of a latch. All theoretical obstructions thus overcome, the only problem was to build the machine, to which end Louis summoned Guidon, the usual carpenter of scaffolds. Guidon submitted an estimate of 5,660 livres. Appalled, the Ministry of Public Contributions turned to a Swiss harpsichord maker named Tobias Schmidt, who tendered the more modest bid of 960 livres. This was accepted with enthusiasm. Schmidt went ahead, even managing to obtain a monopoly of manufacture for all eighty-three departments. The guillotine was tested on living sheep and human corpses at the Hospital of Bicêtre in April 1792, with perfect success, and used for the first time in live execution on 25 April 1792.

The mature decapitation machine therefore resulted from the union of enlightened democratic reason, contemporary technology and medical science, combining to produce an instrument that was both fair and, as far as anyone could tell, completely painless. This accorded perfectly with the contemporary spirit of criminal reform. Had not Marat written against 'cruel torture' even in the gravest cases? Liberticide, parricide, fratricide, murder of a friend or benefactor? The machine has even elicited twentieth-century reactions. Michel Foucault has discerned therein a 'zero degree of torture';[3] Roland Barthes compares it to a camera, repeating 'mechanically that which can never again be repeated existentially'.[4] The nineteenth-century Goncourt brothers stressed geometric aspects: the twin perpendiculars, the perfect triangle, falling through a circle upon a further sphere (the head), itself retained by a horizontal secant. In a more socially conscious vein Victor Hugo perceived it as the law in concrete form. 'The guillotine', one reads in *Les Misérables*, 'is not neutral, and does not allow one to remain neutral. Whoever catches sight of it shivers with the most mysterious of shivers. Every social issue sets a question mark around its blade.' As for the professional entrusted with its use, a grimly prescient Sanson is reported to have said, at the Bicêtre tests, 'A fine invention – as long as it is not abused'.

Less – almost nothing at all, indeed – is made of the fact that this scientifically impressive instrument, invented by male doctors, commissioned by male legislators, built by male carpenters and operated by male executioners – 'this guillotine adopted at the dawning of an era of liberty' and which 'still has the privilege of symbolising the Terror', as Hector Fleischmann wrote in 1912 – this mortal, smoothly functioning machine was rapidly endowed with all the sexual attributes of woman. Not that academics have not studied female revolutionary symbology. Lynn Hunt, for example, brilliantly emphasises the part played in revolutionary iconography by female figures: Liberty and Minerva, who appear on seals and coins; Marianne, who came to be synonymous with the Republic; and the actual live actresses who took part in the 'Festival of Reason'. These allegorical female forms contributed significantly to what Professor Hunt terms 'the imagery of radicalism'. Yet this type of study seldom if ever mentions the guillotine, whose function as guarantor of law was soon to be so eminently practical, and whose femininity was designated in articles, songs, epithets and images almost as soon as the machine was conceived.

Even before the instrument was built, a royalist newspaper had sardonically proposed the 'sweetly flowing name of Guillotine', adding that a Member of the Académie Française had already composed a song for the occasion. Baptised after its inventor much as carriages called 'Turgotines' were named after Turgot, the instrument of death seemingly owed its gender to the innocence of grammar, *machine* being feminine in French. But matters did not stop with a name. Aided no doubt by features of design, such as the victim lying on his stomach with his head in the *lunette*, popular humour did not hesitate to compare loss of the capital member with that of another part. The guillotine inherited from the gallows the nickname of 'La Veuve', the Widow. Chastising this vulgarity, *Le Moniteur* of 18 December 1790 lamented a certain linguistic indecency instilled in its subjects by the old régime, and which the revolutionary French people would do well to be rid of: 'From Charlemagne's sword, nicknamed "The Jolly Girl", to the alias of "The Widow", our nation shows an infirmity of wit whose seat is in the soul. The language of a people must not express anything unworthy of its character.' This high-minded article had no effect at all, although it must be admitted that not all the epithets attached to the guillotine were feminine: there was also 'sneezing in the sack', 'the national razor', and 'looking through the skylight'. But a significant proportion of the jokes and songs celebrated the guillotine as a most gruesome *femme fatale*.

The machine once built and functioning, patriotic wit proved fertile as a hydra's head. Parody became the order of the day, with frivolous obscenity soon grafted onto well-known songs. A historian of the Pont Neuf, where songsters were wont to sing and sell their wares, records a gruesome lubricity echoing across the bridge: 'Every singer then had licence to be simultaneously sinister and obscene.'[5] In the words of a typical *gaudriole*,

> Love fathers our desire
> But Hymen, our pleasure:
>   A godly patriot.
> Love is often fickle
> While Hymen charms and tickles:
>   A real *Sans-culotte*.

Another song entitled 'Landerinette' (one more of the instrument's female names) establishes a crude equivalence between the nude embrace of the knife and that of the desired maiden:

> Her nude breast thrills
> Her kiss kills
> The red blood spills
> And we watch as we die.
> A charming embrace . . .

In keeping with the anti-clerical sentiments of the day the union takes place 'without holy oil', and it is implied that the bride is not a virgin. In fairness to the French, it must be remembered that the guillotine's Scottish ancestress had been dubbed the 'Maiden', while the 'Iron Maiden' and the 'Scavenger's Daughter' were medieval English instruments of torture. Nor was this type of humour confined to the revolutionary period; a drawing of 1887, banned as obscene, retrospectively depicted the guillotine of 1793 as a nude, leering woman, brazenly displaying her charms before the horizontal *bascule* to which victims were attached.

Parallels have also been drawn between the function of the guillotine and motherhood. Daniel Arasse records a traumatic event that may have precipitated Guillotin's own birth: his pregnant mother was apparently out walking when she heard the shrieks of someone being broken on the wheel, which horror induced labour. If Madame Guillotin had the *bourreau* for a midwife, the Republic was delivered by 'Guillotin's daughter', the brand-new Guillotine, who guaranteed its new decrees. As Daniel Arasse sees it, the symbolism of an obscene, political birth was reinforced by the ritual showing of the severed heads, brandished like immense and bloodied new-born babes amid enthusiastic cries of 'Vive la République!'

The guillotine's attributes were not merely sexual and republican: they could be aristocratic and ecclesiastical too. 'She' was also known as 'Dame Guillotine', 'Most High and Mighty Lady Guillotine', and even 'Saint Guillotine', to whom ironic litanies were sung. A specialised press sprang up, commemorating the exploits of the national machine. Citizen Tisset published a parodical court circular, an 'Account rendered to the *sans-culottes* of the French Republic by the most powerful and expeditious Dame Guillotine, Lady of the Carrousel, of Revolution Square, of Place de Grève' – the sites where the instrument was used. Tisset's frontispiece depicted the headless bodies of aristocrats, bishops and generals, all piled up beside a basket of their heads; next to his drawing, Tisset had inscribed:

> These finely diced monsters, through power divine,
> Herald the labours of Dame Guillotine.

The revolutionary committee of Angers referred to the 'sacram sanctam Guillotinam', while the expressions 'to celebrate red mass' and 'sacrificing at the altar of the guillotine' were frequently employed, both in Paris and the south of France. Sometimes the imprecations followed the more orthodox lines of Catholic prayer, such as the 'Ora pro nobis':

> Saint Guillotine, protector of patriots, pray for us!
> Saint Guillotine, scourge of the aristocrats, protect us!
> Amiable machine, have pity on us!
> Admirable machine, have pity on us!
> Saint Guillotine, protect us from tyrants![6]

National anthems, too, were subject to parody. A version of the *Marseillaise* is said to have begun

> O celestial guilloti-i-ne
> You who shorten
> Kings and Queens . . .

While an unrepentant English wit greeted the first royal execution with an alternative version of *God Save the King*. Not even the domestic arts were immune to revolutionary humour: many private homes owned miniature guillotines, used to decapitate chickens before cooking.

The tenor of such pleasantries might lead one to suppose that only men were sacrificed upon the altar of the new, castrating saint; but this was not the case at all, though men were certainly more numerous. Again, it is sometimes thought, even by those who witnessed the daily cortège of tumbrels and decapitees, that victims of the Terror were necessarily clergymen or aristocrats, noblewomen or nuns. But of the 18,613 persons reportedly executed in France at the behest of revolutionary tribunals, 2,567, or just over one-seventh, were women. Of these, 1,447 – more than half – were wives of working men or artisans. According to statistics printed with the memoirs of the Sanson family, there were 2,918 legal beheadings in Paris between 14 July 1789 and 21 October 1796, including 370 decapitations of women. One would naturally expect the more glamorous executions to take place in Paris, and certainly the city rose to the occasion in that respect; yet the actual breakdown is entirely democratic. Of the grand total of 2,918 decapitees, 381 were 'nobles of both sexes', 325 were ecclesiastics, and some 900 were servants, shopkeepers and artisans. There were also sixteen artists, twenty-five 'men and women of letters', 390 military men, and 479 representatives of the liberal professions. The remaining four hundred or so were members of the National Assembly, Convention and Commune, and magistrates from former parliaments. It would therefore seem that members of the government in its various revolutionary phases were executed in about equal numbers with aristocrats. As for the 370 women guillotined in the capital, they included aristocrats and nuns but also working women: milliners, prostitutes, servant girls and bakers' wives.

The best-known – who do not quite fit into any of these categories – were probably, in order of decapitation, Charlotte Corday (17 July 1793); Marie Antoinette (16 October 1793); Olympe de Gouges (3 November 1793); Mme Roland (8 November 1793); Mme du Barry (7 December 1793) and Lucile Desmoulins (13 April 1794); there were also fifteen Carmelite nuns (resuscitated by Bernanos and Poulenc in *Dialogues des Carmélites*), widows, wives, daughters, several actresses and a cartload of peasant women brought in from Poitou. With one signal exception they were brave, proudly aware of the image they would leave to posterity in dying: one is not likely to forget Carlyle's description of Manon Roland at the scaffold. Many uttered final words that have passed into legend, small fictions of history documented only by the *bourreau*, but which often fit the personalities in question better than officially recorded quotes. As important as the images these women bequeathed to posterity, however, are the images the authorities sought to bequeath of them. Almost in every case the better-known women were subject to some form of character assassination, usually centring on their sexual activities; it mattered little whether the maligned victim was an aristocrat or a daughter of the people. The result must count among the great paradoxes of female execution: in the twilight of the Enlightenment, with atheism in vogue, the defaming of famous women at their trials bore a curious resemblance to criticisms made of heretics, or even Renaissance Queens.

DEATH COMES TO THE MAIDEN

'TIS CRIME AND NOT THE SCAFFOLD: CHARLOTTE CORDAY, MARIE ANTOINETTE

When Charlotte Corday was condemned to death for assassinating Jean-Paul Marat in July 1793 she was taken in a tumbril to the Place de la Révolution, now Place de la Concorde. Moved by her courage and her youth Charles-Henri Sanson stood before her, trying to block the guillotine from view; but Charlotte Corday peered right past. 'I have the right to be curious', she said, 'I've never seen one before!'

With this singular utterance did she conclude her singular life. Born on 27 July 1768 to parents of impeccable pedigree and hopelessly diminished revenues, Marie-Charlotte de Corday d'Armont could trace her Norman ancestry to 1077. It was of the nobility of sword, which meant the Cordays were entitled to such doubtful privileges as having the peasants beat the surrounding fields to silence frogs while Mme de Corday was giving birth. Charlotte's father, a third son, was a former army officer turned farmer who had married the equally well-bred and impecunious Mlle Gauthier des Anthieux. This love-match produced several children and eventually killed Charlotte's mother, who died after childbirth in April 1782. Henceforth Charlotte's childhood was stoical and solitary. Indigent, proud and grief-stricken, Jacques de Corday scraped together enough cash to send his elder son to military academy, dispatching the younger to live with grandparents. He then retired into his study with his books: Greek and Roman authors, and Montesquieu and Rousseau. While her liberal father sank into a contemplation of the ideal state, Charlotte was left very much alone.

Before long M. de Corday was too poor even to support his two daughters, and sent them to the Convent of the Trinity at Caen. They were accepted as 'royal pensioners', or scholarship students of impoverished nobility. The education they received was both liberal and careful: like her father, Charlotte read Plutarch's *Lives*, and, more surprisingly, Rousseau. She must certainly have read the works of her ancestor Pierre Corneille, the one bourgeois blot on the family's otherwise pure escutcheon. Corneille extolled the virtues of an active will through a succession of vigorous heroes, often drawn from Roman history: obsessed with his good name and duty to the state, his Horace subdues family feelings and kills not only his brothers-in-law but his sister, who has insulted Rome. As Michelet remarks,

> Miss Corday came of great nobility: she was a close relative of the heroines of Corneille, of Chimène, Pauline and the sister of Horace. She was the great-grand-niece of the author of *Cinna*. The sublime in her was nature.[7]

Addicted to arguments about theology Charlotte had the makings of a minor saint, giving away all her clothes except her convent uniform, spending long, trance-like sessions lost in prayer, assiduously visiting the sick and poor of

Caen. She began to think of taking the veil, and henceforth would never quite resist the appeal of the transcendental, which simply became redirected after an encounter with Rousseau's *Social Contract*.

Revolution came, rendering Charlotte's putative vocation definitively out of the question. In October 1789 monastic vows were suspended and ecclesiastical wealth was put at the service of the bankrupt nation in accordance with the utilitarian ideas of Talleyrand, a bishop-cum-deputy. In February 1791 the Assembly voted to suppress religious orders and congregations altogether. Seals were placed on the charter of the Convent of the Trinity and Charlotte returned home, where she found her father engrossed in his own, unremarkable, political meditations. Bored, Charlotte went to live as a modestly paid companion to her aunt, Mme de Bretteville, who lived in a dark, ill-proportioned house in the most aristocratic street in Caen. Charlotte painted, did needlework, read aloud to her aunt and absorbed more philosophy: Rousseau again, the Abbé Raynal, the philosophers of the *Encyclopaedia*. Anecdotes from this period attest to a republican turn of mind: during a family gathering held at her royalist aunt's house, a toast was proposed to the King, which Charlotte refused to drink. 'How can you refuse to drink to a king who is so virtuous?' a friend whispered to her. 'I believe he is a good king', replied Charlotte, blushing, 'but how can a weak king be virtuous? A weak king can only bring misfortune to his people.'[8] A few months later another friend chided her for living so much in the past, lost in Plutarch and Corneille: 'Perhaps', she answered. 'But I wish I had lived then. In Sparta and Athens were many courageous women.'

Bold, if wistful, words; and yet the Charlotte remembered by her friends in Caen impressed them with her gentleness. She is described by a girl of the same age as 'tall and very beautiful. . . . Her figure was robust but it was noble, her complexion of a dazzling whiteness and of the most wonderful freshness.' Her skin, the friend went on, was very fine:

> She blushed easily, and then she became truly ravishing. Her eyes were deep-set and lovely, but their expression was veiled. Her chin was too long and there was something obstinate about it, but her appearance was full of charm and distinction and had an expression of surpassing purity and frankness. The sound of her voice was indescribably low and sweet. Her hair was light chestnut . . .
>
> (Loomis, *Paris* p. 39).

Hardly, one might think, a candidate for proto-terrorism. Was this the woman who, armed with pure intentions and a knife, was soon to murder Marat?

The motive for Charlotte's deed quite possibly derives from this same 'surpassing purity and frankness'. Four years after the advent of the new society, she was growing disillusioned. Sporadic acts of violence had been occurring in the provinces. Her own father had been chased and almost beaten by a former poacher, now an official of the Republic. A young army officer, the nephew of her Mother Superior, had been stabbed and torn to pieces in the streets of Caen; true, he was arrogant and foolish, and brandished pistols at a hungry mob, but to rip forth his heart and eat it, warm and bloody – as a woman had – did not fit Charlotte's ideal of seemly republican behaviour. Worse still were the events in Paris. In September 1792 there took place the notorious 'September massacres' – a 'purge' of some 1,400 or 1,500 alleged conspirators, summarily tried and butchered in the Paris prisons at the probable instigation of the Paris Commune. To justify the slaughter it was claimed that the Republic, now at war with most of Europe, stood threatened with invasion from without and aristocratic subversion from within: the Fatherland was in danger, the prisons full of plotters. Like many other initially ardent republicans Charlotte was revolted, and did not hesitate to place the blame for this catastrophe in human rights on Marat, the most influential member of the newly formed committee to oversee the Commune. A further shock occurred in January 1793 with the trial and execution of the King. Charlotte may have thought Louis XVI weak, but she did not wish him headless; matters had begun to go too far.

To complete her disenchantment, in June 1793 the leaders of the moderate Girondin party were ousted from the National Convention and declared outlaws. For some months these liberal deputies from around Bordeaux, Marseille and Caen – men such as Vergniaud, Brissot and Buzot – had been involved in a power struggle with Robespierre, Marat, Danton and other members of the more radical party known as the Mountain. Forced at gunpoint from the Convention, some of the proscribed deputies were placed under house arrest in Paris. While many fled to Bordeaux the largest, most important group escaped to Caen, where they set about organising federalist troops to rise against the Jacobins. Charlotte viewed their plans with sympathy but had by this time resolved upon yet more drastic measures of her own. Once again she held Marat responsible for this latest affront to democratic process. 'Sublime and logical', wrote Michelet, '. . . she reasoned thus: the Law is Peace itself. Who killed the Law on June 2? Marat did. Once the murderer of Law is killed, Peace will bloom again. The death of one brings life to all' (Michelet, p. 495). Reasoning thus, the blushing near-nun from Calvados would kill the murderer of law.

With her Norman sense of the practical Charlotte set about her plan. First she made the acquaintance of Barbaroux, the debarred deputy from Marseille, and asked him for an introduction to anyone in Paris who might help her settle the financial affairs of a former friend from the convent, now poor and in Italy. On 8 July she packed a few clothes: two shirts with her initials, two petticoats (one of pink silk, the other of white cotton), two pairs of cotton stockings, four white handkerchiefs, a dressing-gown, two lawn bonnets, four neckerchiefs, some ribbons and a housecoat of striped dimity. Next she reserved a seat in the coach to Paris, telling her aunt she would be going away for a few days. On 9 July she wrote a letter to her father, announcing an intent to emigrate. Clad in a brown dress with a black felt hat, Charlotte then said goodbye to a few friends, gave away her paintbox, put 50 livres in her purse – half her total wealth – and left a Bible on her table, underlined at the passage about Judith and Holofernes. The coach left at two that afternoon; the journey took two days. 'The drowsy diligence lumbers along; amid drowsy talk of Politics, and praise of the Mountain; in which she mingles not', narrates Thomas Carlyle. On the second night while mingling not in Politics Charlotte was approached by an amorous young man, whom she rebuffed in no uncertain terms. 'On Thursday, not long before noon, we are at the bridge of Neuilly; here is Paris with her thousand black domes, the goal and purpose of thy journey!'[9]

In black-domed Paris Charlotte rapidly became aware that her efforts on behalf of the emigrated friend, Mlle de Forbin, were not only useless but would actually compromise the deputies whose help she sought. It was time to go about her business. From her room at the Providence Inn she wrote a 'Letter to the French', a rhetorical piece indicting Marat, whom she apparently considered beyond law:

> Factionism is exploding on all sides, the Mountain is triumphing through crime and oppression. . . . Already the vilest of scoundrels, Marat, whose very name presents an image of his many crimes, in falling to the vengeful steel makes the Mountain totter and causes Danton and Robespierre, the other brigands seated on his bloody throne, to turn pale.[10]

On the morning of Saturday, 13 July, after a hot and probably sleepless night, she went down to the galleries of the Palais-Royal and, practical as ever, bought a knife, with a little leather sheath. This she hid in her bosom, next to the 'Letter to the French'. Then she hailed a cab and drove to Marat's house.

While Charlotte was writing, planning, driving about Paris, Marat sat rotting in his copper bath. He was already dying; Charlotte could not know this. She had, however, found out he was ill and at home, and that she could not therefore murder him in full view of the Convention, as she had warmly hoped. The first attempt to gain admittance failed: Simone Evrard, Marat's common-law wife, and her sister were both suspicious of this well if simply dressed intruder. Undeterred, Charlotte returned to the hotel and wrote Marat a short note: 'I come from Caen. The love you bear the fatherland must make you wish to know the conspiracies projected there. I await your reply.' While waiting she put on a clean dress, had her hair curled and powdered – probably more from a desire to impress posterity, than Marat – and wrote the object of her quest a second note, which he never got: 'It is enough that I am wretched to have a right to your protection.' Once again she set off. This time she managed to advance as far as a small vestibule before again encountering Simone Evrard. 'Hark, a rap again! A musical woman's voice, refusing to be rejected: it is the Citoyenne who would do France a service. Marat, recognising from within, cries, Admit her. Charlotte Corday is admitted' (Carlyle, p. 257).

He suffered from migraines and a painful skin disease, one of whose purulent eruptions stretched along the perineum; the combination of these ills drove him distracted. The malady, as he admitted, was largely caused by nerves: 'An inflammatory illness, a result of the torments I have incessantly given myself in the cause of liberty.' He had been a doctor in the service of the King's younger brother; but his manner had displeased his aristocratic clients. A writer, he had been reduced to fury when Diderot and Voltaire did not appear to recognise his talents. Marat had no money; he gave it to the poor. Fed, medicated and cared for by his devoted Simone, whom he had married in Rousseauesque fashion in 1791 – 'before the sun, before nature' – he slept two hours per night, and gave the rest of his strength to his inflammatory prose. When a deputation of Jacobins, two days before, had told him to take care of his health, he replied – as Charlotte might have done – that he did not care how long he lived if, dying, he could say 'The fatherland is saved'. He was, in his way, her complement.

According to Simone Evrard, Charlotte wept a little when admitted, perhaps out of nerves. Recovering herself, she spoke of Caen.

> Citizen Marat, I am from Caen the seat of rebellion, and wished to speak with you. – Be seated, *mon enfant*. Now what are the Traitors doing at Caen? What Deputies are at Caen? – Charlotte names some Deputies. 'Their heads shall fall within a fortnight', croaks the eager People's-friend, clutching his tablets to write: *Barbaroux*, *Pétion*, writes he with bare shrunk arm, turning aside in the bath: *Pétion*, and *Louvet*, and – Charlotte has drawn her knife from the sheath; plunges it with one sure stroke, into the writer's heart.
>
> (Carlyle, p. 257)

Then she withdrew the knife. Marat, who had often spoken of the need to found a state on blood, was now choking on his own. He called for help to Simone; she appeared, and tried to stem the bleeding. Charlotte made discreetly for the door but Laurent Bas, who had been working in another room with a typographer, picked up a chair and hit her on the head. The black felt hat absorbed much of the blow; stunned, Charlotte rose, without a word. Then Bas grabbed her 'by the breasts' and managed to hold her down. A surgeon came, attracted by the household cries; Marat, he said, was dead.

The authorities arrived. Guellard, a police commissioner, began the preliminary interrogation in the sitting room. Charlotte identified herself and gave her motive: she saw civil war brewing in France, and held Marat responsible. 'I preferred to sacrifice my life to save my country.' Noticing that one of the deputies present, an ex-Capucine named Chabot, had stolen her watch, she asked drily 'Have you forgotten the Capucines' vow of poverty?'

Camille Desmoulins, who had come in with Hébert, later said she made her judges look ridiculous. Her self-possession, astonishing to everybody there, wavered only when they took her to the body; shaken by Simone Evrard's animal despair – it had never occurred to her that Marat could be loved – Charlotte turned very pale, and said only that she killed him. They put her in a coach. The crowd wanted to rip her to pieces on the spot, but Guellard ordered them back and sat down next to her; amazed at still being alive she was afterwards to praise the courage of the officers. Taken to the prison of the Abbaye, Charlotte was extremely polite to her gaolers, expressing regret for walking on the tail of the prison cat – more regret than she would ever show for killing Marat. Wishing to be correctly dressed for the trial she asked Mme Delavacquerie for some lawn to make a bonnet – the black hat had been trampled on – and mended her torn dress and fichu. She also wrote to the Committee of Public Safety to protest against the nocturnal presence of a soldier in her cell, contrary to decency; this she blamed on Chabot, for 'only Capucines can have ideas like that'.

On 14 July the Convention met in extraordinary session to deliver appropriate panegyrics of the slain 'Friend of the People'. In clear contravention of the *Declaration of the Rights of Man* it was recommended that Charlotte be tortured before beheading, but the suggestion went unheeded. The trial was postponed for forty-eight hours on account of Marat's solemn and impending funeral. Charlotte took advantage of the delay to write to Barbaroux. Her letter admitted to having used a rotten trick to gain admittance, but 'Any means is good in such a circumstance'. No-one must weep for her, she said, implicitly comparing herself to the stoic Roman Brutus.

Next day Charlotte was moved to the Conciergerie, a prison that came to be known as 'Death's ante-room' during the Terror, since prisoners were always kept there before trial. Then came the preliminary interrogation, conducted by Fouquier-Tinville and Montané – public prosecutor and president of the Tribunal. She answered their questions with an unnerving frankness that has since been compared to the simplicity of Jeanne d'Arc. Why did she come to Paris? 'To kill Marat.' The idea came to her on 31 May, after the arrest of the Girondin deputies; Marat had attacked the sovereignty of the people and aimed at dictatorship. When her judges tried to prove she could not possibly have acted alone, and must have been directed in this fiendish act, she riposted that they did not know the human heart: 'It is far easier to carry out a project such as this when one obeys one's own hatred, and not the hatred of others.' Back in her cell she wrote to her father: 'Forgive me, my dear Papa, for disposing of my life without your permission. I have avenged many innocent victims and prevented many future disasters.... Do not forget this line from Corneille: *It is crime, not the scaffold, that brings shame.*'[11]

Marat's funeral was held on 16 July, staged by the painter David. At the public viewing Marat was seen with naked torso, writing, propped up on a Roman bed; but the hot July weather had allegedly so decomposed the hero's remains that the arm holding the iron pen had had to be borrowed from another corpse. The mouth would not shut, nor would the eyes; the tongue protruded obstinately and a part had to be cut off. Although regarded as successful, the exhibition was soon outclassed by *Marat Assassinated*, the tragic masterwork commissioned from David by the Convention. Described by Simon Schama as both a 'startlingly realistic account of the murder and a revolutionary *pietà*', the painting is a triumph of inaccuracy. Once again Marat's torso – which in reality was covered by a greasy dressing-gown – is shown naked, implicitly more vulnerable to Charlotte's knife. His features, disagreeable in life, are almost idealised; the skin disease is nowhere to be seen. The plain wood handle of the kitchen knife is now ivory, providing a better contrast with the blood of Marat's wound, but also implying a more aristocratic weapon. To emphasise Charlotte's perfidy Marat is holding in his hand her second note, the one he never actually received: 'It is enough that I am wretched to have the right to your protection.' That the killer is not present at the scene renders this undisputed masterpiece all the more provocative, since every detail quotes her deed; Charlotte's absence permeates the painting's space.

The actual trial took place on 17 July. Charlotte evinced the same simplicity of demeanour and response as in the preceding interrogations, astounding many of those thronging the Salle Saint Louis by her calm resolve. Simone Evrard was called as a witness and once again the only thing that seemed to disturb Charlotte was the sight of this woman's grief. As in the interrogations, she insisted she had acted alone: 'I knew he was perverting France. I killed one man in order to save a hundred thousand.... I was a Republican long before the Revolution, and I have never lacked energy.' Asked what she meant by 'energy', she responded with words that drew a murmur of respect: 'That resolution which is given to people who put their private interests aside and who know how to sacrifice themselves bravely for their country.' When Fouquier-Tinville observed that she had evidently practised the blow – so astonishingly fatal for a single stroke – Charlotte exclaimed in horror 'Oh! The monster! He takes me for an assassin!'

At the last moment her defence had been given to Chauveau-Lagarde, since Charlotte's first choice (a relative of the Mother Superior at Caen) was himself involved in fleeing for his life. Chauveau-Lagarde was in a delicate position, not having even seen the dossier; Montané had given him to understand he should enter a plea of insanity, but Chauveau sensed that such a defence would both humiliate Charlotte and destroy the meaning of her act. Accordingly he delivered a few terse and dignified words which managed to satisfy everyone:

> The defendant calmly admits the horrible murder she has committed. She calmly admits the long premeditation.... Therein, citizen jurors,

is her whole defence. This imperturbable calm, this total dedication of the self which shows no remorse even, one might say, in the presence of death itself, this calm and dedication, *sublime in their way*, are not natural. They can only be explained by that exaltation born of political fanaticism which put the dagger in her hand. It is up to you, citizen jurors, to decide how this moral consideration must weigh in the scales of justice.

The thirty-six citizen-jurors swiftly returned a unanimous verdict, and Charlotte was condemned to be executed later that day. Leaving the courtroom she turned to Chauveau-Lagarde: 'Thank you, Monsieur, for defending me with courage, in a manner worthy of both of us. These gentlemen have confiscated my property. As proof of my gratitude and confidence I ask you to settle my few debts at the prison.'

In the course of the trial Charlotte had noticed a young man sketching her. She asked if he could finish the portrait in her cell, and, since he was a member of the National Guard, he was allowed to do so. Charlotte gave as her reason the habitual public hankering to know the features of great criminals; but she was evidently thinking of the patriotic image she would leave to posterity. She took an active interest in Hauer's drawing and made several suggestions, talking all the while of the days of peace she was bequeathing to the nation.

The execution had been set for five o'clock. Sanson arrived too soon and found Fouquier-Tinville arguing heatedly with Montané, who had managed to omit the crucial words 'with criminal and counter-revolutionary intent' from his summing-up. Worse, he had not hinted at a Royalist–Girondin conspiracy. Sanson also met Mme Richard, the concierge's wife, standing pale and trembling; asked if she was ill, she replied that he too would tremble when he saw the girl he had to kill. Charlotte started a little as he entered the cell – 'What! Already!' she exclaimed – but immediately recovered. When Sanson moved to cut her hair Charlotte herself took the scissors and snipped off two locks, handing them to the painter Hauer and asking him to make a copy of the portrait for her family. She was then dressed in the red shirt reserved for parricides; finally, her hands were tied. 'My final *toilette* was performed rather roughly, but it does lead to immortality.' Sanson would later say she was the bravest he had seen since the Chevalier de la Barre.[12]

There remained the journey in the tumbrel. Charlotte refused the services of the Abbé Lothringer, a priest who had taken the new constitutional oath; then she refused to sit down in the cart. Sanson placed a chair for her to lean on. As this was the most sensational guillotining since the death of Louis XVI a vast, intensely curious, antagonistic crowd had gathered, emitting furious cries; but slowly they were moved to respect as Charlotte passed. Some were even seen to applaud. Students in the *atelier* of the painter Regnault threw down rose petals.... Suddenly a summer storm broke, drenching Charlotte as she stood; the parricidal shirt clung to her breasts, much to the crowd's delight. Adam Lux saw her, and conceived an amorous veneration which caused him to write a poem equating her with Brutus; for this, he too was guillotined, the following November. André Chénier declaimed,

> Belle, jeune, brillante, aux bourreaux amenée
> Tu semblais t'avancer sur un char d'hyménée . . .
> *(La Jeune Captive)*[13]

In the rue Saint Honoré, three other men were watching from a window in Robespierre's house. Robespierre talked animatedly, but Danton and Desmoulins stood silent and distressed.

Analyst of the guillotine Daniel Arasse maintains there is no such thing as an impartial account of a revolutionary execution. Royalist accounts dwell on the final moments of the victim, on his or her last words, as if wishing to perpetuate those hallowed instants when the person was alive. Revolutionary accounts emphasise the happy moment when Sanson or his aides would raise the severed head and show it to the people, brandishing their dripping trophy like Perseus with Gorgon's head. The head of Charlotte Corday was to provide ample matter for Jacobin post-operative comment. Arriving at the guillotine Charlotte had jumped from the tumbrel and run quickly up the steps. She blushed when aides removed her fichu, revealing upper chest and neck, but offered no resistance when strapped to the *bascule*. But this would not be Charlotte's final blush. Held up to the people the head received a vicious smack from one of Sanson's aides: the cheek was seen by many to turn pink, as if smarting from insufferable affront. This incident triggered an alarming thought: Did death absolutely coincide with decollation? Could the head, once severed, *think*? As one surgeon put it, 'What more horrible situation could there be than to perceive one's own execution, followed by the after-thought of one's own death?' Mention was made of Mary Stuart, whose lips had continued to move long after decollation. Of no small interest to an age that had chosen beheading as its *peine capitale*, the debate continued through the Terror. Finally, in November 1795 a German anatomist concluded that '*Feeling*, the *personality*, the *ego* remain alive for some time . . . and there remains a post-operative pain – from which the neck suffers.'[14] The nineteenth century found the problem equally absorbing, and a series of gruesome experiments ensued; as late as 1905 a Dr Beaurieux surmised that the senses of sight and hearing survived about twenty-five to thirty seconds.

Of more immediate interest to the Revolutionary Tribunal was the question of what had been in Charlotte's head while it was still alive. Unable to believe a woman could have conceived of this atrocity alone, the patriotic papers put out she was four months pregnant at her death. It was an odd thing to report because, if known and true, pregnancy would automatically have entailed a stay of execution. To determine whether she was *virgina intacta* the Revolutionary Tribunal had the body conveyed to a nearby hospital to be examined. J.-L. David and several of his students asked to be present at this interesting event, and one of them even made a sketch. The drawing was later lost, but a contemporary description of it states that the head had been put back in its 'normal' position. As a result of the examination the fact of Charlotte's physical integrity was grudgingly, officially made known. The finding was significant, because attempts had been made to link her romantically with Barbaroux or even Henri de Belzunce, the nephew of Charlotte's Mother Superior, butchered at Caen. That a woman could act from conviction alone was evidently as inconceivable as it was politically inconvenient to the Jacobins.

But the adventures of the corpse were not yet over. It seems that the skull was never buried with the rest of Charlotte's body. First of all a former secretary of Danton conserved it in a cupboard. When he died, his widow gave it to a relative who gave it to Prince Roland Bonaparte, who presented it to the Exhibition of 1889. Apparently Prince Roland subsequently retrieved the item, since it remained in the family of the psychiatrist Marie Bonaparte until 1975; at large in the antique market, it then found itself competing with several other purported Corday skulls. Specialists in anatomy have recognised the Bonaparte exhibit as the skull of a woman of 25, preserved in alcohol and never buried. Cesare Lombroso considered its dimensional peculiarities to be typical of male criminals:

> The cranium is platycephalic, a peculiarity which is rarer in the woman than in the man. To be noted also is a most remarkable jugular apophysis with strongly arched brows concave below. ... All the sutures are open, as in a young man aged from 23 to 25. ... The cranial capacity is 1,360 cc while the average among French women is 1,337.

In addition Charlotte's skull – the authenticity and sex of which Lombroso never seems to doubt, although he does admit to inspecting it 'rapidly' – is asymmetrical, has pteroid wormian bones, and an orbital area of 133 mm against an 'average among Parisian women' of 126 mm (Charlotte was not a Parisian woman). All of this fuels Lombroso's contentions that 'female criminals approximate more to males, both criminal and normal, than to normal women' and that 'Not even the purest political crime, that which springs from passion, is exempt from the law we have laid down'.[15]

The Revolutionary Tribunal, which described Charlotte as 'a termagant, fleshy rather than fresh, slovenly like almost all the female philosophers and bluestockings ... above all, hoydenish, with mannish bearing', would doubtless have agreed. Another approach emphasised her delicately feminine aspects. Describing her 'serious beauty, virile in its expression', Michelet praises her 'moral virginity', apparent in the 'intonation of her almost childlike voice', the expression of a being in whom 'nothing had given way'. 'This extended childhood', Michelet continues, 'was a singular characteristic of Joan of Arc, who remained a little girl and never became a woman.' Both points of view would seem to defuse Charlotte's act: no normal woman could have done such a thing, therefore she must have been either masculine or an untouched little girl. Those of Charlotte's contemporaries who first admired her extraordinary courage – Barbaroux, Louvet, Pétion – needed no such distortions of her deed. Quite soon, they simply realised its inappropriate stupidity: the blow would have better been directed against Robespierre. This was also Mme Roland's opinion. 'An astonishing woman, heeding only her courage, came to kill the apostle of murder and piracy: she deserves the admiration of the universe', wrote Mme Roland admiringly from prison. 'But', she went on, 'being ill-informed about the state of things, she chose the wrong time and the wrong victim. There was a greater scoundrel.' As for Charlotte's immediate family and friends, they were totally appalled. Stupefied, her father burnt all her letters, moved to Barcelona and died there in 1798. The convent friend she tried to help, Mlle de Forbin, never spoke her name again.

Hardly more favourable have been the judgements of recent historians. In the view of many the effect of Charlotte's deed was to stir up popular hatred against aristocrats, refractory priests and moderates. Far from bringing peace to France, Marat's murder is often thought to have promoted the atmosphere of paranoia which helped bring about the Terror. Then there is the question of terrorism itself. In *La Machine à Terreur* Laurent Dispot, for example, refers to the 'religion of the dagger' engendered by her deed. Charlotte seems not to have realised that her own justification of both means and end scarcely differed from the reasonings of Marat. It was as if she expected her transcendent idealism to put her deed on a particular, superior plane, while at the same time she employed generalist maxims such as the Abbé Raynal's 'One does not owe the truth to one's tyrants'.

On the positive side may be counted Charlotte's proto-feminism and deep commitment to political action. As Simon Schama remarks, 'It was evidently a point of honour with her – and in deliberate repudiation of the revolutionary stereotypes of gender – to affirm that her sex was both physically and morally more than strong enough to commit acts of patriotic violence' (Schama, p. 738). In Charlotte's Elysian republic, women proved themselves deserving of a patriotic esteem; she looked backwards to the women of Sparta and Athens, while anticipating modern feminists' views of women as capable and equal beings. For Charlotte would show no weakness. That she fully expected to forfeit her life was less a sign of remorse than a recognition of dramatic necessity. Like a devout existentialist, she used her death to determine the sense of a life resolutely thought through. Her deed would not be out of place in the moral climate of Sartre or of Malraux, and in this respect she may be described as more 'modern' than other arguably more famous or respected heroines of her time.

The Tribunal which took so lively an interest in Charlotte Corday's anatomy had become a thriving institution largely through the energy and ambition of its public prosecutor, Antoine-Quentin Fouquier-Tinville. Charlotte's trial was actually one of its more conscientious ventures, quite unlike the slapdash adjudications of late 1793 and 1794. Creation of the Tribunal was proposed in March 1793, its purpose being to judge, without appeal, 'disturbers of the public peace'. Opposed by certain Girondins it was approved by then Minister of Justice Danton, who opined that the infamous September massacres would never have taken place if the Revolutionary Tribunal had been in function. The original plan had been to appoint some fourteen judges from Paris and the surrounding departments, but when many of those chosen declined the honour, or failed to respond at all, the Tribunal made do with less. On 5 April a decree was passed authorising Fouquier to prosecute on the basis of simple denunciations, made either by the authorities or ordinary citizens. Proof was not necessary to secure a condemnation; it was enough if the defendant could not disprove the accusation. Charlotte Corday, of course, had no intention of denying her deed; but not all those arraigned by the Tribunal were condemned with such ceremony. In a fit of drunkenness 56-year-old servant, Catherine Clère, had so forgotten herself one night as to call out 'Vive le roi!' She was guillotined for trying to re-establish the monarchy. On 10 June 1793 the court acquitted two aristocrats, Mme de Virel and Mme d'Allerac, of conspiring in a royalist plot in Brittany, but condemned their younger sister, Mme de la Fouchais. When the gendarmes took her away the other sisters burst into cries of despair, at which three of the jurors ran over and encouraged them – incredibly, given the growing anti-clerical bias – to take solace in religion.

Presently the Tribunal arraigned a more illustrious victim even than Charlotte. As Thomas Carlyle later wrote, with dramatic majuscule and looming present tense,

> On Monday the Fourteenth of October 1793, a Cause is pending, in the new Revolutionary Court, such as these old stone walls never witnessed: the Trial of Marie Antoinette. The once brightest of Queens, now tarnished, defaced, forsaken, stands here at Fouquier-Tinville's Judgement-bar; answering for her life. The Indictment was delivered her last night. To such changes of human fortune what words are adequate? Silence alone is adequate.
>
> (Carlyle, II, p. 276)

Adequate or not, silence was not what was granted. As Stefan Zweig remarks,

> To assail the monarchy effectively the Revolution had to attack the Queen, and in the Queen the woman.... In the very law-court the public prosecutor did not hesitate to compare the 'Widow Capet' with the most notoriously loose women of history, with Messalina, Agrippina, and Fredegond.[16]

One of the few things Marie Antoinette had in common with Charlotte Corday, that heroine of contrary opinions, was that both would see their sexual morality defamed by the Tribunal. Another was that in both cases the outcome of the trial could never be in doubt.

Marie Antoinette de Lorraine et d'Autriche was the fifteenth child of the Empress Maria Theresa. Ever absorbed in statecraft the imperial mother had given birth in an armchair, returning immediately to the duties of the throne. Adored, wilful, inattentive, 'Toinette' romped about in the corridors of Schönbrunn until she was 13, whereupon, as part of an alliance engineered by Choiseul and Prince Kaunitz, she was betrothed to the French Dauphin. Then Maria Theresa realised with some shock that the future Queen of France could write neither German nor French correctly, knew nothing about history and, despite having studied with Christoph Willibald von Gluck, played very little music. She was, in short, little better off than the average teenage student in Reagan's America. But deficiencies of this sort were not an absolute impediment to diplomatic matrimony. Louis XV formally demanded her hand for the Dauphin in 1769; the wedding was set for Easter 1770. Toinette's education was hastily completed, first by French actors, who taught her elocution – of the actors the French court disapproved – then by the more suitably solemn Abbé Vermond, who had been recommended by the Bishop of Orléans. Belatedly, Maria Theresa took her cheerfully distracted offspring to sleep in the same room and exhorted her nightly on the duties of a queen. And then Marie Antoinette was sent into France.

So complete was her necessary renunciation of all rights and privileges Austrian that the little Archduchess – escorted from Vienna by a cavalcade of 340 horsemen, all of them now left behind for good – was taken to a neutral pavilion on an island in the Rhine and stripped to the skin. Dressed hastily in French silks and petticoats she was led to meet the Bourbon delegation. Confronted with the deep formal curtsy of her new lady-in-waiting, the Comtesse de Noailles, Toinette flung herself into that stiff and starchy lady's arms and burst into tears. Inauspicious moments had a way of repeating themselves. Stefan Zweig, whose ingeniously post-Freudian intention is to show that this 'insignificant Habsburg princess' was in every way 'a mediocre, an average woman', nonetheless enumerates an impressive range of portents auguring the disastrous connubial destiny that made her an extraordinary one. The first was the transitional pavilion on the Rhine, which had been decorated with Gobelin tapestries depicting the story of Jason, Medea and Creusa, a choice which enraged the young Goethe. Was it permissible 'thus unreflectingly to display before the eyes of a young queen entering upon married life this example of the most horrible wedding that perhaps ever took place?' Then at the actual wedding the young Dauphine laboriously inscribed her name upon the contract, 'Marie Antoinette Josepha Jeanne', with the ominous addition of an enormous blot of ink. That evening the magnificent firework display, the greatest ever seen at Versailles, was interrupted by torrential rain, driving thousands of poor Parisians home in wild disorder.

Marie Antoinette's marriage was not consummated for eight years. Tucked into bed by Louis XV and practically the entire court her new husband settled into sheets previously, optimistically blessed by a bishop, and fell soundly asleep. It was not the Dauphine's fault; everyone agreed that she was charming. Even the Dauphin himself eventually fell in love with her. The problem was phymosis. Irresolute, short-sighted, stout, 'about five foot six or seven inches tall, square-shouldered and with the worst possible bearing', according to Mme de la Tour du Pin, the young groom suffered from a slight physical ailment which could only be cured by surgery. He managed to put off this minor horror for about seven years, during which Maria Theresa became enraged and Marie Antoinette frivolous and extravagant. Finally the Emperor Joseph II, Louis' brother-in-law, made a special trip to Paris and succeeded in persuading him of the operation's political necessity. By that time the awkward young man was Louis XVI. Marie Antoinette, who had previously written to her mother, rather doubtfully, 'I think our marriage has been consummated', was able to report to the increasingly alarmed Empress that matters were *'parfaitement consommé'*. In 1778, just before Christmas, she gave birth to a daughter, in a room packed with dignitaries, ministers, courtiers and even members of the public, all seated in correct order of precedence; two men actually stood up on a sofa, to gain an unimpeded vision of the bed. Fearing that his wife might suffocate in the crush, the King with unaccustomed vigour tore open the sealed windows to let in some fresh air.

Three other children were to follow: two boys, born in 1781 and 1785, and then a second girl, in 1786. But by this time, according to Zweig, the worst damage was done. It was not just that the King's marital ineptitude had caused his courtiers to giggle, amused most foreign monarchs and been made the subject of lampoons throughout France. The psychological result was more disastrous still:

> When a man is affected with sexual incapacity, he suffers from inhibitions and from irresolution. But when, in the female partner, her readiness to surrender herself to the male does not find its due fulfilment, the inevitable upshot will be irritability and lack of restraint with outbursts of excessive liveliness.

DEATH COMES TO THE MAIDEN

So explains Zweig. Embarrassed and ineffective, Louis increasingly surrendered his domestic authority to the giddy-pated Queen, whose reckless high spirits gradually 'degenerated into a mania for pleasure', bringing with it the misfortune, disrespect and hatred that were to accompany her to the guillotine. Or, as Georges Lefèbvre more discreetly reflects, 'Among the immediate causes of the Revolution the character of the king and queen must be included'.[17]

Of what consisted her excessive liveliness? To begin with, she disdained etiquette. At 15 she had romped with the Dauphin's younger brothers and even, to the shock of Mme de Noailles, the daughters of her chambermaids. She loathed having to sit shivering at her daily dressing ceremony while the ladies in attendance – always in strict order of priority – solemnly passed her clothes: 'It's odious!' she would mutter, through suitably chattering teeth. She insisted on clapping the musicians and dancers who performed at court; this was considered impolite. She thought it absurd always to be driven by a coachman, and so she bought her own cabriolet, driving it herself, extremely fast. Above all she hated being told what to do by Mme de Noailles, her stodgy 'Madame Etiquette'. Once when she fell off a donkey she laughingly refused to be helped up: '"Leave me on the ground", she said. "We must wait for Madame Etiquette. She will show us the right way to get up having fallen off a donkey".'[18] Charming as these lapses seem, in a Dauphine they were fatal. Having scorned the forms appropriate to her station, she could hardly expect them to protect her from censure. Nonetheless, she did.

That was not all. In 1773, while still Dauphine, she received Louis XV's permission to visit Paris – against the protests of the King's elderly sisters, who wished to keep her, unseen and unremarkable, at home in Versailles. The outing was a triumph, serving as a prelude to endless evenings at theatres and opera, but also at gaming tables and masked balls. On all these occasions she was warmly acclaimed. Her popularity was put to a more severe test in 1774, with the première of Gluck's *Iphigénie*, which the court musicians of Versailles had pronounced unperformable. Marie Antoinette championed her old master's cause and despite critics *Iphigénie* went down as a success: the Dauphine brought the entire court, including her recalcitrant spouse, and whenever she applauded, which she did at every aria, etiquette demanded that the court applaud politely too.

More inauspicious politically were the ventures into amateur theatricals. Shortly after becoming King, Louis XVI gave his wife the Petit Trianon, a tiny summer palace tucked away in the park at Versailles, at some distance from the main château. This was soon to be Marie Antoinette's private haven of refined irresponsibility. Decorated to her taste – light, elegant, reserved, graceful and enormously expensive – it was presently embellished by a small private theatre, and a farm. The farm – an otherwise inexplicable rusticity in this rococo paradise – resulted from the current mania for Rousseau.

Without necessarily having read *La Nouvelle Héloïse*, the Queen wanted to have something fashionably natural built, in which she and her friends could collect cow's milk in Sèvres porcelain and watch sheep being led to pasture with ribbons of blue silk. The cost of these and allied pleasures has been estimated at 2 million livres, expended at a time when the Treasury was facing bankruptcy, and when the Queen's real peasants subsisted on boiled chestnuts and struggled to pay taxes, from which the landed aristocracy were exempt. The contrast with real farming – even farming as practised by Charlotte Corday's impoverished parents – could scarcely have been more extreme. But this perilous imperviousness to reality was possibly surpassed by the Queen's espousal of the comedies of Beaumarchais. Banned in 1781 by Louis XVI, who recognised its subversive potential, *Le Mariage de Figaro* was produced in 1784 at the Comédie Française after a private reading for the Comte d'Artois; apparently Marie Antoinette was instrumental in overturning Louis' judgement. Then Beaumarchais' earlier comedy *Le Barbier de Séville* was performed at the Trianon, to his own direction, with Artois himself as Figaro and Marie Antoinette as Rosine. What might appear as a perceptive patronage of art is dismissed by Zweig as another example of the ruling caste's terminal frivolities: for having been forbidden, *Le Mariage* grew irresistibly amusing. Applauding wildly, the French aristocracy had no idea that 'this was the first manifestation of revolt, the herald of the storms of Revolution' (Zweig, p. 158).

This production, which absorbed all Marie Antoinette's attention, coincided with the definitive wrecking of her reputation via another cause: the scandal of the Queen's Necklace. This was an ambitious scam perpetrated by the Comtesse de la Motte-Valois. Claiming to be an intimate of Marie Antoinette, the Comtesse despoiled the court jeweller of an incredibly expensive diamond necklace, using as a pawn the Cardinal de Rohan; this notorious libertine had been tricked into thinking that the Queen was in love with him and wanted the necklace as a present. Such a scheme would have been utterly inconceivable had not Marie Antoinette by this time acquired a reputation for reckless extravagance (the Trianon, her gambling, her diamonds, her dresses) and wild lubricity, the two tendencies being economically connoted in the single word *luxure*. It may seem incredible, considering the Queen's long-time maiden status, that such rumours could have flourished; but that was precisely the problem. The maiden Queen: a sexual oxymoron, fateful in its import. Since the King was known to be inept, it was widely rumoured that his wife consoled herself with every kind of lover. As she wrote gaily to her mother, 'I am credited with tastes of every kind: men and women too'. Foremost among the presumed beloveds were the Princesse de Lamballe – a pretty, highly strung young widow for whom the Queen revived the defunct post of Superintendent of her Household; Count Axel Fersen, a Swedish diplomat; and the Comtesse de Polignac. If Mme de Lamballe made a harmlessly loyal favourite, Mme de Polignac, alas, was both extravagant and ambitious. Then again, there were the post-childhood romps with Artois, the King's brother, and the passion for masked balls, which provided young men to be flirted with from within the safety of disguise. These frolics inspired gossip and, worse than gossip, pamphlets. A certain Pons-Denis-Ecouchard Le Brun wrote, in rhyming couplets,

> Fuckers of all stations, objects of delight,
> Satisfied your tastes with services at night;
> Boundless in desire your far too libertine heart
> Rendered you alternately a Sappho and a Tart.[19]

The three most featured vices of these *libelles* were masturbation, lesbianism and insatiable nymphomania, all of which 'also figured prominently in the medical literature of the 1780's', as Schama records; it was as if Marie Antoinette were scientifically diagnosable as a compulsive nymphomaniac. Her Teutonic origins only furthered the linguistic play. Known increasingly as 'l'Autri*chienne*', the Queen inspired canine puns: in 1790 the amorous confessions of her spaniel appeared, proudly narrating his erotic conquest of the Austro-bitch to a fellow-dog, Mme de Lameth's Constitionnet. Moreover, lesbianism being known as 'the German vice', the Queen's nationality and supposed perversion became one and the same thing. Subjecting the *libelles* to the vocabulary of post-structuralist criticism, one would have to say that Germanism was her signified and signifying sin. Vainly do the memoirs of loyal souls such as Mme Campan deny the charge of sapphism; by the time of Revolution, Marie Antoinette was hopelessly inscribed in the popular imagination as tribade and as tart.

Realising too late the pass to which her disdain for royal propriety had brought her, Marie Antoinette attempted, after the shock of the Diamond Necklace, to set matters straight, giving up gambling, curbing her expenditure and seeing less of the Polignacs. These reforms were scarcely noticed. The Queen's withdrawal to the Petit Trianon had virtually destroyed life at court, thus alienating most of the aristocracy. Her dire reputation, coupled with her total lack of interest in the lives of ordinary subjects, had wiped out whatever natural constituency of sympathy she might otherwise have found in the middle and lower classes: seldom had a monarch been so literally unpopular. Thus, when the Estates-General convened in May 1789 the King was warmly cheered, but the crowd fell silent for the Queen. Private misfortune was adding to her new sobriety; her eldest son was dying of rickets. A pile of cushions had been set above the royal stables for him to watch his parents pass in the procession; his mother turned to him and smiled. He died on 3 June. The Queen had now reached that point in life from which matters could only grow worse.

The ambivalence of the King towards the later stages of his nationalised monarchy was in strong contrast to his wife's reaction to the situation: Marie Antoinette is credited with manifesting a firm, not to say reactionary, disposition to rule. 'She is the only man about the King', declared Mirabeau, who dreamed of engineering a coherent constitutional monarchy through the energy of the Queen. But Mirabeau died, leaving Marie Antoinette with a dignity and determination acquired too late and the problem of her nationality, which never went away. Repeatedly, she had urged the King to flee the country, particularly after the royal family had been transported from Versailles to Paris, to virtual imprisonment in the Tuileries. At Versailles the mob had invaded her apartments, forcing her to flee to the King's room; later she appeared on the balcony with Lafayette, who kissed her hand, prompting shouts of 'Vive la reine!' For all that she mistrusted the commander of the National Guard, considering him a turncoat opportunist. But then, the Revolution mistrusted *her*. It was felt that she envisaged civil war, perhaps conducted from exile and with Austrian troops; the royal family's abortive flight to Metz through Varennes only justified those fears. The King's constitutionally granted veto became a further instrument of Marie Antoinette's fatal unpopularity, for when Louis vetoed decrees against the *émigrés* and non-juring priests it was supposed she had advised him. The detested, dominant woman once known as 'Madame Deficit' was now 'Madame Veto'.

Her situation grew more perilous with actual foreign war. In April 1792 Louis Capet was called upon to declare war on Austria, shattering the vestiges of that imperial alliance forged between Louis XV and Maria Theresa by Prince Kaunitz. Soon France was at war with Prussia too. For some time the royal family had thought their best hope lay in outside help: 'It is for the Emperor to put an end to the disturbances of the French Revolution', wrote Marie Antoinette to Leopold, now Emperor of Austria; 'Compromise has become impossible. Everything has been overturned by force and force alone can repair the damage.' At first it seemed she might be right: deserted by its royalist officers, the French army was in no state to fight, and soon retreated in confusion. But these reverses stirred the Paris populace to violent demonstrations. The Tuileries were invaded, first in June and then, more seriously, on 10 August. Louis, Madame Elisabeth his sister, his wife and children all took shelter in the National Assembly, leaving the King's Swiss bodyguard to be slaughtered almost to a man. On 21 September the National Convention, as it now became, formally abolished the monarchy. Henceforth the ex-King and his family, imprisoned in the Temple, were national hostages of the most embarrassing kind.

The Marie Antoinette who finally stood arraigned before the Revolutionary Tribunal in October 1793 had lived through loss more drastic than the dissolution of the throne. First, her timid but loyal friend the Princesse de Lamballe had been killed and mutilated in the massacres of September 1793, after returning from the safety of London to be with the royal family. An over-sensitive creature who had once fainted at the sight of a dead lobster, the Princess had been led towards a pile of corpses and invited to swear oaths of loyalty to the nation and of hatred of the Queen. Failing in the second of these tasks she had been knocked down and beheaded. The corpse had been raped, the genitalia excised and the head paraded on a pike before the Temple prison. 'Prevent the Queen from seeing', said the King, but she had seen and fainted. Then her husband, whom she had finally learned to love, had been taken from the Temple, tried and beheaded for his crimes to the French people, begging her pardon, in his will, for any offence he might ever have caused. Her remaining little boy whom, it was feared, she now considered King of France, had also been taken away and handed over to the uncertain mercies of Simon, the Temple gaoler; Simon taught him to wear dirty clothes, sing revolutionary songs, and vilify his mother and his aunt. He died from this treatment, but not before his mother's death. Desperate at this abduction Marie Antoinette had kept a lock of her boy's hair, hidden in her bosom with a tiny glove; these things too were taken, at the office of the Conciergerie, where the Queen was transferred in August 1793.

There she had remained for more than two months while the Tribunal prepared her case. When she appeared before the crowded court her hair, prematurely greyed by the death of her first son, was almost white. Her cheeks were pale and sunken; her soul, it seemed, was dead. Only the walk remained, the stiff but lilting carriage of Versailles, leaning backwards slightly from the waist, head high. The witnesses also remained: called into the box, Monsieur de la Tour du Pin did a court bow; asked if he knew her, Bailly the former first Mayor of revolutionary Paris also bowed and said 'Ah yes, I know Madame'. She was questioned on the objects found about her at the Temple: 'Whose hair is this?' asked Herman, the presiding judge. 'It belongs to my children, dead and alive, and my husband.' 'And this paper, covered with figures?' 'It's for teaching my son arithmetic.' 'Whose portrait?' 'Madame de Lamballe.' 'And these?' 'Two ladies I grew up with in Vienna.' 'Their names?' 'The Princesses of Mecklenburg and Hesse.'

That she was guilty, at least in part, of the Republic's charge, is scarcely open to doubt. Michelet quotes an impressive series of autographed documents proving that the King and Queen appealed to foreign powers, for foreign aid, for Austrian troops; thus, she was eminently guilty of the main indictment, summarised at the end of the trial by Herman. Had she participated in communications with foreign powers? Had she participated in conspiracy to bring about a civil war? According to Michelet, she had. Yet at the time the proof was not certain and for two full days, in sessions of fifteen and twelve hours, Marie Antoinette attempted to defend herself. Not once did Fouquier-Tinville or Herman trap her in a contradiction or a lie. And so, frustrated on the political front, they had moved to attack the woman. They had called Hébert, the *Père Duchesne*, to testify. In an imaginative charge, prepared in careful consultation with Simon and the painter David, Hébert accused her of committing incest with her son, of placing him in the bed between herself and Madame Elisabeth, of teaching him to masturbate.

Marie Antoinette had never in her life deigned to refute invective, and did not do so now. The court sat silent and perplexed; Herman himself ignored the clod-hopping words. But one of the jurors wanted the question pressed. With unspeakable disdain the former Queen observed: 'If I have made no reply it is because nature itself refuses to accept such an accusation brought against a mother. I appeal in this matter to all mothers here today'. Indignation gripped the hall. 'The fish-wives', writes Stefan Zweig, privy in a novelistic manner to their thoughts, 'market women, . . .who were busily knitting as they listened, held their breath at the words, for they felt a strange kinship with this ex-Queen of France. In her, all their sex had been affronted.' Robespierre, hearing of it that evening, exploded in rage. 'What a fool that Hébert is', he exclaimed. 'He has thus given her a public triumph during her last hours!'

He need not have been concerned. The following day the Queen's defending counsel – Chauveau-Lagarde, assigned to yet another hopeless cause – spoke bravely for two hours, requesting clemency. She thanked him: 'How tired you must be, Monsieur; I am touched by all the trouble you have gone to.' Then the jury, filing into the court at 4 a.m., unanimously declared the accused guilty of treason as specified in Herman's concluding remarks. Marie Antoinette was brought to hear the verdict. She had scarcely eaten, scarcely slept; once she had asked for a glass of water, which nobody dared bring; Lieutenant de Busne, who finally did, was imprisoned the next day, together with her two defenders. She heard the sentence without emotion, her hands moving on the rail before her as if fingering a harpsichord's keys. Herman asked if she had anything to say. She shook her head.

Two candles stood burning on the table of her cell. The Queen sat down to write a farewell letter to Madame Elisabeth: 'It is to you, Sister, that I am writing for the last time. I have just been condemned, not to a shameful death – it is shameful only to criminals – but to join your brother.' After this Corday-like beginning, she commended her children to Madame Elisabeth's care, asked pardon for her own faults, for any sorrow she had ever caused: 'I had friends. The thought of being separated from them and of their distress is among my greatest regrets in dying. Let them at least know that until the last moment, I thought of them.' Then she fell onto her bed and, fully dressed, in full view of her obligatory gendarme, slept for three-quarters of an hour. When she awoke the gaoler's kitchen maid pressed her to take a little soup. Marie Antoinette asked the gendarme to withdraw while she changed her clothes: this he could not do. And so, crouching between wall and bed, shielded by Rosalie, the Widow Capet dressed for death. For many days, weakened by the lack of air and light, she had been menstruating; rolling her bloodstained under-linen into a small bundle, she hid it behind the stove. Forbidden to appear in widow's weeds on this occasion – it might have seemed provocative – the Queen decided to wear white: the colour of innocence, the mourning of Kings. She wore a piqué gown and bonnet, and her best remaining shoes.

Outside, the drums had been beating since five o'clock that morning. The armed force of the capital stood ready and alert: squadrons of cavalry, infantrymen with bayonets, loaded cannons guarding bridges. At eleven the Conciergerie gates were thrown open and Marie Antoinette was led towards the tumbril. As she saw this vehicle, little better than a manure-cart, her nerves failed, and Sanson untied her hands so that she could hastily relieve herself in a corner of the courtyard. There was no further weakness. The Queen sat upright, jolted but imperturbable, as the tumbril rattled on. Sanson and his aides stood bareheaded at her side. Nothing seemed to disturb her, not the actor-guardsman Grammont, riding by the cart and shouting insults; not the women gathered on the steps of the Eglise Saint-Roch, hailing her with cries of scorn. But not everyone was hostile. Somewhere on the way a woman held up a little boy, the same age as the Dauphin, for Marie Antoinette to see. And then Sanson, as they reached the scaffold, murmured 'Courage, Madame'; 'Thank you, Monsieur', she replied.

It is said that Marie Antoinette mounted the ten steps to the guillotine with as much dignity as the great staircase at Versailles. The instrument had been set up facing the Tuileries; seeing them, she sighed. In the commotion of the moment she is said to have trodden on the executioner's foot. 'I beg your pardon, Monsieur. It was not done on purpose.' Deploring her composure, Hébert wrote next day in the *Père Duchesne*: 'The whore, for the rest, was bold and impudent right to the very end.' It was nonetheless the greatest of his joys, to have seen with his own eyes 'the head of the female veto separated from her fucking tart's neck'.

If final letters constituted in themselves a literary genre, Charlotte Corday and the Queen might have attained to some renown on that basis alone. Marie Antoinette's is thought so masterly that critics have denied it could ever have been written by the once-frivolous French Queen. Politically disparate, the two women did have certain things in common. Both died as if proving themselves worthy of exalted relatives: the dramatist Corneille, the Empress Maria Theresa. Both, on principle, refused the services of the 'sermented' Abbé Lothringer. Both might be described as belonging historically to the Revolution's first phase: the one harking from that liberal aristocracy whose 'progressive' thinking fostered the new ideas, the other an integral part of the constitutional monarchy decreed by the first deputies, and that men like Mirabeau had wanted to preserve. This was not all they shared. The manner in which they imposed their identity on the largely disapproving public's mind may be said to have provoked what is now termed gender anxiety. Both seem to have been perceived as simultaneously masculine and almost excessively feminine. For the Revolutionary Tribunal, Charlotte Corday was hoydenish and slovenly; for Adam Lux, unbelievably sweet and tender. As for Marie Antoinette, her errant masculinity was adequately chronicled while she was living: the presumed lesbian attachments, the frank

Germanic manner. There was also the unwifely domination of her husband and the firm behaviour in crisis: as Simon Schama writes,

> Marie Antoinette – though she could hardly have dreamed of it – represented a threat to the settled system of gender relations. If the King was supposed to be the emblematic head of a patriarchal order, by the same token his wife was supposed to show a face of especial obedience, humility and submission.
>
> (Schama, p. 216)

The unbecomingly decisive Queen may even have run foul of what Antonia Fraser has termed the Shame Syndrome, 'whereby all the surrounding masculine figures are described as failing in courage compared to the Warrior Queen herself'.[20] In Mirabeau's phrase, she was the only man about the King.

At the same time Marie Antoinette may have been unpopular because of the directness with which she represented her own femininity. 'What had been permissible, even expected, in a mistress of the monarch', writes Schama again, 'was somehow intolerable in a queen. It made matters even worse that this femininity was candidly presented and designed, more or less exclusively, by other women' (Schama, p. 216). Among these literally designing women were the dressmaker Rose Bertin, who fashioned the Queen's informal image – abandoning the stiffness of formal court attire in favour of dresses of white muslin – and Elisabeth Vigée-Lebrun, who painted her thus clad. As Germaine Greer comments, Vigée-Lebrun's portraits of the Queen and the Comtesse de Provence 'created a sensation. The malicious said the Queen had been painted in her nightdress.'[21] Oddly enough the final portraits of both Charlotte and the Queen were sketched either by David or by his student: Charlotte's virginity examination, and Marie Antoinette in the tumbril. In the latter drawing David catches the Queen in a pose of rigid dignity, bolt upright with protruding Habsburg lip, but still wearing the white and simple clothes that had once marked her style. The sketch of Charlotte's corpse cannot be consulted, yet something bizarrely obsessive in the very idea of it reflects the ambivalence with which the Virgin-as-Assassin was viewed.

There is, however, an interpretation of Marie Antoinette's death which is less readily applied to that of Charlotte Corday. Commenting on the tendency of societies in the throes of famine, plague, and political or religious conflict to project the cause of such disasters onto some convenient scapegoat, structuralist René Girard finds the characteristics of this habit in both witch trials and the purges of the Terror. When these epidemic or ideological disasters strike, a 'loss of differentiation' between people occurs, resulting in a 'cultural eclipse'. Accusations are levelled, usually of violent crime, parricide, infanticide, incest, bestiality or, depending on the religious climate involved, blasphemy and profanation of the host. Often a king or an authority figure is held responsible; frequently blame falls on minority groups such as foreigners, heretics or Jews. Tension rises and eventually a scapegoat is selected. As Girard somewhat tentatively remarks, 'Marie Antoinette belongs to several categories of preferred victim'.[22] She was foreign and she was a queen. She had been depicted as a harpy in popular prints; at her trial she was accused of incest with her son. As scapegoats go, she was an obvious choice. Charlotte Corday, on the other hand, seems to have elected Marat as her own particular scapegoat, blaming him for the evils besetting France: he was Swiss, his speeches were bloodthirsty and therefore monstrous. But in the posterity of criticism Charlotte may yet qualify, retrospectively depicted as having precipitated the climate of paranoia that in turn nourished the Terror.

CITIZEN BLUESTOCKINGS: OLYMPE DE GOUGES, MANON ROLAND

For Olympe de Gouges, Marie Antoinette was the most detested of women; for Manon Roland she was simply detestable. Olympe de Gouges advocated female equality; Manon Roland did not. These differences did not prevent their sharing the erstwhile monarch's fate. Like her, they were criticised for behaviour thought more suited to a man. Unlike her, both were literary women. Denied office by virtue of her sex, Mme Roland acquired influence by virtue of her salon; this, together with her much-ridiculed ascendancy over her ministerial spouse, incurred resentment. After spending several years 'on quarrelling terms with the whole of the Comédie Française',[23] the dramatist Olympe de Gouges acquired grudging but contemporary celebrity through her political proposals. Both were proud if moderate republicans whose federalist inclinations proved their undoing. Both went to the scaffold in the first days of November 1793.

'The honour of women', wrote the Jacobin *Révolution de Paris* in May 1792, 'consists in cultivating in silence all the virtues of their sex, beneath the veil of modesty and in the shadow of retreat'. The occasion for this pronouncement was a ceremony in honour of the late Mayor of Etampes who had tried to intervene in demonstrations about the cost of grain, only to be killed by the crowd; the Assembly had decided to make a civic martyr of him. Reminding everyone that the 'most renowned peoples' habitually entrusted women with the 'crowning of heroes', Olympe de Gouges had actually been allowed to organise a cortège of women, intended to precede the sarcophagus. She duly set about her fund-raising, even appealing to Marie Antoinette in the name of 'the law to which you, Madame, are subject, and which defends your rights'. Her petition fell first into the hands of Mme de Lamballe, who rejected it; but then Olympe called on the Princess and bullied her into passing it on to the Queen. Intrigued, Marie Antoinette not only came up with the requisite 1200 livres but offered Olympe a pension and a place at court. Unlike Mirabeau, Barnave and possibly Danton, Olympe declined the royal advances. Instead she addressed her co-citizenesses in ringing terms: 'My fellow-women, isn't it time we had a revolution too?' The ceremonial cortège took place, but its dramatic effect was ruined by a thunderstorm – as if the elements were in collusion with Jacobin ideology in dampening the manifestations of Olympe's patriotic feminism. For although the word 'feminist' was not to be coined until the nineteenth century, Olympe de Gouges is often regarded as feminism's first French example.

The woman who thus took it upon herself to petition the Queen had led a life of what Michelet and others refer to as 'gallantry' before devoting herself to revolutionary politics. Born plain Marie Gouze at Montauban near Toulouse, she was held to be the illegitimate daughter of J.-J. Le Franc, Marquis de Pompignan, a writer well known in his day for purity of style and pompous opinions, both of which were mocked by Voltaire. Devoid of sympathy for his putative child and her struggles for recognition, Le Franc's family strenuously defended the Marquis' unblotted and unblottable reputation. Marie Gouze was married off when barely 16 to a cook, Louis-Yves Aubry, whom she did not like. In November 1765 Louis-Yves died – apparently the result of catastrophic flooding of the Tarn, and its epidemic consequences – after begetting a boy, Pierre. Relieved at her widowhood, Marie Gouze began calling herself Olympe de Gouges, Olympe being her mother's name, Gouges an alternative spelling of her stepfather's last name, and the 'de', one can only suppose, in honour of Le Franc de Pompignan. She also started having adventures, acquiring the protection of a wealthy man, Jacques Biétrix de Rozières, who had the monopoly of military transports. From him she obtained a pension for her mother and money to educate her son. In 1788 Biétrix found his monopoly withdrawn by Loménie de Brienne; financial difficulties ensued. According to novelist Restif de la Bretonne, Olympe became a prostitute. Certainly she had affairs. She would not, however, allow anyone to boast of his conquest who had not actually conquered: she once caused a Marquis de Chabillon to admit the truth on his knees, before an entire *salon*. Tall, with an oval face, brown eyes, aquiline nose, medium mouth, and a lot of chestnut hair, Olympe was considered attractive. She was also sensual, imaginative, and terribly extravagant – her biographer Olivier Blanc estimates that Biétrix spent about 70,000 livres on her – endowed with the vivacity of the Midi and a gift for repartee. Chided for her reputation, she declared it better to be known as a frankly 'gallant' woman than a prude: therein lay the difference between the artist and the amateur.

In her middle years Olympe abandoned gallantry in favour of writing. She embarked on her new career with two disadvantages: unlike Charlotte Corday and the dazzling Manon Roland, she had gone through childhood barely able to sign her name. Her native language was not French, but Occitan. She coped with these difficulties by hiring secretaries and dictating to them in bursts of genial spontaneity. Ideas, she felt, counted more than style. Some of Olympe's ideas struck her contemporaries as absurd: an atheist who believed in reincarnation, she was apparently convinced that her dachshund had been a famous man, whose present canine form was punishment for his ambition. She had long conversations about animals' souls with the naturalist Daubenton; in the unkind words of Fleury, an actor, she 'saw herself as giving asylum to all manner of fallen great men and unfortunates; as welcoming science personified in fur and the arts dressed up in feathers'. Her political views were generous and unpopular. In about 1784 she submitted an anonymous manuscript, *Zamora and Mirza, or the Felicitous Shipwreck*,[24] to the Comédie Française, an institution of enormous power, holding a monopoly of the classical repertory and protected by the King; the play's subject was black slavery, to which Olympe was opposed. Her friends had warned her that being a playwright would not be easy; Beaumarchais himself had complained of the actors of his day and their merciless treatment of struggling authors. The Comédie kept Olympe waiting but eventually called her in for a reading in June 1785. Amazingly, *Zamora* was accepted into the repertory on condition that some changes were made. Olympe became dissatisfied with the slow pace of production and meanwhile offered another play to the rival Théâtre des Italiens. Advised to submit this second work to the Comédie, she did so; they refused it, which meant that it could never be performed. This was the beginning of a long and dreadful feud between Olympe and the Comédie Française, in consequence of which the Duc de Duras, gentleman of the King's bedchamber, obtained a *lettre de cachet* and would have had her sent to the Bastille, had not the lieutenant of police refused to carry out the order.

A reconciliation was effected, but not with total success. In 1787 the Comédiens saw fit to remind her of the 'evident danger' incurred by a woman in pursuit of fame. Rehearsals for *Zamora* were interrupted when the leading lady died. Worse, the Comédie depended on the favour of the King and his courtiers, many of whom were slave-owning colonialists. This did not deter Olympe. In February 1788 she wrote her *Reflections on the Negro*:

> I have always been interested in the negro race and its deplorable fate. Those I was able to question on the subject never satisfied my curiosity and judgement. They spoke of those men like beasts, like beings whom the sky had cursed; but as I grew older, I saw clearly that it was force and prejudice that had condemned them to this horrid slavery, that nature had no part in it and that the unjust and powerful interest of the Whites was responsible for all.[25]

In March 1789 she threatened the Comédie with a lawsuit; this, and the uncertain times, prodded them into action. *Zamora* was staged on 28 December, 1789 at what is now the Théâtre de la Nation.

Comparable in its turbulence to that of Jarry's *Ubu Roi* about a hundred years later, *Zamora*'s opening night was attended by colonial factions and 'Friends of the Blacks', all of whom whistled and stamped repeatedly, resulting in a most tumultuous performance. The *Moniteur* gave a favourable account next day, but other critics assailed it:

> To remain entitled to French gallantry, a woman must receive it in her person; the spectator, who becomes her judge, thinks himself dispensed from being chivalrous and no longer discerns what is pleasant in her sex, amid pretensions that veil its graces while calling its weaknesses to mind.
>
> (Blanc, 1981, p. 73)

The play closed after three nights, causing its author to ask justice of Bailly, Mayor of Paris. But Bailly simply reproached her for *Zamora*'s incendiary themes. Olympe then appealed to her fellow-writers for solidarity, without noticeable effect; finally, in August 1792, certain men of letters – La Harpe, Ducis, Chamfort, Mercier, Florian and Chénier – presented a petition to the National Assembly asking for a more liberated theatre and some assurance of an author's rights. Bailly relented, reopening the case of *Zamora*. By this time, however, Olympe had turned to revolutionary politics.

As a Frenchwoman, Olympe had welcomed the convocation of the Third Estate; she hoped the deputies would notice her ardent patriotism. The thought of mobilising patriotic women came to her after the Assembly formally received the wives and daughters of Parisian artists in September 1789. Mirabeau approved of her plan – 'as long as women are not involved, there is no true revolution', he declared – as did the Marquis de Condorcet, who shared her opinions on black rights. Olympe's patriotism soon took on overtones of sympathetic feminism, attesting to a spontaneous and practical compassion for her sex. In her *Patriotic Remarks* of 1788–9 she proposed constructing shelters for the elderly, the homeless, for abandoned children and the widows of labourers killed while at work: 'Often they are pregnant when their husband is brought back on a stretcher, and the unfortunate widows remain without assistance for some time, with no bread for the children who cry out for it.' Her *Useful and Salutary Projects* of 1789 contained thoughts on hygiene and maternity:

> Are there any appalling torments not experienced by women, when they become mothers? And how many lose their lives, giving birth? No art can succour them, and one sees young women dying in the arms of doctors after suffering day and night from keenest pain, after giving life to men, not one of whom has seriously busied or concerned himself in the slightest with the tortures he has caused.
>
> (Blanc, 1981, p. 194)

Realising the importance of cleanliness in obstetrics she demanded proper hospitals. Worried about the problems of unmarried mothers she demanded state assistance, going so far as to propose searching for the father. She was equally concerned about the plight of prostitutes, proposing special areas where they might operate: 'It's not the prostitutes who most degrade morality', she declared in 1791. 'It's the society women!'

To their credit, Marat and Saint-Just had argued in favour of the pregnant and unwed. 'Far from coming to the help of a weak and oppressed woman', wrote Marat in 1780, 'the laws rally with a cruel oppressor, and for a fault he commits with impunity, she must always lose her reputation, frequently her freedom, sometimes her life.'[26] The year of Olympe's death did witness some improvement in these domains. In June 1793 the Convention began giving aid to unmarried mothers. It also granted the right to divorce, of which 3,870 Parisian women availed themselves in the first year alone. Quite possibly Olympe's own illegitimacy had made her more sensitive to the predicaments of oppressed groups – notably, women and blacks; in any case she did not forget bastards, further asking for a law permitting them to inherit from their fathers, and to use their fathers' names. Such a law was indeed passed – on the very day of her trial. On the whole, however, the Revolution showed a certain sluggishness in recognising women's rights. It was this general recalcitrance that prompted Olympe to publish, in September 1791, her *Declaration of the Rights of Woman and the Female Citizen*.

She was not the first to broach the topic. In 1788 the Marquis de Condorcet had suggested that women be allowed to help elect representatives for the Estates General. On 24 January 1789 a royal ruling did permit enfeoffed women to vote in civil and municipal elections, with the result that deputies from the noble and clerical estates owed their election partly to women; but the provision was withdrawn a year later. Robespierre brought the question of female suffrage to the Constituent Assembly, only to see the motion rejected almost unanimously. Again in 1789, *Ladies' Request to the National Assembly* boldly declared: 'You have just abolished privilege.... Abolish then the privileges belonging to the male sex....The French, you maintain, are a free people, yet every day you permit thirteen million slaves to bear the shameful chains of thirteen million tyrants!' – the population of France being about 26 million at the time. The same *Request* suggested that women be allowed to preach in church. Then the *Moniteur* of 29 November 1789 printed a 'Motion to the Assembly in Favour of Women', recommending that men 'be required to marry women without dowry'. In Germany, Theodor von Hippel's *On the Improvement of Woman's Lot With Regard to Civic Rights* appeared in 1790. It was in September 1791, too, that Mary Wollstonecraft began writing her much-acclaimed *Vindication of the Rights of Woman*, translated into French the following year. It certainly seemed as if the time was ripe for change, and yet in France the most relevant and incisive feminist manifesto passed almost unnoticed: the manifesto of Olympe de Gouges.

Olympe had hoped that revolution would bring about equality between the sexes. Two years after it began, she realized that 'Since the Revolution, this despicable and respected sex has become respectable and despised'. It was not, she felt, totally the fault of men. In a play written for Mirabeau's death in April 1791 she had already observed that 'women want to be women and have no worse enemies than themselves. One rarely sees them applauding a fine action or a piece of work done by another woman.' In her view, government would not truly prosper until women were more useful and more serious; once again, feminism merged with patriotism. As Olivier Blanc remarks, Olympe's opinions were more progressive than those of Brissot, Bernardin de Saint-Pierre and Mme de Staël – contemporaries who thought it proper to exclude women from civic affairs. Bernardin de Saint-Pierre, for example, thought that kindergarten was enough for women, but that men needed a thorough education.

The *Declaration of the Rights of Woman* of 1791 comprised seventeen articles, as did the twin male document drafted in 1789 by Lafayette and Jefferson. It called for a civic egality between the sexes, founded on Nature and Reason. It called on all classes of women to react, including 'the most detested' of women, Marie Antoinette, to whom the text was dedicated: 'This revolution will only take effect when all women become fully aware of their deplorable condition, and of the rights they have lost in society'. Following Lafayette's seventeen articles point for point it was almost a parody, in the most literal sense, of the original document: 'Men are born and remain free and equal in rights. Social distinctions may be based only on common utility,' proclaimed the Rousseauesque first article, to which Olympe replied: 'Woman is born free and remains equal to man in rights. Social distinctions may only be based on common utility.' In her second and third articles, Olympe maintained that social authority of any kind could only come from the joint national rule of men and women; her fourth article sought to limit patriarchal authority over girls. Whereas the sixth article of the *Rights of Man* declared that 'All citizens have the right to take part, in person or by their representatives' in the formation of law, Olympe's addition of the feminine gender to its clauses – 'All citizens including women are equally admissible to all public dignities, offices and employments, according to their capacity, and with no other distinction than that of their virtues and talents' – draws attention to the fact that this equal admissibility had not previously applied to women. In article VII, VIII and IX Olympe made clear her *Declaration* did not expect tribunals to extend special favours to the fair sex, repudiating thereby the ambiguous notion of legal chivalry. Even more to the point was her article X: 'Women have the right to mount the scaffold, they must also have the right to mount the speaker's rostrum.' Women were fully punishable, yet denied equal rights: Olympe's ironic formulation exposed this philosophical blunder as no other manifesto of its time had done, exposing the grave oversight of a revolution devoted to egality.

To do the Revolution justice, it did not actually cut off Olympe's head because she was a feminist. It was more her federalist-Girondin tendencies and overall nuisance value that were ultimately responsible: nothing could stop her from pronouncing her opinions, popular or not, on everything that happened. Her plays, though timely in theme, continued to startle. The *Convent of Forced Vows* of 1790, an anti-clerical piece, saw twenty-four performances in Paris and elsewhere, but was received with shock and horror because critics found it offensive to see religious scenes on stage. Continuing to compose texts of impeccable patriotism, Olympe read a funeral oration for Mirabeau at the Café Procope in April 1791; another play, *Mirabeau in the Elysian Fields* was performed in Bordeaux on 1 June. Although she seems to have suspected and disapproved of Mirabeau's secret collaboration with the King, she agreed with him as to the desirability of a constitutional monarchy. But then, allied by temperament and philosophy to the moderate Girondins, she protested when Louis dismissed the three Girondin ministers in June 1792 and seems to have welcomed his subsequent deposition, even writing a pamphlet to proclaim the incompatibility of monarchy and the new laws. Even so, she was taxed with royalism.

More damaging, perhaps, was her instinctive opposition to violence. She was revolted by the September massacres and did not hesitate to say so. 'The blood of even the guilty, shed with cruelty and profusion, stains revolutions for ever, rudely changing people's hearts, minds, and opinions and one system of government is rapidly succeeded by another', she declared in *The Pride of Innocence*. Like Charlotte Corday and Mme Roland she was opposed to Marat and the Mountain and considered them jointly responsible for these atrocities. After the *coup d'état* of 10 August she also opposed the dictatorial ambitions of Robespierre, going so far as to write to him, in a spirit of self-sacrifice, proposing that they swim together in the Seine – with cannonballs attached to their four feet. 'Your death will calm people down and the sacrifice of a pure life will disarm heaven' (Blanc, 1981, p. 145).

The bravado of this outburst, which did her no good whatsoever, was soon surpassed by her impolitic championing of the beleaguered King. Realising the danger in which Frederick of Prussia placed the French monarch by invading France she penned a sarcastic *Address to the Northerly Don Quichotte* inviting him to withdraw. On 15 December 1792 she wrote to the National Assembly protesting against Louis' trial: the English, she said, were dishonoured by the death of Charles I, the Romans immortalised for having exiled Tarquin. Then she topped all this by offering to defend the deposed Capet, adding that a king is only dead when he survives his downfall. These audacious words were unanimously criticised; the general feeling was that Olympe should be quiet and knit trousers for the *sans-culottes*. She was practically attacked in the streets. In an incident related by Michelet a man seized her by the neck and asked if anyone in the crowd would pay 24 sous for the life of Olympe de Gouges. 'My friend', replied Olympe from underneath his arm, 'I'll give you thirty sous'. The crowd laughed, and she was saved to write more of her patriotic prose. On 23 January 1793, two days after the execution of the King, her triumphal

DAME GUILLOTINE

Dumouriez' Entrance into Brussels was performed at the Théâtre de la République. Full of parades and apotheoses, it celebrated the victories of General Dumouriez, a warmongering commander allied with the Girondins. The work was well received, but the memory of it did not help Olympe two months later when Dumouriez was badly defeated at Neerwinde and deserted to the enemy. At the same time the uprising in the Vendée had exasperated tensions between the Mountain and the Gironde; in June, when her Girondin friends were disgraced, Olympe rose to defend them in yet another pamphlet.

Since 11 March of that year it had been a capital offence to suggest any form of government other than the One and Indivisible Republic. Federalism, which proposed giving greater autonomy to the individual departments, was clearly outlawed. It was nonetheless a theory of government favoured by the Girondins, whose idea it was to summon a federalist army composed of patriots from every province (hence the band of *Marseillais* who marched to Paris in the summer of 1792 and gave their name to Rouget de l'Isle's new anthem). In the summer of 1793 Olympe wrote the federalist text, *The Three Urns*, which prompted her arrest. In every department of France,

> Three urns will be placed on the table of the President of the Assembly, each bearing an inscription: Republican Government, Federal Government, Monarchic Government. In the name of the endangered Fatherland the president will announce the free and individual choice of each form of government.

Olympe returned to Paris to print this troublesome document after an idyllic stay in the Loire valley, during which time she bought a house; with its terraced gardens, flowers, four cows and a bull, it was intended as a refuge from Paris, should things go ill – as indeed they did. Olympe had difficulty in finding a publisher in Paris brave enough to print *The Three Urns*, but did discover a hawker who agreed to put it up in poster form. She was denounced immediately.

After her arrest, Olympe displayed her customary audacity and indicated where her papers were; impressed at the quantity of 'patriotic writings', the officials forgot to put seals on them. From prison Olympe managed to write another poster-pamphlet about the deplorable conditions in which she was held – appalling filth, bloodstains from the September massacres still on the walls, no treatment for an infected knee, a 'tyrannical detention detrimental to the *Declaration of the Rights of Man*' – and smuggle it out. It did not attract much notice; by this time sated with her observations the public had a tendency to shrug and say 'Ah, it's Olympe de Gouges again'. But Fouquier-Tinville did authorise her removal to a women's prison, then a clinic, whence she might have escaped; this she elected not to do, thinking it would look like guilt. Instead, she actually asked to be tried, apparently secure in her concept of what patriotic justice ought to be. On 28 October the inevitable happened, and Olympe was transferred to the Conciergerie.

Her trial took place on an exceptionally cold November day. The prisoners had shivered in their cells as temperatures had dropped to below zero the preceding night. Olympe, who coquettishly gave her age as 38 (it was 45) and her profession as 'woman of letters' was accused of harming the sovereignty of the French people by penning texts that questioned the expression of the people's wish, that is to say, a republican government. She was informed that her lawyer, Tronçon-Ducoudray, had refused her case but that she possessed 'sufficient mind' to defend herself. Professing herself a republican, Olympe explained that *The Three Urns* was composed when several of the major towns – Bordeaux, Lyon, Marseille – were in revolt; she felt each province should enjoy the form of government best suited to it. The other charges against her were more idiotic: she was accused of having placed counter-revolutionary speeches in the mouth of Marie Antoinette in one of her plays, *France Saved or The Dethroned Tyrant*. Rolling her eyes heavenward Olympe pointed out that these words were perfectly in keeping with the character of the Queen. In another spirited response she managed to deflect suspicion of conspiracy from her son, to whom she had sent a copy of a pamphlet:

> I'm a woman, I'm afraid of death, I dread your punishment but I have no confessions for you, and I shall draw courage from the love I bear my son. To die in order to fulfil one's duty is to extend one's motherhood beyond the tomb!

The public applauded vigorously here; still, to nobody's surprise, she was condemned.

The Revolution had in common with the *ancien régime* that women expecting babies would be granted a stay of execution. It was something of a mixed blessing. 'The end of Voltaire's century', writes G. Lenôtre in a study of the Revolutionary Tribunal, 'witnessed these monstrous things: while women waited in terror and anxiety for the moment of maternity, there were actually executioners willing to wrest the new-born babies from them; weak and tottering the mothers were then dragged forth to the scaffold'.[27] The officials were said to hate these scenes, but probably not as much as the mothers, whose nine months were carefully counted by the vigilant Fouquier-Tinville. Olympe's cell-mate, Mme de Kolly, had already availed herself of this ambiguous privilege; Olympe herself now announced to the tittering court that she was pregnant. She was examined by prison doctors and a midwife who rather nastily reported the pregnancy to be too recent, if it existed at all, to be assessed. Nonetheless Olympe had gained another night of life, in which she wrote in typical declamatory manner to her son: 'I die, my dear son, the victim of my own idolatry for the fatherland and the people. . . . They have outraged all the laws for the most virtuous woman of the century.' Like most of the other last-minute missives written by Fouquier's condemned, the letter never reached its destination.

On another frigid morning, that of 3 November, Sanson came with his aides. Olympe made a bundle of her effects, looked in the mirror and said she was relieved she did not look too pale. Some witnesses claim to have seen her smile and sniff at a bouquet offered by a young man as she passed by. Once in the tumbril, she cried a little from weakness and from cold; but soon, pulling herself together, decided to take advantage of the captive audience, stood up and, 'in a feverish, declamatory voice', as Sanson put it, harangued the crowd on politics. An eye-witness on the steps of Saint-Roch recalled seeing her as 'lovely and courageous as Charlotte Corday'. In the Place de la Révolution she turned to the marble statue of Renown and enquired, 'Fatal desire for Fame, why did I aspire to *be* something?' Then, turning contemptuously towards the guillotine, 'They're going to be pleased, they'll have cut down the tree as well as the branch'. Someone in the crowd – drawn hither by curiosity, to see the 'former gallant woman' die – conceded that 'they killed a lot of spirit there'. Her son, Lieutenant Pierre Aubry, admitted less. In Tours when she died, he put posters in the city (her son at least in that) declaring that her blood was justly shed and that he himself was happy to sacrifice his mother to his country.

Although Olympe was technically convicted of federalism, there was among the diverse accusations one which suggests her feminist activities may in fact have entered into the motives for her arrest: she was accused of founding women's clubs. The Tribunal was not the sole authority to link her with these. After enumerating her more 'ridiculous' ventures, Michelet's editor Gérard Walter declares that she had 'also undertaken to found popular societies for women', ostensibly to throw mud in the eyes of the Jacobins, who had 'ejected' her from their club. Michelet, too, asserts that 'This ardent woman from Languedoc had organised several societies for women'. After his remark about the clubs Walter goes on to explain that Robespierre and his colleagues 'eventually got fed up with her and sent her to the scaffold', indicating a direct connection between the founding of the clubs and this latter calamity. The charge is disputed, both by Olympe's biographer Olivier Blanc and Marc de Villiers, author of a study of such societies. According to Villiers, Olympe scarcely went to women's clubs but was one of the first to think of forming a female National Guard, the 'Amazons of the Queen', whose mission would have been to watch over Marie Antoinette. Olivier Blanc suggests that the Revolutionary Tribunal brought up the subject of women's clubs in an attempt to trap her; incarcerated as she was, she could scarcely know that they had been outlawed just before her trial.

Although Olympe seems to have reacted to this charge as to a manifest absurdity, it would not have been surprising if she had been active in the clubs: female societies were among the most visible forms of women's revolutionary activity, occasionally martial and often feminist. One such club was the Society of Female Friends of Truth, founded by Etta Palm d'Aelders. In April 1792 Etta Palm, whom Walter disagreeably describes as a Dutch 'adventuress', approached the National Assembly at the head of a deputation of women and asked – in the spirit of Olympe's *Declaration* – for women 'to be admitted henceforth to all civil and military employment'. Women shared in the dangers of revolution, she went on; should they not share in its advantages too? Her manifesto called for girls to receive a proper education, for women to be declared adults at 21, for liberty and political equality to be granted to both sexes, and for the right to divorce. Etta Palm was also a member of the Fraternal Society of Patriots of Both Sexes, which admitted men and women. Dubbed the Hermaphrodite Society by its enemies, this club was frequented by many persons of influence including Danton and Roederer, the *procureur syndic*; here Hébert met his future wife, the ex-nun Marie Goupil. Other prominent female members were Théroigne de Méricourt, Mme Robert-Kéralio and Pauline Léon; even Manon Roland went a few times. On the other hand, Villiers adds, the men tended rather to desert its meetings.

There were also several high-profile female para-military organisations. In February 1792 Théroigne de Méricourt – who had already tried to found several political clubs and, attired in a dashing red riding jacket, been active in the march on Versailles in October 1789 – set about organising a female battalion: 'It's time women emerged from their shameful nullity', she said. 'Do men claim the right to glory for themselves alone?' Her plan was for women to take up arms and perform manoeuvres three times a week on the Champs-Elysées, for which proposal she was presented with a sabre by the consul general of the Paris Commune. Nor was this an isolated dream. In 1792 the citizenesses of the Charente-Inférieure offered to form a body of National Amazons. Women performed auxiliary services in Angers, dealing with baggage and provisions, while Villiers records several instances of their taking up arms to defend 'the endangered Fatherland' during the war when France was threatened with invasion.

Unfortunately for Théroigne and like-minded females, women's clubs were often confused in the contemporary view with the infamous *tricoteuses*, of scaffold-knitting reputation, and gained a bad name. Most violent among these diverse organisations was the Club of Revolutionary Republican Citizenesses, founded in February 1793 and lodged at the Jacobin club in the rue St Honoré. One had to be 18 to belong, of good morals and presented by three female citizens; even so, the club was unflatteringly described by its contemporaries. The Girondin Buzot thought the members were prostitutes; Chaumette of the Paris Commune termed them 'shameless viragos', and Fabre d'Eglantine said they were 'female grenadiers'. Scarcely had the club been formed, writes Villiers, than the

Revolutionary Citizenesses went, on May 12, to the Jacobin club to invite the women of all Paris sections to fight and encourage their husbands to take up arms. Preaching by example, they then proposed arming all patriotic women aged between eighteen and fifty and organising them into an armed body to fight the brigands from the Vendée.[28]

Later on that May they proposed creating revolutionary tribunals in every section of the Commune, arresting all suspect persons and moderate deputies – that is, the Girondins – and forming a phalanx to destroy the aristocrats.

It is Villiers' conclusion that the Jacobins and the Commune found the Revolutionary Citizenesses useful in overturning the Girondins (whom the red-bonneted, striped-panted *citoyennes* deemed too moderate) but then hastened to disband them. In October 1793 male voices were raised in the Assembly, demanding the 'abolition of all societies, of women forming clubs, because it was a woman who plunged France into misfortune', the woman being Charlotte Corday, who had not the remotest connection with female societies other than her convent. Still other speakers feared that women's clubs would 'divide the Revolution'. Accordingly, on 23 October and on the grounds of public safety, female clubs were outlawed, 'at least during the revolution'. Besides, Villiers remarks, the Girondins were being guillotined next day.

The effect of this prohibition was to discourage theoretical feminism for the remainder of the Revolution and some time beyond. 'Before the end of 1793 the feminist movement was crushed', bluntly states Claire Tomalin in her biography of Mary Wollstonecraft. Olympe de Gouges was dead; Théroigne de Méricourt, the other charismatic female leader, had gone mad. In that same May, when the Revolutionary Citizenesses were at their most active, Théroigne had been making speeches on the terrace of the Tuileries, apparently in favour of the Girondins. She had been attacked, stripped, and beaten about the buttocks and the head by some female supporters of the Mountain. This brutal humiliation cost Théroigne her wits: she spent the rest of her life being moved from one asylum to another, dying at La Salpétrière in 1817. Condorcet, the principal male theorist of equal rights for women, was proscribed with the Girondins and arrested in 1794; he committed suicide. Discussing the bad faith of the aristocracy in the French Revolution's early stages, Georges Lefèbvre contends that the Revolution could not tolerate the retention of nobiliary feudal privilege – the existence of a nation within a nation. The Revolution of 1789 was 'above all the conquest of equal rights', he maintains. But it would seem that the Revolution could no more tolerate a revolution within a revolution that might have led to equal female rights. Had women achieved full civic egality from the very outset the startling behaviour of some female clubs might never have occurred – and if it had still occurred, might not have seemed so startling.

Five days after the execution of Olympe de Gouges the Revolutionary Tribunal tried Manon Roland. Although she had attended a few meetings of the Society for Both Sexes and been a friend of Mary Wollstonecraft, Manon was scarcely a feminist. Women, she declared, wished to govern only through men's hearts: 'You have strength, courage, perseverance, great vision and great talents; it's up to you to make the laws in politics: govern the world.' Thus did she apostrophise the male sex in a letter to botanist Louis Bosc. She was herself to govern through a male heart, that of her husband, the Girondin minister Roland, and it killed her.

Marie-Jeanne Phlipon, better known as Manon, was born into the class of petty bourgeois and artisans which played such a major role in the Revolution. Her father, Gatien Phlipon, did engravings for the Compte d'Artois; he was also a mediocre painter. Her mother, Marguerite Bimont, was poor, charming, and quite pretty. Marie-Jeanne was the only one of their seven children to survive infancy. As her more than slightly Rousseauesque memoirs inform us, she disliked using a chamber-pot and used to ask if salad bowls and soup tureens were used for the same purpose; she herself preferred a corner of the garden. Extremely good at lessons, she was obstinate in the sense that she would not agree to anything she did not see the point of. Once when she was ill she refused to swallow some particularly revolting medicine. After being spanked – twice – by her father, a sudden calm came over the 6-year-old girl: she turned, and silently offered him her bottom. 'They could have killed me on the spot without obtaining a single sigh.' Then, to please her mother, and after being left alone with the medicine for two hours, she drained it at a single gulp, only to vomit it all back fifteen minutes later. Her father never spanked her again, which was probably as well for him since she had a habit of biting his thigh when he did. The episode was still vivid in her mind when she came to draft her memoirs in the prison of the Abbaye, thirty-two years later: 'It's the same inner stiffening I've felt in solemn moments since; and it wouldn't cost me much more of an effort to ascend the scaffold proudly than it did to yield to this barbaric treatment, which could kill me but not conquer me.'[29]

This resolute infant soon became a tiny bluestocking. She read Plutarch, Tasso and Voltaire. Her father gave her Locke and Fénelon; as for her mother, the one author she positively banned was Rousseau. 'I discovered him late', Manon would write, 'and this was a good thing, for he would have driven me mad; I should have read no one but him.' Parents in the *quartier* cited Manon as a model of studiousness to their own offspring. At the age of 11 she developed a sense of religious vocation after one of her father's students attempted to seduce her. This was a boy of 15 or 16 whose parents were not in Paris, and to whom Manon's mother was therefore especially kind. One day when Manon went into the studio the youth seized her hand and pressed it against 'something quite extraordinary'. Manon screamed and tried to withdraw; the student loosed his grip, turned on the chair and exposed himself. Manon looked away. 'In truth, Monsieur, how horrible!' The student apologised and there the scene ended, except that Manon, pale and trembling, felt obliged to hide the cause of her emotion from her mother.

On another occasion the youth took Manon on his knee and tried to caress her indecently. This time the child was sufficiently upset to tell Mme Phlipon. Manon's mother merely kept them apart, avoiding the scandal of dismissing the young man. Unfortunately she also obliged Manon to confess the matter to a priest, as if the sin were hers. Manon became in consequence timid, self-effacing, and terrified of men, particularly those who seemed at all pleasant. Thus, at 16, she skipped all the sections of Buffon's *Natural History* that dealt with reproduction, and their attendant illustrations; at 25, and wedded to Roland, she had 'so thoroughly avoided the development of that instruction whose beginnings were so premature, that the events of my wedding night seemed to me as strange as they were disagreeable'. The seduction episode proved so shocking to Manon's editors that several omitted it from her memoirs; even the admiring Sainte-Beuve criticised her frankness. Despite these discouraging beginnings Manon was not uninterested in sex. 'No-one', she wrote, 'was more disposed to enjoy pleasure than I am; and no one has enjoyed it less.'

Manon's youth was marked by her friendship with the Cannet sisters, who went to the same convent school; by the discreet lapsing of her Catholicism; and by her mother's death. 'Religion', she remarked in her Memoirs,

> is like so many other human institutions; it does not alter an individual's mind, but blends with his nature, growing stronger or weaker with him. The ordinary man thinks little, believes what he's told and acts according to instinct, so that a perpetual contradiction develops between the precepts that are taught and a person's actual line of conduct.
>
> (*Mémoires*, p. 227)

The first thing to perplex her in Christianity was the 'universal damnation of all those in ignorance or mis-knowledge of it'. Reading Bossuet's defence of religion had the unexpected side-effect of acquainting her with some of the arguments against it. Diderot, d'Holbach, d'Alembert and Helvétius added to her perplexity; by June 1775 she was quite 'incrédule'. Aware of this rational young woman's growing doubts her confessor managed to keep her a practising Catholic, at least for a while. Though the adult Manon preferred the company of atheists, she always found them lacking in a depth of personality that she felt the religious sense provided.

When her mother died, Manon was inconsolable. She fell ill; her own life was despaired of. 'It is a fine thing to have some soul', said her practical confessor, 'but it is certainly uncomfortable to have so much.' Somehow she recovered and plunged back into study. Her life from that time changed greatly. Having acquired a mistress he felt he could not introduce to his daughter, Gatien Phlipon became debauched and spent all his cash. Manon, whose mother had told her to marry, began to attract proposals.

At this point in the story her own view of herself – 'A sweet character, a strong soul, a very affectionate heart and looks which betokened all of this' – begins to differ from the opinion of modern historians, at least of Stanley Loomis in *Paris in the Terror*. 'Manon Phlipon', Loomis bluntly declares, 'was an intellectual as well as a social snob.' Ridiculing her rejection of a neighbourhood butcher – she despised 'men who made their fortunes by overcharging people in the market' – Loomis quotes the reaction of Monsieur Phlipon, who sighed at the refusal, saying he would like some grandchildren: 'Manon's father appears to have been a sensible man.' Yet it seems the prodigal father had by this time spent Manon's dowry on his unpresentable mistress. The man his erudite daughter finally decided to marry was Roland de la Platière, a liberal philosopher from Lyon sent to her by the Cannet sisters. Manon was reading *La Nouvelle Héloïse* when she met Roland: doubtless a fine portent. Her new suitor was 40, balding, of scrupulous probity, and an inspector of commerce with unsuccessful aspirations to nobility, his mother having been an aristocrat. He was also, in Loomis' view, a 'pedant and a bore of such proportions that even to read about him 170 years after his death is enough to deplete the room of its air'.[30] Or, in Sophie Cannet's less dismissive presentation: 'He is an enlightened man with excellent morals, and the only fault to be found in him is his great admiration for the Ancients at the expense of the Moderns, and a weakness for talking about himself.' But Madeleine Clemenceau-Jacquemaire, who quotes the Cannet letter, warns against condemning Roland as a bore. That *we* might find him so does not mean that Manon did.

The marriage did not take place for four years, owing to the objections of Manon's father and the dithering of the groom; when it did occur, it seems not to have been particularly jolly. Almost immediately Roland forbade Manon to see her female friends. In Michelet's phrase, it was to be 'a marriage of work'. Manon helped Roland prepare his technical writings, and together they produced a *Dictionary of Arts and Crafts*. 'He made me his copyist and his proof-reader. I performed this task with a humility at which I cannot help smiling ... but it came from the heart', explain the Memoirs. In October 1780 they produced a baby girl, Eudora, who grew up to be extremely pretty and quite indifferent to books, and was thus a disappointment to her mother.

After three years in Amiens they moved to near Lyon, spending time at Roland's inherited small property, the Clos de la Platière. Here Manon became an unofficial village doctor and acquired a taste for gardening. Often consulted by women of the village when doctors had given up, she was horrified by the hardships the villagers endured:

Nothing but poverty! ... these people suffer for whole months without stopping their work; they go to bed without a word ... never think of a doctor, or, fearing the expense of having one, call in the priest and in agony depart this life thanking God for having delivered them.[31]

These words were written in 1787. Two years later, on the eve of social change, Manon nursed Roland through a near-fatal illness, spending ten sleepless nights beside his bed. Scarcely had he recovered than incredible news arrived from Paris: Necker was dismissed, the Bastille taken, a national militia had been formed. The capital was in a ferment.

As a first patriotic offering the Rolands chopped their name in half; from Roland de la Platière it became plain and simple Roland. As a second contribution, Manon continued an exchange of letters begun in 1787 with Brissot, another future voice of the Gironde who presently invited her to contribute to his patriotic review. Having 'in youth, at study, wept for vexation at not being born a Spartan or a Roman', Manon dispatched to Brissot her 'Letters from a Roman Lady', full of enthusiastic plans for a federated France. 'The Revolution, imperfect as it may be, has altered the face of France. It has given her a character, and we had none before', she wrote in 1790. Brissot, who had thought that such exalted missives could not have been the work of a woman, was much impressed.

This epistolary friendship stood the Rolands in good stead on their visit to the capital in 1791. Now a Notable of Lyon, Roland was sent to Paris to negotiate the public assumption of his city's debt, which amounted to 39 million francs. One must suppose he was partly successful in this task since the state agreed to accept thirty-three and a half of those millions that same year. While in Paris the Rolands lived in the Hôtel Britannique on the rue Guénégaud, and their apartment – thanks to Brissot – rapidly became a meeting place for politicians of the Left. 'It was arranged that the deputies who were accustomed to meet and confer together should come to my house four times a week after the session at the Assembly and before that of the Jacobin club.' This was Manon's influential *salon*, one of the main focal points of the Gironde, the others being the Committee of the Place Vendôme, which boasted Vergniaud; and the *salon* of Mme Sophie de Condorcet, of atheist, Encyclopaedic tendencies, which boasted Pétion. But it was Mme Roland's *salon* which became the most brilliant and the most frequented. Even Robespierre came, although he seems to have liked Mme Roland about as much as she liked him: 'Robespierre ... spoke little, sniggered a great deal, uttered a few sarcasms and never gave an opinion. But on the morrow of these discussions he took care to appear in the Tribune of the Assembly and turn what he had heard his friends say at my house to good advantage', she wrote in a letter to a friend.[32] Manon herself was tactful in the conduct of her *salon*: 'Sitting by the window ... I would work or write letters . . . because that made me appear more distant to the matters discussed, but enabled me to listen.' Except for polite compliments on the arrival and departure of the gentlemen, she uttered not a word.

In March 1792 Loomis' boring pedant was named Minister of the Interior. He owed his elevation to the King's determination to appoint a Ministry which could, he thought, unite the Left; to the loyal offices of Brissot; and to a rule preventing deputies from becoming ministers, which meant that the chief members of the Girondin party – Brissot, Condorcet, Pétion and Vergniaud – were automatically disqualified. It is not impossible that his wife's discreet stage-managing had some effect on the appointment, since Clemenceau-Jacquemaire baldly remarks that she, and not Roland, was the real appointee. Certainly Mme Roland is credited with influencing the most controversial event of that ministry: its dismissal.

Manon was no monarchist. When she was 20 her mother had taken her to stay at Versailles for two days, in the apartment of a lady-in-waiting to Marie Antoinette.

> Two rooms, rather poorly furnished, and at the top of one an arrangement where a valet might sleep, the approach to them made detestable by the odour of the privies – such was the habitation that a Duke and Peer of France was proud to possess so as to be able to grovel more readily every morning at the rising of Their Majesties,

recollected the righteous Manon. Versailles, she told her mother, made her 'feel injustice and look upon absurdities'. Loomis even suggests that Manon's 'personal and unrelenting' hatred of the Queen resulted from 'some fancied slight' that took place during this visit. Her prison portrait of the King suggests no such grudge: Louis, she observed, was neither the total fool nor the good and kindly man he was made out to be, but an excellent geographer with a firm grasp of French history and foreign policy. Even so, she doubted his good faith with regard to the Republic, and had criticised the Jacobins for their 'softness' in not bringing him to trial after Varennes. Her deep mistrust resurfaced during the Girondin Ministry over the question of the royal veto. Whether or not her fears were justified is still subject to some debate.

In contrast to Michelet, who praises Manon's 'virile heart' and considers her 'the soul of the Gironde', Loomis views Manon's whole effect on the Girondins as a disaster: 'Her erudition, her considerable reading in the classics and those philosophic speculations to which her years of boredom and frustration had driven her, gave her the appearance, entirely false, of having a "man's mind",' he writes disparagingly of her *salon*. As for the Ministry, 'the rock on which it sank was that issue, always close to Mme Roland's enthusiastic heart, of a "federated France"' – that is, a France defended by a confederate army. The Rolands had ardently supported war with Austria. But when war came what France needed was not a bevy of autonomous departments, but strong and central authority. When

Mme Roland stubbornly insisted – via her spouse – on summoning a federal force to Paris, the King resisted with his infamous veto. When Mme Roland, via her spouse, penned him an 'insulting letter', he dismissed the Ministry. Ever critical of Manon's presumed obsession with upward mobility, Loomis damns her once again: 'women of her kind rarely learn that first lesson of statesmanship and of good manners: the control of one's temper' (Loomis, p.191). Manon's 'rudeness' was too much even for the 'patient' King. The somewhat royalist opinion here implied seems upheld by Simon Schama, who sees Louis as being impelled by his conscience to veto the Girondist proposals.

A different view is held by Paul de Roux in his edition of Manon's Memoirs. The Girondin Ministry placed the party in a difficult situation because it had only three portfolios (Servan and Clavière being the others) and could not therefore control the entire cabinet. At the same time the war was complicated by the duplicity of Dumouriez and Lafayette, who would have liked to help restore the King to his former absolute power; the Girondins had no such intention. When Louis XVI refused to sanction the deportation of refractory priests and to approve the formation of the new confederate guard near Paris, the three Girondists rebelled. Mme Roland's famous letter of 10 June, read in public by her husband, had the effect of unmasking the King's anti-constitutional bad faith. Dismissed, the three Girondins became, at least for a while, symbols of patriotic honesty. Manon had, Roux concludes, 'magisterially extracted her husband' from his ministerial predicament.

Where lies the truth of it? Manon's own text at least demonstrates her grand concept and her grasp of the crisis. 'Sire', it begins, 'the present plight of France cannot long endure. A critical state exists, wherein violence attains its height.' Placed in a position which compels him to speak the truth, 'Roland' bluntly does so: 'The French have given themselves a Constitution; it has made enemies and malcontents. The greater part of the nation wishes to uphold it, has sworn to defend it at the cost of its own blood, and joyfully accepted war as a means of making it secure.' A minority having resisted, combining all its efforts to secure the upper hand, 'an intestine struggle against the law' has been the dire result. The King, it is none too tactfully implied, belongs to that minority: 'Your Majesty enjoyed great prerogatives which you believed were the rights of Royalty. Brought up to the idea of preserving them, you naturally were not pleased to see them go.' This reaction had 'entered into the calculations of the Revolution's foes'.

Blaming the conduct of the nobility, the letter continues with a justification of measures taken against priests: 'In the clash of interests all emotions acquired the intensity of passion. Fatherland is no longer a mere word to be embellished by the imagination; it is a being to whom we have made sacrifices.' It is clear to the nation that its Constitution can only be effective if the King resolves fully on upholding it; already it is too late to temporise or withdraw. Criticising the King's action with regard to the priests and confederate camp, Manon proceeds to the epistle's most injudicious words: 'I know that the stern language of truth is rarely welcomed by the throne; I know too that it is because truth is almost never heard there that revolutions become necessary.' One cannot but recall that Roland had been appointed against the private advice of Manon's great friend Sophie Grandchamp, who feared the effects of Manon's candour and felt the Rolands, in their ignorance of the court, would fall into all manner of traps. Yet such words could scarcely have been employed in ignorance of their probable effect. The letter is Manon Roland's version of the Pascalian bet: either the King would see reason, or he would dismiss the Girondists and turn them into martyrs. Either way, Manon's moral loftiness would win.

Roland was not absent from the Ministry for long. Reappointed after the deposition of the King on 10 August, he was presiding at the Interior when there occurred that litmus test of revolutionary zeal, the September massacres. Manon was horrified, especially at the atrocities to women: 'If you knew the appalling details of the expeditions!' she wrote to a friend. 'Women brutally violated before being torn apart by these tigers, their bowels cut out, then carried like ribbons, human flesh devoured bleeding. ... You know my enthusiasm for the Revolution; well, now I'm ashamed of it.' Though probably referring to the rapes committed at the female prison of La Salpétrière, Manon may also have heard of the fate of Marie Gredeler, who had once kept an umbrella stand in the courtyard of the Palais-Royal. Gredeler had been tied to a stake and her bosom been cut off with a sabre; her feet were nailed to the ground while a fire was lit between her ankles.[33] Or Manon may have been thinking of the unfortunate fate of Mme de Lamballe, a woman she had hitherto detested as an appendage of the abhorred Marie Antoinette, but whose bodily integrity she would certainly respect: the Princess had been mutilated, bits of her eaten, and her severed legs shot from cannon. Whatever precise horrors Manon had in mind, the September massacres were the beginning of a long disillusion.

Who was responsible? The Rolands themselves are held partly to blame, if only because they had obstinately insisted on bringing to Paris the ardent *Marseillais* confederates from whom the Commune would recruit its murderers. So contends Loomis, who argues that 'The registers of the Commune ... indicate very clearly that the greater part of the assassins were hired, at twenty-four livres each, a sum equivalent to twenty-four dollars'. Dismissing leftist pleas of collective panic brought on by the nation's embattled state, of provocation and conspiracy indulged in by the royalist prisoners, Simon Schama is more scornful even than Loomis: 'chief among' those who looked away and did nothing to prevent the killings 'when they were incontrovertibly in a position to have done so' were, in his opinion, Danton and Roland. Mme Roland seems to have anticipated this judgement of posterity, since she claims in her memoirs that her husband did register a protest on the morning of 3 September. But by this time many of the massacres had already been committed; even the sympathetic Paul de Roux admits that no trace of Rolandian remonstrance was found before 4 September.

Manon herself had no doubts about who was behind the killings: she blamed Danton. 'Danton', she declared, 'is the secret chief behind the horde', the horde being Paris, 'city of lies, lust and blood' which had let the disaster happen. 'I no longer hope that liberty may be established among cowards, cold spectators to crimes that the courage of fifty men might have prevented.' She had always mistrusted Danton, repelled by his ugliness, his overt sexuality, his bull-like physique: 'I would look at this repulsive and atrocious face and ... could not apply the idea of a worthy man to such a countenance', she wrote from the admittedly jaundiced vantage-point of prison. Loomis claims this revulsion masked a latent attraction: 'Her final loathing of him ... seems to have been informed by passions not unlike those of lust', he muses. One cannot suppose that Manon herself could have approved this perception, but Loomis is on firmer ground when he remarks that Manon suspected Danton of wanting to become a dictator. She was additionally revolted by his tendency to enrich himself while preaching *sans-culottism*. Hence she rebuffed his political overtures, until the exasperated Minister of Justice joked publicly that Roland 'was not alone in his Ministry'. The result was a political quarrel that, again in Loomis' view, destroyed all possibility of unity between the Girondins and Danton, an alliance that might have saved the Gironde, thwarted Robespierre and, by extension, put a brake upon the Terror.

But the downfall of the Girondins and the onset of the Terror cannot be ascribed entirely to Manon's hormones and snobbishness. 'Historians', writes Madeleine Clemenceau-Jacquemaire, 'do not always approach Mme Roland with the serenity which befits them nor the neutrality which is her due'. They posthumously debate with her and ultimately resort to ridicule. Moreover, the favourite target of their wit – Manon's falsely masculine grasp of affairs – distracts the reader from the very real dithering of her masculine associates. 'This woman of sense, plucky-spirited, clear-minded, was to associate all her life with men who were incapable of considering the varied aspects of a case and coming to a definite decision' (Clemenceau-Jacquemaire, p. 34). Phlipon, and Roland himself, had dithered over her marriage; the Gironde would dither with regard to the King. Rather than blaming Manon for the Terror, Clemenceau-Jacquemaire argues that the Girondins, who helped Danton engineer the *coup* of 10 August, were so dazed by having overthrown the throne that Robespierre was able to take quick advantage of them.

Restored to the Interior, Roland had favoured the monarch's deposition rather than decapitation. At the same time his economic measures had been violently unpopular; his propagandist Bureau of Public Education, which a feverishly active Manon largely ran, had irritated his enemies. On the day of the King's execution Roland was deprived of his letters of credit for developing the 'civic mind'. Next day he resigned. Both he and Manon withdrew from politics, Roland wanting to return to the Clos de la Platière but obliged to remain in Paris intil his ministerial accounts were formally examined. Manon's remembrances of government are thoroughly disillusioned: 'I should like to see my garden and my trees again after so many fools!' she had exclaimed, early in the Revolution. In prison she wrote: 'I would never have believed, had not circumstances put me in a position to judge, how rarely one encounters a sound mind and a firm character; how few men, in consequence, are fit to deal in business and still less to govern.'

Her final months were both lightened and complicated by a new event: in late 1792 or early 1793, she fell in love with the Girondin Buzot. The passion was reciprocal. Manon remained, as she would say, virtuous, but high-mindedly told Roland of her feelings, only to be baffled by his jealous rage:

> I cherish my husband the way a sensitive girl reveres a virtuous priest, for whom she would sacrifice even her lover; but I have found the man who could be that lover. . . . My husband, rendered excessively sensitive by his affection and his pride, could not tolerate the thought of the slightest weakening of his authority. . . . I sacrificed myself to him, and we were unhappy.
>
> (*Mémoires*, p. 23)

Manon had chosen matrimory as her vocation; in today's terminology we would probably say this was the script she had written for herself. That she later viewed it as 'a strict bondage, a partnership in which the woman took upon herself the responsibility of two people's happiness' did not diminish her commitment. Disillusioned and work-weary she might be; nothing would bend her stoic rectitude. Nonetheless some sentimental change must have been apparent since Lanthenas, a friend from the early days of her marriage, grew jealous too, and vented his wrath to some third person, enabling the Jacobin newspapers to mount their usual character attack. 'I doubt if more horrors were printed about Antoinette, to whom they compare me and whose names they call me', she wrote that winter to Servan. Nor would later generations hold back their criticism. Sainte-Beuve disapproved of her blunt honesty towards Roland, and even Madeleine Clemenceau-Jacquemaire considers this unwelcome announcement the probable cause of Roland's resignation.

Spring came, and with it the Girondins' collapse. After her friends were forced into hiding Manon stayed in Paris. Eight times the painfully honest Roland submitted his accounts; the authorities still would not 'release' the ex-minister by deigning to examine them. Manon would not leave him, and that willed constancy cost her her life. Braver than anyone, in Michelet's glowing view, the Rolands 'did not condescend to move from their home', even for the safety of one night: 'Madame Roland feared neither death nor prison, but only an outrage to her person; to remain mistress of her destiny, she never went to sleep without a pistol at her bed-head.' When finally a deputation from the Commune came to the house Roland manfully refused this 'unlawful' arrest; the officers withdrew, allowing him to escape through the back door. Manon then found a cab and 'rushed to the Tuileries, with the heroic – rather than rational – intention of quashing his accusers, of striking the Mountain with lightning bolts of eloquence and courage, of wresting from the Assembly the freedom of her spouse'.[34] Her attempt failed, and Manon herself was arrested in the night.

She was already asleep when the officers returned. 'My maid came into the bedroom and announced that some gentlemen from the section were begging for my presence in the study.' Knowing what this meant, she emerged fully dressed. The servants and Manon's daughter Eudora began to cry. Chaos ensued as about 150 men tramped through the apartment for the rest of the night, affixing seals even to her piano. At seven o'clock next morning Manon was marched past a double row of guards and put into a coach. A few women called out 'To the guillotine with her!' Asked if she would like the blinds to be drawn, Manon declined: 'No, gentlemen, innocence, no matter how oppressed, never assumes an air of guilt.' Spartan words, impressive to the guards: she had, they said, more character than most of the arrested men.

The prison of the Abbaye housed her reasonably well, in a cell that would soon be occupied by Charlotte Corday, later on by Brissot. Disgusted by its filth, Manon set about scrubbing down the walls and 'establishing cleanliness upon my person'. Years before she had written to a friend that it was 'injudicious for women to despise housework, for it is better to do common things well than to show one's incapacity for higher matters'. But higher matters were not neglected either: sending for volumes of Plutarch, Hume and an English dictionary, Manon began composing her memoirs. As offended by the violation of liberty as by her own arrest she also wrote numerous letters to the authorities, complaining of her illegal detention. One day she was visited by a committee of *sans-culottes* who asked if she had any complaints. Yes, responded Manon, she was in prison. Was she ill or bored? No; she suffered from the injustice of being arrested for no reason. Ah, they replied, there was so much to see to in a revolution, one could not think of everything. A king, she rejoined, had once said something similar to a woman in his kingdom who shot back 'If you haven't time to treat me justly, you haven't time to be king!'

When not studying English and willing herself to eat ever smaller quantities of chocolate and green beans – prison, she thought, must be met with appropriate self-discipline – Manon went on writing protests about her unjust treatment and the absurd things being said about her in the newspapers. Unfortunately these letters may actually have given their recipients the idea of releasing her, the better to rearrest her with due and proper process. On 24 June 1793 she awoke, rather groggily, to be greeted by her maid who, weeping with joy, had come to fetch her home. Scarcely had Manon sprung from her carriage and mounted the stairs to her apartment than two men appeared from nowhere. 'Citizeness Roland? In the name of the law we arrest you.' She was taken to Sainte-Pélagie, prison of prostitutes and thieves.

This second detention tried her courage more; Manon termed it a bitter refinement of cruelty. She now spent hours at a time weeping and depressed and had to make a great effort to show composure to the world. The word DEATH, in capitals and with enormous margins, appears in her papers. Nonetheless she re-established her brave regimen, sending for a piano, studying English before lunch and drawing in the afternoon, besides finishing the memoirs. Though horrified to find herself penned in with 'creatures' such as a procuress and promiscuous women, she enjoyed the company of Mesdames Pétion and Montané, arrested for 'uncivic' behaviour following the disgrace of their husbands. She wrote passionately to Buzot, who had succeeded in getting letters to her; the terms of her missive finally reveal the shackles of domestic life falling free:

> July 7, [1793,] Sainte Pélagie
> You cannot imagine, my friend, the charms of prison, for here the heart alone takes one to account for the manner in which the moments have been employed. No diversions that pall, no arduous sacrifices ... none of those duties that are the more exacting because deemed worthy of respect by an upright heart; none of those contradictions between society's laws and prejudices, and nature's sweetest instincts. ... Restored to oneself, restored to truth ... one's soul is at liberty to assert its own integrity and, though apparently a captive, one can retrieve one's moral independence and employ it with an entirety that social relations usually impair. ... How I prize those shackles which grant me the freedom to love you unreservedly and to think continually of you.
>
> (Clemenceau-Jacquemaire, p. 290)

In late August she wrote 'Farewell! Never was man more loved by heart of women!' and advised him to leave for America. She also wrote farewells to her daughter and her servants. In mid-October it grew impossible for friends to visit her; on 24 October she was transferred to the Conciergerie. Manon had contemplated suicide through opium, but Bosc begged her to remain alive as long as possible, persuading her that death on the scaffold would better serve the cause of liberty.

The Girondins were tried in later October, a week or so after the execution of the Queen. No doubt this calendrical proximity was designed to lend credence to the principal charges brought against them: that they had always been devoted to royalism, and done their best to preserve it, through

Dumouriez and Lafayette. As Michelet observes, 'There was no hypocrisy about the trial: everyone could see at once that the intention was to kill them'. There was no defence attorney, and several of the accused were not allowed to speak. Sentences were read on 30 October and carried out next day. Mme Roland's young men mounted the scaffold singing the *Marseillaise*, its volume diminishing as, one by one, their heads were removed. One of them, Valazé, had previously committed suicide; his corpse was guillotined with the rest.

Manon herself was tried on 8 November. It was not a difficult task for Fouquier to connect her to the Girondins, so recently condemned; Manon had already been called upon to testify at their trial, and come away smarting at 'questions which outraged her honour' – presumably centring on her attachment to Buzot. Having chosen Chauveau-Lagarde for a lawyer she later decided not to compromise him; perhaps it suddenly seemed better to avoid parallels with the late Queen. When she attempted to speak she was interrupted, and told she could not take advantage of her own defence to praise the criminal Brissot and his friends. Turning to the public to appeal against the violence being done her, Mme Roland was greeted with insulting shouts and whistles. After the sentence she said simply, 'You judge me worthy of sharing the fate of the great men you have murdered. I shall try to show the same courage they did at the scaffold.'

Dusk was falling on the bitterly cold day when Manon was led out. Like Marie Antoinette, she wore white: an elegant bonnet, a dress of English muslin, set off by a black velvet belt. She had not wanted Sanson to cut her splendid hair, but when he delicately explained the necessity, she plunged her hands into the thick chestnut curls exclaiming 'At least leave enough to show my head to the people, if they ask to see it!' Unlike Marie Antoinette, she did not die alone. A terrified forger named Lamarche made the journey with her. Perhaps grateful for the distraction he provided, Manon now devoted her energies to putting a smile on the trembling creature's face, encouraging him to eat something and complimenting him on his Roman appearance after the final haircut. He stepped into the tumbril before her, and she reproached him: 'You're not very gallant, Lamarche; a Frenchman must never forget his behaviour to a woman.' On the Pont Neuf the cart drove past the red and white house where she had spent her childhood. An old friend, Sophie Grandchamp, was waiting to wave goodbye: Manon was still 'fresh, calm and smiling', still encouraging Lamarche. When they arrived at the scaffold the terrified man collapsed and was seized with violent shivers. Manon looked at him with pity. The only thing she could do was ask Sanson if he could be beheaded first – sparing him the sight of her own blood – and Sanson agreed, ignoring his own orders.

'Like a white Grecian Statue, serenely complete, she shines in that black wreck of things;– long memorable', enthuses Thomas Carlyle. Thus Mme

Roland entered history, entirely conscious she was about to do so. She had asked for pen and paper to be brought in order to record 'the strange thoughts that were rising in her'; this was denied. Soft and white against the stark trees of the Tuileries she had turned to the great colossus of Liberty, gravely addressing it: 'O Liberty, so many crimes committed in your name!' Pushed towards 'the terrible *bascule*' Manon resisted long enough to bow 'to the emblem that had been her idol'; a moment later, as Sanson himself records in Roman style, 'she had lived'. Manon and the statue were as one.

The news was brought to Roland at his hiding-place near Rouen. He took an isolated path, stopped beneath an oak and fell upon a sword, three times. The blade broke off, remaining in the wound; probably his death was slow and painful. A note found with his body exhorted passers-by to 'respect the remains . . . of a man who died as he lived, virtuous and honest'. Another note explained 'Not fear, but indignation, made me leave my retreat, on learning that my wife had been murdered'. Manon Roland's manuscripts were hidden in a rock by her friend Bosc until they could be published. The same Bosc then acted as guardian to Eudora Roland until the time of her marriage.

Not all accounts of Manon's death glow with antique virtue. 'Michelet idealised her beyond measure', complains Gérard Walter, who has scarcely a good word for any woman of the Revolution. 'She died admirably, indeed; but even there, with her white dress and her fine hair falling on her shoulders, she posed for posterity as a perfect tragic actress.'[35] Of course the splendid hair had previously been cut, and the courage needed to strike Plutarchian postures in the shadow of the scaffold was probably greater than Walter seems to imagine. Many guillotined women were quite aware that they were posing, not merely for the largely hostile crowd, but also for posterity: it was all that was left to them. They owed it to themselves, as participants in the momentous event of Revolution, to leave an image that would linger. Thus we have Charlotte Corday calling for her portrait and standing to be seen in the tumbril; Marie Antoinette in white, sitting on her plank as if daring it to be a throne; Olympe de Gouges sniffing a bouquet, speaking out on politics; Manon Roland, asking how her severed head would look and bowing to a statue. The semantics of demeanour and attire were still within their control – that, and their pride. 'Posing' was more than a theatrical whim; it was the willed completion of a life.

Nor would Mme Roland's domestic existence probably meet with the approval of some modern feminists. Compared to Olympe de Gouges she was extraordinarily unliberated. Her comments on male superiority, the sacrifices made to matrimony, her willed self-effacement while discreetly making known her remarkable abilities – all this is disappointing to anyone who favours a direct frontal assault on male prerogative. And yet the Jacobin journals of the day found Manon far too assertive. Hébert's targeted readership was undoubtedly meant to see resemblances between the power behind the throne that was Marie Antoinette and the power behind the ministry that was Marie-Jeanne Phlipon; thus Manon in the tumbril was hailed with as many hostile cries as the detested Austro-bitch. An article addressed to Republican Women in *Le Moniteur* of 19 November 1793 drew quite explicit parallels between the recently felled females and their unfeminine behaviour. Marie Antoinette was castigated for 'sacrificing her spouse' to the Habsburg ambitions, and Olympe de Gouges criticised for her federalism, her exalted imagination and her wish to behave as a 'man of the state'; the law had 'punished this conspiratress for forgetting the virtues appropriate to her sex'. Mme Roland was termed a 'monster', whose desire to be learned made her, too, forget the virtues of her sex, a lapse which, 'always dangerous', brought about her execution. The implicit virility of three vastly different women, of differing opinions and beliefs, was thus held up to the public as an example of behaviour likely to lead to Dame Guillotine. Remembering that Charlotte Corday was posthumously chided by the Revolutionary Tribunal for her masculine ways, one begins to wonder whether the all-important popular imagination was not being subliminally groomed to find 'masculinity' in women a capital offence. If this were true, decapitation by the Widow would be symbolically quite apt.

On the other hand women were also guillotined who, by the standards of the time, led lives of utter femininity. Their significance in terms of revolution resides less in their effect on politics than in their effect on public guillotining, a process which, in the minds of one sentimental historian, they managed utterly to subvert. A few weeks after the execution of Manon Roland there died a woman who had risen from the obscurity of part-time whorehood – it was said – to the ambiguous and splendid state of mistress to the King, a woman whose only claim to masculinity in an otherwise matchlessly feminine career was that she had once been painted in hunting clothes by Drouais, a woman who came to represent, perhaps even more than the dread Marie Antoinette, the excesses of the *ancien régime*. This woman, to the great glee of her detractors, died extremely badly. She was the Comtesse du Barry.

THE SLEEP OF INNOCENCE, OR WIVES, WHORES AND PARRICIDE

An accomplished courtesan is but she who can conform as closely as possible to man's image of the perfect woman. Her function is to alleviate boredom, to amuse, beguile and sympathise, as much as it is to arouse and assuage passion. She is what wives are supposed to be but after a few years of marriage are not. She is a pearl beyond price.

So observes Stanley Loomis early in his biography of Jeanne Bécu, Comtesse du Barry, a courtesan he terms fitted for her august calling by birth, training and inclination – and a character he seems to find infinitely more sympathetic than the ministerial Manon Roland.

In terms of birth, Jeanne was the illegitimate daughter of Anne Bécu, a seamstress who apparently supplemented her meagre earnings with occasional ventures into paid love. Born in Vaucouleurs in 1743 she was of father unknown, though a certain Brother Angel – a monk named Gomard – is thought the most likely candidate. When the child was five her mother moved to Paris, becoming cook to a rich contractor there; struck by the 'extraordinary beauty and breeding' of the tiny girl, Anne Bécu's new employer decided to sponsor her. Aided by his own mistress (herself a famous courtesan) he arranged for little Jeanne to be brought up in a convent. She remained at the convent of Saint-Aure until she was 16, emerging with an education probably superior to that of Marie Antoinette but a future less assured. Apprenticed first to a hairdresser, she found herself in legal trouble when the master tried to seduce his ravishing *élève*. Next, she became companion to Mme de la Garde, resident of the Château de Corneuve and widow of a tax collector. Here again scandal struck. Mme de la Garde's two sons – and probably one of her daughters-in-law – began too warmly to admire the new companion. Though court spies were later unable to rend the 'veil of reticence' drawn across the whole affair, Jeanne found herself dismissed.

Jeanne's next employment was in a millinery shop, the Maison Labille, where she stayed until she was 19. It would be asserted at Versailles that she was a woman of the streets during those years, but evidence was never found. A libertine piece penned in 1775 by Pidansat de Mairobert purportedly quoted a description of the future Mme du Barry's charms as set down by a well-known procuress, Mme Gourdan:

> I saw her naked as she was born! I drew closer. I saw a ravishing body, a throat ... well, my hands have caressed a good many throats in their time, but never one of this elasticity, of this shape, of this irresistible softness. The plunge of her breasts threw me into an ecstasy; her dazzling white thighs, her delicious little buttocks – the Sculptors themselves have never produced anything more perfect. As for the rest, I was connoisseur enough to realise that the *pucelage* was in a very equivocal condition ... but with the application of certain astringents it might be sold a few more times!

The entire scene is apparently pure invention but as a curiosity piece it bears comparison with similar examinations as conducted by an another equally well-known connoisseur:

At the beginning, when I take a look, it's a question of seeing if the silhouette and the gestures are pretty. Then there was a disagreeable moment. I said 'I'm sorry about this unpleasantness but I have to ask you to get undressed, because I can't talk about you unless I see you.' Believe me, I was embarrassed, just as they were, but it had to be done, not out of voyeurism, not at all – I don't like *les dames horizontales*.[36]

The lady evincing such professional reticence and objectivity in the mid-twentieth century is Mme Claude, granting an interview to the London *Sunday Times*. No sculptures, no ecstasy. 'I could judge their physical qualities', she said. 'I could judge if she was pretty, intelligent and cultivated, but I didn't know how she was in bed. So I had some boys, good friends, who told me exactly. I would ring them up and say, "There's a new one". And afterwards they'd ring back and say, "Not bad", "Could be better", or "*Nulle*". And I would sometimes have to tell the girls what they didn't know.'

In the case of Jeanne Bécu the significant educator seems not to have been the ambivalent Mme Gourdan, but Comte Jean du Barry, a rake on a spectacular scale whose eccentricity it was to instruct beautiful young girls in aristocratic niceties before selling them off to his fashionable friends. Enthusiastic about his protégée's potential, du Barry covered her with diamonds, kept her as his hostess and eventually sent her on a business errand to Versailles. The court was in deep mourning, for Queen Marie Leczinska had just died. Jeanne du Vaubernier, as she now called herself, was hidden somewhere in the palace. Even so the widowed Louis XV saw her and was instantly entranced. By the end of the month her presence was desired at court.

To attain to the honour of being publicly disgraced by His Majesty – who seems from the outset to have wished her to be his titular Royal Mistress – it was necessary for Jeanne to be married. Jean du Barry already had a wife, and could not oblige; he remembered that he had a brother, Guillaume, who lived with his mother and two sisters in remotest Levignac. The brother and sisters were hastily summoned to Paris and the wedding took place on 23 July 1768. Rewarded for his part in the ceremony with a pension of 5,000 livres, Guillaume returned to Levignac. The new Comtesse du Barry said goodbye to her husband and then proceeded to join the King at Compiègne, at Fontainebleau, and even at Versailles, where she was ultimately installed in apartments of some opulence. 'From the ceiling of the central room blazed a lustre of rock crystal which had cost sixteen thousand livres', writes Stanley Loomis of her wages of sin;

> Two commodes faced each other, one in gold lacquer of a kind no longer found on the face of the earth, from which two baboons rose in gilded relief; the other ornamented with five placques of Sèvres porcelain which nowhere had their peer. Marbles, bronzes, porcelains, crystals and lacquers were gathered together in this 'asylum

of voluptuous pleasure' in a profusion and selection such as had never before been seen.

Such an asylum was not created overnight. Mme du Barry's rise to eminence was marked by two small wars, waged in some part by the King: the battle for her formal presentation to himself – necessary, in a titular Royal Mistress – and her struggle to be recognised by Marie Antoinette, then Dauphine of France.

Both events were marked by aristocratic feuding of virulent intensity. Fortunes rose and faltered with the question of the presentation. The Duc de Choiseul – the King's chief minister and former ambassador to Austria – had risen to prominence with Mme du Barry's predecessor, the late Marquise de Pompadour. Choiseul energetically opposed the new favourite, even proposing an alternative candidate for the King's bed: his own sister, Béatrix de Choiseul-Stainville, with whom he was said to be incestuously linked. At the same time he mobilised the writers of malicious pamphlets, generating almost as much mud as would soon be hurled at Marie Antoinette. But Mme du Barry was supported by the Duc de Richelieu – the libertine, aptly named First Gentleman of the King's Bedchamber – who managed to defuse much of the worst gossip. Richelieu even succeeded in finding a sponsor of impeccably noble quarterings to present her in the person of his aunt, the Comtesse de Béarn. Thus, after several false starts, the King was able to announce that on 22 April 1769 he would formally receive the Comtesse du Barry. For this momentous occasion she was late. The irritated monarch was about to order the assembly dismissed when horses' hooves were heard to clatter in the courtyard below. After a further eternity of waiting Richelieu flung open the door and announced to a silent, spellbound room the Comtesses de Béarn and du Barry.

> Blazing in a half million dollars' worth of diamonds she advanced with that peculiar lilting movement which was the stamp of Versailles, and made a deep curtsy before the enamoured Sovereign. Her hair, after the custom of these ceremonies, was powdered to a snowy white that brought forth the fragile rose of her skin and the sapphire of the half-closed, slightly slanting eyes . . .
>
> (Loomis, 1959, p. 66)

So relates Stanley Loomis. Less enthusiastic was the eye-witness account of Mme de Genlis, whose own aunt was received at the same time. 'Never had there happened anything quite so scandalous', wrote Mme de Genlis, herself the mistress of the Duc de Chartres at the time. '. . . This with many other instances of unparalleled undecency cruelly degraded Royalty and consequently contributed to bring about the Revolution.'

Mme du Barry's reception at court probably did not cause the Revolution, but her struggle with the new Dauphine did have political consequence.

DAME GUILLOTINE

Spurred on by Richelieu and his nephew d'Aiguillon, Mme du Barry managed to obtain an invitation to the pre-nuptial dinner given for Marie Antoinette in May 1770 – an event it was felt she could not decently attend. There, seated at a table with the royal family and persons of great rank, the young Archduchess beheld Mme du Barry and wondered who she was. Instructed by the embarrassed Dauphin and his maiden, spiteful aunts, Marie Antoinette conceived a shocked dislike for this woman with her murky past and decided to cut her publicly whenever she could. Versailles tittered gleefully; Mme du Barry's private humiliation grew. She appealed to the King. Thinking to restore domestic harmony, the monarch dismissed Choiseul, who had been partly responsible for engineering the Austrian alliance and was now encouraging the Dauphine in her icy blue-eyed silence. The court of Vienna went into shock. Maria Theresa wrote letters exhorting her wayward daughter to a more diplomatic comportment. The King spoke strong and private words to the Dauphine's Mme Etiquette and to the Austrian Ambassador: in vain. Finally Maria Theresa put aside her remaining moral delicacy and bluntly ordered Marie Antoinette to humour the King.

By this time it was New Year's Day 1772. Among the courtiers thronging to pay their respects to the royal family were seen Mme du Barry and the Duchesse d'Aiguillon. Slowly they advanced down the receiving line; they reached the Dauphine. Would she speak? She did. After addressing a few words to Mme d'Aiguillon, Marie Antoinette turned more or less towards Mme du Barry and said 'There are a lot of people at Versailles today'. It was done. The King, the Comtesse and the party of d'Aiguillon went mad with delight. Vienna breathed with relief: the alliance had been saved. Shortly thereafter, Maria Theresa's armies marched into Poland, a country she had decided to partition with Frederick of Prussia and the Empress Catherine. The move would normally have been opposed by France, but the tacit price of Marie Antoinette's stupendously banal remark was Louis XV's silence. 'Not only was Marie Antoinette humbled', Zweig remarks, 'but a whole country had thereby been laid low.'[37] The trifling war of etiquette had permitted a great political crime.

Far from gloating at her victory the essentially good-natured Mme du Barry now tried to make amends. The Comtesse had fought for the Dauphine's word without animosity, merely as a salve to wounded pride; having obtained it, she seems to have been rather ashamed. Quite possibly, she realised the folly of her deed: the King might suddenly die, leaving her vulnerable to the disfavour of the future Queen – a *lettre de cachet* and the Bastille. She took to attending Marie Antoinette's evening parties, even though the Habsburg hostess never spoke to her again; she offered her enormously expensive gifts of diamonds, that being the one thing they had in common. All this was disdained. Many years passed before Marie Antoinette, herself wounded by *libelles* and other blows of fate, began to relent.

In fact Mme du Barry was by nature kind. She did not, like Mme de Pompadour, use her influence as mistress to meddle in statecraft, and when she did ask favours of the King it was rarely for herself. Early in her curious tenure she had heard about a young woman condemned to death for concealment of pregnancy, and written furiously to Chancellor Maupeou: 'I understand nothing of your laws; but they are barbaric and run counter to all reason and humanity when they condemn to death a poor creature because she gives birth to a still-born child without having given formal notification.' The girl, Mme du Barry reasoned, was either unaware of the law, or else failed to carry it out through 'a very natural modesty'. Her thoughts on the subject are not unlike those of Voltaire, whom she admired enormously. His writings lined her library along with volumes of history, Shakespeare, Homer, Ovid, Villon, Pascal and Montaigne – and numerous pornographers.

Soon after the matter of the still-born baby she was approached on behalf of an elderly and hopelessly impoverished couple, the Comte and Comtesse Pé de Louësmes. Poorer even than Charlotte Corday's parents they had mortgaged their castle and lost it to a wealthy tradesman. When he came to claim it, they had opened fire. In the course of a two-day siege Mme Pé de Louësmes had shot and killed a policeman before being hurt herself; she and her husband were condemned to be beheaded. Wishing to maintain the law, the King rejected all appeals. In despair the Pé de Louësmes daughters turned to Mme du Barry, who duly fell at the King's feet and threatened never to get up again. 'I am delighted, Madame, that the first favour you ask of me should be an act of mercy', murmured the monarch, raising her. On another occasion she interceded to save a soldier who, in an access of homesickness, had run off to his farm; the wretch had been condemned for desertion. But her generosity was most apparent in her treatment of an implacable foe, the Duc de Choiseul, who found himself faced with financial ruin after his dismissal. Made aware of his plight, the Comtesse approached the King – no easy task, for he now loathed the former minister – and succeeded in obtaining a reasonable pension. 'Neither I nor Madame de Choiseul said a word of thanks to her', wrote the indebted Duke. 'The injustice and above all the harshness with which we were treated exempted us from any gratitude' (Loomis, 1959, p. 100).

In 1774 Mme du Barry was dismissed from court, though not by Marie Antoinette. That April Louis XV contracted smallpox, and Mme du Barry's reign – the warm-heartedness, the diamonds, the admiration for Voltaire – abruptly reached its end. Bloated and disfigured the King lay at Versailles in a state of living putrefaction, attended by his daughters by day, and Mme du Barry at night, until it was decided that His Majesty should repent him of his sinful worldly ways and repudiate the Mistress before receiving absolution. She was sent to d'Aiguillon's castle at Rueil. That evening the King asked for her as usual. 'She is gone, Sire.' 'What, already?' sighed the King, a tear on his cheek. Before expiring he signed a letter exiling to a safe distance from court the one person he still cared for – presumably to protect her from the wrath of the new Queen. Escorted by two inspectors of police, Mme du Barry was removed to the fortified Abbey of Pont-aux-Dames in Brie, where her captor nuns were pleasantly surprised to find their scandalous charge possessed a sweet and kindly face and almost saintly disposition. Perhaps that was what had endeared her to the world-weary King.

By slow degrees her exile was rescinded. Joined in the convent by her sister-in-law, the loyal Chon du Barry, she was presently allowed to move to the estate of Saint-Vrain and, in November 1776, to her own castle of Louveciennes – the most magnificent of many gifts received from Louis XV. Here she lived quietly until Revolution struck, receiving friends both old and new: Elisabeth Vigée-Lebrun came, and painted her three times. Drawn by curiosity foreign dignitaries came too: Marie Antoinette's brother, the Emperor Joseph II, went to Louveciennes during the momentous journey to Versailles in which he persuaded Louis XVI to undergo a small and painful operation. Though not to the Emperor's Germanic taste, Mme du Barry was still a beautiful woman, unaffected, slightly plump, lightly clad even on the coldest winter day, her radiant health sustained by vigorous walks. In 1781 she embarked on a passionate, affectionate liaison with the Duc de Brissac, a liberal and dreamy sort of aristocrat who looked with generous intent upon the coming social change. Inspired by her benevolent lover, Mme du Barry emerged slightly from retirement and began going to the opera.

Mme du Barry's kindness did not cease upon her loss of power. During her two years at the Château de Saint-Vrain she showered gifts upon the poor girls of the village, attending to their needs as best she might; these 'tactful acts of charity', as Loomis calls them, continued at Louveciennes. 'To this day', wrote Mme Vigée-Lebrun in her memoirs,

> I can remember her anger when she visited a woman who had just given birth and who had nothing in the house. 'What!' she cried. 'You have neither linen nor soup nor wine?' 'Alas, nothing, Madame.' As soon as we had returned to the Château Madame du Barry summoned her housekeeper and other servants who had not obeyed her orders. I can't describe to you the indignation she was in. She had them make up a parcel of linen on the spot and bring it at once to the poor woman, along with soup and Bordeaux wine.
>
> (Loomis, 1959, p. 219)

Her villagers were grateful for such deeds, and for a while their gratitude deflected Revolution's wrath. But acts of individual kindness do not always mollify the architects of social reform; they have the ring of charity, demeaning to the recipient. Mme du Barry was not intellectually equipped to conceive the abstract kindness of a new order. Would it have been less mutually demeaning not to send the woman soup?

DEATH COMES TO THE MAIDEN

For a while, after July 1789, Mme du Barry lived as she had before, and as she might have continued to do, had it not been for the curious and monumental theft of her jewels. This occurred at Louveciennes on the night of 10 January 1791 while she was staying with Brissac in Paris. Discovering the theft the Comtesse was unwise enough to publish a list of the lost items; the disastrous inventory – several pages long and fabulous in cost and content – had the effect of bringing her once-notorious name before a restless, starving populace, attracting the righteous fury of the revolutionary journalists. Even worse, the jewels began turning up in London and the Comtesse had to go and identify them, thereby incurring suspicion of being a go-between for the French court and the emigrated royalists who had flocked to England. Mme du Barry's conduct did nothing to dispel such notions: she moved in the highest circles of English society and entertained the exiles. Like the Princesse de Lamballe, she would have done better to remain in London, but was drawn back to France by her devotion to Brissac and his daughter, Pauline de Mortemart. By the time she returned from her third visit the royal family had concluded its inept flight to Varennes and was confined to the Tuileries. A new Constitutional Guard had been created, and for its commander the King had chosen Brissac.

This honour, the last the monarch could bestow, cost Brissac his life. On 30 May 1792 the guard was disbanded and a warrant issued for the 'royalist' Brissac's arrest. Taken to Orléans and imprisoned there for several months, he was brought back to Paris with fifty-three other prisoners in a convoy of ten carts. It was the week of the September massacres. In the streets of Versailles the crowd broke through the escort and fell upon the carts. Brissac was cut to pieces and his flesh devoured. His head was brought to Louveciennes and hurled through a window, coming to rest almost at Mme du Barry's feet; like Marie Antoinette in a parallel predicament, she fainted.

A month later she left again for London, sharing a house with Brissac's daughter. This time her activities, although curtailed by deep mourning, were unabashedly royalist. She gave the Archbishop of Rouen 200,000 livres, to be given to the more penniless *émigrés*. She ordered her bankers, the Vandenyvers of Paris, to advance an equal sum to the Duc de Rohan-Chabot, who may have used the money to help fund the Vendée uprising. In January she went to a funeral service for the recently beheaded King – an indiscretion duly noted by the Jacobin spies in London. In March, for reasons nobody seems able to divine, Mme du Barry returned once more to France, only to find that Louveciennes had been placed under seal and she herself declared an outlaw. Aware of her reputation for benevolence Lavallery, vice-president of the department, returned the castle to her care. But before long this same Lavallery was denounced to the Committee of Public Safety and committed suicide by drowning in the Seine. In vain did fifty-nine 'citizens of Louveciennes' draw up a petition on her behalf:

We have seen her in every kind of weather come to the help of the sick and the poor. Since the Revolution we have also seen her conform to every law, making financial contributions either obligatory or voluntary.

On 22 September Mme du Barry was arrested for incivism and 'aristocratic leanings' – an odd phrase, that neatly circumvented her plebeian origins – and taken to Sainte Pélagie. Meanwhile the man who had arrested her, a citizen Greive, took up residence at Louveciennes. (Loomis thinks he was driven by a peculiar obsession, and probably raped her while conducting the arrest.) Once again the villagers got up a petition, which Greive countered by arresting her Paris bankers. On 4 December she was transferred to the Conciergerie. Two days later, in company with the Vandenyvers, she was brought to trial.

Predictably, Fouquier-Tinville began with a character assassination, serving up Mme du Barry's undeniably colourful past. Then he accused her of sheltering and protecting priests and former aristocrats, of inventing a jewel robbery as pretext for espionage in London, of advancing sums of money to the counter-revolution, of attending a memorial service for the Tyrant – most of which was true. The Vandenyvers he charged with being 'enemies of France'. Mme du Barry did not totally abandon her aplomb: when one of her less loyal servants testified against her, she explained she had dismissed him not for being a good patriot, as he made out, but because he had stolen quantities of china. After Lafleurtrie and Chauveau-Lagarde concluded an inadequate defence, Fouquier rose once more.

> The vile conspiratress who stands before you today was able to live in the lap of luxury acquired by shameless debauchery.... The Liberty of the people was a crime in her eyes.... This example, joined to many others, proves more and more that lewdness and evil morals are the greatest enemies of Liberty and the happiness of the people.

Together with the three Vandenyvers 'the woman Dubarry' was now condemned 'to the penalty of death', as much, it would seem, for her shameless debauchery as for having given 400,000 livres to the enemies of the Republic. The Messalina of the People collapsed on hearing the verdict and was borne fainting to her cell by two gendarmes. Her execution had been set for the next day.

That Mme du Barry died badly cannot be disputed. Most victims of the Terror were killed immediately after judgement; Mme du Barry had had a night to think. Next morning, in an extremity of terror, she tried to bargain for her life. In a scene reminiscent of pre-revolutionary confessions at the Hôtel de Ville she offered to reveal the whereabouts of treasure hidden at Louveciennes if they would spare her life. The officials sent by the Committee of Public safety apparently agreed. Scarcely had they done so than the executioner arrived to cut her hair, so that 'to a natural dread of decapitation was now added the suspicion that a terrible mistake had been made'. As soon as Sanson appeared with his aides Mme du Barry began to scream 'No, I don't want to go!', resisted the cutting of the hair and wept all the way to the scaffold while the Vandenyvers and Sanson himself tried to give her courage. The order was for her to die last, but in view of the state she was in Sanson decided to guillotine her first; feeling the hands of the aides on her she revived and began to struggle, so that it took four men three minutes to strap her to the plank. Then, as he succinctly adds, 'we executed the others'.

It was possibly her finest hour. According to Sanson she had appealed to the crowd along the route: 'Good citizens, deliver me, I'm innocent! I'm one of the people, like you! Don't let me die!' And the crowd, initially as hostile and as numerous as it had been for Marie Antoinette, for Manon Roland, the crowd had stopped hurling insults; many of its number bowed their heads. During the scuffle at the scaffold spectators fled in all directions 'like a routed army'; her screams, Sanson felt, must have been heard across the Seine. It is customary to see this undignified conduct as proof of Mme du Barry's common origins, as contrasted with the icy aplomb of aristocrats and the noble posturing of bourgeois republicans. But Mme du Barry was concerned neither with pride nor posterity; she seems, simply, to have loved being alive. Her desperate struggles confronted the crowd with the equally desperate immediacy of mortality as no noble sang-froid ever could; indeed, the more composed the victim, the easier it was to project hate, to treat the stricken heads as stone. Had all condemned persons protested as she did, Sanson felt, the Terror could never have gone on as long. Michelet considers her the Terror's most unworthy victim; yet, because of the visceral pity she aroused, 'people remembered that death was something after all'. Mme du Barry's subversion of the guillotine was arguably her great achievement.

If a Queen and an ex-Royal Mistress were depicted at their trials as whores, one should not overlook the use made of the genuine article. In October 1793 Chaumette, *procureur* of the Commune, had the inspired idea of bringing two prostitutes to trial with Marie Antoinette. 'The spectacle of three whores sharing the same tumbril would provide an eloquent symbolic statement of the sans-culotte view of the ex-queen', as Simon Schama puts it. Perhaps Chaumette, soon to achieve equal renown for his anti-Christian activities, was thinking it would also provide a feminised parody of another famous death, in which a noted male was killed between two thieves. Whatever the case, whoredom was on his mind: on 1 October he had delivered a ringing indictment of public prostitutes, drawing protests from the women whose only means of subsistence was threatened by his zeal. On 10 October he instructed the police to deal most severely with 'these monsters, the shame of their sex and the scourge of society'. Presumably they did so, for a few days after Mme du Barry's death Sanson noted that 'Chaumette is hounding the prostitutes excessively'. Strange to relate, the various judiciary committees decided Chaumette's plan for the execution of the Queen was too extreme; but they did not entirely give up on the two prostitutes. In December 1793 Claire Sévin, widow Loriot, and Catherine Halbourg, known as Eglé, found themselves on trial for entertaining 'conspiratorial relations' with Marie Antoinette. Condemned, Claire Sévin excused herself from the scaffold by virtue of pregnancy. Eglé disdained this solution. 'Go ahead, tell them your state', she said to her colleague. 'As for me, if I've got to croak I'd rather do it right away.'[38]

These were not Eglé's only words to the authorities. A cheerful royalist, she had been wont to criticise the new régime to anyone who would listen, on street corners. In the social promiscuity prevailing at the Conciergerie she had encountered the Duc de Châtelet, weeping and tottering with fright, and berated him for his unaristocratic bearing: 'You must learn, Monsieur le Duc, that those who have no name acquire one here, and those who have a name must know how to wear it' – causing those who overheard to think she was a 'person of quality'.[39] Acknowledging her royalist leanings at the trial, Eglé decided to hoist her accusers on the petard of class distinction.

> Me, accomplice of the person you call widow Capet and who was very much the Queen, me who earned my living on street corners and would never even have made the humblest maid in her kitchen, that's really worthy of a bunch of crooks and imbeciles like you.
>
> (Schama, p. 795)

This outburst made one juror think she must be drunk, but Eglé riposted that she meant every word. She leapt into the tumbril with alacrity, sharing that vehicle with two aristocrats – Geneviève and Madeleine Vernin d'Aigrepont, convicted of corresponding with an *émigré* – so that Chaumette's original symbolism was in some measure reversed. Nor did her verve diminish in the cart, whence she saw fit to yell back insults at anyone who insulted her. 'Farewell, friends', she called from the scaffold. 'Long live Louis XVII!'

According to police reports spectators were 'indignant' at Eglé's unrepentant conduct. Were they the same onlookers as those dismayed by Mme du Barry's piteous appeals? From the Sanson memoirs it would seem that crowds identical in composition showed extremely different responses to different executions. This impression is also conveyed by Daniel Arasse. Spectators, he says, were capable of two basic reactions: 'hatred or vengeful joy, exploding very visibly'. Occasionally a third response was manifest, that of the public's 'sublime enjoyment'. This latter, lofty mood pervaded the last ride of Charlotte Corday; also that of Manon Roland, for whom the public was plunged into 'admiration and a sublime, profound silence'.[40] Unhappily this pleasing picture does not entirely tally with the accounts of the actual executioner, who describes a group of determined inveighers running alongside Charlotte's tumbrel hurling insults; as for the 'sublime, profound silence' accorded Mme Roland, Sanson asserts that 'the Queen, Charlotte Corday, the Girondins – none had been as subject as Madame Roland to the fury of what was known as the people' (Sanson, t.iv, p. 307). But in their comments on female executions as barometers of public reaction both Sanson and Arasse are far outdone by the gallant and romantic Michelet. For Michelet purely and simply blames the spectacle of female death for the demise of the Republic.

How could this have been? Michelet anticipates and answers the question in a long and most peculiar footnote. 'Against women', he declares, 'there is no serious means of repression.' Women corrupt everything; even putting them in prison is a risky undertaking. But as for exposing them on the scaffold, 'a government which commits that folly guillotines itself'. The fault lies with nature; in perpetuating the species nature has given rise to the paradox – 'absurd at first glance' – that women are eminently *responsible* but they are not *punishable*. Why is this? Because young women make one think of love and fertility; old women have grey hair and invariably remind one of one's mother. As for pregnant women, they pervert the law altogether, for to strike them makes the law seem like an 'enemy of God'. At this point Michelet seems to remember the protests of republican feminists, for he suddenly admits that women themselves may say they 'want to act, and suffer the consequences of their acts'. This problem is dismissed by a return to nature; it is not men's fault, he goes on, if nature has made women 'infirm, periodically ill' and thus unsuited for certain functions of political society. Even so, they may have political influence – often, he concludes, with calamitous results.

Having defined women's function exclusively in terms of procreation, Michelet now resorts to a negative metaphor of birth: women's bad influence 'has appeared in our revolutions. It is generally women who have caused them to abort'. For women's intrigue, women's deaths, 'often deserved', have served as potent aids to counter-revolution. Michelet's abortion image is all the more interesting if set against Daniel Arasse's depiction of the guillotine as midwife to the Republic: according to Arasse the death of counter-revolutionaries (including women) engenders the Republic, whereas for Michelet the death of counter-revolutionary women aborts that Republic. But Michelet does not finish here. Strategically inserted in his narration at the point where things begin to go awry for the Jacobins, the long footnote is indeed a scholium to Michelet's startling assertion as to the effect of female execution: 'The impression grew and grew. The most elementary politics should have abolished the death penalty for women. It was killing the Republic.'[41] The women whose deaths most drove him to this utterance were Mme du Barry – 'poor aging daughter of the flesh, who felt death beforehand in her flesh . . . arousing all the fibres of brute pity' – and Lucile Desmoulins, 'the young, courageous, charming wife of good Camille'.

'I shall say just this of my wife', declared Camille Desmoulins to a cynical colleague, 'I had always believed in the immortality of the soul, but my marriage is so happy I'm afraid I've had my reward here on earth.'[42] Lucile Duplessis was 13 when she and Camille met; she was playing with her mother and sister in the Luxembourg gardens. At the time Camille was an impoverished lawyer with a stammer so pronounced he could hardly plead his infrequent cases. All the same, Mme Duplessis must have liked him since he was soon invited with his friend Fréron to the Duplessis home in the Cordeliers section of Paris, near today's Odéon. The little girl grew up, and Camille fell in love with her. As a match, it looked hopeless: he was extremely poor, she was comfortably rich. He was about thirteen years her senior, with dark, bilious, irregular features; she was blonde, and very pretty. Eventually he summoned enough courage to declare his passion. Lucile blushed violently, eloquently lowering her gaze; she also confided in the diary she wrote each night by candlelight. '*I* don't feel love', she had written, before Camille's avowal. 'When then shall I love? They say that everyone must love. Will I be twenty-four before I love? I'm made of marble. Ah, how peculiar life is.' After the declaration, her confessions took a different tone: 'I daren't confess even to myself what I feel for you; I spend all my time concealing it. You tell me that you suffer. Oh! I suffer more; I see you constantly in thought; your image never leaves me, I look for faults in you, I find them and I cherish them.' Informed of this inner turmoil Mme Duplessis eventually succeeded in overcoming the resistance of Lucile's father: on 11 December 1790 he relented. Camille went to find Lucile in her room, fell on his knees and said he loved her. Lucile wept and laughed, overcome with happiness; Camille wept and laughed; the household went half-mad with joy.

The misgivings of M. Duplessis, middle-class if liberal, were understandable. Not only was Camille extremely poor, he was a fervent revolutionary. At a dinner given by a proud relative in his studious youth he had been so provoked by a royalist guest as to leap onto the table and kick dishes while declaiming about liberty and despotism.[43] When the Estates General convened in 1788 he had hoped to be elected deputy for Guise, but failed when his own father, a local magistrate, did not support him. He rose to fame at the Palais-Royal in July 1789, in the scene preceding the storming of the Bastille: leaping once again onto a table Camille announced the dismissal of Necker, pulled out a pistol and, apparently without stammering, incited the crowd to its heroic deed. Thereafter he acquired additional celebrity as a witty and acerbic journalist, sending frequent letters to his father to prove how well he was doing. Unimpressed, Desmoulins senior eventually sent him enough money to buy a bed. Some of his more cynical contemporaries suggested he had married Lucile for her money; Michelet's editor Walter inclines to this opinion too. 'Lucile Desmoulins brought him 100,000 livres of dowry plus silverware valued at 10,000 livres ... this young scatterbrain was not entirely devoid of practical sense and some of his "follies" were quite remunerative' (Michelet, t.ii, p. 1362).

Certainly his life was transformed. They were married in the sacristy of Saint-Sulpice; among the witnesses were Robespierre and Pétion. With Lucile's dowry he rented an apartment near the Luxembourg gardens and bought furniture, including a big round table to celebrate the wedding breakfast. They spent weekends at the Duplessis' country home in Bourg-la-Reine, inviting Fréron; frantically busy while Camille and his friend stood lazing in the sun, Lucile would run up to the two men and stuff herbs into their mouths. They were carefree; they were deliriously happy.

In the summer of 1791 Lucile's husband stopped his newspaper, thinking to take up law again. The Revolution seemed well established in its course and Lucile was now a mother. But in August 1792 the Republic was proclaimed; Camille became Secretary-General in Danton's Ministry of Justice. His political disposition of that time in no way predicts the appeal for clemency that soon would cost his life: he was silent on the September massacres, voted for the execution of the King, and generally opposed the Girondins. When the latter were tried and sentenced Camille realised his mistake, blaming his own writing for their fate: 'I'm the one who's killed them! I'll never forgive myself!' he exclaimed at the verdict. Inspired perhaps by Danton, encouraged by Lucile, he embarked thereafter on the fatal series of attacks on Robespierre, writing articles that drew none too obscure parallels between Rome under its tyrants and Robespierre and the Terror. With so many Committees of Justice, he enquired, could there not be one for Clemency as well?

Robespierre was not amused, denouncing his friend to the Jacobins. In wild alarm Lucile wrote to Fréron, himself at the siege of Toulon:

> Come back, Fréron! Come back as quickly as you can! Bring all the Old Cordeliers you can find; we need them badly.... The wild thyme is ready, I picked it with a thousand worries. I've stopped laughing... I no longer play the piano, I no longer daydream, I'm just a machine.... Come back, come back quickly!
>
> (Clarétie, pp. 296–8)

Despite her private concern, she continued to support Camille in public. When General Brune visited them and tried to warn Camille of his danger, Lucile ran over to intervene. 'Let him be: let him carry out his mission: he'll save France.... Anyone who thinks otherwise won't taste of my hot chocolate!' Michelet credits Lucile with the courage shown by her husband in the explosive, irrevocable seventh issue of the *Vieux Cordelier*, in which Camille compared Danton to an heroic Mark Antony and Robespierre to a despotic Augustus. Or, as Chateaubriand would add, 'In making him capable of love a young and charming woman made him capable, too, of virtue and self-sacrifice'.

Sacrifice it proved to be. On 20 March 1794 Camille received a black-bordered envelope from Guise. 'Your mother died today at noon; she loved you tenderly. My love to my dear daughter-in-law and little Horace, in sadness and affection.' Camille was still weeping over his bereavement when he heard the soldiers in the street. It was late; Lucile had gone to bed. Camille rushed to embrace his wife and little boy before surrendering. He was taken to the nearby Luxembourg prison, where his cell overlooked the gardens he had seen Lucile play in as a child. From prison he wrote the most emotional letters of his life:

> Sleep suspended all my troubles. One is free when one sleeps. . . . Heaven has pity on me. Just a moment ago, I saw you in a dream, I was kissing you in turn, you, Horace and Daronne who was at home with us; but our boy had lost an eye . . . and the pain of this mishap woke me. I found myself here in my cell. . . . O my dear Lucile, I was born to write poetry, to defend those in misery, to make you happy.[44]

After a perfunctory trial, cut short by Fouquier-Tinville – 'End!' bellowed Danton, who was tried at the same time, 'How can it end? It hasn't even begun. You have not read a single document! You have not called a single witness!' – a distraught Camille was executed amid the shouts of those who had once hailed him as Father of the Revolution. Danton, who also left a wife he loved, tried vainly to comfort him, placing in his bound hands a lock of Lucile's hair which Camille clung to all the way to the scaffold. Augmenting his distress was the certainty that she would be arrested too: 'They are going to murder my wife!' he had cried out at his trial. He was right. Lucile had been seen standing near the prison with her little boy, hoping that Camille would catch a glimpse of them; she had been to Robespierre's house to plead for Camille's life. Had not he and Camille been to school together? Wasn't he the witness at their wedding? Hadn't he once asked for her own sister, Adèle, to marry? Robespierre refused to have her admitted, and the Revolutionary Tribunal found it convenient to present her conduct as conspiracy. She was, they would later say, intriguing with the prisoners, who were suspected of plotting a new royalist coup. Thus Lucile was arrested and brought to trial a few days after Camille's death.

Until the moment of her arrest accounts of Lucile's life dwell more on her marriage, on her husband: Camille the stammerer, the frivolous, the sarcastic, the Voltairean, the brilliant classical scholar whom she had made as happy as only devotees of Rousseau were supposed to be. But in narrations of her trial and death it is Lucile who overshadows her journalist husband, setting new records in courage and compassion at the scaffold. Of the ill-assorted batch of defendants who faced trial on 13 April 1794 – Lucile, the royalist General Dillon, the widow of Hébert, Chaumette, the actor-soldier Grammont and his father – Michelet maintains that only she was truly brave. 'She appeared intrepid, worthy of her great name. She declared she had told Dillon and the other prisoners that if there was another 2 September it was their duty to defend themselves' (Michelet, t.ii, p. 826). Sanson relates how, taken back to the Conciergerie, Lucile devoted her remaining instants to making herself as beautiful as possible, 'as if this day should have been a second wedding day'. No doubt existed in her mind that she would soon be with Camille. As the prisoners were getting into the tumbrils, Arthur Dillon came up to her; knowing that her name had proved most useful in framing the conspiracy charge, Lucile apologised for being the cause of his death. Dillon replied that she had only been the pretext, and began lamenting the fate of one so young and charming as herself. She interrupted him. 'Do I look like a woman in need of consolation? For the past week I've thought only of joining Camille. If I didn't hate those who condemned me, because they also murdered the best and most honest of men, I'd bless them for the favour that they're doing me today' (Sanson, t.v, p. 98).

It was a glorious, hot spring day. Once in the cart, the radiant Lucile set about consoling the others, laughing and joking until the youngest and most frightened began to smile with her. This grace and courage were wasted on the younger Grammont, who sat blaming his father for their deaths. 'Monsieur', said Lucile, 'They say that you insulted Marie-Antoinette in the tumbrel, and I readily believe it. But you would do better to conserve some of your boldness to confront another queen, the queen of death, whom we shall soon be meeting.' Grammont replied with swearwords; Lucile turned her back on him disgustedly. When they reached the guillotine she mounted the steps with 'unaffected pleasure', receiving the final blow 'without appearing to notice what the executioner was doing' (Hibbert, p. 245).

Before leaving the Conciergerie she had written to her mother. 'Good night, dear Mummy; I have wept one tear, and it's for you. I shall fall asleep in the calm of innocence.' Her parents never received the note; like Marie Antoinette's final letter to Madame Elisabeth, it was seized by Fouquier's minions and spirited into locked files, where it remained for years. Camille Desmoulins' father died of grief in Guise; Lucile's father died shortly after, also of grief. Mme Duplessis, 'Daronne', survived to bring up Horace, who sailed for Haïti in 1817. Horace married and had two daughters whom he named after his parents, Camille and Lucile; widowed, they lived in penury to a great age.

> There was not a single man, of whatever opinion, whose heart was not wrenched by this death. She was not a political woman, like Corday or Roland; she was simply a woman, a young girl, to look at her; a child, one would think. What had she done, alas? She wanted to save her lover? . . . Her husband, the good Camille, the advocate of mankind.
>
> (Michelet, t.v, p. 141)

Her innocence was devastating; her condemnation most confusing. What was the crowd to make of a procession of tumbrils that contained Lucile Desmoulins, royalist generals, the anti-whore, anti-Christian, anti-feminist Chaumette, the revolutionary Bishop of Paris, the Dantonist Simon, and the Hébertist Grammont? 'The people, despite their wont, could not but be astonished when they saw, mixed up in the tumbrels, this horrible *plum-pudding*, wherein had been muddled every nuance, party and opinion' (Michelet, t.ii, p. 827). Such astonishment bred discontent – discontent that facilitated the eventual overthrow of Robespierre and his élite.

In the same incoherent tumbril with Lucile on 13 April was Marie-Françoise Hébert, née Goupil, whom Lucile with customary kindness had befriended in the prison. Marie-Françoise Hébert was an ex-nun. The Revolution, which discouraged the celibate waste of manpower, disbanded convents and monasteries and exhorted their former occupants to marry and lead a useful life; Françoise had left her convent in June 1790. But what was a former nun to do? She was 36 and alone; she frequented the Fraternal Society of Both Sexes. She met Hébert, 'Father Duchesne'. Like Camille Desmoulins, whom he disliked intensely, Hébert was poor and over-educated when the Revolution commenced; like Camille, he rose to prominence as a journalist. As Père Duchesne his literary persona was that of a man of the people, equipped with oaths and pistols, a sort of good bugger speaking street argot. He was good-looking; he was cold and hungry; his friends sometimes fed him. Marie-Françoise Goupil had a small income inherited from her parents, besides a pension from the state of 700 livres as a secularised nun. She married Hébert early in 1792. Her husband was very proud of her, writing to his sisters that he had married 'a proper person'. He was happy and well, he said; 'wedded to a woman in whom all the good qualities are joined to her mental charms, whose education is complete, whose character is perfect. . . . I lead the gentlest and most peaceful life.'[45]

The portrait contrasts strikingly with Hébert's tirades against other women of the hour. In his newspaper Charlotte Corday was the 'slut from Calvados', Mme Roland became 'Queen Cocotte', and Marie-Antoinette the 'Austrian Tigress who . . . ought to be chopped up like sausage meat for the blood she's caused to be shed'; Hébert promised his readers the Queen's head if he had to cut it off himself. For her part Marie-Françoise, who was given to domestic peroration on the role of Christianity in revolution – 'All justice emanates from God' – wrote of her husband that 'his hands are as pure as his soul'.

On 8 February 1793 Marie-Françoise gave birth to a daughter, named in the Roman manner of the time Scipion-Virginie, or Scipio-Virginia. A suitable bride for little Horace Desmoulins, perhaps, but for paternal strife? Odder things would come to pass. Scipio-Virginia's parents were arrested on 14 March 1794 within a few hours of each other. Mme Hébert left her daughter to the care of Citizeness Gentille, together with some earrings and a watch. As for Hébert he found himself accused of plotting to restore Louis XVII, the infant son of Marie Antoinette. The charge could hardly have been more ironic, remembering Hébert's own testimony at the Queen's trial; but by spring 1794 Father Duchesne had been outmanoeuvred in the course of political re-alliances with Robespierre. At his own particular judgement Hébert was far from exhibiting the insolent audacity he had deplored in the Austro-bitch. Perhaps, like a dentist suddenly reduced to patient status, he knew what was coming, but too afraid to speak he could only answer 'yes' or 'no'. Contrary to what one might expect the crowd was delighted at his death and roared its approval when Sanson kept him waiting at the scaffold; strapped to the *bascule*, Hébert screamed hysterically as the knife dangled for a few extra seconds above his head. It was the sole recorded instance of Sanson deliberately being cruel.

Herself already in the Conciergerie, Marie-Françoise heard about his epic fright from other prisoners, and wrote to the authorities asking to go home. There was no reply. The only consolation for her misery seems to have been the friendship of Lucile, who hugged and tried to comfort her. Dragged before the Tribunal on 13 April, Mme Hébert was found guilty of being 'a conspiratress with her husband, an immediate agent of the system of corruption set up by the horde of foreign bankers and aimed at several unworthy representatives of the people'. Marie-Françoise burst into tears and claimed to be pregnant, but that hope failed when the prison doctors Bayard and Thery pronounced her fit for execution. While Sanson's aides were cutting her hair a witness heard her say to Lucile: '*You're* very fortunate, there's no blot on your record. You'll leave life by the grand staircase.' Another witness said she chatted with Lucile in the tumbrel, seemingly indifferent to the hostile cries that designated the guillotine with the epithets invented by her husband: 'Ah! Mother Duchesne! Off to the guillotine, rum tum tum! She's off to put her nose in the little window!' Still other eye-witnesses claim that she collapsed at the Place de la Révolution and had to be carried to the knife, providing the spectators with a death they could rejoice in as much as they bemoaned the execution of Lucile.

As for Scipio-Virginia, she was brought up first by her uncle, then by a printer in the rue de Vaugirard. She married a Protestant minister, dying in Paris in 1830.

No other batch of victims proved as ideologically motley as the *fournée* of 13 April. There would, however, be several more large convoys of alleged conspirators, some of whom seemed so improbable that their executions provoked further adverse comment. On 24 April Sanson and his aides had the task of decapitating thirty-two 'male and female bourgeois' of Verdun who had welcomed the King of Prussia on his conquest of that town the year before. Some of the younger girls had offered him candies and bouquets of flowers; others had danced with Prussian officers. Twelve of the condemned were women: four were adolescent girls. These last were dressed in white for their execution and sang canticles while riding to the scaffold. 'Our usual crowd', reported Sanson, 'showed only mediocre enjoyment of this spectacle'. Much to his distress the executioner had been obliged to accept the services of a macabre acrobat who habitually performed somersaults alongside the tumbrils, drawing laughter from the bystanders. On this occasion the only person who seemed entertained was young Hélène Vatrin, one of the teenaged girls: 'Look sister, look how amusing he is!' The following day Sanson was obliged to 'expose' on the guillotine Barbe Henry and Claire Tabouillot; being only 17 years old, the two girls had been spared actual execution. The exposure was supposed to last six hours, but after being strapped for a mere sixty minutes to the instrument which, the day before, had killed her sisters, Barbe Henry fainted and had to be untied. Claire Tabouillot was similarly pale, and the crowd began to shout 'Enough' – feebly, it is true; but, Sanson wrote, 'Given the general state of mind, this cry is a symptom that warms an honest heart'. Sanson sent to Fouquier for instructions and a substitute prosecutor ordered the girls be taken back to their prison.

If most of the Verdun victims had been solidly middle class – Barbe Henry's father was a former president of the bailiwick, Claire Tabouillot's a prosecutor – the spring of 1794 saw the executions of a number of aristocratic women, all of them condemned for some species of counter-revolutionary activity, not necessarily connected with each other. Béatrix de Choiseul-Stainville – once Mme du Barry's rival for the favours of Louis XV – found herself brought to trial with the Princesse Lubomirska, Mme du Barry's friend. Accused of corresponding with an *émigré* the former duchess hesitated for a second, then faced her judges with indomitable contempt. 'I was going to lie,' she said, 'but it simply isn't worth it.'

Escorted to the scaffold with twenty-three purported co-conspirators Madame Elisabeth, sister to Louis XVI, was beheaded on 10 May. She had responded calmly to Fouquier's more peculiar accusations: Had she not participated in royalist orgies with the Flanders regiment? Had she not bitten on the bullets destined to be fired at patriots, the better to ensure their death? Had she not dressed the wounds of palace guards injured when the Tuileries were stormed by brave *Marseillais*? Denying the 'indignities' imputed to her name the former princess went on to explain that she had tended wounds out of simple humanity: 'I didn't need to determine the cause of the wounds in order to relieve the suffering. I don't praise myself for that; but nor can I conceive how it can be turned into a crime.' Before being prepared for execution Mme Elisabeth had spoken at some length with Mme Richard, the gaoler's wife, asking to know every detail of the captivity and death of Marie Antoinette. She took leave of Mme Richard kindly, Sanson wrote, but without that last-minute impulse that prompted Marie Antoinette, 'seemingly far haughtier', to hug her little maid. When

Sanson went to cut her hair he found a pale blue-eyed woman, inclined to plumpness like her brother, reading a prayer book. As leader of the presumed conspiracy Mme Elisabeth was executed last. Despite having to watch the preceding twenty-three beheadings she remained calm until the end but, like Charlotte Corday, was shocked when an aide removed her fichu to give the blade an unimpeded fall: 'For pity's sake, Monsieur,' she remonstrated, in a 'sublimely modest tone' (Sanson, t.v, p. 147). Her death, in Sanson's view, served no political purpose whatsoever.

Common to most of the trials, male or female, conducted by the Revolutionary Tribunal was the obsession with conspiracy. Conspiracy had been the justification for the September massacres; in one form or another, conspiracy had justified the creation of the Tribunal itself. Unable to believe that Charlotte Corday had acted alone, her prosecutors had looked not for a woman but for a plot; the accusation of plotting figured in most of the subsequent trials. But this juridical fixation reached its peak in the summer of 1794. On 10 June (22 Prairial in the revolutionary calendar) Robespierre's henchman Couthon introduced a new decree that considerably extended the definition of 'enemies of the people' while considerably relaxing the standard of proof deemed necessary for a conviction. Proof was now defined as 'any kind of documentation, be it material, moral, oral or written, that can naturally obtain the consent of all just and reasonable minds'. In practice this often meant nothing more than a simple denunciation of counter-revolutionary activities, which any citizen had the right, indeed duty, to make. Since all such denunciations had now to be approved through the Committees of Public Safety and Public Health, those two political bodies were guaranteed virtual control of the death penalty. The summoning of witnesses was formally abolished; the only 'rule of judgement' was henceforth the 'conscience of the jurors, enlightened by patriotic love' and aiming at the 'triumph of the Republic and the ruin of its enemies'. Aided by this open-ended decree, Fouquier had little difficulty in supplying batches of decapitees of up to sixty a day.

A pretext for this shameless extension to the Law of Suspects had been provided by the Cécile Renault plot. Here, as in many other cases, an element of truth was grossly inflated to serve political ends: the young woman in question had entertained some mild intention of murdering Robespierre. Towards nine in the evening on 23 May,

> Cécile Renault, Paper-dealer's daughter, a young woman of soft blooming look, presents herself at the Cabinet-maker's in the Rue Saint-Honoré; desires to see Robespierre. Robespierre cannot be seen; she grumbles irreverently. They lay hold of her. She has left a basket in a shop hard by: in the basket are female change of raiment and two knives! Poor Cécile, examined by Committee, declares she 'wanted to see what a tyrant was like;' the change of raiment was 'for my own use

in the place I am surely going to.' 'What place?' 'Prison; and then the Guillotine', answered she.

(Carlyle, vol.ii, p. 332)

As if anticipation of the guillotine were not incrimination enough, there was a precedent, which nobody forgot: 'Such things come of Charlotte Corday; ... Swart choleric young men try Charlotte's feat, and their pistols miss fire; soft blooming young women try it and, only half-resolute, leave their knives in a shop.' Resolute or not, Cécile was not mistaken as to her eventual destination. Although she had not laid a finger on the 'tyrant', she was arrested with her father and 'entire kith and kin' and sent off to the places she had mentioned.

They dressed her, as they had Charlotte Corday, in a crimson smock: 'red shirts and smocks, as Assassins and Factions of the Stranger . . . red baleful Phantasmagory they flit on, towards the land of Phantoms'. The problem with Carlyle's image is that Cécile and her family were not condemned as mere assassins; they were considered parricides. And the rhetoric of parricide had functioned in the voting in of Couthon's new decree: political crimes, he had argued, were more reprehensible than non-political ones because they threatened not mere individuals but 'the existence of free society'; whenever the Republic was threatened with conspiracies, 'indulgence is atrocity . . . clemency is parricide'.

It was no small Freudian irony that the Revolution had maintained the *ancien régime*'s punitive parricidal smock. Before the Revolution parricide had been the eighteenth century's worst crime, surpassed only in the rigour of mandatory punishment by regicide, to which it was symbolically related. The century ended by legally decapitating a king, the symbolic father of his people. This irrevocable act must at some subconscious level have engendered rampant insecurity. 'Liberty, Egality, Fraternity – or Death': so promised Ministry of Justice notepaper. In a Fraternity – a community of brothers, would it not be, of rebellious but united sons? – one might reasonably expect plots to be termed fratricidal. Historian Lynn Hunt has pointed to the absence of paternal figures in revolutionary iconography. By late 1793 the dominant figures on seals and medals were abstractly female – Liberty and Equality – and, dwarfing them, a virile and fraternal Hercules. 'The masculinity of Hercules', she writes of a seal designed by David, 'reflected directly on the deputies themselves; through him they reaffirmed the image of themselves as the band of brothers that had replaced the father-king.'[46] At least in the imagination of David there would be no more fathers.

Curiously, in view of these fraternal aims, the rhetoric of justice preserved the more Oedipal notion of parricide, which the *Petit Robert* defines as murder of a king, a father or mother or any other ancestor. Could it be that the brothers in power were rapidly identified as fathers? Marat's murderess had worn the smock of parricide; Couthon's rhetoric referred not to fratricide but parricide. The literal murder of a parent had been replaced in the hierarchy of horrors by parricidal plotting, whether against the new fathers of the infant Revolution, or against the all-important Fatherland, *la Patrie en danger*. Stemming partly from a genuine paranoia the obsession seems to have been coldly manipulated by Couthon and the Jacobin élite: the more improbable the conspirators, the better they served to illustrate that enemies were lurking everywhere. Cécile Renault had comported herself at the last minute like a proper young woman and left her knives next door; but the intention had been there, and that was all that justice needed. For punitive purposes, Cécile could be taken every bit as seriously as a fraternal suspect.

Thus not only Cécile but her 63-year-old father, one of her brothers and an aunt who had been a nun were all taken to the tumbrils. Fouquier found them an escort of fifty male and female accomplices. All were condemned and executed on 17 June 1794. The batch included the former governor of the Invalides and his son; a grocer, a merchant woman, a musician, a pottery painter and some servants; a teacher, a concierge, some military men; a priest, a lemonade-seller, an 'ex-prince' and several former police officers. Forty-three of the condemned were men: many of them had been behind bars at the time of the supposed plotting. Among the eleven women was Jeanne-Françoise Desmiers de Saint-Amaranthe who had kept a gambling house, acquiring both a fortune and a number of Dantonist clients. Her daughter – a pretty girl, but married – was variously credited with rejecting the advances of Saint-Just, Robespierre's brother, and even Robespierre himself, which was popularly interpreted as a reason for her arrest. In general, however, the prosecution of conspiracy was rather less romantic. Entire families were arrested on the extirpation principle, as if they had been kin of witches. Thus the younger Saint-Amaranthe was seized with her husband, her husband's mistress Maria Grandmaison, and her husband's mistress' maid, Nicole Bouchard. The crowd, it seems, showed quite an interest in Maria Grandmaison, who had been an actress at the Théâtre des Italiens. Michelet places her in the tumbril next to her lover's wife: 'the two unhappy women, sisters in death, dying in the love of the same man'.

Unprecedented consternation was caused by the death of Nicole Bouchard, an 18-year-old girl who looked 14. First of all the man sent to arrest her in her seventh-floor garret had almost failed in his task, reporting to the Committee of Public Safety that 'this child should not die'. To Sanson she appeared so fragile, thin and delicate that 'a tiger would have pitied her'. One of the aides who came to bind the tiny wrists enquired, in some alarm, 'This is just a joke, isn't it?' 'No, Monsieur', replied Nicole, smiling through her tears, 'it's real'. The aide refused to tie the cords, leaving one of his colleagues to complete the task. In the journey to the scaffold Nicole asked to sit with her mistress, who was weeping, and did her best to cheer her up. As the tumbril containing five or six young and pretty women and Nicole rumbled past, the crowd began to vent its indignation: 'No more children!'

Many wept; Sanson himself did not dare look at her. In the Conciergerie he had felt her black eyes on him: 'You won't make me die!' they seemed to say. 'And yet, she died.' In Michelet's account 'a very tough strong man, of an athletic build, one of those people who are all muscle and no nerves' wagered that he could watch the execution from close by, but when Nicole was being strapped to the plank he fainted. In Sanson's version, a man had to leave the scaffold and go home: that man was the executioner himself.

The carnage continued. On 25 June twenty-two peasant women from Poitou, brought in on the usual charge, were decapitated:

> Overcome by the fatigue of their long journey, they lay in the courtyard of the Conciergerie, sleeping on the paving stones. Their glances betrayed no understanding of the fate that awaited them, resembling those of oxen herded together in the market-place. . . . At the moment these unhappy women were going to their deaths, a guard took from one of them the baby she was nursing.
> (Loomis, 1964, p. 329)

Stanley Loomis asserts that the 'story' of the peasant women is confirmed by an English witness, Helen Williams, a friend of Mary Wollstonecraft; but one need only look to Sanson's records.

> Condemned and executed on the 7th of Messidor: *Louise Fleury*, farmer's wife, aged forty; *Marguerite Sapin*, widow *Duplessis*, private income, sixty; *Jeanne Boissard*, day worker, eighteen; *Marie Guillotte*, widow Boissard, sixty; *Marie Thibault*, day worker, aged forty; *Anna Grande*, seamstress, aged eighteen; *Louise Sibut*, widow *Lienard*, servant, aged thirty; *Juliette Raffin*, widow *Regnard*, day worker, thirty; *Caroline Bonnin*, widow *Picard*, seamstress, sixty.
> (Sanson, t.v, p. 243)

And so on, down to the twenty-third woman who was not a seamstress or a day worker but a *ci-devant noble*, Mme Occard de Corberon. These women behaved as Mme du Barry had done, wailing, weeping and begging to be saved; their supplications, Sanson noted, 'sickened the most determined' of the bystanders. 'Three or four times I saw the crowd disperse and the street become deserted.' Three weeks later a comparable list contained the names of fifteen former nuns, but Sanson does not record the effect their deaths had on the crowd.

Messidor, Thermidor: although the victims could not know it, the Terror was drawing to a close. Its final weeks witnessed the demise of several august ladies, their names sufficiently sonorous to foster the myth that only aristocrats were guillotined. In the prison diary she composed retrospectively in 1801, the Duchesse de Durfort-Duras recalls her anguish at being arrested and taken from her parents, the Maréchal and Maréchale de Mouchy; feeble and infirm they had refused to emigrate, remaining to obey the dictates of the new régime with a religious resignation. Arrested in their turn they were incarcerated together in the Luxembourg, where they were greatly liked. On the day of her trial, 27 June, Mme de Mouchy was too ill and old to grasp what was happening. Her husband told her gently: 'Madame, we must go now. God wishes it, let us therefore honour His will. I shall not leave your side. We shall depart together.'

With them in prison had been three women of the Noailles family: Henriette-Alexandrine d'Aguesseau, Duchesse d'Ayen; the Vicomtesse Louise de Noailles; and Charlotte-Françoise-Caroline de Cossé-Brissac, who was none other than the widowed Maréchale de Noailles and Marie Antoinette's 'Madame Etiquette'. If ever anyone deserved her sobriquet it was surely the Maréchale, who had lost her wits in old age and taken to corresponding with the Virgin Mary on the subject of etiquette in heaven. Her confessor humoured her, replying to the letters and signing himself Mary, as if of ducal rank. On one occasion he made a slight error of form, immediately pounced on by Marie Antoinette's ex-lady-in-waiting: 'Ah well, one cannot expect too much of her, she was only a bourgeoise from Nazareth. It was through marriage that she became attached to the House of David. Her husband Joseph would have known better.' She was arrested with her daughter and daughter-in-law on 6 April – the day after the execution of Danton and Desmoulins – and taken to the Luxembourg. The Maréchal de Mouchy is said to have blanched when he saw her: 'That demented old woman will get us all beheaded', he groaned, lamenting her eccentric indiscretion. As if to justify his forebodings Mme de Noailles hastened to visit the Duchesse d'Orléans, snubbed prisoners of lesser rank and took to lecturing the prison guards on intricate points of genealogy.

The three Noailles women were executed on 22 July 1794 after a heavy thunderstorm. They were attended to the last by their faithful Abbé Carrichon, who had previously promised that he would do his utmost to wait along the tumbrils' path and give them absolution. This he bravely did, trotting before the carts at great risk to his person until the rain cleared the streets and the ladies finally noticed him; he was then able to make the prearranged, absolving sign. Thus died the arbiter of protocol of old Versailles, witless, hands tied behind her, jolted by the cobbles, buffeted by wind and rain.

Robespierre, Couthon and Saint-Just: within a week, they followed her. For some time Robespierre had been losing control of the Convention, which he rarely visited; the Jacobins were no longer of a single mind. Maximilian the Incorruptible was on the wane, his position undermined by the very events designed to bolster it: the Feast of the Supreme Being, the Law of 10 June, the ever-swelling *fournées* of conspiratorial executees. Stanley Loomis suggests

Robespierre may even have gone mad, his rationalised paranoia blossoming into religious mania. On 7 May he had attacked revolutionary atheism in a major speech; on 8 June he celebrated the Supreme Being's return to France in festivities as redolent with symbolism as the American Super Bowl. But 8 June, the Feast, did not go well for Robespierre. Mutterings had reached him, of colleagues comparing him to Brutus, to tyrants; a *sans-culotte* had said 'The bastard isn't satisfied with being boss, he's got to be God as well'. Then, at the execution of Cécile Renault, the procession of parricidal conspirators took fully three hours to cross Paris, a show of pomp not seen since the beheading of Louis XVI. '"All this," people said, "to avenge a single man! What more might they do, if Robespierre were King?"' (Michelet, t.ii, p. 899). Perhaps even more pertinently, his colleagues were afraid for their lives. Couthon's Law of 10 June demonstrated irrefutably that everybody was denounceable: apart from Robespierre himself, the ideologically pure person was nowhere to be found. Furthermore, the country's military situation no longer left excuses for the Terror. The French army was now winning battles; order was more or less restored in the Vendée. Matters reached a critical point on 26 July when Robespierre addressed the Convention for the final time, calling for a purge of the conspirators still in its ranks; he was shouted down and arrested on the following day – Charlotte Corday's birthday. On 28 July, his jaw shattered by a bullet, he was guillotined.

It is said that women in the streets danced for joy, that one determined female pushed her way to his tumbril and cursed him as he lay, pale and bloodied: 'You monster out of hell!' she shouted, presumably driven to these uncharitable sentiments by grief. 'Go down into your grave burdened with the curses of the wives and mothers of France' (Hibbert, pp. 267–8). Those executed with him were in equally pitiful shape. His brother Augustin had tried to commit suicide by jumping from a balcony, and failed; Hanriot, commander of the Paris guard, died covered with manure, his right eye hanging from its socket. As for the cripple Couthon, it took ten minutes to strap him to the *bascule*; and as they tried to straighten him, he screamed.

Was this a victory for the wives and mothers of France? Had they won then, the women, the resolute Corday, the soft and blooming Cécile? Perhaps, if it was vengeance that they wanted. Despite the efforts of some moderates to forestall a vengeful purge the executions continued for months: seventy members of the Council General of the Commune, fifteen from the Revolutionary Tribunal and, ten months later, Fouquier himself. It is estimated that the Paris prisons contained 8,000 suspect persons at the time of Robespierre's arrest; all might well have perished had he lived.

These numerical considerations did not of course help the women who were executed in the last hours of Robespierre's rule. There was Mme de Quérhoënt, condemned and beheaded on 26 July or 8 Thermidor. She had written to Fouquier-Tinville:

> Until this moment, citizen, I did not know of what I stood accused. I now see I am accused of emigration, although I have never in my whole life been outside French territory, even for a minute. Please authorise me to send for my certificates of residence.
>
> (Blanc, 1984, p. 90)

There was the Princesse de Monaco, who died the next day, *after* the crowd had tried to stop the progress of the tumbrils. Though technically a foreigner she had been compromised by her husband's participation in the Vendée uprising. Condemned, the Princess pleaded pregnancy, using the moment of reprieve to cut her own hair with a piece of broken glass. Then she wrote to Fouquier:

> I inform you, citizen, that I am not pregnant . . . I wanted to secure a day's grace so that I, and not the executioner, could cut my hair. It is the only legacy that I can leave my children. It should at least be pure. (Signed) Choiseul-Stainville-Joseph-Grimaldi-Monaco, foreign princess, killed through the injustice of French judges.
>
> (Blanc, 1984, p. 92)

She was being driven through the streets when rumour came of Robespierre's fall. The crowd pressed forward, stopped the convoy, trying to prevent the superfluous executions. But clemency was not on everybody's mind. In his final day of power Hanriot came galloping, cleared a path, gave orders to proceed to the scaffold. The Princess was the third to mount, her 'youth resplendent in the blinding July light'.

Then there was Mme Mayet, who had been confused with her more aristocratic phonetic twin, Mme de Maillié, brought to judgement on 26 July and executed anyway 'because she was there'. The real Mme de Maillié survived to give evidence at Fouquier-Tinville's trial ten months later. She complained not only of this unconscionable muddle but of the treatment accorded to her 16-year-old son, who had never even been arrested, but had insisted on accompanying his mother to the prison. He was tried with Mme Mayet, and condemned. When Mme de Maillié came to trial she was overcome with emotion at finding herself standing on the spot where her boy had been sentenced, and fell down in a faint. Roused to indignation the *spectators* – as she was careful to insist at Fouquier's trial – carried her outside. By the time she recovered it was 27 July, 9 Thermidor; Robespierre had fallen, she was saved.

Had Mozart lived longer, and been moved to write an opera about the Terror with Commendatore-like, retributory motifs, he might well have looked for his stone statues to the women who returned from certified death to testify against Fouquier-Tinville. Mme Saint-Pern and Mme Sérilly had both been granted stays of execution on account of pregnancy – and then been issued death certificates. Confronted with these and other instances of prosecutorial confusion, Fouquier-Tinville coolly complained that instead of judging him, the court was actually judging the trial process of the Revolutionary Tribunal. The distinction did not help him. Like many he had prosecuted, he wrote a farewell letter to his wife.

> I bid you farewell for the last time, your aunt too and my poor children, I kiss you all a thousand times. Alas! What sweetness it would bring me to see you and press you in my arms. But, dear friend, it's finished; I must no longer think of that.
>
> (Blanc, 1984, p. 240)

For Fouquier, like Hébert, had been a tender family man. He died protesting his innocence: 'I always conformed to the laws, I was never the pawn of either Robespierre or Saint-Just. . . . One day, my innocence will be recognised.'

Michelet's *Histoire de la Révolution française* ends with Robespierre's death. Its tone is bitter. Particularly horrifying to Michelet were the windows, rented at great cost, with shameless women, 'half-naked in the pretext of the July heat', leaning forth to celebrate. The same women, he complains, then dressed ceremoniously for dinner; not long after began the balls in honour of the victims. This unseemly gaiety 'paved the way to the great tomb where France immured five million men', Michelet concludes, referring to the Napoleonic bloodbath to come. It is not difficult to comprehend his rage. There had been other histories of the Revolution, all 'essentially monarchist'; there would be marxist versions too. But Michelet's was the first to make the French people its protagonist. Frivolous Paris, dancing on the tombs of its dead men; men of 'implacable utopias' who died to set France free. Having thus narrated the tragic outcome of a noble dream, what idealist of the people would wish to devote equal space to military imperialism?

One does not entirely forget, for all that, Michelet's exasperated cry that 'it is generally women who have caused our revolutions to abort', as if the inequality of law and the mismanagement of men counted for nothing in these disasters. On the other hand, in a conclusion published posthumously by his widow, Michelet's favourite revolutionary women rest in the cemeteries with the heroes of utopia: Manon Roland at Clamart, near Mirabeau; Charlotte Corday in the Madeleine, with the Gironde; Lucile Desmoulins at Mousseaux, with Camille, Danton, Robespierre and Saint-Just.

For some female patriots, the struggle had not quite finished. As the Thermidorian Convention that replaced Robespierre pursued its bumpy course towards the right, renascent famine and the violent behaviour of right-wing youths inspired fresh popular protest. On 20 May 1795 a group of women from the Paris sections invaded the Convention calling for 'Bread and the Constitution of 1793'; one of them, Marie-Françoise Carlemigelli, was later guillotined. It would be the final showing of the Parisian *tricoteuses*. The Convention responded with a decree confining women to their homes until otherwise permitted. Meetings of more than five females were to be broken up by force of arms; women could not attend political gatherings. Justifying these prohibitive manoeuvres the framers of the decree maintained that male agitators had taken to dressing up as women, thereby benefitting from the 'impunity' enjoyed by their sisters; as for the actual females, whether provoked by 'enemies of freedom' or else frankly deranged, they too were taking advantage of the 'indulgence shown to their sex' and were disturbing military and police operations.

It would be difficult, says Paule-Marie Duhet who chronicles these particulars, to proceed further down the path of anti-feminist repression. Napoleon nonetheless succeeded, since article 312 of his civil code of 1804 ordered women to obey their husbands, a 'progressive degradation' of female civil rights explained by Duhet in terms of increasing anti-feminism. The period of 1793–1804 thus offers the spectacle of three ideologically different governments – Jacobin, Thermidorian, Napoleonic – doing their best to suppress the political agitation of half of their citizens. A generation of patriotic Frenchwomen was left to mutter that 'there hadn't been much point' in having a revolution. True, there had been some gains: the right to inherit, the right to divorce, the possibility of equal education. But the divorce laws were quietly repealed in 1816, and women were not granted suffrage until 1945.

As for Madame Guillotine, that castratory midwife of democracy, she continued to function for almost 200 years, executing fewer women as the chivalrous nineteenth century wore on, none at all in the early twentieth century, and five during the German occupation. Her nickname of the Widow survives to this day. There would be changes in her code: in 1810 Napoleon restored amputation of the right hand as part of the ancient penalty for patricide, thus revoking the revolutionary prohibition of bodily mutilation other than that caused by capital punishment itself. The same code of 1810 felt it necessary to reiterate that pregnant women need only be executed after giving birth, reminding one that the oldest survivor of the Terror, a Mme de Blamont, had escaped the guillotine by being with child; saved by Thermidor, she lived until 1870, outlasting several more revolutions. Unremarkable except in her survival, Mme de Blamont might well be considered a candidate for having had the last word, were it not for the advent of Napoleon Bonaparte. Napoleon, who was not a feminist, completed the revolutionary cycle by making himself Emperor and marrying another Habsburg archduchess. Asked by Germaine de Staël to name the world's best woman, he replied 'The one who produces the most children'.

5

THE ART OF IMMOLATION

> The death of a beautiful woman is, unquestionably, the most poetical topic in the world.
>
> (E.A. Poe, *The Philosophy of Combustion*)

TRAGEDY, ROMANCE: ANTIGONE AND JOAN

Dramatically, the situation is a simple one: a woman is condemned to death. There will be characters: a judge, perhaps an executioner; a victim too; and possibly spectators, or witnesses of some kind. There will be a cause – why is she condemned? – and an outcome: the sentence is or is not carried out. Then, the human feelings. The victim may deplore her fate, or she may welcome it – may actually have chosen it, as a necessary consequence of self-defining deeds. Perhaps she has broken laws; if she admits that she was wrong, she may be spared. Then again, her sense of self may not permit this. Depending on the religious or philosophical context of events, her choice gives rise to tragedy or martyrdom. A happy outcome will be relatively rare.

With bleak beginnings such as this, what scope is there for poetry? Great scope. A number of executed heroines have been celebrated in drama or in verse, Antigone and Jeanne d'Arc being the preferred subjects: some thirty operas have been composed around the story of Antigone alone. Renaissance and revolution have provided additional heroines, as have wars and the files of contemporary criminology. The dramas they inspire are tragical, more or less historical, or else even romantic. While it has not become a commonplace of literary theory to prove genre by reference to female execution one might broadly state that the death sentence, when carried out, is conducive to tragedy; when not, to Romance.

The model for these operatic and theatrical Antigones was Sophocles' play of that name, produced in Athens in 441 BC when Sophocles was 54. The first of the author's three Theban plays, *Antigone*, depicts events which take place after those in Sophocles' other two Oedipal dramas, the *Oedipus Rex* of 429–420 BC and the *Oedipus at Colonus* of 401 BC. The audience watching the *Antigone* would have been aware of its background:

after unknowingly committing patricide and incest a disgraced, abhorred Oedipus, former King of Thebes, has died in exile at Colonus. His two sons, Eteocles and Polynices, have been waging a furious civil war that culminates in their killing each other. The deed which directly precipitates the events of *Antigone* is committed by Creon, Oedipus' brother-in-law and new King of Thebes, for Creon now decrees that Eteocles, who was loyal to the city, shall receive honourable burial; the rebel Polynices shall not.

As the play begins Oedipus' daughter Antigone is explaining the unholy horror of the edict to her sister, Ismene: Polynices must lie unburied and unmourned, 'a feast of flesh for keen-eyed carrion birds'. Convinced that Creon has aimed this decree at her, Antigone resolves to bury her brother as religion and duty both prescribe, even though Creon has ordered that anyone caught disobeying his law will be publicly stoned. Recalling the disasters that have already befallen their incestuous, parricidal and now fratricidal family, Ismene remonstrates:

> O think, Antigone; we are women; it is not for us
> To fight against men; our rulers are stronger than we,
> And we must obey in this, or in worse than this.[1]

Antigone is not put off by these considerations and proceeds to cover Polynices' body with earth. She is arrested, brought unrepentant before Creon, and condemned to death.

Complications now enter the story in the person of Haemon, Creon's son and Antigone's fiancé. Haemon attempts to reason with his father, claiming to be concerned for his father's good name and pointing out that many in the city think Antigone acted properly in burying her dead; when all such argument proves futile, Haemon departs in rage. Undeterred, Creon orders Antigone to be walled up in a rocky cave – a form of burial alive. The blind prophet Tiresias arrives and berates Creon for leaving his nephew's corpse unburied and for burying a living soul; he predicts appalling consequences for this doubly sacrilegious deed. Seriously alarmed, Creon hastens to complete the burial and to halt the execution of Antigone. This action comes too late. Creon enters the cave to find that Antigone has hanged herself, thus cheating his decree, and Haemon has committed suicide beside her body. Hearing this, Creon's wife also kills herself. The tragic focus shifts from Antigone and the house of Oedipus to Creon.

Antigone is invariably viewed in terms of a clash between the individual and the state, Antigone against Creon, religious duty against politics. While modern audiences tend to justify Antigone and sympathise more with her youthful and defiant martyrdom, this was not always so. Several translators and critics comment that the Athenian public would probably have found Creon's tragedy the more affecting:

To see statecraft misdirected into blasphemous defiance of piety is for him (and for the Athenian audience) the greater tragedy; the sacrifice of a well-meaning woman, the less. Thus the King's final humiliation and chastening through the loss of his son is of higher dramatic significance than the fate of the woman.[2]

Or again, 'To the original audience Creon's position must have seemed sounder than Antigone's'. Could a conscientious ruler honour 'a traitor who had come to destroy the city equally with the patriot who had saved it? And should not Antigone have accepted the authoritative decree, as Ismène says it was proper for a woman and a subject to do?'[3]

The objection to this seemingly reasonable view is that Sophocles did not call his tragedy after Creon, but Antigone. Evidence within the text moreover suggests that Sophocles sympathised less with his figure of authority than did his presumptive audience – and that he was not intrinsically opposed to a woman's assuming an extraordinary role.

First, there is the question of punishment, deriving from authority itself. Before Creon first appears, the Chorus hails him as its new *basileus*, or king – a word denoting one with charge of public worship and the conduct of criminal trials. But Creon's behaviour proves to be that of a ruler who asserts criminal law at the expense of piety. In his opening tirade Creon justifies the punishment he has already ordered for the rebel Polynices: he is to be eaten by dogs and vultures, 'a horror for all to see'. Creon considers it treason to put friendship or love before the state and vows he will never permit evil to triumph over good. To this the Chorus replies dutifully that Creon's 'will is law'. Almost immediately, however, the Sentry arrives with news that Polynices has been covered up with earth; the Chorus begins to express warning doubt:

> My lord, I fear – I feared it from the first –
> That this may prove to be an act of the gods.
> (Watling, p. 133)

At this, Creon cuts in impatiently and threatens to have the Sentry 'racked and tortured' unless he finds out and tells 'the whole truth of this outrage'. Incredulous at hearing himself suspected of untruth and veniality the Sentry protests: 'To think that thinking men should think so wrongly!' and hurries away to remove the earth from Polynices' corpse. The Chorus is left to comment on the wondrous subtlety of man, who has found a remedy for every ill 'save only death'.

The Sentry soon returns, accompanied this time by Antigone under guard: the soldiers have found her pouring ritual earth on the rotting naked body they had previously uncovered. Interrogated by Creon, Antigone makes plain that she was perfectly aware of Creon's order and its consequences and chose to disobey it:

> I did not think your edicts strong enough
> To overrule the unwritten unalterable laws
> Of God and heaven, you being only a man.
> (Watling, p. 138)

Enraged, Creon argues with her: one should not give equal honour to the good brother and the bad. Who knows? responds Antigone; in the country of the dead, that may be the law. Ignoring the pleas of both Ismene and Haemon, Creon pronounces sentence:

> I will take her where the path is loneliest and hide her, living, in a rocky vault with so much food set forth as piety prescribes, that the city may avoid a public stain. And there, praying to Hades, the only god whom she worships, perhaps she will obtain release from death.[4]

This, the third of Creon's punitive pronouncements, proves the most calamitous, precipitating the triple suicide. The tragedy which eventually befalls Creon is certainly great and pitiable, but its causes appear clearly in the confrontation with Antigone. He has divided humanity into two, the good and the bad, and punished the bad. He has ignored religious law in favour of the state. True, Antigone ignores the state in favour of religion, but has lucidity enough to see that the eternal, natural laws precede the other kind. Intent on asserting his authority in this first crisis of his rule, Creon on the other hand derives his power from his personal qualities and his position. And when Haemon indicates that the people of Thebes may well support Antigone, he is subtly indicating that many points of view obtain in a democracy such as Athens.

The actual image of the punishment is crucial to the structure of the play. Polynices lies unburied, dead, his soul lingering between this world and the next; Antigone will be entombed alive. This penalty is more severe than the public stoning originally announced in Creon's decree, for it condemns Antigone to an equally unhallowed state. She herself evokes this ambivalent fate in her final utterances:

> O monstrous doom,
> Within a rock-built prison sepulchred,
> To fade and wither in a living tomb,
> An alien amidst the living and the dead.[5]

For violating the natural order of things above and below ground – 'you have lodged a living soul in the grave but keep in this world one who belongs to the gods infernal' – Creon has two debts to pay, as Tiresias informs him. Losing both his wife and son, Creon comes to suffer the same fate he prescribed for Antigone:

> Now all is lost, for life without life's joys
> Is living death, and such a life is his
> (Watling, p. 157)

the Messenger remarks. Creon's wealth and power count for nothing, weighed against his shattering loss.

Apart from its religious import the burial cave has marital connotations too. With double irony the Chorus terms Antigone's rocky cell the 'bridal-bower of endless sleep', evoking the marriage to Haemon which will never take place, and unwittingly anticipating the final scene in which Haemon commits suicide beside his dead fiancée:

> So there they lay
> Two corpses, one in death.
> His marriage rites are consummated
> In the halls of Death.
> (Storr, p. 409)

The 'Bride of Hades' theme accumulates power from the multiple connotations of the Greek word for marriage-bed, which can also mean both sleep and the grave. Not only does the cave turn out to be a bitterly appropriate bridal chamber, but the manner of Antigone's demise has sexual implications. Entombed, Antigone would have been joined with the traditionally female element of earth; hanged, she symbolically separates herself from it. But hanging – as one recalls from Eva Cantarella's article on 'Dangling Virgins' – could also symbolise the passage from virginity to womanhood, besides being the means resorted to by virgins when threatened by some menace. In Antigone's case the menace is not rape, but an unnatural sentence which would have alienated her from both the dead and living worlds.

Should Antigone have behaved like a woman and obeyed Creon's edict, as Ismene first maintains? This would scarcely have solved the problem of her decaying brother. As she observes to Creon,

> This punishment will not be any pain.
> Only if I had left my mother's son
> Lie there unburied, then I could not have born it.
> (Watling, p. 189)

Antigone's tragedy is that her only dignified choice entails death; compromise, and her sense of self, her duty to her foredoomed kin are compromised in turn. Possibly Sophocles elected to place a woman in this plight in order to accentuate the enormity of her revolt: 'We'll have no woman's law here, while I live', says Creon in disgust; and later, ordering the Chorus to take Ismene and Antigone inside: 'Take them and keep them inside – the proper place for women.' In his line-by-line commentary on the *Antigone*, Kamerbeek deems these responses typical of Creon's coarse masculinity – a coarseness that suggests a certain antipathy for Creon, felt by his creator. Professor Kamerbeek further demonstrates that Sophocles was the first to introduce into the legend the problem of Polynices' burial and Antigone's disobedience; Sophocles' probable sources mention neither Polynices' burial, nor Antigone's response, so crucial to the play. In other words, Sophocles' treatment of this part of the Oedipus legend was original, and the focus on Antigone deliberate.

Certainly Sophocles was not one to shrink from depicting unusual domestic situations. In the *Oedipus at Colonus* the normal hierarchy of gender is reversed by the appalling behaviour of Oedipus' sons, savagely bent on fighting while Ismene and Antigone are left to lead their blind, decrepit parent on his path of exile. Oedipus knows that their nomadic existence has been physically harsh. 'You would have seen me dead', says Oedipus in fury to a suppliant Polynices, 'but I had daughters, whose never-failing care has nursed my life. *They* are my sons; you are some other man's' (Watling, pp. 112–13). Clearly Sophocles was quite aware that the proper place for women was within domestic walls, and chose to contemplate other roles that they might play, superior, essential and disastrous.

Theatrically and ideologically, the Antigone legend has been subject to all manner of revampings. Among the thirty or more operas written on this subject one might select an early work by Marie Antoinette's music teacher, Christoph Willibald von Gluck. Based on Sophocles, Gluck's *Antigono* had a libretto by Metastasio and was first performed at the Teatro Argentino in Rome in 1756. It does not count among the master's more frequently performed pieces. In the 1920s Jean Cocteau took up the subject and 'adapted' the Greek version into the idioms of his eclectic and iconoclastic age. The result

> follows Sophocles closely, often speech by speech, the greatest cuts being in the choruses: it was something he could do quickly, and he accomplished the feat of preserving considerable nobility of language in his modernising. He called his text 'a pen drawing after an old master' . . .

writes Steegmuller, Cocteau's biographer. Cocteau had seen *Antigone* performed at the Comédie Française, and found it 'incredibly boring,' mainly for the flaws in the production. 'The age of the actress playing Antigone made her walk to the tomb all too natural, and consequently anything but touching. Old men – quite obviously chorus boys in white beards – sang unintelligible words to music by Saint-Saëns. That was a true *scandale*.'[6]

Cocteau's own 'contraction' of the play, which he described as an 'aerial view of the Acropolis', opened in Montmartre on 20 December 1922 and ran for about a hundred nights. Arthur Honegger provided 'a little score for oboe and harp', and the sets were designed and painted by Picasso. Costumes were by Coco Chanel. 'I wanted Mlle Chanel because she is our leading dressmaker and I cannot imagine Oedipus' daughters patronising a "little" dressmaker. I chose some heavy Scotch woollens. . . .' The director Charles Dullin played Creon, and Cocteau himself delivered the lines of the Chorus from an opening in the violet-blue backdrop. The Antigone was a young Greek dancer, Genica Atanasiou, whom Cocteau had chosen for her rare 'quality of nobility'; she spoke practically no French and had been coached by Cocteau. 'Her Greek accent, which made the French language more sonorous than it really is, drove the author's words deep into our hearts', wrote an admiring Maurice Sachs. Critical opinions were divided. At the opening night a worldly, glittering audience laughed at what it took to be wittily updated lines that were in fact from Sophocles. On the third night proceedings were interrupted by a shout from André Breton about Creon: 'He attaches the greatest importance to the execution of his orders. He's wrong!' According to Steegmuller Cocteau had been drawn to *Antigone* 'because of its attractive theme – disobedience to the establishment'. In Cocteau's mind the aesthetic establishment apparently meant Breton and the Dada avant-garde, whom he caused to be ejected from the performance. Of a later night André Gide wrote in his *Journal* that he

> suffered unbearably from the ultra-modern sauce poured over this admirable play, which remains beautiful despite Cocteau rather than thanks to him. However, we can understand what he was trying to do, and he concocted it with consummate skill.
>
> (Steegmuller, p. 299)

The composer of the 'little score' apparently had fewer reservations, since in 1927 he used Cocteau's 'rapid and violent' text as the libretto for a fully scored tragic opera.

Equally basted with modernity – but without the benefit of Honegger, Picasso and Chanel – Sophocles' austere masterpiece reappeared in 1942 in Occupied France, recreated by the pen of Jean Anouilh. This time the modifications are those imposed by Anouilh's personal tone and deliberate theatricality. The action of the play is enclosed in a frame: 'These characters are going to act the story of Antigone', the Prologue tells the audience. 'Antigone is the little thin one sitting over there, who doesn't speak.'[7] The romance between Antigone and Hémon has been considerably updated: Ismène is blonde and sexy, Hémon something of a playboy, given to parties and dancing. Everyone expects him to marry Ismène but for reasons no one can divine he has fallen on his knees in the course of an especially brilliant ball and asked Antigone – thin, dark, compelling – to be his wife. The settings are of a supposedly timeless neutrality: the characters wear modern evening dress. At one point Antigone borrows a pretty dress from Ismène and uncharacteristically daubs herself with lipstick, thinking to please Hémon. Créon's palace guards play cards, discuss salaries and make jokes about women: one they recently arrested claimed to be the Police Commissioner's girl.

Anouilh has also restructured the play, adding some characters and subtracting others. Like Cocteau, he retains most of Sophocles' plot while cutting the role of the Chorus. But he now equips Antigone with a Nurse – an inevitable and pathetic reminder of the childhood from which the heroine has barely emerged. The Nurse does not know Antigone has spent the night pouring soil over Polynice with the toy bucket he played with as a little boy, and thinks she has a secret lover; thinking she has failed in her duty to the late 'Madame Jocaste', the old woman bursts into tears. Adding to the author's calculated enhancement of the general poignancy is a scene between Antigone and Hémon in which Antigone informs her baffled but obedient fiancé that she can never be his wife. Having been informed by the Prologue that Antigone will shortly die the audience knows what is going on; Hémon and the Nurse do not.

Gone from Anouilh's version is the confrontation between Creon and Tiresias; gone, indeed, is the entire character of Tiresias, with his message of eternal law. On the other hand Anouilh has considerably expanded the confrontation between Créon and Antigone. The scene begins with comic misunderstanding as the guards bring in Antigone, who has just covered the body for the second time: 'Imbeciles!' bellows Créon, thinking they have made a mistake. When he finds out there was no mistake, that Antigone is quite prepared to cover the corpse again and expects no favours for being the daughter of a king, he attempts to save her. 'Look at yourself!' he tells her. 'You're too thin to be put to death! Put on a bit of weight and give Hémon a nice baby boy. Thebes needs that more than it needs your death, I assure you.' He reveals that her brothers were obnoxious cads who punched Oedipus on the nose and tried to have him murdered; Antigone did not know this and is stunned. Quietly, obediently, she agrees to return to her room, see Hémon and get married. It seems that Créon has won – until he commits the strategic blunder of evoking daily happiness. 'Life is a favourite book, a child playing at one's feet. . . . Life is perhaps nothing else but happiness!' Far from reassuring his exacting niece, these words serve only to disgust her.

> You all disgust me with your happiness! With this life of yours one has to love at any price. . . . *I* want to be sure of everything today, and I want everything to be as beautiful as when I was a little girl – or else die.

Antigone has admitted that burying her brother was an absurdity; but she has also realised that it is not in her nature to accept a life of compromise. Antigone chooses death.

The effect of this expanded scene is to focus more sharply on the conflict between the heroine and the king; but whereas Sophocles presented a conflict between religion and politics, or personal truth and public order, the long scene between Antigone and Créon now appears as a clash between two individuals of more or less valid but irreconcilable points of view. The conflict has become less a matter of universals and more a question of personality. Moreover, the death-quest of his adolescents obsessed with purity has earned Anouilh some criticism: his tragic vision is often castigated in terms of infantile regressiveness. The deliberate evocations of childhood – Polynice's toy bucket, for example – reinforce the primary impression of a juvenile nobility. But for what, really, do Anouilh's youthful heroes die? Conspicuously absent from Antigone's long scene with Créon is any serious discussion of eternal truths, or higher duty. Créon even makes Antigone confess she does not believe in the efficacy of ritual burial; her deed, she admits, is absurd. Gone and vanished is the original Haemon's implied point about democracy; Anouilh's Hémon confronts his father in a state of amorous despair, and when he commits suicide it is with the glowering expression of a rebellious little boy. As Germaine Brée remarks, Anouilh's tragic heroes evince fidelity to little more than 'the role one is designated to play, the acceptance of oneself in a given part whatever its absurdity'.[8] In Sophocles, Antigone and Oedipus persist in their disastrous conduct because their whole beings would be negated if they did not; in Anouilh, the tragic fate becomes a matter of casting. 'Each of us his part to play', Antigone tells Ismène. 'Créon has to kill us, and we have to bury our brother. That's how it's been assigned.' The implacable natural law of Sophocles has been replaced by a theatrical convention.

That is not to deny the play's undoubted effectiveness in a political context. Staged in Occupied Paris in 1944 *Antigone* enjoyed considerable success.

> For 645 consecutive performances Frenchmen crowded into the Atelier Theatre, often without electricity, to see Antigone confront Créon in the narrow patch of light falling from the stage's skylight. And for once Anouilh's theme – the preference of death to compromise – seemed terribly immediate.
>
> (Harvey, p. viii)

Although the figure of the king was still viewed as sympathetic, it was not hard to see the Antigone-Créon conflict as reflecting the humiliating circumstances of a divided France. Performed at the University of Wisconsin-Madison in 1974 during the student protests against the Vietnam war, Anouilh's *Antigone* seemed to mirror the schism between youthful objectors and 'mature' university administrators. Nor is it impossible to imagine an *Antigone* – whether by Anouilh or Sophocles – set in Tiananmen Square.

A dramatist who left no doubt as to his political intentions was Bertolt Brecht. *Die Antigone des Sophokles* – Brecht's 1947 adaptation of a previous translation by Hölderlin – boasts a prologue of ninety-three lines, set in the Berlin of 1945. Two sisters are faced with the familiar dilemma: their brother has deserted from the German army, and his body been found hanged. Are they to cut it down, and risk being seen by the S.S.? In the play itself, which largely follows Hölderlin, Brecht has effected subtle changes in the unrhymed verse; new passages are woven in. Creon becomes 'a brutal aggressor, who has attacked Argos for the sake of its iron ore; Polyneikes deserts in protest against this war which has killed his brother; and Antigone is partly moved by a like disapproval of her uncle's policy'.[9] Brecht retains the character of Tiresias, but more as a cynical analyst of the present than as one who prophesies the future. The play's ending is even more catastrophic than in its models. Not only do Antigone and Hamon die, but a wounded messenger announces the death of Megareus, Creon's only loyal son. Disaster threatens Argos, while the fall of Thebes itself looms imminent.

First produced in Switzerland in 1947, Brecht's *Antigone* was published the following year with notes by the author and a foreword which indicates Brecht's existential, self-deterministic humanism: 'According to the picture of the ancients man is delivered more or less blindly to Fate; he has no power over it. In Bertolt Brecht's adaptation this picture has given way to the view that man's fate is man himself' (Willett, p. 58). The manner of production paralleled the contemporaneity of Brecht's philosophy. Brecht's comments on the acting style he desired in *Antigone* accentuate his departure from tradition; the verses are broken and asymmetrical, and must be delivered accordingly:

> The essential was to avoid that revolting convention which demands that the actor should tackle any fairly long verse passage by, as it were, pumping himself full with some emotion which will roughly cover the lot. There should be nothing 'impassioned' either before or after speech or action. We move from verse to verse, and each must be carved out of the character's *Gestus* [or underlying attitude].
>
> (Willett, p. 101)

Asked how the rhythm was managed technically Brecht replied that one applied 'the syncopation common to jazz. This brings an element of contradiction into the flow of the verse, and allows the regular to prevail against the irregular.' Delivered in this way, concludes John Willett, the unrhymed verse is common to the didactic pieces of Brecht's various periods, corresponding 'not only to the austere aesthetics and sharp political argument of the early 1930's, but also to the deliberately stumbling dialectic of Brecht's late plays' (Willett, p. 101).

But in staging *Antigone* Brecht aimed at more than a destruction of declamatory style. According to Frederic Ewen, he was trying to restore a dramatic repertory that had been mangled and distorted by the Nazis. Hölderlin's *Antigone* – one of the great classical translations of all time – had been used in Viennese productions to illustrate Fascist doctrine, the 'female sensibility' of Antigone being played against Creon's more admirable 'masculine reason', while the text in general was underscored by Bacchic frenzies. Reacting against this type of spectacle, Brecht's own version tends more to emphasise the collapse of a tryannical régime, rather than focussing sympathy on the individual act of resistance so recently distorted in the Nazi productions.

The sombre emotions of the Second World War thus engendered several *Antigones*. In 1949 Carl Orff of *Carmina Burana* fame wrote his own libretto based on Hölderlin's translation of the Sophocles. The result was staged in Salzburg on 9 August of that year. Orff – who, like Cocteau, also wrote an *Oedipus* – employed a 'primitive' style to promote the drama's Greekness: rhythmic speech, chants in monotone, and driving rhythms provided by an unusually large percussion section predominate; although comprising but a single act the opera takes three hours to perform. Bearing in mind Brecht's comments on jazz rhythms and the numerous operas based on the Antigone legend it would seem that music is seldom far from the treatment of this story: few heroines can have inspired such a wide range of works. An obvious competitor is Jeanne d'Arc who, as Saint Joan, Jeanne, Johanna, Giovanna or simply Joan the Maid provided an evident vehicle for nationalist sentiments in a variety of contexts. A source for dramas historical, religious, marxist and tragic, Jeanne's exploits have also fallen into the unlikely sphere of burlesque Romance.

'Without tragedy', writes Northrop Frye, 'all literary fictions might plausibly be explained as expressions of emotional attachments, whether of wish-fulfillment or repugnance: the tragic fiction guarantees, so to speak, a disinterested quality in literary experience.'[10] This disinterested quality, Frye adds, derives largely from Greek tragedy, which introduces the 'sense of the authentic natural basis of human character'. Romance, on the other hand, 'the nearest of all literary forms to the wish-fulfilment dream', is the medium by which the ruling social and intellectual class of every age projects its cultural ideals: thus, chivalric Romance in the Middle Ages, but also bourgeois Romance from the eighteenth century on. Although Frye does not here make mention of buried, burned, hanged or decapitated women, one may discern the aspect of wish-fulfilment in the near-burnings of Romance: accused of treason and adultery, Queens Guinevere, Halis and Yseult are making ready for the stake when lo and behold a peerless knight arrives and frees them, whether in single combat or by daring rescue. Since the knights involved – Lancelot, Joufrois, Tristan – are or will be the Queens' lovers, the rescue appears satisfactory from all points of view.

An ideal and definitive thwarting of the law, it would seem, except that the lady's problems do not usually end with the rescue. So it is with Yseult in the twelfth-century *Tristan* of Beroul. Betrothed to King Mark of Cornwall whom she has never seen, the Irish princess Yseult is being taken to Tintagel by the King's nephew Tristan. Thirsting for wine, they accidentally drink the love potion prepared by Yseult's mother to ensure a happy marriage to

King Mark. A mutual and irresistible passion ensues, which continues after Yseult's marriage to Mark; discovered by an indiscreet dwarf their adultery is revealed first to some jealous barons, then to the irate King. Tristan and Yseult are taken, bound, and threatened with the stake: 'The King orders a ditch to be dug and filled with knotty boughs and piles of white and black thorn bushes, torn up with their roots' – a painfully slow bonfire (Beroul p. 26, 1.867–72). Secure in the knowledge that he could easily defeat any knight in Cornwall Tristan demands trial by combat to clear himself and the Queen, and indeed, this should have been his normal recourse under the law, as the people of Tintagel vainly point out to Mark. Although scheduled to be burned first, Tristan manages to escape by leaping from a church built on a precipice. Yseult is being led to the stake when a band of lepers presents itself and asks for the Queen to be handed over as their communal whore: 'No woman ever met with a worse end. Sire, there is such heat in us no woman under heaven could endure being with us: the cloth burns on our very backs . . . .' There are more than a hundred of them, and besides being metaphorically appropriate the punishment is so horrible that Mark actually agrees. But no sooner is his wife committed to their care than Tristan and his faithful squire, Governal, emerge from behind a clump of trees. Governal chases the lepers away – Tristan being too honourable to smite sick men himself – and Yseult is set free.

There follows a gruelling interlude in the forest of Morrois. For three years they eke out an uncomfortable existence 'without salt or milk', their clothes in tatters, constantly fleeing from place to place, building fragile shelters of branches and leaves, eating nothing but venison which Tristan manages to hunt with the aid of his dog Husdent, who has followed them, and the ever-loyal Governal. Eventually the love-potion begins to wane and a sympathetic hermit, Ogrins, negotiates the Queen's return to court, even buying her an expensive dress so that she may be socially correct for the occasion. But matters do not end there. The three disagreeable barons renew their accusations, Mark sighs and Yseult bravely takes it upon herself to clear her name. Asking Mark to summon Arthur, his court and all his valiant knights, she promises to swear on holy relics she is innocent. At the same time she sends word to Tristan, who disguises himself as a pilgrim and waits by a ford on the way to the swearing-place. The Queen requests the 'pilgrim' to carry her through the water, then proceeds to swear in front of man and God that no one but King Mark and this obliging stranger have intimately grasped her person. Since this is the literal truth, Yseult passes the relics test and impresses the assembled knights.

God does not strike her dead, but has he not been mocked? By no means. In Beroul's version of the Tristan legend God has the extreme good taste to side with the lovers; he knows, as society does not, that they have unwittingly drunk a fateful potion and he knows that they are faithful to him. This would seem to have the effect of pitting God against the teachings of the Church, which did not approve of extramarital romps. As mythologist Joseph Campbell explains, the troubadours, 'very much interested in the psychology of love', did not countenance the type of union so often sanctioned by the medieval Church: loveless, arranged by society for temporal and political gains. In the view ascribed by Campbell to the troubadours, Tristan and Yseult – unconsciously in love even before they drank the potion – were ideally suited; Mark and Yseult were not. 'The true marriage', declares Campbell, 'is the marriage that springs from the recognition of identity in the other, and the physical union is simply the sacrament in which that is confirmed. It doesn't start the other way around. . . . It starts with the spiritual impact of love.'[11] Marriage violated this spiritually inspired love when it was socially arranged; it is the union of Mark and Yseult which is immoral, not that of Yseult and Tristan.

Unfortunately Campbell does not specify which version of the Tristan Romance he has in mind, and indicates only vaguely what he means by troubadours. But, though not as 'courtly' as some versions, Beroul bears out his concept. The troubadours' view of love thus presupposes a spiritually superior type of God who is capable of appreciating it: one who might, without apparent blasphemy to himself, permit Yseult to be rescued from the stake and pronounce technically correct oaths on holy relics, thereby deceiving the most valiant military males in two kingdoms. This does not mean that Tristan and Yseult can love with impunity. 'There's no possible fulfilment in this world of that identity one is experiencing', says Campbell of this myth. The love-potion – the Irish witch-queen's solution to the problem of loveless matrimony – contains a death sentence. 'Wretches!' exclaims the servant on the ship, seeing they have drunk the potion, 'You have drunk your death'. For lovers who have taken the potion cannot, thereafter, bear to be long separated. Tristan dies in France, wounded in body and mind, thinking Yseult has failed to answer his summons; Yseult dies on his body. United in death lie Yseult the Blonde, who has inherited her mother's healing arts, and Tristan the Knight, who is also an artist in his way, a musician and a master of disguise. In more ways than one the double death links witch and troubadour, both of whom recognise the value of ideal love and its incompatibility with the social institutions of the time.

Given the example of Yseult, the transformation of Saint Jeanne d'Arc, bellicose and virginal, into a heroine of Romance would seem a literary feat defying credibility. Nonetheless Voltaire accomplished it – almost; he took the liberty of adding satire to the tale. Challenged at the Duc de Richelieu's dinner table to write a poem on the subject of the Maid, Voltaire declared there were so many absurdities in the story that it was better suited to the mock-heroic burlesque form than to that of the epic, which a minor poet had recently attempted. Taking up the challenge he produced several cantos quickly – there would be twenty in all – beginning in 1730. The poem proved so entertaining that several hundred spurious cantos soon appeared, causing Voltaire such endless inconvenience he eventually felt obliged to bring out his own edition in 1762.

Voltaire's intention in *The Maid of Orleans* was not so much to satirise Jeanne as the forces which tended to 'foster and magnify' the mythical elements in her story. Casting aside the historical facts of Jeanne's trial and execution, Voltaire concentrates on the chivalric aspects of her life, limiting himself to the period of military splendour that followed her arrival at Chinon and elaborating a series of adventures involving French and English knights and their respective ladies. He parodies those elements of medieval romance which seemed to his age so ridiculous, and to a later age so charming: dragons, magicians and supernatural events. Voltaire's Jeanne flits around on a flying ass provided by her protector Saint Denis and, with heavenly assistance, repels numerous dastardly attacks on her maidenhood, mostly undertaken by priests. His cantos abound in burlesque battles, single combats and ladies threatened with extinction at the stake, Jeanne herself surviving a grotesque near miss in the castle of Hermaphrodix.

The problems one might expect to result from the presence of a maid in armour amid hordes of lustful men are thoroughly explored; Voltaire was visibly amused by the pomp and ceremony attending Jeanne's virginity. In Canto I, Saint Denis announces to the warriors Xaintrailles, Dunois and La Hire his intention of saving France through a virgin. This commodity proves very difficult to find, but in Canto II the saint encounters Jeanne. He gives her a splendid coat of armour and a flying ass and together they proceed towards the Loire where Jeanne is presented to the Dauphin Charles. Asked the inevitable question the heroine cheerfully replies:

> Oh! great sire, give orders now
> That doctors sage, with spectacles on nose,
> Who versed in female mysteries can depose,
> That clerks, apothecaries, matrons tried,
> Be called at once the matter to decide.[12]

Once affirmed, the famous maidenhood is rapidly subject to a series of assaults by English knights and naughty priests: Sir John Talbot engages her in single combat, and prevails. He then sets about raping her while the French knights watch helplessly, bound by the rules of combat not to intervene. At the crucial juncture honour is preserved by Saint Denis who renders Talbot impotent. The saint intervenes again later to ward off catastrophe when Gribourdon, a lubricious monk, attacks Jeanne while she is asleep.

Despite these humiliations Voltaire's Jeanne performs several military feats. On her way to Chinon she steals an English knight's breeches and large codpiece from his tent. When Agnes Sorel, jealous of the Maid's success, puts on Jeanne's splendid armour and the stolen breeks and sets off to join

THE ART OF IMMOLATION

Charles she is captured by the trousers' owner, Sir John Chandos, who tries to ravish her; the practical Jeanne quickly dons inferior armour, summons the French knights and frees Agnes in a mighty battle. But while returning from the fray Jeanne and Dunois are led into peril by a seemingly friendly dog, and it is at this point that Voltaire satirically raises the other problem inherent in her donning warrior's attire: androgyny. The well-trained canine leads them to the castle of his master Hermaphrodix, a lavish host who tries to seduce both of them. The two refuse his pleasure, are stripped naked and condemned to an obscene fate:

> Our tyrant wronged thus, in a twofold way,
> Resolved upon revenge without delay:
> Pronouncing to his myrmidons thus hailed
> The dreadful sentence: 'Let them be empaled'.
> (Voltaire, 1901, p. 152)

This fate is all the more terrible in that Jeanne and Dunois have, unknown to each other, fallen in love, and are forced to contemplate each other's nudity with pitying eye. They are saved from the sharp stake by Friar Gribourdon who arrives opportunely and offers to ravish Jeanne – and Hermaphrodix as well – as price of ransom; Jeanne is engaged in an unseemly struggle with the friar when the flying ass swoops down and rescues her. 'Praise be to God! My charming ass is here!' Since the ass, too, has formed tender feelings for the Maid Saint Denis thinks it a good moment to send the beast into Italy, together with the amorous Dunois; a repentant Gribourdon is turned over to Jeanne as substitute mount.

Voltaire now takes aim at the Holy Inquisition. Dunois arrives in Milan to find that Dorothy – mistress of his friend La Trémouille – is about to be burnt at the other kind of stake. A boastful demon called Sacrogorgon offers challenge to anyone who would save her, and Dunois accepts. But before engaging in combat, he listens to Dorothy's tale of woe. Her uncle, an archbishop, has fallen in love with her:

> He breathed his flame – heaven, what was my surprise!
> I placed his rank and duties 'fore his eyes,
> His sacred calling, and what further stood
> As bar – his consanguinity of blood.
> (Voltaire, 1901, p. 231)

Discovering that Dorothy has had a child by La Trémouille (who is away fighting the English) the prelate is incensed and tries to rape her. Dorothy calls for help, only to be denounced as a 'public strumpet' and 'staunch heretic': she is arrested, tortured and tried by the Inquisition. Many knights offer to defend her, only to be threatened with excommunication by her uncle. Outraged by this narration, Dunois is thirsting for the fight when he finds himself ambushed by a hundred archers and condemned as a sacrilegious knight. He is about to be burned with Dorothy when the ass performs another airborne rescue, swooping down to free him. Dunois then kills the Sacrogorgon and restores Dorothy to a grateful La Trémouille; the reunited pair's adventures take up a good part of the remaining cantos.

It may come as no surprise that *The Maid of Orleans* was bitterly attacked by clerics – so bitterly that the editors of Voltaire's American translation feel impelled to claim Voltaire was no more an atheist than Rousseau. (They had in mind Rousseau's missive to the Archbishop of Paris, an orthodox Catholic who kept a mistress and insisted he believed in Christianity because of the numerous miracles contained in the Roman legend: 'You, my Lord', wrote Rousseau, 'believe in the Christian faith on account of those miracles, and I, my Lord, in spite of them' (Voltaire, 1901, p. 11).) Yet Voltaire says nothing at all about the most damning feature of Jeanne's case: that she really was tried and condemned by an ecclesiastical court. In taxing his clerics with mere lustfulness he may have led them into a judgemental trap. Possibly not all priests were lustful; in any case Voltaire's are fictional; but the Church *did* hand Jeanne over to be burned. Ironic comment is left to the American translator. The *braguette* or codpiece, he remarks in a note,

> was the peculiar prerogative of the most noble of the sexes; wherefore the Sorbonnic doctors presented a petition that the Maid of Orleans might be burned for having worn short clothes with the braguette: six French bishops, assisted by their mitred brother of Winchester, condemned her to the stake; which, considering all things, was very proper; nay, it is to be regretted that this does not occur more frequently; but let us despair of nothing.
>
> (Voltaire, 1902, p. 134)

Satirical exaggeration of the Church's minor sins implicitly recalls the far greater crime, as the translator is aware.

Seventy years after Voltaire began his burlesque poem Schiller composed his 'Romantic tragedy', *Die Jungfrau von Orleans*. Written between June 1800 and 16 April 1801 *Die Jungfrau* was first produced in Leipzig on 18 September, praised by Goethe and admired by two generations – the generations of German Romanticism. Since accorded rather lukewarm accolades, it is considered to contain only occasional pages of genius. Nonetheless Schiller has the honour of being the 'first literary man to accord dignity and sympathy to Joan', who had hitherto been considered a 'ludicrous trollop'.[13] Blame for this circumstance falls largely on Voltaire, but should probably extend to Shakespeare too: in *Henry VI Part One* the Pucelle degenerates from being valorous and eloquent (she defeats several men in single combat, persuades Burgundy to rejoin the French and cleverly invades Rouen) into a terrified strumpet who tries to save herself from burning by claiming to be pregnant by half the French court. Schiller was no more faithful to history than Shakespeare and Voltaire, but strove to replace their unflattering depictions with something nobler and eternal, aiming at the greater, more poetic truth through factual inaccuracy.

In subtitling the play a 'Romantic tragedy', Schiller apparently envisaged an excursus into those fanciful Middle Ages which Voltaire and the rationalists found so barbarous and absurd, but which Rousseau and the Romantics admired for their imaginative qualities and simple faith. Like Voltaire, Schiller avoids all mention of Joan's execution and concentrates on the problem of her femininity-at-arms, but there the similarities end. Schiller's play comprises a prologue and five acts of unmitigated high-mindedness. Behaviour is impeccably chaste and the villain of the piece is not some lecherous monk but Joan's own father, who suspects her of commerce with the Devil. The action begins in Domremy with Thibaut d'Arc – as Schiller inexplicably calls him – lamenting the English occupation of the region, and marrying his daughters to suitably protective swains. Joan shows no inclination for matrimony, a fact distressing to Thibaut, who fears she may indulge in some morally disastrous rise above her station. Joan prophesies a miracle: a tender virgin will inspire the French knights and drive forth the English through God's will. Left alone beside the oak tree, she then bids the bucolic scene a sentimental farewell.

She next appears at Chinon, where things are going very ill for Charles VII; he has no money to pay his troops, and his own mother, Queen Isabeau, has just declared him a bastard. Dunois encourages him to keep fighting and so does Agnes Sorel, who actually offers her jewels to finance the war. But word arrives that a mysterious maiden has inspirited the troops; brought before Charles, Joan astonishes everyone by revealing the contents of his dreams. Describing her holy mission, she says the Virgin has assured her of success as long as she remains without 'all earthly love'. In the ensuing battle she leads the French into the heart of the English camp, kills a young Welshman and – as in *Henry VI Part One* – succeeds in charming the renegade Duke of Burgundy back to the French side. As a reward for these services Charles knights her and ennobles her forebears. He also proposes finding her an aristocratic spouse, at which Dunois and La Hire, who are both in love with her, step forward. Joan blushes, causing Agnes Sorel to think that this lofty and unfeminine creature has at last been overcome with womanly confusion and would like to confide in Agnes alone. But Joan explains that she is bound to her virginity:

> I have been summoned for a different task
> Which no-one but a maiden can perform.
> I am a warrior of highest God
> And may not be the wife of any man.
> (Schiller, *Maid*, p. 73)

When the Archbishop of Reims tells her it is woman's lot to marry, Joan explains that her task is still unfinished, since her King is not yet crowned; when Charles adds his voice to the entreaties, she becomes enraged.

DEATH COMES TO THE MAIDEN

> The majesty of heaven shines about you,
> Before your eyes its miracles are wrought
> And you see nothing in me but a woman.
> ... A man's eye desiring me
> Is horrible to me, and sacrilegious.

Unhappily for Joan, terrestrial affections are soon to leave their imprint. As the battle continues she encounters the ghostly Black Knight who warns her to stop fighting and then vanishes. Joan nonetheless vanquishes the English commander Lionel in single combat, rips off his helmet, sees his face – and falls helplessly in love. Overcome with horror she calls upon the Virgin for assistance before collapsing in a faint as Dunois and La Hire arrive on the scene.

In Joan's pure mind the damage is now done. She sees herself as tainted, stained and doomed. Reluctantly assuming her place for the coronation at Reims, the Maid embraces her sisters and their husbands and thinks of returning with them to her father. But Thibaut d'Arc has not relinquished his earlier suspicions, and chooses the coronation ceremony to denounce his glorious daughter in front of King and court and all of Reims:

> You think you have been rescued by God's might?
> O Prince betrayed! O blinded Frankish people!
> You have been rescued by the Devil's arts.
>   (Schiller, *Maid*, p. 102)

Through nicety of conscience Joan feels unable to disculpate herself, for she is still thinking of Lionel. Dunois offers to fight as her champion, but heaven answers with a thunderclap and everybody stares in horror; the Maid is dismissed from the city. As she explains to Raimond (a friend from Domremy who now accompanies her), the accusation came from her father, thus from God, and therefore could not be denied. Even so the disgrace has had its advantages, since she is now cleansed of passion. In the middle of her explanation the treacherous Queen Isabeau enters with English soldiers and takes Joan prisoner. Raimond hurries back to tell Dunois and the Archbishop, who admit that Charles and his knights are beginning to regret their hasty action; hearing that Joan has been taken they sound the alarum and attack. Informed by the gloating Isabeau that Charles and Dunois are losing the fight, Joan bursts her chains with superhuman strength and rushes to their aid. The tide immediately turns, but Joan is mortally wounded. With her dying breath she tells Charles she is no sorceress and asks for her standard. As the sky flushes with a rosy glow the King gestures for banners to be laid across her body.

Thus did Schiller plunge his Joan into the 'raging cauldron of Romance', as G. B. Shaw was to remark. Nevertheless *Die Jungfrau von Orleans* is not totally impervious to fact. Joan's father is known to have been distressed at the thought of his daughter consorting with soldiers, while the superstition surrounding the tree in Domremy is quoted even by twentieth-century commentators on witchcraft. Then again, there is the historical mystery of Joan's declining fortunes after Reims. Schiller seems to interpret a fall from military grace in terms of earthly passion, providing his heroine with the semblance of a tragic flaw. Essentially Schiller ponders the same problem as Voltaire: what Joan's presence on the battlefield would mean in terms of lust, both for her and for the soldiers. The conclusions reached are as different as the two heroines' costumes. Whereas Voltaire's Jeanne romps in a *braguette*, Schiller's Maid appears in helmet and breastplate but 'otherwise in women's clothes'. That she manages in single combat to vanquish Montgomery and Lionel in a gracefully flowing skirt is seemingly attributed to the omnipotence of the Virgin. But Schiller has also given some thought to what might conceivably be termed Joan's feminism, had the word existed then:

> Only a strong woman can be loved
> By a strong man

opines Dunois, who finds Joan's natural nobility quite equal to his own royal, if illegitimate rank. Paradoxically, while subjecting his heroine to Romance, Schiller simultaneously preserves her from it: women can rise above their biological lot to accomplish great things, but at the apparent cost of what lesser minds regard as their normal marital destiny.

Some resemblance to Schiller's drama is borne by Verdi's *Giovanna d'Arco* of 1844. The libretto, by Temistocle Solera, reproduces elements of *Die Jungfrau* – most notably, the problems caused by Giovanna's over-zealous father. In Solera's version Giacomo d'Arc witnesses a patriotic exchange between Charles VII (Carlo) and Jeanne (Giovanna) underneath a haunted oak. Misunderstanding the situation entirely he concludes that Giovanna has given herself to the Devil out of demented passion for the King; in fact she has simply found Carlo's armour, taken it for herself, and fired the discouraged monarch with nationalist resolve. The haunted tree provides Solera with a pretext for competing choruses of good and bad spirits: as if borrowing from Schiller, the good spirits warn Giovanna that she must at all costs beware of 'terreno affetto', earthly love. For operatic purposes Solera reduces the number of Jeanne's admirers to the single, amorous person of the King, who is not only unmarried but conveniently divested of Agnes Sorel. When Carlo declares a lofty passion for his breastplated maid, a tormented Giovanna avows she loves him too. Still fearing the worst Giacomo is driven by paternal despair to denounce his daughter in mid-coronation and, as if that were not enough, to the English army too. Captured by Sir John Talbot's men Giovanna prays for help to the Virgin. Giacomo overhears her and, correct in his assumptions this time, realises she is innocent. He repents and frees her, enabling Giovanna to return to the fray. Mortally wounded, Giovanna dies as light pours from the heavens and the French army lowers its banners and falls before her in the dust.

The first performance took place on 15 February 1845 at La Scala and was a huge success. Even so, *Giovanna d'Arco* is not often performed in the modern repertory; modern audiences possibly find Giacomo a bit excessive, to say nothing of the haunted tree. The fault lies not with Verdi, who produced credible musical expression for the struggle between satanic and celestial forces. In the overture a rapidly enunciated motif of brooding Romanticism vies with a slower, more angelic theme, presaging the supernatural match; the opposition is resolved in a triumphal march. As Verdi's student and devoted friend Emmanuele Muzio wrote admiringly,

> If with her exploits she had not made her memory eternal, the Signor Maestro's music would have made her immortal. . . . The awesome introduction . . . the magnificent number 'Maledetti cui spinse rea voglia', are two things that will startle any poor man. The choruses of the devils are original, popular, truly Italian; the first ('Tu sei bella') a very pretty waltz, full of seductive tunes . . .; the second ('Vittoria vittoria s'applauda a Satana') is a music of diabolical exultation, a music that makes you shiver and tremble; in short they are divine things.[14]

Yet despite the packed, happy audiences described by Muzio strange things befell *Giovanna*. A poster made later on in 1845 shows that, syllable for syllable, the opera was now entitled *Orietta di Lesbo*. Embarrassed by Verdi's nationalistic Jeanne (Italy was divided at the time), censors from the papal state had the action moved to Lesbos. Here Giovanna became Orietta, a Genoese heroine rousing the Lesbians (in the geographical sense) to repel the Turks.

These modifications in no way deterred other composers and librettists from tackling the topic of Jeanne. In 1881 Tchaikovsky's *The Maid of Orleans* premiered in St Petersburg with a libretto by the composer, based on Schiller's play. Five years later Emil von Rezniček wrote an opera with the same title. Jeanne's canonisation in 1921 prompted a rash of plays, beginning with Shaw's *Saint Joan* and Brecht's *Die Heilige Johanna der Schlachthöfe*; there have also been several operatic versions. The most consistent feature of these twentieth-century works is the emphasis placed upon Jeanne's trial – almost as if, now that she was safely canonised, one could remind the audience that she had actually been burned. Thus Honegger's *Jeanne au bûcher* of 1938 – an opera-oratorio with a text by Paul Claudel – is normally performed on two separate stages, Jeanne being attached to the stake on one while flashbacks from her life are re-enacted on the other. In Norman Dello Joio's *The Trial at Rouen*, which was first performed on NBC television in 1956, Jeanne's trial takes up the whole of Act II, and the opera ends with her execution.

The first three scenes of Shaw's *Saint Joan* of 1923 – a 'chronicle play in six scenes and an epilogue' – follow Joan's career from her masterly conquest of Robert de Baudricourt to her arrival at Chinon and subsequent effect on military events. Although he emphasises his heroine's earthy common sense, Shaw does not neglect the miraculous aspects of her achievement. Hens that would not lay suddenly produce scores of eggs when Baudricourt gives Joan a horse; the wind changes as she meets Dunois at Orléans, enabling the French forces to attack. In the ominous fourth scene the focus shifts to the English camp. Warwick, the Chaplain and Cauchon are seen discussing the desirability of bringing Joan to trial. Apart from the defeats she is inflicting on the English 'goddams', Joan alarms the Earl of Warwick because her policy of installing Charles as King and God's representative on earth bypasses the entire aristocracy – just as her claim to direct celestial inspiration alarms Bishop Cauchon because it bypasses the Church. She is, Cauchon declares, the advance guard of a terrible heresy to come; equally dreadful, her protonationalism represents another means of dividing the Church, which should know 'only one realm, and that is the realm of Christ's kingdom'.[15]

Bestowed by the author on Joan's judges almost five centuries after the event, these predictions of nationalism and heresy lend a prophetic air to the proceedings; in Scene 5, Shaw offers a psychological explanation for Joan's subsequent downfall. The heroine is seen after the coronation at Reims, magnificently attired as a man, no longer engaged in battle but missing the excitement of war. She thinks of 'retiring' to Domremy but then decides not to until she has captured Paris. Realising the tactical advantage no longer lies with her, Dunois tries to dissuade her, as do Charles, the Archbishop, and Gilles de Rais (Bluebeard); all warn that they will do nothing to save her if she is caught. But Joan persists in knowing best – which is precisely why they are criticising her.

The effect of this criticism is to place some of the responsibility for Joan's capture on the saint herself, so that the long trial scene which follows seems a natural consequence of her 'superbity'. In the trial Joan appears less arrogant, but defends herself 'boldly' as her voices have instructed. Many of the questions and replies are drawn from the historical trial: Joan refuses to tell the whole truth, because 'God does not permit it'; she frankly declares her intention to escape if she could; she states that there are many other women to do women's work, but no one else to do hers. Asked if Saint Michael appeared naked, she proffers her celebrated reply: 'Do you think God can't afford to dress him?' Pressed repeatedly about her own male attire she either says 'Ask me something else' – as she did historically – or else insists upon the common-sense aspect of the question. Seeing her still obdurate her judges summon the executioner. The pyre is higher than usual, he confirms: Joan will suffer more. At this, Joan finally realises they mean to burn her *now*; she begins to lose faith in her voices, and recants. Cauchon and the Inquisitor, who have laboured in good faith to save her, are relieved. But when Joan learns that they intend keeping her locked up for the rest of her days she withdraws her recantation. She cannot, she tells them, live without the 'wind in the trees, the larks in the sunshine, the young lambs crying through the healthy frost'. 'You wicked girl', exclaims Brother Ladvenu, 'If your counsel were of God would he not deliver you?' 'His ways are not your ways', replies Joan. 'He wills that I go through the fire to his bosom; for I am His child, and you are not worthy that I should live among you' (Shaw, p 408). She is taken out and burned, to the great terror of the Chaplain, who compares himself to Judas: 'I let them do it. If I had known, I would have torn her from their hands. You dont know: you haven't seen.'

The play ends with an epilogue set in 1456, after Joan's rehabilitation trial. Though dead, Joan casually walks in on a discussion between Ladvenu and Charles. They are joined by Cauchon, Dunois, the Executioner and the English soldier who made a cross from two sticks and held it to her at the stake. The latter is now in Hell, whither he must return before midnight; because of his good deed he is allowed out for one day each year. A gentleman dressed in the top hat and frockcoat of 1920 appears and declares Joan a saint; everybody praises her, much to her alarm. 'And now tell me: shall I rise from the dead, and come back to you a living woman?' Her interlocutors slink off in embarrassment. 'The heretic is always better dead', observes Cauchon, 'And mortal eyes cannot distinguish the saint from the heretic. Spare them.' Joan is left rhetorically to enquire when the earth will be ready for God's saints.

Apart from the Epilogue, and the few homely 'miracles' that seem to follow Joan, Shaw's play is conspicuous for its realism. No trace remains of chivalric romance, witches' choruses or superstitious fathers. Joan's voices are ascribed to her imagination or her innate practicality: 'even if they are only the echoes of my own commonsense, are they not always right?' she asks in Scene 5. In the same exchange Dunois recognises God's part in helping Joan and the French, but also his own hard work: 'Do not think, any of you, that these victories of ours were won without generalship.' God, he reminds them, has to be fair to the enemy as well; Joan's reckless bravery, relying on ten men to do the work of a hundred, will one day lead her into trouble. Thus Shaw rationally explains Joan's military setbacks after Reims in simple terms of overconfidence and inadequate numbers. The Epilogue, with its anachronistic Gentleman visitor from 1902, seems alien to this practical mode until one realises it is Shaw's witty and theatrically effective way of dating his play – of indicating that its perspective necessarily derives from recent events in Basilica Vaticana. It also establishes Joan's posterity as an important element in her story, a step followed by other dramatists later in the century.

The first of three plays the distinguished Communist wrote inspired by the new saint, Brecht's *Saint Joan of the Stockyards* is set in the slaughterhouses of Chicago. It reflects a view of the forces Brecht considered operative in the world in general and Germany in particular. Completed in 1930, the play was in some ways more timely even than the Shaw: 1931 was the 500th anniversary of Jeanne's martyrdom, while in 1932 there were 6 million unemployed in Germany and Hitler was a rising menace. In Brecht's play the Franco-English struggle has been replaced by a complex economic war among the meat packers; as meat king Pierpont Mauler sighs to a colleague, 'Ah, Cridle, our business is a bloody one'. The heroine, Joanna Dark, is a Salvation Army lieutenant, a soldier of God who thinks the Word of the Lord is more essential and more nourishing than the soup she and her fellow 'Straw Hats' also provide. Dispatched by Mauler on a descent into Hell – that is to say, a visit to the labouring classes – Joanna discovers that poverty and degradation destroy moral behaviour. She also realises that the meat-king class finds the Salvation Army most useful in pacifying the workers. Her consciousness is raised, but not in quite the way that Mauler intended.

Meanwhile, the economic situation grows more desperate: starved and unemployed, the workers organise a strike. The sympathetic Joanna is sent to deliver an important message. But despite her pity for the strikers she is beset with bourgeois doubts, and fails to deliver it. Troops break up the strike; Pierpont Mauler, who has succeeded in cornering the market, defeats his competitors. Joanna collapses and dies heartbroken, only to be canonised by Mauler and the cattle barons. 'Thus, in Brecht' – concludes critic Frederic Ewen drily – 'capitalism canonises its useful martyrs.'[16]

Sometimes described as Shakespearian in form, *Die Heilige Johanna* comprises eleven scenes of classical blank verse, prose, irregular unrhymed verse and Salvation Army hymns. There are frequent choruses of workers, cattle dealers and Salvationists. There also echoes of both Goethe and Schiller, whom Brecht parodies with visible glee. In Schiller's *Die Jungfrau von Orleans* Charles asks Joan how she managed to recognise him after he changed places with a courtier. 'I saw thee, where no-one else but God saw', replies Joan. In Brecht's play Joanna goes to seek out Mauler, effecting a similar miraculous reconnaissance:

Joanna: You are Mauler.
Mauler: No, I'm not. (*Points to Slift*) He is.
Joanna (Points to Mauler): You are Mauler.
Mauler: No, he is.
Joanna: You are he.
Mauler: How do you know me?
Joanna: Because you have the bloodiest face of all.[17]

When Joanna dies, Mauler signals for flags to be laid across her body, as in Schiller; her 'apotheosis' recalls the end of Goethe's *Faust*. For all the savage parody, Joanna nonetheless emerges as an 'active', heroic woman, on the scale of Mother Courage or Grusha in *The Caucasian Chalk Circle*. Such qualities did not help the work in pre-war Germany: it was given only a partial radio broadcast in 1932, with Peter Lorre, Carola Neher and Helen Weigel.

If *Die Heilige Johanna* draws ironically on the themes of her 'mission' and canonisation, Brecht's second dramatisation involving Jeanne d'Arc resets her visions and her nationalism in another twentieth-century context. Though not performed until 1957 *Die Gesichte der Simone Machard* was written in exile in 1942–3. Simone Machard is a young cripple working at a hostelry in Touraine in June 1940, at the moment of the German advance. Her employer gives her a life of Joan to read, cynically remarking that the country needs another Maid. Simone then has a series of visions in which her 17 year-old brother – the only one in the whole town to volunteer for the French army – appears as an angel and encourages her to resist. When the town spinelessly welcomes the invaders Simone explodes the petrol stores, preventing the gasoline from falling into German hands. In her final dream she sees herself condemned to death; then one by one her accusers – who first appear in medieval garb – turn into Frenchmen. Simone demands a hearing, in the course of which she is teased about the angel, who no longer visits her. At this point Marshal Pétain proclaims a truce 'which does not at all touch the honour of France'. Simone is committed to an insane asylum run by nuns. The play's concluding events nonetheless suggest that others are beginning to follow her example and resist the Germans.

Brecht's third venture into sanctified intertextuality was the relatively straightforward adaptation of a radio play by Anna Seghers – an old acquaintance, and the best-known Communist writer to settle in East Berlin, after Brecht himself. The *Trial of Joan of Arc at Rouen in 1431* was produced by the Berliner Ensemble in November 1952, Brecht's previous two Joans being still unperformed. Seghers' radio play provided material for eleven out of the final sixteen scenes, using crowd noises and shouts to create a popular feeling. Brecht amplified this aspect of the work, adding three new crowd scenes, besides opening and closing sections which reflect the people's view of Joan. Apparently he felt his task was threefold: to expand the radio text into a full-length, performable play; to establish and develop a connection between Joan's voices and the people; and to depict the said people as individual, performable beings. Brecht's own notes consistently underline Joan's reliance on popular support: 'Cut off from the people, Joan *suddenly* breaks down (in the eighth scene). But it can be observed (in the sixth) how her isolation keeps undermining her resistance.' Or again, 'It is not the church's threats but her own mistaken assumption as to the people's passivity that temporarily breaks down Joan's resistance.'[18] Hearing of popular unrest in Rouen stirred up by her plight Joan recovers, resumes her male attire and is martyred.

Of Brecht's three plays about Joan, the Seghers adaptation most develops the idea of 'the great patriot' as a rebel and a populist. The play is perhaps even more historically realistic than Shaw's *Saint Joan*, although Seghers seems to follow Shaw in emphasising the trial scene (Brecht in fact shortened the Seghers text here). Once again Joan refuses to swear to the whole truth, evades certain questions and honestly admits she would like to escape. She also offers to wear female clothes if they will let her hear Mass – a question to which her interrogators return almost obsessively. Seghers goes further than Shaw in including a scene (retained by Brecht) in which Joan is threatened with torture; she is also more ironic at the expense of the Church scholars. 'Joan, the torturers are ready to lead you to the truth by force, for the salvation of your soul', says Chation, Professor at the Faculty of Theology in Paris. Joan faints at the sight of the instruments, but then declares that whatever confessions they manage to extract, she will 'say afterwards that it was torn from me by force'. Despairing of her obstinacy Cauchon announces that the judges fear 'torture can no longer benefit her' (Brecht, 1972, pp. 171–2). In Brecht's adaptation the execution is seen through the eyes of the crowd, who are matter-of-fact but sympathetic in their curiosity: 'Swine!' exclaims a fishwife, speaking of the pyre, 'They've piled it high to make her suffer more'. 'Don't cry now', says a peasant to his wife, 'She can't feel anything now', to which the Loose Woman replies 'She's still screaming'. Whereas the Seghers text ends with Joan's death, Brecht adds a scene showing the liberation of France five years later; Joan leads a procession, young girls sing her glory (a song adapted from a poem by Christine de Pisan) and the peasant Legrain explains how she used her trial and death to change defeat 'into our greatest victory'.

Another twentieth-century play which resuscitates Jeanne for the concluding scene is Jean Anouilh's *L'Alouette* (*The Lark*), written in 1953. As in his *Antigone*, Anouilh presents a heroine who refuses a mundane existence and affirms her true identity by choosing death. Like Shaw, Anouilh dramatises a series of events from Jeanne's past, but in more complex form: the re-enactment of her life is framed within the trial, and the trial itself is framed – as in *Antigone* – in conscious theatricality. When the play begins the cast is seen picking up props left lying around after a previous performance. The Earl of Warwick, who represents English political interest, briskly enquires 'Are we all here? Good. Then let's get on with the trial. The sooner she's judged and burned, the better for all of us.'[19] It is the play's particular convention that Jeanne cannot be condemned until she has recreated for her judges the principal scenes of her short life. Her own awareness of the two levels of theatricality – play and trial – appears when the Inquisitor asks if she considers herself in a state of grace. 'When do you mean, sir?' she replies,

> It's hard to know just where we are. Everything's confused. Do you mean, at the beginning when I hear my voices or at the end of the trial when I've understood that my king and my friends have also abandoned me, when I've begun to doubt, when I've abjured and then taken it back?
> (Anouilh, 1957, pp. 27–8)

Since most of *The Lark's* action is anticipated in these lines, the principal task of the audience is now to sit back and appreciate the various *coups de théâtre* served up by its author.

Among the first scenes to be re-enacted is Jeanne's departure from her parents' farm. Anouilh deals with the problem of her father's reaction to the divine mission, but instead of making the father-as-God the pivotal figure in her denunciation, as nineteenth-century authors did, he simply presents an enraged peasant who, hearing his daughter wants to 'go with soldiers', beats her black and blue with his trusty leather belt. The question of male lust is personified in the lecherous Beaudricourt (*sic*), whom Jeanne must charm into lending her a horse and escort; while flattering him into thinking that the idea of saving France is really his own, she makes him admit she is not his type, that he is 'like all men' and 'doesn't want to pass up the opportunity' of seducing a girl in return for some favour. Her next task is to bring courage to the dithering Dauphin Charles. The best way to overcome cowardice, she says, is to be mortally afraid *before* the event, so that when the moment comes to act, one has already had all one's fear. Romance there is none; Jeanne's friendship with her fellow-warriors is limited to the figure of La Hire, a good-natured brute reeking of wine and onions who provides a foil to Jeanne's humanism. 'Fat-head! Bumpkin! Blockhead! Paradise is full of fools! Our Lord said so. Perhaps they're the only ones who get in' she tells her over-respectful captain, who is worrying about his chances in the next life. In Jeanne's view the sinner who dies doing a good deed is just as dear to God as anybody else: heaven is full of lusty swearing Englishmen as well as saints.

Such views are anathema to the Inquisitor, a venomously holy intellectual who is largely Anouilh's own creation, the historical prototype having been an ineffectual fellow who did his utmost to get out of this inconvenient trial. For Anouilh's Inquisitor God is everything; to love mankind as Jeanne does is to neglect God. Worse, it is not so much the Devil who must be feared – he is, after all, a fallen angel, a member of the Church in a sense – but Man. 'In matters of faith', declares Jeanne, 'I submit to the Church. But as for my own deeds, I shall never forswear them.' The Inquisitor sees this remark as quintessentially human and sinful:

> There they are, the words they all utter at the stake or on the scaffold, or while they're being tortured, each time we manage to get hold of them! The words they'll say again centuries from now, and just as insolently, for this manhunt will never end. . . . No matter how powerful we become . . . there'll always be a man to hunt down somewhere, one who gets away, who'll be captured and killed and who will yet again humiliate the Idea at the height of its power, just because he looks us straight in the eye and says 'no'.
>
> (Anouilh, 1953, pp. 146–7)

It is not, however, the Inquisitor who persuades Jeanne to recant but Cauchon, a fairly kindly man sincerely concerned with returning the stray sheep to the fold of Mother Church. He overcomes Jeanne's resistance by explaining that God wills her to submit, and that Jesus certainly suffered more on the cross than she is suffering at her trial. Pressed to abandon her boy's clothing Jeanne blushingly explains the English guards would rape her if she wore a skirt. Warwick promises to take care of the matter. Jeanne signs the necessary document and the churchmen sigh with relief.

Congratulated by Warwick for surviving the trial, Jeanne becomes despondent. She has no wish to grow fat, old and complacent, as will Charles, Agnes and Warwick himself; visited in prison by Charles and Agnes she sees – though too loyal to admit it – that their mediocrity contrasts depressingly with all that she has done for France. Realising her mistake she reassumes her identity, calls for male pants and is taken to be burned. At the last minute Beaudricourt rushes in and stops the execution, reminding everyone they have not done the coronation scene, as had been promised. *The Lark* thus concludes with the triumphal tableau in Reims Cathedral, for the real Jeanne d'Arc – as Charles declares – is not the cornered animal of Rouen, but 'the lark circling in the sky, or Joan at Rheims in all her glory'. Jeanne d'Arc is a story that must have a happy ending.

This final, posthumous tableau implies that, choosing death, Jeanne chose correctly; her martyrdom defines the image that posterity will keep of her and reaffirms the sense of her whole life. For the audience this is no doubt less depressing than watching some simulation of the saint being burned to a cinder. Structurally speaking, it provides a closure in keeping with the play's conventions: as Beaudricourt points out, they had promised to show everything. But this resort to convention – structural convention, convention of the history books – ultimately suggests a certain dramatic shallowness; Jeanne 'survives' in the pretty tableau much as Antigone dies in Anouilh's earlier work, that is to say, because the play's self-conscious frame has decreed it. Shaw's *Saint Joan* and Brecht's adaptation of Anna Seghers' text similarly include 'posthumous' scenes in an attempt to dramatise the phenomenon of Joan's appeal to posterity; but Anouilh's coronation is perhaps less effective than Brecht's poetic myth of nationalism and Shaw's ironic treatment of Joan's canonisation.

ROMANTIC MADNESS

Nineteenth-century drama did not always spare its condemned women execution; but on those rare occasions when the scaffold could not be plausibly avoided it did permit them to go mad. The tendency was marked in opera, particularly if the victim was of noble birth. Thus, in Donizetti's *Anna Bolena* of 1830, the disgraced Queen's reason is made to collapse under the double pressure of forthcoming execution and remembered romance. Despite her loss of wits she dies with seemly grace, a quality shown by other beheaded heroines of the period whether mad or sane.

Donizetti's librettist, Felice Romani, has not necessarily followed fact in bringing Anne Boleyn's story to the stage. The villain of the opera is unequivocally Henry VIII, Enrico, who sets a Machiavellian trap for his unhappy Queen and her innocently stupid friends. In the opening scene

DEATH COMES TO THE MAIDEN

Anna and her court wait vainly for the King to pay an evening visit; finally Anna dismisses everyone and goes to bed. Only then does Enrico appear, through a secret door, to keep a tryst with Giovanna (Jane Seymour) whom he has taken as his mistress. Distraught at betraying Anna's confidence Giovanna wants to break off her amorous bonds, but Enrico sweeps her objections aside and promises she will be Queen. Then he springs his trap. Recalling from exile Riccardo Percy, to whom Anna was once engaged, Enrico informs the naive young man that the Queen is responsible for his return to court. Unable to think of anything except his passion for Anna, Percy falls to his knees and thanks her effusively – thereby arousing the King's all too ready suspicion. Desperate to see her alone Percy begs his friend Rochefort, Anna's brother, to arrange an interview. This Anna reluctantly grants, only to tell him they cannot meet again. Demented with grief Percy draws his sword and is about to kill himself when Anna's musician, Smeton, bursts in to defend the Queen from what he thinks is Percy's mad attack. Just at this moment Enrico enters, furious at seeing naked weapons in his palace. Smeton protests that all present are innocent and with an impulsive gesture bares his chest (or her chest, since the part is sung by a mezzo-soprano), inadvertently causing a locket with Anna's picture to fall at the King's feet. Delighted at this evidence of guilty passion Enrico orders everyone arrested and tells Anna she can explain herself when judged.

Sent to visit Anna in prison, Giovanna Seymour informs her that the King will spare her life if she confesses to loving Percy. Anna refuses, even when Giovanna reveals that she herself is now the royal mistress; Anna also pardons Giovanna, who becomes distraught with guilt. Meanwhile young Smeton is tricked into a confession of adultery: he has been told that this will save Anna's life, but instead she is condemned. Giovanna pleads vainly for the Queen to be spared. Percy and Rochefort, now in the Tower, refuse all offers of clemency that fail to include Anna; confronted with the King, Percy actually declares that he and Anna were once married! None of this in any way helps Anna who goes mad in her cell. As the sheriff comes to take Anna, Percy, Rochefort and Smeton to the block, news comes that Enrico is about to marry his new mistress. As the opera ends, Anna recovers her lost wits sufficiently to forgive the royal pair and pray for their future bliss.

Despite his departures from fact – the real Percy, one recalls, figured among Anne's judges, not among the condemned – Romani no doubt conveys a certain popular judgement of Henry VIII, marrying Jane Seymour a few days after Anne Boleyn's execution. It is hard to reconcile Romani's sweet, forgiving Anna with Henry's jealous and sarcastic second Queen, at least as portrayed by Nora Lofts – let alone with the depictions of Anne as a witch; but the actual mad scene appears less than a figment of Romani's imagination if one considers that both Edith Sitwell and Retha Warnicke deem Anne to have been under nervous strain by the time she reached the Tower. Even so, the demented bursts of laughter – 'I have a lyttel neck' – recorded by Governor Kingston contrast oddly with the touching melancholy shown by Romani's Queen. For Romani's Anna has only one visible fault: she has valued the throne above the loyal heart of Percy, as she herself confesses in her reluctant meeting with the former sweetheart. Even this failing is inaccurately depicted, since in reality it was not Anne but Henry VIII and Percy's father who broke up the romance. As far as the opera is concerned, however, Anna's attitude to Percy is a precipitating factor in her madness. Unhappy, and neglected by Enrico, she has struggled to repress a rush of tenderness for Percy; condemned to death, she blames herself for having rejected him. Apart from her 'disordered clothes' and 'uncovered head', the first sign of Anna's madness is that she thinks it is her wedding day:

> The King awaits me . . .
> the candles on the altar are lit,
> it is decorated with flowers.
> . . .That Percy know nothing about it,
> the King has ordered it so.[20]

Imagining that Percy then scolds her, Anna withdraws into images of the past, begging for a single day of their lost love. Her head clears to the discovery that she herself must die, and that wedding bells are ringing for the King. Summoned to the block, Anna faints – as if Romani wanted to spare her consciousness of the full horror.

With Giuditta Pasta in the title role *Anna Bolena* was an immediate success, although it subsequently fell into neglect. Revived for Maria Callas in 1957 it still boasts a mad scene second only to that of *Lucia di Lammermoor*, in which matrimony itself fulfils the structural function of a death sentence: obliged by her brother to marry Arturo, whom she does not love, and forget Edgardo, whom she does, Lucia goes mad on her wedding night and stabs her unwanted groom, dying shortly after. Variously combined, the elements of madness, romance and execution recur in several works by Vincenzo Bellini, notably *Il Pirata* (adultery and madness) of 1827, and *Beatrice di Tenda* (adultery and execution) of 1833, both with libretti by Romani.

Five years after *Anna Bolena* the formula of madness and execution is given an interesting twist in Bellini's *I Puritani*, with a libretto by Peppoli based on a novel by Sir Walter Scott. In *Puritani* the woman condemned to death – Queen Enricchetta, widow of the recently beheaded Charles I – is not the woman who goes mad. That distinction falls to Elvira, the angelically frail daughter of Roundhead Sir Walter Walton, governor of Enricchetta's prison. Betrothed by her father to the Roundhead Riccardo, Elvira has finally been allowed to marry the man she really loves: Lord Arturo, a dashing Cavalier. As the bridal day dawns Arturo arrives at the castle with bridal gifts and, alone among those present, recognises the soon-to-be executed Enricchetta as the Queen. Realising what a wonderful disguise Elvira's veil would make, he escapes with Enricchetta – ignoring the Queen's percipient plea to give some thought to his poor bride. Elvira returns from her matrimonial preparations just in time to see her fiancé departing the ramparts with another woman, and is unhinged by the shock.

Elvira's first reaction to the horror of Arthur's desertion is to split away from her own sense of identity:

> He looks at her, sighing,
> And calls her his bride.
> Is Elvira that lady?
> I'm Elvira no more?[21]

In the second phase of the delirium she rejects harsh reality altogether, thinking that her marriage to Arturo is about to take place. According to some critics, the dramatic plausibility of Elvira's madness was secondary to the opportunities it afforded for brilliant 'coloratura' – at least, until Maria Callas. 'Her inflections', writes J.B. Steane of the Callas *Puritani*, 'had a gentle pathos which brought out something different in the music... the dramatic situation became real rather than nominal; those descending chromatic scales were the haunted sighs of a clouded mind' (*Puritani*, p. 11). Bellini, who translated Elvira's emotional shock into these mournfully sinuous melodic lines, died at the age of 34 of intestinal fever. Delirious on his deathbed, he thought he saw a performance of *I Puritani* taking place in his bedroom.

In recent years the phenomena of female madness and death in opera have begun to attract feminist critics. Catherine Clément's *Opera, Or the Undoing of Women* subjects to Lacanian analysis à la Hélène Cixous the plots of thirty well-known operas, including *Norma, Aida, Carmen, Der Ring des Nibelungen, Tristan und Isolde* – and *I Puritani*. Observing that 'All Bellini's work is moved by broken unions', Catherine Clément stresses the moment when wild joy takes over in the aria:

> Bellini suddenly breaks the slow pace of delirium to launch the woman into the outrageous joy of wild, uncalled for, vertiginous notes. Little sparkling trumpets sound the joyful onslaught of fantasies. Elvira, like Lucia, passes rashly into the magical order of her desires. And what do the madwomen find in their delirium? The marriage that eludes them.[22]

The madness of Anna Bolena seems at first sight to 'elude' this remark, for in her delirium it is marriage with Enrico that she imagines first; later on, however, she longs for a single day of her lost love for Percy. Taking issue with the common view of operatic madwomen as 'pretty feebleminded', Clément contends that, on the contrary, they are stubborn and determined in their song; hardheaded, 'holding onto their desire even when everything else gets in the way'. *O rendetemi la speme, o lasciatemi morir*: give me back my hope, or let me die.

THE ART OF IMMOLATION

In the view of Susan McClary, who introduces Catherine Clément's book, her aim is to transmit to the reader 'some sense of opera that does not passively accept the stories it articulates', while recognising that her heroines 'are the victims of an art form that demands the submission or death of the woman for the sake of narrative closure' (Clément, p. xi). Strangely, Clément ignores the very operas which most explicitly demand the heroine's death through legal, if immoral, execution: *Anna Bolena, Maria Stuarda, Dialogues des Carmélites* – to say nothing of most of the *Antigones* and certain of the *Joans*. One is tempted heretically to suggest that perhaps those heroines are omitted because, with the exception of Antigone, it was not Opera but History that called for their death. The works to which Catherine Clément gives analytical preference are fictitious, sometimes based on myth, and probably serve better to illustrate the tyrannical structures of their creators' imagination: familial, paternal, racist, imperialist and so on.

Not actually attacked by madness at the block (or at the altar) the heroine of Schiller's *Maria Stuart* (1800) was subject once again to all the passions of Romance: she must physically repel an amorous would-be rescuer at one point. Besides being fatally attractive, Mary Stuart is endowed with considerable mental agility. As a prisoner at Fotheringay she argues spiritedly with both her gaoler, Sir Amias Paulet, and Elizabeth I's Lord High Treasurer, berating them on points of law. When Burleigh defends the probity of the forty male peers who have already condemned her, Mary sarcastically asks how she, 'a woman and unlearned', is to compete against a speaker of such skill: if the lords of the Commission were the erudite paragons of conscience Burleigh describes, her case would be hopeless. Mary however sees those 'high aristocrats of England' acting like seraglio slaves before her Uncle Henry; she sees them

> Enact laws and revoke them, now dissolve
> A marriage, now enforce it, at the mighty
> Man's bidding, disinherit England's Princesses
> Today and shame them with the name of bastards,
> And then again tomorrow crown them Queens.
> I see those worthy peers with swiftly changed
> Convictions *four times* alter their religion
> Under *four* regimes.[23]

Clearly, there is nothing wrong with this woman's wits. Yet Mary's gift for uncontrollably spirited replies soon proves her undoing. Taking liberties again with history, Schiller constructed his whole drama around a scene which never took place in reality: Mary's meeting with Elizabeth in the park at Fotheringay, a scene in which the two Queens spar, and which only leads to confirmation of Mary's sentence of death.

Occurring in the very middle of this symmetrically ordered play, the encounter is the result of duplicitous manoeuvring by Leicester, Elizabeth's most ambitious courtier. Unknown to Elizabeth, her favourite has been corresponding with Mary, promising her both matrimony and freedom. These causes he hopes to promote by engineering the meeting Mary has humbly requested through her gaoler, Paulet. Appealing to Elizabeth's vanity, Leicester gains her assent: how splendid it will be for her to trample on her wretched rival, when Elizabeth herself has just been betrothed to a French duke! But despite Leicester's cunning the meeting is a disaster. Elizabeth finds Mary, supposedly a suppliant, too proud, while Mary finds the English Queen arrogant, discourteous and unforgiving. Elizabeth cannot forget that Mary plotted to murder her (the Babington plot is still on everybody's mind); Mary on the other hand considers her cousin responsible for nineteen years of imprisonment, not to mention an illegal and outrageous trial. Tension mounts until Elizabeth insults her unruly adversary:

> Are all your plots done? No other murderer
> Is on his way? Will no adventurer
> Attempt his sorry chivalry for you?

This is too insulting for Mary, who retaliates by referring to the English Queen's 'secret lusts' and Anne Boleyn's adultery. Elizabeth departs in rage, leaving the prisoner's friends to bewail their lost hopes – even though it seems tacitly agreed that Mary got the best of the exchange.

To make matters worse a young Catholic knight named Mortimer, also in love with Mary, now tries to kill Elizabeth; he fails, and is betrayed by Leicester, who uses the betrayal to deflect suspicion from himself. Pressed by Burleigh to sign Mary's death warrant Elizabeth reluctantly does so, wrathfully ordering Leicester to arrange the execution. At the same time she commits the troublesome document, rather ambiguously, to her secretary Davison. Burleigh hastens to carry out the order before Elizabeth can change her mind. There is nothing left for Mary but to die. She does so with a serene grandeur, disposing of the shame-faced Leicester in a few dignified words and leaving Elizabeth, whom she magnanimously blesses, to the torture of remorse.

In penning his animated confrontation of the monarchs Schiller was not thinking merely of conflicting religious and political interests, but of antithetical psychological types. Mary is made to seem passionate and human – she admits, in confession, to an adulterous complicity in Darnley's murder; she is a sinner who has greatly loved and who is therefore lovable. Where the historical Mary was plump, balding and bewigged at the time of her trial, Schiller's Mary is so irresistible that men will die for her – Mortimer sacrifices himself, and Leicester wishes that he had. She is charming, without calculation, and entirely spontaneous. By comparison the English Queen is cold and vain, a prisoner of duty, rational intellect and contrived virtue. Men make excuses for Mary, whereas they simply flatter Elizabeth:

THE ART OF IMMOLATION

> She threw herself into the strongest, bravest
> Man's arms – compelled by what devices, who
> Can tell? For woman is a frail creature,

declares Shrewsbury, apologising for the blot on Mary's conduct that was Bothwell. Although the historical Elizabeth was wont to criticise her sex, Schiller makes her angrily retort:

> Woman is not weak. There are strong souls
> Among the sex. – I will not tolerate
> Talk of that sex's weakness in my presence.

Mary, in short, is seen as a 'natural' woman, frail and adorable, where Elizabeth is unbecomingly rational and strong. The play's ending reflects its emotional preference: a victorious Elizabeth is deserted by her officers of state while Mary's friends, as execution looms, have literally to be wrested from her side.

Posterity has preferred Schiller's Mary to his Joan; *Maria Stuart* is still regarded as his greatest work. Stripped of its political complexity, its intellectual power and most of its characters it presently provided the basis for another opera by Donizetti, his *Maria Stuarda* of 1835. Donizetti had seen Maffei's translation of the play performed in Milan, and being at the time engaged by the Conservatory of Naples to compose an opera each year he hastened to approach his favourite librettist. Romani, however, was tiring of the theatre and had immersed himself in journalism. The impatient Donizetti turned to a 17-year-old law student, Giuseppe Bardari, of no known ventures into literature and music either before or since: Bardari became a Neapolitan magistrate, and died as prefect of police.

Young Bardari managed astonishingly well, retaining the main episodes of Schiller's play but shrinking the drama from five acts into three. Act I is taken up with Leicester's efforts to persuade a wildly jealous Elizabeth to meet Mary; Act II presents their calamitous encounter in the park at Fotheringay; Act III includes Mary's confession, final meeting with a distraught Leicester, and preparation for execution. The cast was similarly pruned from seventeen characters to six, providing Donizetti with an excellent pretext for a sextet – though not such a good sextet as in *Lucia di Lammermoor* – before the disastrous confrontation, on which the action hinges. In Act I Mary has already been condemned; her only hope is mercy from Elizabeth, hence Leicester's efforts to obtain the meeting. Bardari followed the outline of Schiller's confrontation, but the insults uttered by his Queens are more succint and vituperative. Since political considerations are simplified and romantic ones exaggerated, the resulting dialogue suggests that Elizabeth I condemned Mary Queen of Scots from nothing more than jealousy, and rage at being called a bastard; statecraft plays no part in the disaster, as if women rulers had nothing more significant to ponder than the favours of the Earl of Leicester. Although Mary emerges from the meeting liberated by her outburst, the only practical result is an emphatic repetition of her condemnation.

The royal trade of insults had repercussions for Donizetti too. When the opera went into rehearsal in August 1834 the *prime donne* cast as Mary and Elizabeth sang their tirades with such conviction –

> Unchaste daughter of Anne Boleyn,
> do you speak of dishonour?
> Base, lascivious harlot,
> let my shame fall on you.
> The English throne is profaned,
> despicable bastard, by your presence![24] –

that Anna del Sere (Elizabeth) took the awful utterance personally and did Giuseppina Ronzi de Begnis (Mary) physical violence. Donizetti calmed the divas by remarking that 'those two queens were whores, and so are both of you'. Next the Neapolitan censors demanded changes in the text. After they had been made, King Ferdinand of Naples banned it altogether. He and his Queen (who had been reluctantly extracted from a convent to marry him) disliked public entertainment, especially sad and bloody plays depicting the beheading of monarchy. Moreover, they were both descended from Mary Queen of Scots. Faced with grafting the music of the opera onto another subject – as Verdi had to do a decade later, with *Orietta di Lesbo* – Donizetti first thought of Lady Jane Grey, but from the viewpoint of the court this was scarcely an improvement. The internecine strife between the Guelphs and Ghibellines in thirteenth-century Florence seemed a harmless choice and a second libretto was hastily concocted. The resulting opera, *Buon del Monte*, did not profit from the changes. To Donizetti's relief *Maria Stuarda* was finally performed in its original form at La Scala on 30 December 1835, with Malibran as Mary. After three performances the censors struck again; Acts II and III were replaced by bits of Rossini's *Otello*. After six performances the authorities once again banned the work completely, apparently objecting to Mary's confession scene – the sacraments, they said, should not be viewed on stage – and the word 'bastarda' in the royal exchange. As for *Buon del Monte*, it has never been revived.

Donizetti never saw his *Maria Stuarda* again, dying in 1848 after a period of insanity. In 1865 the San Carlo Opera staged the work with reasonable accuracy; after that it disappeared from the repertory until revived in Bologna in 1958. This hiatus by no means signalled the literary end of Mary Stuart. In Italy alone her irremediably romantic personage had inspired works by Sogner, Carafa, Palumbo and Carlo Coccia. There was also Mercadante's *Maria Stuarda Regina di Scozia*, and Capecelatro's *Davide Riccio*. Into the English-speaking world came three dramas by Algernon Charles Swinburne: *Chastelard* (1865), *Bothwell* (1874) and *Mary Stuart* (1881). The trilogy has lapsed into obscurity, suffering – unlike Schiller's plays – from loose construction and too great a faithfulness to history. In 1933 Maxwell Anderson, better known for his *Key Largo*, wrote a *Mary of Scotland*. In the post-war period *Mary Queen of Scots*, an opera by Thea Musgrave (who also wrote the libretto), made Mary arguably the most popular executed heroine after Antigone and Jeanne d'Arc.

Fourteen years after Mary Stuart died at Fotheringay, Beatrice Cenci was beheaded by the *mannaia* in Rome. Just as the sanguinary events of the English Renaissance seem to have fired the imagination of Italian librettists, so did the dark and passionate undercurrent of the Italian Rinascimento appeal to the English Romantics – not the elegantly idealistic Renaissance of Marsilio Ficino or Baldassare Castiglione, but the Renaissance evoked by the name Borgia, a Renaissance of murder and intrigue not untinged with incest. Such a world is conjured up in *The Cenci*, a 'fearful and monstrous' story which Shelley began to cast into tragedy in Rome in May 1819, and finished in September of that year.

Although written in Italy, *The Cenci* was conceived with production in England in mind: Shelley wanted it staged at Covent Garden with Eliza O'Neill as Beatrice. Kean was to have played Francesco Cenci, even though Shelley had disliked his Hamlet; 'too furious', he thought, but then fury was an appropriately dynamic asset for Count Cenci. This production was never to be. For the Tory establishment controlling English theatre, a drama written by a radical left-wing atheist dealing with incest was hardly likely to please. As the reviewer of *The Literary Gazette* remarked, 'Of all the abominations which intellectual perversion, and poetical atheism, have produced in our times, this tragedy appears to us to be the most abominable. We have much doubted whether we ought to notice it.'[25] Yet notice it the *Gazette* deigned to do, if only to set up a warning beacon to this 'noisome and noxious publication'. *The Cenci* was not staged in Shelley's brief lifetime, which meant it could not be revised in the light of rehearsal and production. Finally given twenty-six performances in Moscow during the 1919–20 season, it was put on in Prague in 1922, the centenary of Shelley's death, and then, with Sybil Thorndike as Beatrice, in London.

The action of *The Cenci* was drawn from one of those now highly suspect *relazioni* that tended to depict Francesco as a frenzied, sodomitic monster who despised his children, and Beatrice as a ravished martyr. It seems to have assumed Francesco raped his daughter, though no-one can be absolutely certain as the one surviving copy of this particular account is the handwritten script of Mary Shelley, whose pen refused to record more than a series of asterisks for the parental crime. While viewing Beatrice as a victim – first of paternal oppression, then of corrupt papal authority – Shelley nonetheless meant to show her as he thought she was: an energetic, strong-willed girl capable of violent revenge. His honesty may have been prompted by his own feminism: he had, after all, married the daughter of Mary Wollstonecraft and William Godwin. In 1818 he had written a *Discourse on the Manners of the Ancient Greeks* attacking the degraded state of women in Greek culture, which granted men rigorous intellectual training while keeping its women as ignorant slaves, consequently incapable of full development. His own age, he felt, was much improved but still 'remote from what an enlightened mind cannot fail to desire as the future destiny of human beings'. As for marriage, it derived from a simple relationship of property: in primitive times men subdued women by force, then treated them as mere possessions.

Though not of Ancient Greece, Lucrezia and Beatrice Cenci are scarcely better off than slaves at the hands of Shelley's debauched patriarch. In *The Cenci*'s early scenes the wicked Francesco is seen first in conflict with Cardinal Camillo, who is trying to reform him, then at a banquet scene whose purpose, he informs his startled guests, is to celebrate the recent murders of his sons. When Beatrice reproves his horrid flippancy he responds with chilling words: 'I know a charm shall make thee meek and tame.' In Act II Francesco extends his evil domination of the household, mistreating both Lucrezia, stepmother to the surviving children, and his younger son Bernardo. He also intensifies his threats against Beatrice who, fearful and distracted, seems to divine her father's foul intent:

> Oh! He has trampled me
> Under his feet and made the blood stream down
> My pallid cheeks...
> And I have never yet despaired – but now!
> What shall I say?[26]

With an effort she recovers herself: she must keep her wits together for Lucrezia's sake. Indeed, the remaining male characters are not likely to provide much help. Her other brother Giacomo is irresolute and poor, lacking money to feed his children; Francesco has stolen the young wife's dowry. Beatrice has asked the prelate Orsini, who was once in love with her, to present a petition to the Pope on her behalf; but Orsini intends only to seduce her. A figure of ruthless corruption, he provides a sinister glimpse of the external world with which Beatrice presently must cope.

When Beatrice appears in Act III she is temporarily insane. It slowly becomes clear to the audience, as it had done to Orsini and her family, that Cenci has raped her. That the resulting mad scene owes something to the conventions of Elizabethan drama does not inhibit its effectiveness. It must and does convey the violence done to Beatrice's emotional integrity; the threat of execution will terrify her less. She enters 'staggering', and 'speaking wildly':

'My brain is hurt', she says, 'My eyes are full of blood'. From the initial shock she moves to disassociation from herself:

> I thought I was that wretched Beatrice
> Men speak of, whom her father sometimes hales
> From hall to hall by her entangled hair; . . .
> At others, pens up naked in damp cells
> Where scaly reptiles crawl, and starves her there
> Till she will eat strange flesh. . .
> (Shelley, p. 276)

Slowly she returns to an apprehension of reality:

> Why so it is. This is the Cenci Palace;
> Thou art Lucretia; I am Beatrice.
> I have talked wild words, but will no more.

Thereafter revenge emerges as her dominating obsession. Together with Orsini, Giacomo and Lucretia she plots to kill Francesco by making use of Marzio and Olimpio, two henchmen of Petrella who loathe their former lord.

From Cenci's bullying words in the first and second acts it appears that he rapes Beatrice mainly to break her spirit. In Act IV, he goes further, explaining that he wants to degrade her soul eternally: give her a taste for incest, damn her before God, make her 'Body and soul a monstrous lump of ruin'. He even hopes that she will bear a child, whose likeness to herself – and him – will cause her constant anguish:

> Quick Nature! I adjure thee by thy God,
> That thou be fruitful in her. . . May it be
> A hideous likeness of herself; that as
> From a distorting mirror, she may see
> Her image mixed with what she most abhors.

More ominously still, he seems to hope the child will outrage her as its father did, repaying her maternal care with pain and hate 'Or what else may be more unnatural'. These and similar expectations put him in a frenzy of lust: 'A fearful pleasure' in his blood 'makes it prick and tingle'. Exhausted by so much feverish anticipation, he falls deeply asleep. Beatrice then sends the hired murderers, Marzio and Olimpio, into his room to kill him. But the two men are overcome with pity and fail in their task; Beatrice has to threaten to do the deed herself before they find the courage.

The murder immediately proves to have been precipitate. A papal legate arrives moments later with a warrant for Cenci's arrest, and quickly discovers the crime; although Clement apparently intended prosecuting Cenci, he will show no mercy to his murderers. Thrown into prison, Beatrice and her family now find themselves pitted against the judicial resources of the papal state. When those around her are tortured and confess, Beatrice continues to deny everything: in her own mind she is guilty not of crime, but of an act of justice. Threatened with the rack herself she berates her judges for their cruelty, and Giacomo and Lucretia for their weakness in confessing:

> Tortures! Turn
> The rack henceforth into a spinning wheel!
> Torture your dog, that he may tell when last
> He lapped the blood his master shed – not me!
> My pangs are of the mind, and of the heart . . .
> To see, in this ill world where none are true,
> My kindred false to their deserted selves.
>
> (Shelley, p. 304)

When the Supreme Pontiff rejects Bernardo's plea for mercy Beatrice realises she must die, and once again her mind clouds with horror: isn't she too young to go 'Under the obscure, cold, rotting, wormy ground?' Like Racine's Phèdre she imagines herself meeting her father in the after-life, not in her case as the judge of Hades but in the form he tortured her on earth, 'Masked in grey hairs and wrinkles', coming to

> Wind me in his hellish arms, and fix
> His eyes on mine, and drag me down, down, down
> For was he not alone omnipotent
> On earth and ever present?

Even in this extremity her strong spirit rises to the occasion. Regaining her composure Beatrice dies with grace and dignity, comforting those around her – both those who must perish, and those who remain. Her final words manage to wring peaceful domesticity from the grim necessity of putting up her hair:

> Here, mother, tie
> My girdle for me, and bind up this hair
> In any simple knot; ay, that does well.
> And yours I see is coming down. How often
> Have we done this for one another! now
> We shall not do it any more. My lord,
> We are quite ready. Well, 'tis very well.

Thus Beatrice gently dies, accepting her destiny.

Although Shelley's preface to *The Cenci* makes clear he disapproved of Beatrice's vengeful deed, his sympathetic presentation of her fate suggests he disapproved even more of papal justice. Beatrice must face two forms of tyranny, and her efforts to free herself from both prove futile. The corrupt atmosphere of the Palazzo Cenci, Shelley implies, eventually taints her own proud character; the outrage to which she is subject momentarily destroys her sense of self. Her tragic achievement is to reassert her wounded self, but at the cost of proving she is cast in Cenci's mould. Heroically, she keeps faith in the justice of her act until the very end. Her dire imaginings when faced with death indicate, horribly, how papal harshness – paternalism of another sort – betrays her to the ongoing celestial domination of her earthly father. When reason returns, acceptance is her one recourse.

Thus Donizetti's Anna Bolena, Schiller's Maria Stuart and Shelley's Beatrice Cenci represent three versions of the Romantic executed woman. All three are sorely tried and, despite their varying degrees of criminality, leave the audience with the feeling they have been unjustly condemned. All die evincing saintly humility and grandeur of soul: Anna, while still almost mad; Beatrice, having been mad; Maria, never having been mad, but having shown a passionate pride beyond her control. The heroines' chronology is troublesome in that the historical order in which they were executed naturally does not match the sequence in which the plays and operas were composed. There is in Anna Bolena's madness an anticipation of late nineteenth-century attitudes: woman is a frail creature, mad almost by birth; passion is too much for her and, combined with injustice and the block, will certainly unhinge her. That Anna faints at the last provides a ladylike exit from the gruesome scene, hinting, besides, that women should not really be subject to such horrors.

Created earlier in the century, Maria Stuart and Beatrice Cenci are far more complex characters. If Maria embodies the attractive paradox of the lovable sinner, Shelley's Beatrice is both delicate and violent: 'Beatrice Cenci appears to have been one of those rare persons in whom energy and gentleness dwell together without destroying one another', wrote Shelley in his preface. In both cases this paradox of character lends dynamism to the play. In *The Cenci*, Beatrice's temporary alienation of wits has implications that transcend the conventions it is derived from: the chasm of the imagination opens up to the alienated, outraged self, at once victim and perpetrator of familial crime.

SISTERHOOD AND SACRIFICE

Beatrice Cenci was not the sole beheaded heroine to be celebrated by Shelley. As a student at Oxford he had written fragments of verse in the name of Margaret Nicholson, a demented laundress who had tried to kill George III, and subsequently been confined to Bedlam. The fragments took the form of an Epithalamium featuring François Ravaillac, murderer of Henry IV, and Charlotte Cordé (*sic*); on the principle that 'Congenial minds will seek their kindred soul', the spirits of the two assassins meet and fall in love:

> Yes, Francis! thine was the dear knife that tore
> A tyrant's heart-strings from his guilty breast...

So apostrophises Charlotte, while Ravaillac responds,

> Soft, my dearest angel, stay;
> Oh! you suck my soul away!
> Suck on, suck on; I glow, I glow!
> ... Endless kisses steal my breath,
> No life can equal such a death.[27]

Published as a practical joke upon the English public, the poetry is not of Shelley's finest. Nor is it typical of literature dealing with the heroines of revolution. While passion continues to be present at the scaffold, victims tend to be animated less by the spirit of assassination than by the spirit of self-sacrifice.

Thus the heroine of Giordano's opera *Andrea Chénier* (1896) and the hero of Dickens' *A Tale of Two Cities* (1859) both immolate themselves for love. Numerous adaptations into film and television series have made the metamorphosis of Sydney Carton, Dickens' dissolute London lawyer, into a paragon of altruistic love exceedingly well known: by pointing out his own astonishing resemblance to Charles Darnay, defendant in a treason case, Carton is able to confuse a prosecution witness and save Darnay from death. When Darnay is later condemned by the French Revolutionary Tribunal, Carton visits his *alter ego* in prison, drugs him, dresses up in his clothes and – taking advantage once again of their uncanny likeness – is guillotined in Darnay's stead. This noble deed is inspired by love for Darnay's wife, the angelic Lucie Manette; the hopeless, disreputable Carton had once promised he would give his life for her.

Maddalena di Coigny, the aristocratic heroine of Giordano's opera *Andrea Chénier* (1896), might well be termed the female counterpart of Sydney Carton. For reasons of love she, too, succeeds in replacing a prisoner condemned to death, and dies joyfully. But whereas Carton sacrifices himself that another may live, Maddalena gains admittance to the prison of Saint-Lazare to die *with* her beloved – the poet André Chénier.

The opera presents the usual departures from fact. The historical André Chénier was arrested almost by mistake by an illiterate fool after disdaining to flee, and guillotined after a period of imprisonment. Maddalena, or Madeleine as she would have been in French, seems to have been created *ex nihilo* by Giordano's librettist, Luigi Illica. The opening section of the work takes place before the Revolution: Chénier, a gifted poet of democratic views, meets Maddalena at a fashionable reception held in her mother's house. Challenged to recite some of his work, Chénier at first refuses; poetry, he says, is quite as capricious as love and cannot be forced. Maddalena giggles, for she has laid a bet with her friends that the poet would inevitably speak of love. Stung, Chénier launches into his aria 'Un di all' azzurro spazio', a bitter denunciation of both Church and nobility:

> I crossed the entrance of a humble cottage.
> There a blaspheming man maligned
> the soil that barely satisfies his taxes
> and against God and against man
> he hurled the tears of his children![28]

Mostly noblemen or clerics, the Contessa di Coigny's guests are appalled and enraged, but Maddalena is deeply moved; apologising for her frivolity, she excuses herself from the reception.

Act II finds the protagonists in mid-Revolution. At first admired by the revolutionary leaders – who include Gérard, a former servant of the Coigny family – Chénier now finds his influence has declined. He nonetheless refuses to flee from Paris until he has kept a rendezvous with a mysterious woman who has been sending him love letters. The woman turns out to be Maddalena, herself in great peril and sheltered only by a devoted maid. She asks for Chénier's protection, and the two exchange rhapsodic vows: 'We will be together until death!' – a fate soon realised. Their duet is interrupted by the arrival of Gérard, a powerful Jacobin enamoured of Maddalena whom he has been spying on. Thinking to protect his beloved, Chénier draws his sword and wounds the former servant. Recognising the poet, whom he still admires, Gérard generously reveals that Chénier is now on Fouquier-Tinville's proscribed list and tells him to flee and to protect Maddalena.

The opera's third act comprises a trial scene of epic scope. Required to pen a denunciation of Chénier, Gérard shows that he is not a jingoistic monster but a conscientious man who has begun to have doubts:

> Once it was joyous to me to walk
> among hatred and vengeance,
> pure, innocent and strong.
> I believed myself a giant!
> But I am still a servant –
> I have merely changed masters!
> (*Andrea Chénier*, p. 56)

While ruminating thus, Gérard is approached by Maddalena who offers to sleep with him if he will save the poet. Moved by this self-sacrificial evidence of love, Gérard explains to Fouquier and an incredulous court that he has falsely accused Chénier. This brave gesture is quite useless, for Gérard promptly hears himself denounced as a traitor by the spectators. Chénier is condemned and taken back to prison. In the final act Gérard enters the prison with Maddalena, who bribes the jailer into letting her take the place of a condemned woman:

> I am here so that I may never leave you.
> This is not a farewell!
> ... I have come to die with you!

After another idyllic duet they are executed together; as Chénier proclaims, 'Our death is a triumph of love!'

Although fidelity to fact is certainly no guarantor of aesthetic felicity – and the actual love story seems to have been an invention of the librettist – the historical background of *Andrea Chénier* was admirably researched, containing few inaccuracies of style and tone. Giordano has woven contemporary quotations into his score: snatches of the Carmagnole and Marseillaise blend with his own soaring melodies. Musically and dramatically, the opera conveys a certain authenticity in its depictions of revolutionary fervour and amorous idealism: Maddalena's sacrifice is not inherently impossible, given the lax policing of some prisons and the amorous inclinations of a good many prisoners, spurred into passion by the probability of death. One thinks of Adam Lux falling in love with Charlotte Corday at the scaffold, and wishing to die with her; of Chénier's lines for the same heroine. Illica's protagonists are persons of some depth, all capable of sacrifice: Maddalena moves from worldly levity to a more socially conscious sort of love; Gérard defends Chénier at risk of his life and at loss of hope of love. Nor does Chénier, poet of the poor and oppressed, hesitate to risk his life for an ideal passion. Love and death, love overcoming death: thus, a century after the event, Illica meditates on the Revolution, with generosity of heart pitted against the murderous zeal of Jacobin ideology.

A less terrestrial spirit of sacrifice animates the heroines of Georges Bernanos' *Dialogues des Carmélites* of 1947. Based on the martyrdom of the Carmelite sisters of Compiègne in July 1794 and written in the months preceding Bernanos' own death, this austere text has been adapted for theatre, opera and television. The original source was the *Relation* of a senior Carmelite, Mother Marie of the Incarnation, who had entered Carmel after being – miraculously, it seemed – cured of a paralysis in early life. Expelled from their convent on 14 September 1792 by the revolutionary government, the Carmelites of Compiègne had lived on in small groups in the town until arrested in June 1794. Absent on personal business at the time of the arrest, Mother Marie escaped the mass guillotining which occurred on 17 July – ten days before the fall of Robespierre. The fifteen sisters mounted the scaffold singing the *Salve Regina* and the *Veni Creator*, apparently pausing only to curtsey to their Superior. Mother Marie lived for some time in hiding, re-entering the Carmel of Sens in 1823 as a paying guest; evidently a woman of means, she is thought to have been the illegitimate offspring of a royal liaison. She died in 1836. Her martyred colleagues of Compiègne were beatified by Pius X in 1906.

THE ART OF IMMOLATION

Few novelists would seem more fitted to treat such a subject than Georges Bernanos, a patriotic Catholic whose books had always reflected a religious preoccupation with the struggle for salvation. As a young man his interest in sanctity verged almost on the droll: in 1914, in Rouen, he had met and married Jeanne Talbert d'Arc, daughter of the president of the right-wing Dames de l'Action Française and a direct descendant of Joan of Arc's brother. In later life he kept beside him the *Novissima Verba* of Saint Thérèse of Lisieux, and it is said he felt closer to this child-like figure than to any other saint except Jeanne d'Arc herself. Yet it was not Bernanos but a German writer, Gertrud von Le Fort, who first took up the tale in her *novella, Die Letzte am Schafoott* of 1938. To the original complement of fifteen martyred nuns Le Fort added two youthful novices, Sisters Blanche and Constance, both seemingly modelled on Marie-Geneviève Meunier, who was the youngest of the historical nuns. Marie-Geneviève had chosen the name of Sister Constance but, owing to the decree of the Constituent Assembly, never took her actual vows. Of Blanche, who was very much her own invention, Le Fort wrote that she was 'born of the profound horror of a time in which the shadow of presentiment pointing to future events was falling upon Germany' and that she 'rose up before me as the incarnation of the mortal anguish of a whole period approaching its end'.[29] In the *novella* Constance and Blanche are both afraid of martyrdom, but overcome that fear: when her sisters are being guillotined Blanche voluntarily joins them, thus becoming the 'last one at the scaffold' of the title.

When asked in May 1947 if he would write dialogues for a screenplay based upon the *novella* Bernanos hesitated; he had never worked in film. Indeed, when his manuscript arrived in Paris a year later it was deemed 'too interior' for celluloid and the project was postponed. After Bernanos died the *Dialogues* were rediscovered in a trunk and arranged for stage performance by a friend; in 1955–6 they were pruned into a libretto for the opera by Poulenc.

Aware, as he wrote, that he was dying, Bernanos drew upon his own fear in elaborating the *Dialogues*' main theme: the anguish felt by Blanche de la Force during the revolutionary upheavals. A delicate, timorous aristocrat tormented by her own weakness, Blanche might well have been expected to go mad had she experienced an *affetto terreno* and found herself in an Italian opera a century before. But Bernanos had other plans. To the alarm of her father and brother – already disturbed by her fragility – Blanche announces that she is going to enter Carmel. Interviewed by the convent's Mother Superior, she defines the purpose of Carmel as 'overcoming nature' and asks to be known as Sister Blanche of the Agony of Christ. This reference to Christ's terror in the Garden of Olives startles the Superior, for it is the name she had once chosen herself. Admitted to the order Blanche makes friends with Constance, a young, aristocratic novice; Constance terrifies her new friend by remarking that she has always had the feeling they will die together, very young. Shortly thereafter the Mother Superior dies after committing Blanche to the care of her second-in-command, the resolute Mother Marie. The Superior's painful death, full of anguish and despair, astonishes everyone except Constance, who observes that God must have given her this difficult death to make dying easier for someone else – someone who would not normally expect to die bravely at all.

The new prioress is not Mother Marie, as Constance hoped, but the far more down-to-earth Mother Lidoine, whose father was a merchant; it is implied that the choice was made to placate the egalitarian new authorities. Even so the small convent is soon rocked by revolutionary intrusions. Himself about to join the *émigré* army, Blanche's brother tries vainly to persuade his sister to return to their father. When Mother Marie begins to hint at possible martyrdom she is rebuked by the practical new prioress for her aristocratic heroism: 'Carmel is not, as far as I know, an order of Chivalry'. Urging her charges to the less spectacular occupation of prayer, Mother Lidoine announces she will not resist the government's suspension of monastic vows. This prudence is opposed by Mother Marie, who takes advantage of a day when Mother Lidoine is absent to extract a vow of martyrdom from all the nuns. Realising the strain this will place upon the younger sisters, Mother Marie concedes that one dissenting voice will cause her to retract the vow. One sister does in fact dissent: not Blanche, as everyone expects, but Constance, who does not want her friend to appear the only coward. Seeing, however, that Blanche has voted with the others, Constance asks permission to change her vote. As the nuns line up to solemnise their vow Blanche flees in distress. Mother Lidoine returns and rebukes Mother Marie for her thoughtless bravery, reminding her that the 'strong are strong at the expense of the weak, and weakness will finally be reconciled and glorified in the universal redemption'.[30] Mother Marie apologises, prays that God may punish her severely and begs permission to go and look for Blanche in Paris.

In the play's concluding scenes Blanche's father, the Marquis de la Force, is guillotined a week after being freed from the Conciergerie. Visiting her, Mother Marie is horrified to find Blanche as fearful as ever, and terrorised by the servants. 'The real misfortune', Mother Marie tells her, 'is not to be despised by others, but to despise oneself.' The remaining nuns have meanwhile been arrested with Mother Lidoine. Hearing they have been condemned to death Blanche urges Mother Marie to do something to save them. Mother Marie does not agree: on the contrary, she is all for dying with them. Horror, she declares, lies only in crime, which can be effaced by the sacrifice of innocent lives. Revolted by this talk of death Blanche rushes out. Mother Marie, who feels 'dishonoured' at not fulfilling her vow of martyrdom, is restrained from dashing to the scaffold by the convent's former Almoner, who points out that precipitous action could further endanger her Carmelite sisters.

THE ART OF IMMOLATION

At the Conciergerie Mother Lidoine assumes responsibility for the vow she did not take and comforts those who are unnerved; as their mother, she explains, she was unwilling to sacrifice them even to God himself, but now that martyrdom is imminent she gives them her maternal blessing. In the final scene the Carmelites descend from the tumbrils and mount the scaffold singing the *Salve Regina* and the *Veni Creator*. Disguised in a Liberty Bonnet the Almoner gives surreptitious absolution. One by one the sisters' voices diminish until Constance alone remains; suddenly Blanche emerges from the crowd and makes her way towards the guillotine. Constance catches sight of her, smiles, and is beheaded. Blanche calmly sings four lines of the *Veni Creator* before her voice, too, is silenced.

In writing his *Dialogues* Bernanos reduced the forty sequences of the original scenario to twenty-two, cutting external action and concentrating mainly on Blanche and her fear. The libretto, as cut into scenes by Poulenc himself in 1953, presents an even tighter drama, focussed almost wholly on Blanche's inner fight. Poulenc omits much of the 'worldly' material – revolutionary interventions, events at the La Force home – leaving only what is strictly necessary to indicate the heroine's background and the effects of revolution on the convent. Vocally, there results an interesting opposition between sexes: except for the Almoner, the male voices heard belong entirely to the world outside Carmel – in striking contrast to the voices of the female sanctum. Yet Poulenc has also cut a number of dialogues between the nuns themselves. The effect is to reduce not only the range of opinion within Carmel but also the broader sense of the eventual martyrdom. Most notably, he cuts Mother Marie's remark about crime being effaced by the sacrifice of innocent lives, which in Bernanos' text is the main point of the sisters' death.

On the other hand Poulenc's libretto expands the indications given by Bernanos for the harrowing final scene: lightly and serenely the diminishing voices of the sisters sing the full text of the *Salve Regina* while sickening orchestral thuds announce the operation of the guillotine. Throughout this last scene, which has been described as a long march to the scaffold, inexorable rhythms build; the sombre momentum of the music suggests the wrenching of the soul from its human frame. The opera has no distractingly brilliant arias; each individual utterance relates to the texture of the whole. Discreetly the orchestration yields to the voice, as if it were exhaling the soul. Opera or play, seldom has a work been so well named: dialogues between the sisters, dialogues between the sisters and the world, dialogues in the Platonic sense, dialogues by Bernanos written for a film. And, although Bernanos specifies that only the foot of the scaffold should be seen, seldom has a work conveyed so graphically the horror of the guillotine as the singers' voices cut out one by one, often in mid-word.

An impressive work undoubtedly, in all its forms. But as Blanche herself remarks, isn't all this emphasis on martyrdom a touch revolting? Doesn't one begin to feel, like the revolutionary officer who visits the convent in the play, that there are sequestered persons living there who would do better liberated, in the world? Bernanos admits this view, only to reject it in favour of the spiritual imperative. For him the Carmelites are a devout élite for whom the ultimate elegance is to give themselves, like saints, in a gesture at once perilous and total. 'A saint doesn't live on the interest of his income,' he wrote in 1947, not too long before the *Dialogues*, 'or even on his income; he lives on his capital, he gives all of his soul.' Nonetheless 'saints are not heroes in the manner of Plutarch's heroes' who seem to surpass humanity. 'The saint doesn't surpass it, he assumes it.' Hence his respect for Blanche's terror, since Christ 'wished to open up to His martyrs the glorious opportunity of a death without fear; but He also wanted to precede each of us in the darkness of mortal agony'. The dying Bernanos saw a world increasingly debased by technology – 'that degraded form of intelligence' – and threatened in its inner life, against which our 'inhuman civilisation is conspiring'. In the mid-twentieth century saints seemed to him significant because they maintained 'the interior life without which humanity must debase itself to the point of extinction'.[31] Blanche and Constance, those literary sisters of Saint Thérèse and Jeanne, militate, like saints, against such debasement.

Written at Sorrento in 1938, Marguerite Yourcenar's classic short novel *Le Coup de grâce* is also concerned with the values of an aristocratic élite in time of revolution. Like *Die Letzte am Schafoott* it is one of the few works about executed females penned by a woman; unlike the Le Fort *novella* it has practically no religious elements and is based on an incident which took place in our century. Set in an isolated part of the Baltic states following the Russian Revolution, Yourcenar's tale concerns an impossible romantic passion with an unusually disastrous termination – military execution. The incident was narrated to the author some twenty years after the event by a friend of one of the protagonists. As Yourcenar comments in her retrospectively written preface, it 'seemed to lend itself to the frame of the traditional French *récit*' – a form which has retained 'certain characteristics of tragedy'. Apparently she was thinking of the old classical unities of time, place and 'danger', and of the 'inevitably tragic outcome to which passion always leads'.[32] Classical unities notwithstanding, her *récit* has also lent itself to cinematic adaptation in the form of a black-and-white film by Volker Schlöndorff.

Like certain first-person *récits* by another master of the genre, André Gide, *Le Coup de grâce* is given a conventional explicatory frame. An unidentified observer hears the story as related many years later by its hero, Eric von L'Homond, in the buffet of Pisa railway station one morning before dawn. Eric is described as fortyish, handsome in a petrified sort of way, a professional soldier of fortune. These particulars given, the story shifts into Eric's own narration of the 'interminable confession he was really only making to himself'.

THE ART OF IMMOLATION

In the indecisive anti-Bolshevik campaign that follows on the First World War, Eric and his friend Conrad – blond, titled, pale-eyed and muscular – return to Conrad's family castle at Kratovicé, where they had stayed as adolescents. The castle is full of soldiers; of Conrad's family only his sister Sophie and an aunt remain. Unaware that Eric and Conrad are lovers, Sophie – spontaneous, chivalrous and pure – falls deeply in love with her brother's friend, and tells him so. Eric does nothing to enlighten her, just as he fails definitively to encourage or reject her; instead, flattered and intrigued by her valiantly ingenuous charm, he becomes her friend and confidant. Except for Conrad, who notices nothing, the other officers assume they are engaged. But the closest Eric and Sophie ever come to passionate reciprocity occurs during a nocturnal bombardment of the castle. Intoxicated by the danger they have shared, Sophie flings herself against Eric's chest and for a moment the young man succumbs to a seductive sweetness. Unfortunately for Sophie this changes quickly to revulsion and he pushes her away. Wounded to the core, Sophie takes lovers, without pleasure to herself, mainly to exasperate Eric. She almost succeeds: at Christmas he punches a particularly detestable 'rival' who is kissing Sophie underneath the mistletoe. Eric is painfully aware that if he commits himself to Sophie it must be for life; he does not see himself as Conrad's brother-in-law, and once again does nothing to resolve the situation.

Next morning the entire garrison departs on a campaign, in the course of which Eric sends his 'rival' back to the castle on a mission of some danger. When he returns he finds Sophie going down the stairs with a bundle of clothes. Informed by the rival of Eric's relations with her brother she is leaving in immense disgust. A furious confrontation follows in which the two say wounding things to each other. Having done nothing to prevent her from leaving, Eric eventually makes enquiries and finds she has deserted to the Bolsheviks. The war drags on. In a subsequent campaign Conrad is fatally wounded in the stomach and dies at dawn in agony; Eric thinks of shooting him to end his pain, but lacks the necessary courage. Instead, he bullies a frightened priest into giving Conrad absolution and buries him in the Baltic mud. Not long thereafter Eric and his soldiers find Sophie, dressed as a man, trapped in a granary with a handful of Bolshevik troops whom they take prisoner. There can be no quarter given; besides, Sophie has defected. There is not even a trial, just an intelligence-gathering interview which disgusts Eric himself. The peasants and Sophie tell him nothing. He has them shot at dawn, singly, by revolver, the deed being carried out by Kratovicé's former butcher. Sophie is the last to die. She has lost nothing of her aplomb and at the last moment orders Eric to execute her; his first shot destroys part of her face, preventing him from seeing 'what expression she adopted in death'. The second one kills her.

Yourcenar insists in her preface on the nobility of her three principal actors, all of whom belong to that social caste whence knights were once recruited.

Burying Conrad, Eric has the feeling he has brought him safely home: dying in battle, blessed by a priest, it is an end Conrad's ancestors would have found acceptable. But for Yourcenar nobility is not a simple matter of aristocratic birth. It is a quality of disinterestedness, 'a total absence of calculation', extending to a scrupulous generosity towards one's adversaries. Such an attitude soon blurs distinctions – so clearly delineated in chivalric Romance – between good and bad, friend and foe, noble and commoner. It is no accident that Eric, though German, has French and Baltic ancestors; Sophie and Conrad are Baltic and Russian. Eric's father, an admirer of things French, is killed by a Frenchman at the battle of Verdun. Though anti-Semitic by upbringing, Eric comes to admire Grigori Loew, a young Jewish pro-Bolshevik intellectual who lends Sophie books and later dies in battle with a volume of Rilke in his pocket – a poet Conrad had liked. At the same time Eric feels nothing but disdain for certain aristocratic fellow-officers. For Sophie the 'supreme elegance' in a war devoted to preserving the interests of her class was to 'prefer the enemy'. And a blond Russian peasant boy who befriends Sophie in her Bolshevik phase and becomes her lover joins 'the young countess', as her former servants persist in calling her, in the nobility of the heart.

This disinterested quality coexists in the *récit* with a gruesome realism. A dog sniffs out a hand-grenade as if it were a truffle and is blown into a bloody stew; a horse burns to death with fearful screams during the bombardment of the château. Completely undercutting those vestiges of chivalry that might remain in such a war, Sophie is raped by a drunken sergeant who humiliates her further by begging her pardon in front of thirty people the next day. In this ambiguous battleground the real adversaries are not the warring armies floundering in the mud but Sophie and Eric, two kindred if hopelessly divided spirits matched blow for blow in a refined and tragic duel. Eric's scrupulous regard for Sophie appears in the lucidity with which he narrates behaviour that can only make him look bad; Sophie's fairness to Eric in the frankness which causes her to appear before him with unbraided hair – thus making it a point of honour not to look attractive – the day after he has had to put her to bed, hopelessly drunk. Contrary to what Sophie assumes, Eric was not at all repulsed by her drunken state, as it reminded him of taking care of similarly afflicted male comrades; but it is part of the irony inherent in Eric's first-person narrative that Sophie cannot know this.

It is a peculiarity of Marguerite Yourcenar's better novels – *Memoirs of Hadrian, Le Coup de grâce, L'Oeuvre au noir* – that they are all narrated from a man's point of view, whether in the first or the third person. Was this a factor in her becoming the first woman ever elected to the Académie Française? Probably not. One might wonder, all the same, whether this derives from professional virtuosity or if it is merely a form of narrative chivalry to men. If the latter, the apparent narratorial privilege is surely undermined in *Le Coup de grâce* by the very technique employed. The unreliability of the first-person narration is recognised by Eric himself when he warns against believing people who claim to remember every word of conversations. As in Gide's *The Immoralist*, a subjective narration ends by resembling an objective condemnation of the narrator: Eric's 'endless confession' takes the place of the truth which, revealed to Sophie early on, might have forestalled the eventual catastrophe.

Is Eric as bad as he himself makes out? It is after all Sophie who falls in love with him, Sophie who orders him to execute her, Sophie who, in refusing his offer of help, casts him as her judge. But in the last two instances he fails to understand her. 'Don't you want to owe me anything?' he asks when she declines to be saved. 'It's not even that', she replies, without it occurring to Eric that she might actually want to share the fate of her comrades-in-arms. Evidently feeling impelled to make some sort of final effort he touches her breast: 'Don't try any more, Eric', says Sophie, 'It doesn't suit you' – without his being sure whether that refers to his offer to save her or to his amorous gesture. When the disastrous interrogation is over he realises she has taken his cigarettes, which she then chain-smokes till the time of execution. The last to be killed, she turns away from what is going on beside her 'like a woman turning from an obscene gesture'. Her paradoxical command over the situation appears when she asks Eric to kill her: 'Mademoiselle *orders* it to be you', says one of Sophie's former servants, now Eric's orderly. At the time Eric thinks she means this as a proof of love, final and definitive; later he realises it was vengeance, to make him suffer from remorse. 'She judged correctly: I do feel remorse at times. One's always caught in a trap with these women' (Yourcenar, p. 157).

Possibly this was Sophie's way of making him assume responsibility for his acts; possibly, of making him confront a hidden wish to kill her. In any case, the consequences of the judgement endure beyond the grave. Something of Eric dies with his *coup de grâce*, as appears from the testimony of the unidentified observer in Pisa: Eric is 'petrified' in a kind of everlasting youth. In this he differs from Conrad, who reaches a maturity beyond his years while dying of his stomach wound, and whom Eric did not have the heart to finish off. Nor has Eric changed professionally. Incapable of committing himself to a 'sentimental' cause, as Sophie could, he remains a mercenary who eventually fights for Franco. As he remarks early on, his 'vice' is 'not so much the love of boys, as is often thought, but rather love of solitude'.

Killing what one loves is the theme of another twentieth-century masterpiece: Jean Genet's *Les Bonnes* (*The Maids*) of 1947. Though the author does not specify its provenance *The Maids* is thought to have been inspired, like the preceding texts, by a real event – in this case the 1933 killing of two 'honourable bourgeois women' of Le Mans by their hitherto impeccable domestics, Christine and Léa Papin. The story differs from preceding examples in that its heroine Christine, although condemned, was never executed; in chivalrous pre-war France the practice of beheading women was long since obsolete. Christine herself did not expect such mercy. She was not a martyr, or a victim of politics or incest: she had committed bloody murder. The crime itself was so appalling that any form of sympathy for those who had committed it would seem precluded from the first.

Before being made into high literature by Jean Genet the case attracted much attention from the press. It also drew outstanding articles from two masters in their respective fields: Janet Flanner, pseudonym Genêt, urbane reporter for the *New Yorker*, and Jacques Lacan, psychiatrist, of subsequent New Critical fame. In her missives from Paris Miss Flanner returns often to the subject of French execution: one of her numerous sprightly pieces concerns Eugene Weidmann, the last man to be guillotined in public. Another deals with Mata Hari, German spy, shot by a French firing squad in 1917. It is not so much Mata Hari's death as her life that primes Miss Flanner's wit, in particular the spy's exciting career as a salon dancer:

> Certainly one of Mata Hari's most astonishing performances was held in the Neuilly garden of an American lady over a long period noted for her intellectual energy and sardonic social indifference. While duchesses gaped, the spy-dancer made her entry, nearly nude, on a rented, turquoise-blue caparisoned circus horse. (She had wanted to make her entry on a rented circus elephant, which the American thought would be difficult to manage, since there were tea and cookies to follow.)[33]

On another occasion, a 'more intimate feminine fete', Miss Hari agreed, for a suitably enormous sum, 'to dance entirely nude before ladies only'. The dance was a Javanese warrior's dance, with weapons, and was going fairly well when Miss Hari noticed, 'because of the large shoes, that one of the assembled ladies was a lady's husband, disguised'. Outraged at this contractual breach Miss Hari all but ran him through with her spear. 'She was', Miss Flanner states, 'always courageous'. When found out as a spy and led before the firing squad Mata Hari wore an Amazonian suit, specially tailored for the occasion, 'and a pair of new white gloves'.

The Le Mans murder finds the journalist for the *New Yorker* at the summit of her powers. On the day of the crime Monsieur Lancelin, husband and father to the victims, returned home from his club to find the doors firmly bolted and the windows dark – but for a furtive glimmer from the maids' room in the attic. The husband went for reinforcements: some policemen and his brother-in-law. Having forced an entrance the men of law crept upstairs and then 'humanely warned the husband not to follow'. On the third step from the landing of the second floor, 'all alone, staring uniquely at the ceiling', they had found an eye. On the actual landing lay the female Lancelins, strangely arranged, their heads 'like blood puddings'. Beneath their 'provincial petticoats', Miss Flanners continues, their 'modest limbs'

THE ART OF IMMOLATION

had been cut 'the way a fancy French baker notches his finer long loaves'. The Lancelin finger-nails had been torn out, as had another eye, and teeth. 'Blood had softened the carpet till it was like an elastic red moss' (Flanner, *Paris*, pp. 98–104).

The third policeman, whose name was Truth, was sent towards the attic. He found the Papin sisters – Lapin, or rabbit, in the early press reports – sitting in a single bed, dressed in blue kimonos. They had washed their hands and faces and, 'being well-trained servants', also the carving-knife, hammer and pewter pitcher used in their deed. Christine, the older girl, confessed: 'They had done it'. It was all the fault of the electric iron, which had fused, she said. Committed to prison Léa, the younger sister, proved incapable of intelligible speech and Christine had 'extraordinary holy visions and unholy reactions'. The trial took place in Le Mans six months later and became a national event, covered by regiments of journalists, and guards with bayonets.

In the course of this judgement, for which Miss Flanner reserves her best irony, the

> diametric pleas of prosecution and defense were clear: either (1) the Papin sisters were normal girls who had murdered without a reason, murdering without reason apparently being a proof of normalcy in Le Mans, or else (2) the Rabbit sisters were as mad as March hares, and so didn't have to have a reason.

The jury were 'twelve good men and true, or quite incompetent to appreciate the Papin sisters'. In a woefully inept attempt to find persons who *might* appreciate them the prosecution had consulted three local insanity experts who had seen the defendants twice, for half an hour. This familiarity enabled them to swear in the witness stand that the girls were of 'unstained heredity'. As Miss Flanner then adds, their father was a dipsomaniac who had raped another sister, 'since become a nun'; their mother, an hysteric. A cousin had died in a madhouse and an uncle had hanged himself because 'his life was without joy'. Ignoring this, the court also disdained the testimony of a Parisian psychiatrist, Professor Logre, because he had not met the girls at all. Unlike almost everybody else he had, however, considered the evidence of Christine's prison visions, which led him to pronounce the two sisters a 'psychological couple'. 'Sometimes', Christine had said, 'I think in former lives that I was my sister's husband.' In one of the visions she had seen Léa hanging from an apple tree, with broken limbs; she had then leapt ten feet into the air to the top of a barred window, and remained there until Léa – whom she had not seen for five months – was called in as a sedative. At this point Christine 'cried with strange exultation, "Say yes, say yes"', which Joycean imperative no one understood at all.

The judge, who had satisfied himself they were not Bolsheviks, since only books of piety were found in their room, was unimpressed by these details, as by Christine's having wriggled out of a straitjacket, something that had never previously been done in a French prison. The jury, who gave Léa ten years in prison and twenty of municipal exile, was likewise unimpressed. Christine was sentenced to be guillotined in the main square of Le Mans. Unaware that women were no longer decapitated in France she heard the sentence on her knees, as if it came from God.

Dr Jacques Lacan arrays the same set of facts, adding a few details: the Papin sisters were considered model servants, their only strangeness being that they spent their days off together in their room. On the other hand their employers seemed unusually devoid of human sympathy; neither maids nor employers ever exchanged a word. Perhaps, on the fatal day, Mme Lancelin had scolded the maids about the blown fuse; the servants, reacting in a sudden paranoid paroxysm, had torn out their employers' eyes, bashed in their heads, and cut into the thighs and buttocks, exposing the sex. In prison, Christine had tried to tear out her own eyes – vainly, as it happened, but damaging herself – before succumbing to erotic exhibitionism, followed by depression.

According to prevailing concepts, paranoia (which seemed to be the sisters' problem) resulted either from the development of congenital morbidity, or else from disturbances of perception which the mind tried rationally to explain. This rational effort was followed by a 'passionate reaction', an explosive criminal act whose particular nature derived from the delirious conviction involved. Finding both notions inadequate Lacan refers to an essay by himself, written the preceding year, which recognises the influence of social relationships or tensions in the phenomenon; the particular balancing or rupturing of social tensions, he explains, defines each individual personality. At the root of psychosis lies an aggressive impulse, invariably murderous in its intent, often with overtones of vengeance or punishment – in other words, deriving from socially sanctioned ideas about justice.

How does this relate to the Rabbit Sisters? Turning to the other side of the social equation – that of society offended by the murderous deed – Lacan explains that the strong emotions generated by the Papins' crime stem from its horrid symbolism. The sisters had given literal execution to a metaphoric expression of rage: 'I'll scratch your eyes out.' Reassuring those persons who feared that psychiatric interpretations of crime might lead to a literal application of another expression, 'To understand is to forgive', Lacan points out that in the context of local justice – necessarily limited by its specific ability to comprehend – the reverse is true: to understand is to condemn.

As for the Papin sisters Lacan, like Professor Logre, takes into account the prison visions of Christine, particularly the remark that she was once, in a former life, her sister's husband. Rejecting contemporary assertions that the diagnosis was impossible he concludes that the girls were afflicted with a shared delirium. Such cases did exist, he affirms, particularly between close relatives of the same sex; and the forms taken by the Papins' psychoses were almost identical. One had only to look at the duplication of the tortures: whatever Christine did to Madame, Léa did to the daughter. Questioning the idea of incest between the sisters as a physical reality, Lacan praises Logre's term of a 'psychological couple' for its revelatory restraint: the persecution complex itself, he goes on, results from the suppression of a *latent* homosexuality. Having sought out the object most like itself, the suppressed desire identifies the beloved in the presumed persecutor. Thus, on the fateful afternoon when the iron fused all the Lancelin lights and the servants were, perhaps, scolded, Christine exacted her terrible revenge on the mother–daughter couple that beset her. Following her example Léa – as she said in her one lucid comment at the trial – notched her 'little carvings' on the daughter's thighs, probing, as Christine told her, for the 'mystery of life'.

This was not all. Presumably because of the repressions to be countered, the murderous impulse could be complicated by self-punishment. Blinding has long been recognised as a symbolic substitution for castration; the girls, Lacan writes, 'castrated as the Bacchae would'. As they did to others, they were doing to themselves: in prison, Christine tried to blind herself, and only after this symbolic act of expiation was she able to pronounce those 'words of passion laid bare: yes, say yes'.[34]

Janet Flanner put the thing more simply: 'The Papins' pain was the pain of being two where some mysterious unity had been originally intended.' Or, as one of the sanity experts said, they were 'Siamese souls'.

Of these elements of social calamity – a revolution, Janet Flanner called it, though of minor proportions – her near namesake Jean Genet retained seemingly little in his *The Maids*. In Genet's triangular drama the two domestic sisters thought to be inspired by the Papins do plan to kill their employer; but it is, precisely, a carefully premeditated deed, ritualised and heavily symbolic. There is no explosive violence, no blood-stained stair, no madness. The murder weapon is not a carving-knife, but an elegantly served cup of herbal tea. On the other hand the suicidal struggle of the 'psychological couple' striving to assert their identity is given tragic recognition, as is the social rage implicit in the sisters' plight.

The first astonishing thing about *The Maids* is that its heroines are women. In Genet's previous work the distinction of committing a crime worthy of the death sentence is granted only to men – mostly homosexual murderers guillotined in glory, the glory conferred on them by Genet's sumptuously metaphoric prose in *Notre-Dame-des-Fleurs, Miracle de la rose*. The second astonishing thing is that his celebration of a female crime assumed dramatic form: 'I don't like it', he declared in a letter to his publisher Pauvert, referring not to his play but to theatre in general. What kind of theatre did he like? Japanese, Balinese, Chinese: something splendid and symbolic, and preferably not western. 'The western actor does not try to become a sign charged with other signs', he wrote in the same letter; 'he simply wants to be identified with a character in a comedy or play.' Current occidental theatre tended to reflect the visible world of men, and not the invisible world of gods; theatre had become trivial and frivolous, like the people in it, whereas it ought to have the power of a poem – 'that is to say, a crime'. How to arrive at this effect? Children could: he cites the example of some small boys playing at soldiers in a park. Darkness was needed to cover an attack; by common accord, the youngest and most fragile was chosen to play Night. But when darkness came too soon the leaders suppressed Night, and returned him to the ranks. As for adult theatre, 'in the Western world, ever more touched by death and turned towards it, it can only grow more refined in the "reflection" of one play of another, of reflections of reflections that a ceremonious style might render exquisite, and close to invisibility'.[35] While Genet's 'Letter' purports to have little to do with *The Maids* it actually provides an aesthetic key to two of the play's main concepts: the designation of identity, and the infinitely complex play of reflections encountered in its form.

The action begins in the conventional bourgeois luxury of Madame's bedroom. Claire, a servant, is putting on Madame's clothes and giving her sister Solange orders, addressing her not as Solange but as Claire; in other words, Claire is playing at Madame and Solange is playing Claire. It soon becomes clear that this double masquerade is a private and habitual ritual, emanating from the imagination of the maids: something they do whenever Madame is out. But on this occasion imagination has affected reality. It transpires that Claire has written letters to the police accusing Madame's boyfriend, Monsieur, of being a thief. Under the stress of this revelation Claire slips into a schizophrenic mode, speaking both as herself and as Madame. Solange, too, speaks with a dual identity – Solange and Claire at once. A current of erotic tenderness emerges from the dialogue, as does a mutual hostility, and once again the ambiguity obtains since both these contrary feelings characterise the relationship between the sisters and the relationship between Madame and her maids. Genet, who does not mention the Papin sisters as a model, has in effect dramatised the essence of their psychological predicament.

This first phase of the drama ends abruptly when an alarm clock rings, warning the maids that time is running out for their game. They revert to being themselves, that is, to being Claire and Solange. Yet even the cessation of the role-playing is disturbing, since it implies that identity can be assumed or dropped at will, like a mask. A further sinister aspect of the reversion is that Claire now accuses Solange of not having 'finished' her allotted task – the murder of Madame, which the two maids must carry out at least in thought in order to acquire the dignity necessary for loving each other. Renewed and virulent accusations accrue, heightening the tension: Solange is really in love with Monsieur, as if she were Madame herself; Solange *really* wants to kill both Claire and Madame. This verbal violence gives way to an emotional lull interrupted by another ring: the telephone. It is Monsieur, calling to say he has been released, provisionally, and will wait for Madame at the Bilboquet.

THE ART OF IMMOLATION

At this point the sisters realise that matters have taken an irremediable turn for the worse – freed, Monsieur will naturally wonder who accused him and soon suspect the maids. In response, they decide they must *really* kill Madame. But how can they, as mere servants, effect change in the real world? They don't even have a motive. Passing over this difficulty they resolve to put gardenal in Madame's herbal tea. Once again a bell rings – the front door, this time – and in walks Madame.

Madame, it has been pointed out, is a kept woman, a being scarcely more substantial in the social scheme of things than her imaginative maids. Nonetheless she dominates in her domain. One would improperly conceive of her as having a Mme du Barry's kindness and charm; she is more likely a graduate of Mme Claude's who has struck a solid vein of gold. A woman given to exaggeration and flights of fancy, she revels in detailing the extremely humble circumstances she supposes she will live in when Monsieur has gone to prison. She will follow him to Siberia (not a French penal colony, though the play seems set in France); she will give her designer dresses to the maids – indeed, she starts to do so. Intent on getting her to swallow the *tisane* Claire and Solange fail to tell her that the all-important male has been set free. But Madame notices the phone is off the hook, necessitating an explanation. Immediately keen to join Monsieur, Madame sends Solange out to fetch a taxi. Claire's final effort – 'Madame must drink her tea, even if it's cold' – is brushed aside. Madame exits in triumph.

Down in the street the taxi honks, triggering the fifth phase of the play like the last act of a tragedy. Claire and Solange must now confront the fact that they have failed to kill Madame and that their feeble attempts at poison-pen writing will certainly be discovered; they will be known as mediocre, common-place criminals and not famous murderesses. Inspired by Solange's vision of herself marching to the scaffold at the head of all the servants of the district, Claire suddenly perceives the only dignified way out and reassumes her role as Madame; Solange must kill her with the gardenal and live on as the celebrated criminal, *Mademoiselle* Solange Lemercier. Solange must be very strong and carry Claire within her, for only thus will she be able to form 'the eternal couple of the criminal and the saint'. The play ends with Claire slowly drinking the lime tea, poured in 'the best, the richest tea-set', while Solange stands with wrists outstretched, anticipating handcuffs.

The Maids, which rapidly attained to classic status, has been analysed from almost every point of view known to academe. Its five, bell-punctuated acts have been compared to the five acts of classical French tragedy, as has its richly elegant language. (So splendidly was Genet's prose perceived that an early critic complained maids did not talk that way; Genet replied that in the language of their hearts, they did.) But there is more to tragedy than formal division into acts. *The Maids* is worthy to sit beside *Antigone* because in the end the sisters' quest for selfhood leaves them no other dignified choice but the immolation of Claire-as-Madame. Only thus can they escape from the demeaning rank of servitude, of being perceived as maids by Madame; only thus can their divided self become one. By means of this sacrifice the imagination emerges victorious and love is preserved. As Claire puts it, 'Above all don't forget, when you've been condemned, that you carry me within you. Like a treasure. We shall be happy, beautiful and free.'[36]

This miracle is accomplished despite the structural and aesthetic factors which would seem to vitiate the notion of identity entirely. There are several layers of illusion in *The Maids*: there is the level of the actress playing Claire, and the level of Claire-as-Madame. To these veils of disbelief Genet added a third, proposing that the parts be played by boys – a recommendation not always adopted in production. By no means mere frivolous misogyny, this direction aimed at distancing the actors from the essence of the roles assumed. For Claire and Solange *have* no identity; they are 'signs charged with signs'. Indeed, the success of their role-playing is measured by the response of the other; the identity assumed is constantly modified in terms of the reflection in the *alter ego*'s eyes. The play is like a walking illustration of the master–slave dialectic in that the official identities of all three characters depend on mutual perceptions of two interdependent notions, Madameness and Servantdom, while the constant play of reciprocal perceptions corresponds to the 'reflections of reflections' evoked in Genet's *Letter to Pauvert*.

That Claire dies as Madame strikes symbolically at the prevailing bourgeois rule of Madameness. It is like the burning of the American flag: the material destruction of a symbolic object wounds those for whom the object signifies something quasi-sacred. Killing Claire while she is behaving like Madame is perhaps even more insulting than slaughtering Madame herself. The social subversiveness of the deed appears in Solange's long and fanciful evocation of her own execution, which she describes in eighteenth-century terms: clad in red, like parricides, and carrying a torch, followed by a procession of exultant servants and an admiring executioner.

> First of all come the butlers, in livery, but without their silk lapels. They're bearing wreaths. Then come the footmen, the lackeys in knee breeches and white stockings. They too are bearing wreaths. Then come the valets, then the chambermaids, dressed in our colours. Then the doormen, and the delegates from heaven. And I am leading all of them. The headsman caresses me. I'm hailed with acclaim. I'm pale and I'm going to die!
>
> (Genet, pp.174–5)

At once ridiculous and grand the vision marks the victory of Servantdom as, charged with the liveried *signs* of the *ancien régime*, the hordes of domestics march towards the scaffold. In the imagination of the maids, revolution has arrived.

O rendetemi la speme, o lasciatemi morir: give me back my hope, or let me die. These words, which herald the beginning of Elvira's famous mad aria in *Puritani*, constitute what might be termed an emphatic quotation in Catherine Clément's book; they reflect the fundamental plea of all her operatic heroines. Summarising dramatic and narrative treatments of executed heroines generally, one might rewrite it thus: give me back my sense of self, or kill me, because, dying, I affirm myself. This is the spoken or unspoken challenge hurled by tragic women put to death.

For the executed heroine's affirmation of her chosen self is a factor in drama and narrative from Sophocles to Yourcenar, from Anouilh to *The Maids*. Such exceptions as occur are not tragic; they are burlesque Romances (Voltaire's *La Pucelle d'Orléans*, in which Jeanne is not killed), chivalric Romances, or plays in which a historical model is adapted to ideological aims, such as Brecht's first two treatments of the Jeanne d'Arc story. Yet even a Romance may contain tragic elements: in the various versions of the Tristan legend Yseult's eventual death is both an inevitable consequence of her having drunk the potion, and a profound affirmation of her identity as Tristan's lover. The society which thwarts their love emerges as inferior to the passion it seeks to kill; as in tragedy, the gap between the tyrannical 'what is' and the transcendental 'what might be' fosters the sentiment of loss.

In the early Romantic period, 1800-45 or so, a number of authors either spare their heroines the execution history prescribed (Schiller in *Die Jungfrau von Orléans*), or imply that they should have been spared by representing them as literally maddened by their tribulations. Madness appears as a temporary exit from a mind overburdened with horror, while generating audience sympathy for the afflicted victim and seeming a biologically feasible development in the fragile female creature. In the case of Beatrice Cenci the alienated mind is presently restored to the self and Beatrice makes a noble end. Beatrice, Anna Bolena and Maria Stuart are all invested with some form of guilt – even Anna has abandoned the man she loved in favour of ambition – but do not 'choose' to die in the sense that Antigone does, or G.B. Shaw's Saint Joan; all three Romantic heroines would have preferred to live. Their heroism lies in their acceptance of an unjust death, and the effect of the injustice is to place blame on the social forces that condemn them, whether they are individual monarchs or a style of justice.

In other cases the sacrifice of the self is linked not only to the quest for an acceptable identity, but to an heroic attempt to reconcile opposing forces. This attempt is hinted at in Sophocles' *Antigone* when the heroine contests Creon's different treatment of the good and the bad brother; in the land of the dead, she remarks, equal treatment may be the rule. A 'control' example of male execution, Sydney Carton's sacrifice in *A Tale of Two Cities*, is set against an epic dualism – it was the best of times, it was the worst of times – that Carton's death alone cannot heal; but his generous deed anticipated a brighter future. The sacrifice of innocent lives to militate against surrounding evil is explicit in Bernanos' *Dialogues des Carmélites*, in which the heroine overcomes personal terror to find her place within the small community of martyred nuns. In Marguerite Yourcenar's *Le Coup de grâce* distinctions between foe and lover blur among the chivalrous, mud-bound protagonists, disinterested descendants of the knightly caste of old.

A seemingly improbable vehicle for human salvation, Jean Genet's *The Maids* presents a tragic affirmation of identity in which the two main protagonists struggle to reunite halves of a self that can only be salved by its own immolation. Formally destroying conventional western theatrical notions of identity while simultaneously presenting the quest for identity as its main theme, this extraordinarily complex play presents a victory of the imagination in which love and revolution come together to assert the eternal co-dependence of Genet's favourite odd couple, the criminal and the saint. For the saint cannot be immolated without the active participation of the criminal, who then faces immolation of a different kind. Claire and Solange do not try to pay for 'bad' humanity by immolating themselves, they try to assume human contradiction within themselves as a couple, criminal and saint but also mistress and employer, murderess and lover, other and self. Once again, the heroines' situation is tragic in that no other resolution to the problem can be found but to require their death. The paradox, in Genet's case, is that from this emotion, this tragic sense of sacrifice and loss, derives the potent and subversive reaction of revolt.

CONCLUSION

This book was not written to illustrate any particular theory. From the outset it appeared that so many executions of such different types of woman, from different periods of time, could not be expected to fit into a single concept, even considering the relatively few countries discussed. Nonetheless certain patterns have emerged. One is mankind's persistent tendency to split itself into two Manichean camps, in which Evil is always located on the side of the Other: Christian and pagan, Christian and Jew, Christian and heretic. Less noticeable in primitive religions, whose gods are permitted to be both good and bad, this grandiose projection had a significant effect upon the witch trials of the late Middle Ages, Renaissance and seventeenth century; it recurs in rationalist form in the executions of the Terror. While a more or less equal persecution of men and women characterised the early phases of the witch-hunts, the publication of the *Malleus Maleficarum* in 1489 signalled an increased tendency to view women as sexually in league with Satan; thereafter the execution of witches and female heretics assumes almost sexocidal proportions, especially in Germany, resulting in burnings, hangings and beheadings so numerous as to defy accurate calculation even today.

This attitude to women left its mark on justice for some centuries. Even ostensibly powerful females were not immune to charges of rampant, criminal sexuality, as can be seen from the fates of Anne Boleyn and Mary Stuart; accusations of treason and adultery were too expedient politically to be ignored. What distinguishes the decapitations of these two Queens from ecclesiastically pronounced judgements is that the question of guilt or innocence, though so emotionally charged, was in practical terms irrelevant; what mattered was to remove them from the scene. During the Renaissance, as in the Middle Ages, the notions of chivalry by which aristocratic, sword-wielding males were supposed to protect the fair sex were sacrificed in a second when political interest dictated a more Machiavellian course. Nobility, which protected noblewomen only to the extent of guaranteeing them a relatively painless death by beheading, might, however, encourage their rehabilitation after death: no matter how lewd or frankly murderous an aristocratic woman had seemed when alive, she had a tendency to become a martyr after execution. So it was with Mary Stuart and Beatrice Cenci, the one martyred for the sake of papal authority, the other because of it. Even the world-class criminality of the Marquise de Brinvilliers was compensated in some measure by depictions of her repentant end. Exceptions do of course occur in thirteenth-century accounts of the early Christian martyrs, whose chastity is greatly stressed.

Punitive efforts to discredit or repress women sexually are apparent as late as the Enlightenment. While the more appalling torments, such as breaking on the wheel, were reserved for men, a number of capital crimes – abortion, concealment of pregnancy – concerned only women. Again, character assassination with potent sexual overtones reappears in the French Revolution, notably in the trials of Charlotte Corday, Marie Antoinette and Manon Roland, all of whom were credited with lustful activities. And, at a time when patriotic Frenchwomen were beginning to demand a say in the affairs of the state, the same three women – together with the sprightly Olympe de Gouges – were taxed with unfeminine behaviour of one sort or another: as *Le Moniteur* put it, with 'forgetting the virtues appropriate to their sex'. For aspiring to be men they were given the appropriate symbolic punishment by the guillotine, a machine whose geometric design made it approach abstraction but which popular wit endowed with the castrating body of a female. In the gruesome case of Mme de Lamballe, the castration was quite literal. During the September massacres the Princesse de Lamballe – Marie Antoinette's supposed paramour, and presumed counsellor in the unfeminine business of dominating the King – had been beheaded, stripped, and mutilated by bystanders. In Michelet's words, the assailants, 'driven by an unworthy curiosity which was perhaps the principal cause of her death', acted as if to determine 'some shameful mystery which would confirm the rumours that had circulated'.[1] Although these misfortunes were not legally imposed, the Princess had suffered a primitive form of trial by ordeal that required her to stand on a pile of corpses and swear anti-royalist oaths. Her impromptu judges seem to have been groping for a form of justice that simultaneously satisfied patriotism and the hidden obscene motives of psychological necessity.

A structuralist explanation for both large-scale persecution and certain types of individual execution is provided by René Girard, who analyses how societies threatened by natural, political or religious catastrophe tend to project the cause of such disasters onto some convenient scapegoat; Girard finds the characteristics of this habit both in witch trials and the purges of the Terror. Typically, the disastrous threat is blamed on minority groups such as foreigners, heretics or Jews; but once-powerful figures such as kings and queens are also likely candidates. Such paradoxical polarity is characteristic of the scapegoat mechanism for, as Girard adds, 'All persecutors attribute to their victims a harmfulness capable of turning into positiveness, and

CONCLUSION

vice versa'.[2] By this reasoning, victims in the scapegoat category might well include Marie Antoinette and even Manon Roland.

Related to the scapegoat mechanism is the phenomenon of human sacrifice, whereby the designated victim dies that others may be absolved. The topic of sacrifice, animal or human, has absorbed the superstars of French intellectualism for more than a century. As Joseph de Maistre argues in his *Eclaircissement sur les sacrifices*, the idea of original sin - apparently common to all races - engendered the idea of expiation: the gods are just but we are guilty, and must therefore pay for our crimes. The surest way of expiating them was to offer up a sacrifice. At first the sacrificial object was a human being, often from a special criminal caste; gradually, the human victims were replaced by beasts - lending credence, one would think, to Schopenhauer's suggestion that humans are actually demons put on earth to torment animals. Discussing the Christian theory of sacrifice, whereby innocence could sacrifice itself as a propitiatory offering, de Maistre even implies that Marie Antoinette's hapless spouse entertained this notion of himself, a theory supported by incidents accompanying his death. Brought to the guillotine, Louis XVI resisted attempts to remove his coat and tie his hands until the executioner cast imploring glances at the King's confessor; the Abbé Edgeworth then persuaded Louis to resign himself to this indignity by remarking that it established a further resemblance between the King and the God he was about to meet. Before being guillotined the King tried to address the crowd: 'Pray God my blood brings happiness to France' - words that suggest a certain sacrificial awareness. That revolutionary decapitations could in general be construed, at least in casual metaphor, as sacrifices of a kind is apparent from the words of the executioner's son, Henry Sanson, who later referred to the beheadings of the Terror as 'these horrible sacrifices'.[3] In the domain of literature this opinion is echoed by such divergent voices as the Marquis de Sade - himself condemned to death under both the ancient and the revolutionary régimes, and saved from guillotining by the advent of Thermidor 9 - and Georges Bernanos, apologist of saints. Published in 1795 de Sade's philosophical novel *Aline et Valcour* boasts a benign savage, King Zamé, who unhesitatingly equates capital punishment with barbaric sacrifice: instead of being sacrificed to gods, Zamé explains, men in civilised countries are sacrificed to laws. In a more mystical vein, Georges Bernanos has dramatised the execution of fifteen Carmelite nuns in terms of the propitiatory self-sacrifice of innocence, offering itself to atone for the surrounding wickedness.

On the other hand the orthodox Christian view of self-sacrifice is contested both by Thomas Szasz and René Girard. Describing the ancient Jewish ceremony of Yom Kippur, in which the collective guilt of the community was ritually transferred to an animal, a 'scapegoat', Szasz is led to comment:

When the Temple stood in Jerusalem, the scapegoat was a real goat. His duty was to be the embodiment, the symbol, of all the sins the people of Israel had committed over the past year, and carry those sins with him out of the community.[4]

According to Szasz, the Jewish tradition seems to culminate in the legend of Jesus Christ, 'mankind's most illustrious scapegoat, who suffered for and redeemed all men for all time'. Lofty though the ideals of Christianity undoubtedly are – the good and innocent suffering for the bad – Szasz feels that they ask more than human beings can provide. In his opinion the Christian scapegoat ethic may do actual harm, engendering additional guilt among those witnessing the sacrifice; furthermore, it reinforces the sacrificers' chronic inability to shoulder moral responsibility for their own conduct. As Szasz concludes, 'So long as men engage in the ceremonial destruction of symbolic enemies – whether these be animals, alien peoples, or individuals who formerly belonged to the group – man will not be safe from his fellow predators'. Societies which think themselves advanced and maintain the fiction 'that they engage in no ritual acts' are thus, in effect, blind.

A similar view is expressed by René Girard in the concluding chapters of *Le Bouc émissaire*, except that Girard rejects the common identification of Jesus as the sacrificial lamb. In Girard's analysis Jesus himself, a man of 'superior intelligence', is at frequent pains to 'undo' the sacrificial mechanism, as if anticipating an era in which the most enthusiastic of his followers would themselves apply the logic of persecution to those they deemed un-Christian. The violent, satanic cultural order shown throughout the gospels cannot, Girard thinks, survive being revealed: 'Once the founding mechanism is revealed, the mechanism of the scapegoat – the expulsion of violence through violence – is rendered obsolescent through its own revelation' (Girard, p. 278). But in Girard's view this is not totally understood, even by Christians. For if the early Christians were themselves persecuted, they have subsequently persecuted Jews, witches, heretics and numerous other enemies.

What has this to do with execution? For one thing, there is the problem of public lust. According to some postulators of sacrificial theory, the presence of Eros at the altar is as old as sacrifice itself. Relying heavily on his own, sometimes questionable interpretations of de Sade, Georges Bataille has sought to connect the phenomenon of violent death with erotic experience. 'In sacrifice', he observes in *Literature and Evil*, 'the victim is divested not only of clothes but of life. . . . The victim dies and the spectators share in what his death reveals. This is what religious historians call the element of sacredness.' Explaining the interdependence in primitive mythology of death and sex, Joseph Campbell remarks that

> The world lives on death. . . . As we learn from other myths and mythological fragments in this cultural sphere, the sexual organs are supposed to have appeared at the time of this coming of death.

CONCLUSION

Reproduction without death would be a calamity, as would death without reproduction.

Accordingly, many sacrificial rituals involved erotic acts. The sacrificial kings of the Sudan, for example, were strangled by the priests, then buried with a living virgin at their side. Both Campbell and his source, Leo Frobenius, suggest that this cruel practice may have been at the origin of the Scheherazade legend; but if this was indeed the basic structure of that tale, it has certainly undergone radical modifications – most notably, that in the *Thousand and One Nights* the freshly married virgins were all killed while the sultan remained alive. In many African tribes, the death of the king was followed by the public copulation of naked and pubescent boys and virgins, holding sticks of fire, after which they were tossed into a trench, and buried alive. In Dutch South New Guinea, the male puberty rites terminate in general orgies, lasting several days, at the end of which the initiates all copulate with one finely painted girl. As the last of the youths embraces her, the couple are suddenly crushed to death by heavy logs. They are then cut up, roasted and eaten.

True, records in the Archives Nationales do not imply that citizen-virgins of France were cast into the lime-pits, still alive, with Louis XVI, or ceremonially eaten by Robespierre. However, certain incidences of lubricity accompanying revolutionary executions – judges in Brest, for example, copulating with the bodies of decapitated girls in a dissecting theatre, in full view of the public – suggest the release of bloody and erotic impulses similar to those noted during ritual sacrifice. Such impulses appear to have been manifested at public executions from the earliest times, particularly when the victim was a woman. A misguided concern with modesty and decency could not entirely mask the fact that women were viewed as sexual objects – as one put it in the sixties – even on the scaffold.

Objectification of the victim is a feature of both punishment and sacrifice: the mob is quite unmoved by the victim's sufferings. If anything, it tends to enjoy them, forgetful for the moment of its own human identity. Since Freud and Jung we have become accustomed to the notion that we project onto others those tendencies most feared and repressed in ourselves, that we punish someone not so much because of what he or she has done, but because he or she represents the literally unthinkable possibility that we might do the same. The 'projective' theory of punishment seems particularly applicable to the French *ancien régime*, when criminal codes emphasised the 'crimes of luxury' or 'crimes against chastity' and prevailing religious views were relatively repressive. The crowd's erotic interest in executed women suggests a perception of the criminal female as a sort of sacrificial temptress, while the indecent epithets applied to decapitation machines would seem to indicate that, before and during revolution, male executions were viewed as a form of castration.

Though much has been said here of the cruelty of religions, significant religious thinkers seem to have been aware of the tendency to objectify victims, and spoken out against it. Invited to justify the stoning of the woman taken in adultery, Christ recommended that 'he who is without sin' should cast the first stone, and when the hostile crowd sheepishly dispersed, allowed her to go. The Compassionate Buddha wrote: 'All men tremble at punishment, all men fear death; remember that you are like unto them, and do not kill, not cause slaughter.' Yet the Christian injunction not to kill has been rationalised into 'thou shalt do no murder', while followers of Buddha have included the Samurai warriors of Japan. Considering the problem of objectification from a non-religious point of view, psychiatrist Thomas Szasz comments, 'I believe that intelligent self-interest, conscientious self-restraint, and sympathetic identification with others would engender less inclination to hatred than traditional religious teachings based on the promise of redemption through the sacrifice of scapegoats'.

Unsatisfactory as the Revolution may at first have seemed, in terms of political equality for women, egalitarian notions have been slowly gaining ground over the last two hundred years, at least in western democracies. Whereas both the French and American constitutions of the late eighteenth century denied women the vote, suffrage has now come; women vote, they sit on juries, study law. There is even a woman on the Supreme Court of the United States, although her opinions may not be wholly satisfactory to feminists. But that is not to say that where capital punishment is concerned, the problems posed to the judiciary body by the female body have been smoothly erased.

A number of books and articles – by Freda Adler, most notably – appeared in the 1970s in America, arguing that liberation and equality had so influenced women that they were emulating men in their greater criminality. This view was refuted by Ann Jones in her 1980 study, *Women Who Kill*, which postulates, on the contrary, a reaction on the part of law enforcement officials irritated by feminism and suddenly eager to arrest: 'If it's equality these women want, we'll see that they get it.' Violent crimes committed by women, Jones maintains, have not in fact increased; the only increase has been in non-violent offences, such as larceny or fraud, a statistic easily explainable in terms of increasing poverty in certain female social groups. But Jones and Adler concur in pointing to a number of states whose laws actually provide stiffer penalties for misdemeanours committed by a woman (this apparently despite the declaration, in 1968, that discriminatory sentencing practices are unconstitutional), a situation unlikely to be modified without the Equal Rights Amendment. In particular, crimes traditionally perceived as masculine – armed robbery or felony murder – often draw heavier sentences when carried out by women. Freda Adler devotes some considerable space to the plight of the American black woman, several times more likely – at least in the 1970s, in Philadelphia, where Mrs Adler's doctoral dissertation was compiled – to resort to crime than her white sisters. The reason, she contends, lies in the socioeconomic position of the black woman, a position which, together with her innate resourcefulness, provides both the necessity and opportunity for crime. Even in the late 1980s, opponents of capital punishment in the United States quote racial inegality in sentencing as a basis for abolition: black people, already disadvantaged socially, are in a sense doubly scapegoats.

As for the physical reality of execution, it is easy to think of contemporary American practices as relatively enlightened. Hanging is no longer an ungainly matter of strangulation; it has been refined to the point where the knotted rope snaps the cervical vertebrae, as soon as the feet are unsupported. Some pain is thought to be experienced in the neck, but death occurs quite quickly, at the very worst, through slow strangulation, in three to four minutes. On the other hand the electric chair, which causes smoke to rise from the victim, can only be described as revolting. No wonder that the late Andy Warhol saw fit to paint its image, again and again, with titles such as 'Lavender Disaster'. In May 1990 the execution by electric chair of Jesse Joseph Tifero caused media consternation when the application of three electric jolts resulted in three spurts of flame: Tifero's body was slammed back against the chair, while reddish flames appeared on the left side of his head. It was later discovered that the synthetic flammable sponge attached to the electrode had caught fire. In the view of the execution consultant who appeared on ABC's Prime Time to discuss the apparent mishap, electrocution is humane – providing the equipment is up to par.

The most recent American method of execution is lethal injection, by which the condemned person resembles a mad dog rather than a scapegoat. This is the method adopted by the states of Delaware and New Mexico. Delaware actually uses an injection machine, guaranteeing anonymity to the executioner. A similar incognito obtains in modern gas chambers, where three executioners are used; the controls are set up in such a way that no one knows who has thrown the switch. (Gas is perhaps not as humane as it seems, if we remember that Himmler prescribed gas after nearly fainting at the execution by firing squad of scores of Jewish women; rather than halting the executions, he substituted the gas chamber.) And how long does it take? At the prison of San Quentin in California the gas chamber's operating manual declares a maximum of ten minutes; even so, an executioner's notebook recalls a 'coloured guy' who 'took about fifteen minutes to die'. At the execution of Aaron Mitchell at San Quentin in 1967, the victim apparently went mad and called out, as they slammed the chamber shut, 'I am Jesus Christ'. According to one witness, when the gas hit him his head immediately fell to his chest. Then his head came up and he looked directly into the window I was standing next to. For nearly seven minutes, he sat that way, with his chest heaving, saliva bubbling between his lips. He tucked his thumbs into his fist, and, finally, his head fell.[5]

A doctor was listening to the heartbeats; twelve minutes passed before they stopped.

Clearly, and despite these little mistakes, the old heroic days of confrontation between the *bourreau* and his victim are long gone. Gone, too, are the days of public hanging described by John Pritchard, when crowds strained forward to catch sight of the victim's convulsed face. From being a society given to public spectacle, in which the many watch the few – a few objects, a few people – we have changed into a society in which the few observe the many. So explains Michel Foucault, referring to the improvements in nineteenth-century prison design, which enabled a handful of prison guards, stationed on a central tower, to keep watch over numerous prison inmates, arranged all around in flights of open cells, the inner prison wall consisting only of bars: Bentham's panopticon. Thus, movements of reform also initiate change: no longer do executions take place in the open, before an appreciative multitude, but behind prison walls, before a select few. This despite Sam Donaldson, host of Prime Time, who, perhaps ironically, commenting on the Tifero execution, declared that in his view executions should be telecast, enabling those in favour of the death penalty to face their responsibilities.

Despite these advances in anonymous technology, odd parallels between the new and the ancient practices remain. For one thing, when confrontation does occur, and on those rare occasions when a woman is put to death, the *bourreau* is still male. Whereas grudging advances are being made in the armed forces, and the possibility of women acceding to combat duty is openly discussed on public television, the question of women being employed legally to execute members of their own, or even the opposite, sex, does not seem to have been raised.

For another, there is curiosity of the familiar less than seemly kind. Although a limited number of witnesses are normally invited to observe executions, the number can become excessive. This appears from accounts of executions in the forties and fifties when women were involved. In 1947 a 58-year-old grandmother, Louise Peete, stepped into the San Quentin gas chamber with eighty official witnesses – all men – packed into the tiny observation chamber, straining to catch a glimpse. On 3 June 1955, Barbara Graham was executed for a murder she consistently maintained that she did not commit. Her story was twice committed to film under the title *I Want to Live*. In both versions, her innocence is stressed. As a prison attendant recalls, 'God, she was a beautiful woman. . . . When she started in for the third time

CONCLUSION

[after two stays of execution] she asked for a blindfold. . . . I don't think she wanted to see anyone in the witness room.' Ferretti, the attendant, strapped her in, patted her knee and told her to take a deep breath, 'and it won't bother you'. 'How the hell would you know?' she replied (Kroll, p. 27).

Then there are the stays of execution. In *I Want to Live* Barbara Graham is shown taking brave but tearful leave of her little boy, whose existence did not sway the judge to clemency. In 1990, as in 1789, women who are pregnant at the time of condemnation are granted a stay of execution, until such time as they give birth; then, they are executed. The stay, of course, is granted to spare the life of the innocent child. The possible psychological effects of the child's growing up to know its mother was once put to death are not necessarily taken into consideration.

There once again, the actual female body is the problem. There is something repugnant about destroying a body which gives life, even when strict egality requires that women should be punished just as men. Would the average feminist wish to see women executed, as a sign of progress in equal rights? For articles have been written, pointing to a disparity in conditions obtaining in male and female prisons; Rita James Simon, for one, has suggested that women might be willing to see their prisons downgraded to the level of the men's, if this will foster egality. But how does one equalise an execution? Either one is killed or one is not; and if not, when the crime is murder, one is faced with chivalry again, and the problem of women having the right to sit in government, but not in the electric chair.

Finding it repulsive to kill women, egalitarian and humane societies might well decide to extend the benefits of this chivalry reciprocally to men, abolishing the death penalty altogether. But these do not seem to be the motives which impel diverse countries to take that step; rather, they decide for some reason that the death penalty is ineffective as a deterrent, and that it is philosophically inconsistent, as Beccaria observed, to punish killing with killing, no matter how symmetrical the practice may seem. Alone among the western democracies, the United States of America has yet to make that decision.

NOTES

INTRODUCTION

1 Elizabeth Cady Stanton, Susan B. Anthony, Matilda Joslyn Gage, editors, *A History of Women's Suffrage*. New York, Fowler and Wells, 1881, vol.I, p. 675.

1 BURIALS AND BURNINGS

1 See Jacques Delarue, *Le Métier de bourreau*. Paris, Fayard, 1979, p. 102.
2 Quoted by Jules Loiseleur, *Les Crimes et les peignes dans l'antiquité et dans les temps modernes*. Paris, Hachette, 1863, p. 156.
3 Carl Riedel, *Criminal Law in the Old French Romances*. New York, Columbia University Press, 1938, p. 38.
4 Jules Michelet, *Les Guerres de religion*. In *Oeuvres complètes*, vol. viii, edited by Paul Villaineix. Paris, Flammarion, 1980, p. 99.
5 See John Laurence Pritchard, *A History of Capital Punishment*. New York, 1963, p. 9.
6 'Si l'en menrai en ma contree, Car molt me semble preuz et sage; Se vous l'ardez, ce ert domage.' *Les Romans de Claris et Laris*, edited by Dr Johann Alton, Tübingen 1884, p. 263.
7 Not only in the medieval mind. According to Thomas Szasz, a twentieth-century psychiatrist, 'The late senator Joseph McCarthy thus equated the social sin of Communism with the sexual sin of homosexuality and used the two labels as if they were synonymous. He could not have done this had there been no general belief that, like medieval heretics, men labelled "homosexual" are somehow totally bad.' *The Manufacture of Madness*, New York, Harper and Row, 1970, p. 166.
8 George Bernard Shaw, preface to *Saint Joan*. In *Complete Plays with Prefaces*, vol. ii. New York, Dodd, Mead and Company, 1963, p. 265.
9 Margaret Murray, *The Witch Cult in Western Europe*. Oxford, 1921, p. 177.
10 Helen C.White, *Tudor Saints and Martyrs*, pp. 59–60.
11 Montague Summers, *The Geography of Witchcraft*. New York, Alfred A. Knopf, 1927, pp. 484–5.
12 Barbara Ehrenreich and Deirdre English, *Witches, Midwives and Nurses*, pp. 5–6.
13 Michelet, *La Sorcière*. Paris, Garnier-Flammarion, 1966, p. 164.
14 Henry Charles Lea, *Materials Towards the History of Witchcraft*. 1939, p. 233.
15 Quoted in the introduction to James Sprenger and Henry Kramer, *Malleus Maleficarum*, translated and edited by Montague Summers. London, 1928.
16 Robert Mandrou, *Magistrats et sorciers*. Paris, Plon, 1968, p. 101.
17 Margaret Murray, *The God of the Witches*, p. 145.

NOTES

18 *A Discourse on the Damned Craft of Witchcraft*. Cambridge, 1608. Quoted in Christina Hole, *Mirror of Witchcraft*. London, Chatto and Windus, 1957, p. 219.
19 Muriel Joy Hughes, *Women as Healers in Medieval Life and Literature*. New York, Columbia University Press, 1943, p. 93.
20 Ann Jones, *Women Who Kill*. New York, Ballantine, 1980, p. 171.
21 Lang and Maclaurin quoted in Sackville-West, p. 334.

2 BEHEADING

1 Jacobus de Varagine, *Legenda Aurea*, pp. 34–7 (Lucy) and 110–13 (Agnes).
2 Edith Sitwell, *Fanfare for Elizabeth*. New York, Macmillan, 1962, p. 8.
3 Retha M. Warnicke, *The Rise and Fall of Anne Boleyn*, p. 59.
4 Betty Travitzky, *The Paradise of Women. Writings by Englishwomen of the Renaissance*. New York, Columbia University Press, 1989, p. 170.
5 Anne Askew, *The first examinacyon*. Quoted in *The Paradise of Women*, p. 174.
6 *The Paradise of Women*, p. 190.
7 Antonia Fraser, *Mary Queen of Scots*, p. 13.
8 Ronsard, *Poésies choisies*. Paris, Garnier, 1963, p. 354.
9 Stendhal, *Chroniques italiennes*. In *Romans et nouvelles*. Paris, Gallimard, 1982, pp. 706–7.
10 From Labat's *Voyage en Italie* of 1730. Quoted by John Laurence Pritchard in his *A History of Capital Punishment*. New York, p. 71.
11 Corrado Ricci, *Beatrice Cenci*, vol. I, p. 19.
12 K.N. Cameron, *Shelley: The Golden Years*, p. 399.
13 Hugh Stokes, *Mme de Brinvilliers and her Times*.
14 Mme de Sévigné, *Lettres*, vol. II Paris, Gallimard, p. 157.
15 Cesare Lombroso and William Ferrero, *The Female Offender*. New York, Appleton, 1895, pp. 150–1.
16 Marie Vassiltchikov, *Berlin Diaries 1940–1945*. New York, Alfred A. Knopf, 1947, p. 223. Italics mine.

3 HANGING

1 Carl Riedel, *Criminal Law in the Old French Romances*, p. 37.
2 Roger Anchel, *Crimes et châtiments au XVIIIe siècle*.
3 Eyewitness account quoted by Jacques Delarue in *Le Métier de bourreau*. Paris, Fayard, 1979, p. 242.
4 Marguerite Yourcenar, *Oeuvres complètes*. Paris, Editions de la Pléiade, 1982, p. 982.
5 Montague Summers, *The Geography of Witchcraft*, p. 112.
6 Carol F. Karlsen, *The Devil in the Shape of a Woman*, p. 247.
7 Chadwick Hansen, *Withcraft in Salem*, p. 15.
8 Roger Anchel, *Crimes et châtiments au dix-huitième siècle*, p. 66.
9 Voltaire, *Commentaire sur le livre des délits et des peines*. In *Oeuvres complètes*. Paris, Gallimard, 1961, p. 787.
10 The *Globe Encyclopaedia*, London, J.S. Victor, 1890, vol. III, p. 494.
11 Quoted by Ann Jones in *Women Who Kill*, p. 48.
12 George Eliot, *Adam Bede*. London, William Blackwood and Sons, c. 1875, pp. 402–3.
13 Thomas Hardy, *Tess of the d'Urbervilles*. New York, Harper and Bros, 1950, p. 505.
14 Michel Foucault, *Punir et surveiller*. Paris, Gallimard, 1975, p. 16.

DEATH COMES TO THE MAIDEN
4 DAME GUILLOTINE

1. Preface to *The Coming of the French Revolution* by Georges Lefèbvre. Princeton, Princeton University Press, 1947, p.v.
2. Simon Schama, *Citizens*. New York, Alfred Knopf, 1989, p. xiv.
3. Michel Foucault, *Punir et surveiller*. Paris, Gallimard, 1976, p. 38.
4. See Daniel Arasse, *La Guillotine et l'imaginaire de la Terreur*. Paris, 1987.
5. Edouard Fournier, *Histoire du Pont Neuf*, vol. II, p. 163.
6. Quoted in Jacques Delarue, *Le Métier de bourreau*. Paris, Fayard, 1979, pp. 160–1.
7. Michelet, *La Révolution française*. Paris, Gallimard, Editions de la Pléiade, 1952, p. 68.
8. Told by Stanley Loomis, *Paris in the Terror*, p. 68.
9. This and surrounding quotations from Thomas Carlyle, *The French Revolution*, vol. II. London, Chapman and Hall, pp. 256–7.
10. Melchior-Bonnet, *La Vie de Charlotte Corday*, p. 175.
11. Loomis, p. 12. Apparently the line is from Thomas Corneille, not Pierre Corneille.
12. Anecdotes recorded by Sanson are taken from the six-volume family memoirs, *Sept Générations d'exécuteurs 1688–1847*. Paris, Dupray de la Maherie, 1862–3, or from the more recent edition of Charles-Henri Sanson's revolutionary diary: *La Révolution française vue par son bourreau*. Paris, l'Instant, 1989. Though much of the 1862 edition is apocryphal, Charles-Henri's revolutionary diary is relatively reliable.
13. Young, beautiful and brilliant, soon the headsman's prey
You seemed to be proceeding to your wedding day...
14. This history of this debate is given in Alistair Kershaw's *A History of the Guillotine*.
15. Cesare Lombroso, *The Female Offender*, pp. 33–4.
16. Stefan Zweig, *Marie-Antoinette: The Portrait of an Average Woman*. New York, Garden City, 1933, p. xi.
17. Lefèbvre, *The Coming of the French Revolution*, p. 25.
18. Christopher Hibbert, *The Days of the French Revolution*. New York, Quill Paperbacks, 1981, p. 26.
19. Quoted by Hector Fleischmann in *Marie-Antoinette Libertine*. Paris, 1911, p. 122.
20. Antonia Fraser, *The Warrior Queens*, p. 12.
21. Germaine Greer, *The Obstacle Race*. New York, Farrar, Strauss and Giroux, 1979, p. 272.
22. René Girard, *Le Bouc-émisaire*, p. 32.
23. Claire Tomalin, *The Life and Death of Mary Wollstonecraft*. New York, Meridian, 1874, p. 154.
24. The originals of Olympe's work are conserved at the Bibliothèque Nationale in Paris. I have translated the titles.
25. The performance of *Zamore ou le naufrage heureux* is discussed in Olivier Blanc's *Olympe de Gouges*. Paris, Syros, 1981, pp. 59–73.
26. J.-P. Marat, *Plan de législation criminelle*. Paris, 1790.
27. G. Lenôtre, *Le Tribunal Révolutionnaire*. Paris, Flammarion, 1937, p. 53.
28. Marc de Villiers, *Histoire des clubs des femmes et des légions d'Amazones*. Paris, Plon, 1910, p. 233.
29. *Mémoires de Madame Roland*. Paris, Mercure de France, 1966, p. 210.
30. *Paris in the Terror*, pp. 178–9.
31. Quoted in Madeleine Clemenceau-Jacquemaire, *Life of Madame Roland*, p. 109.

NOTES

32 Quoted by G. Lenôtre, *Paris révolutionnaire*, vol. I, p. 181.
33 G. Lenôtre, *Le Tribunal révolutionnaire*. Paris, Flammarion, 1937. According to Lenôtre, this was the only case of a woman being put to death in the massacres which took place at the Conciergerie; thirty-six men and seventy-four other women were set free.
34 Michelet, *Histoire de la Révolution française*, vol. II, p. 377
35 Notes to Michelet's *Histoire de la Révolution française*, vol. II, p. 1545.
36 James Fox, 'Madame Claude'. Interview-portrait, *Sunday Times Magazine*, 26 July 1987, p. 27.
37 Zweig, *Marie Antoinette*, p. 56.
38 *Mémoires des Sanson*, t.iv, p. 366.
39 Quoted by Olivier Blanc in *La Dernière Lettre*, p. 77.
40 *La Guillotine et l'imaginaire de la Terreur*, p. 123.
41 *Histoire de la Révolution française*, t.ii, pp. 900–2.
42 G. Lenôtre, *Paris révolutionnaire*, pp. 33–4.
43 See Jules Clarétie, *Camille Desmoulins, Lucile Desmoulins*, p. 27.
44 *La Révolution française vue par son bourreau, Charles-Henri Sanson*. Paris, l'Instant, 1989, p. 170.
45 G. Lenôtre, *Vieilles Maisons, vieux papiers*, t.i, p. 374.
46 Lynn Hunt, *Politics, Culture and Class in the French Revolution*, p. 104.

5 THE ART OF IMMOLATION

1 Sophocles, *The Theban Plays*, translated by E.F. Watling. London, Penguin Classics, 1947, p. 127. I quote from several translations, however, according to the respective merits of each version; Jebb and Storr are footnoted for later passages.
2 E.F. Watling, introduction to *The Theban Plays*, p. 14.
3 Moses Hadas, introduction to Sophocles' *Antigone*, translated by Sir Richard Claverhouse Jebb. New York, Bantam, 1967, p. xiii.
4 *The Complete Plays of Sophocles*, translated by Sir Richard Claverhouse Jebb, p. 135.
5 *Antigone*, translated by F.A. Storr. Cambridge, Loeb Classics, 1959, p. 381.
6 See Francis Steegmuller, *Cocteau: A Biography*. New York, Little Brown, 1970, pp. 292–3.
7 In *Nouvelles Pièces noires* by Jean Anouilh. Paris, La Table Ronde, 1957.
8 Quoted by John Harvey, *Anouilh. A Study in Theatrics*. New Haven, Yale University Press, 1964, p. 98.
9 John Willett, *The Theatre of Bertolt Brecht*. New York, New Directions, 1959, p. 57.
10 Northrop Frye, *Anatomy of Criticism*. New York, Atheneum, 1968, p. 186.
11 Joseph Campbell, *The Power of Myth*. New York, Doubleday, 1988, p. 190.
12 Voltaire, *The Maid of Orleans*. In *The Works of Voltaire*, vols 40–1. New York, The St Hubert Guild, 1901, p. 83.
13 Charles E. Passage, introduction to Schiller's *Maria Stuart. The Maid of Orleans*. New York, Frederick Ungar, 1967, p. iv.
14 Quoted by William Weaver, *Verdi*. New York, Thames and Hudson, 1977, p. 162.
15 G.B. Shaw, *Saint Joan*. In *Complete Plays with Prefaces*. New York, Dodd, Mead and Company, 1963, p. 369.
16 Frederick Ewen, *Bertolt Brecht: His Life, His Art, His Times*. New York, Citadel Press, 1967, p. 266.

17 Bertolt Brecht, *Die Heilige Johanne des Schlachthofe*. Frankfurt, Suhrkamp Verlag, 1960, p. 28.
18 Brecht, *The Trial of Joan of Arc at Rouen in 1431*. In *Collected Plays*, vol. 9. New York, Pantheon Books, 1972, pp. 401–2.
19 Jean Anouilh, *L'Alouette*. Paris, La Table Ronde, 1967, p. 11.
20 Felice Romani, librettist, *Anna Bolena*, translated by William Ashbrook. Angel Records AVC 3401, 1972, p. 25.
21 Carlo Peppoli, librettist, *I Puritani*. Angel CDC 7 47308 8, 1987, pp. 76–7.
22 Catherine Clément, *Opera, Or the Undoing of Women*. Minneapolis, University of Minnesota Press, 1988, p. 91.
23 Schiller, *Mary Stuart*, translated by Charles E. Passage. New York, Frederick Ungar, 1961, p. 26.
24 Giuseppe Bardari, librettist, *Maria Stuarda*. English version by Diana Reed. Philips CD 426 233–2, Philips Classical Productions, 1990, p. 128.
25 Quoted in K.N. Cameron's *Shelley: The Golden Years*. Cambridge, Mass., Harvard University Press, 1968, p. 396.
26 Shelley, *The Cenci*. In *The Poetical Works of Percy Bysshe Shelley*. London, Frederick Warne, no date, p. 271.
27 Shelley, 'Posthumous Fragments by Margaret Nicholson'. In *The Complete Poems of Percy Bysshe Shelley*. London, Frederick Warne, no date, pp. 641–2.
28 Luigi Illica, librettist, *Andrea Chénier*, translated by Martin L. Sokol. RCA CD 2046-2-RG, 1977, pp. 31–2.
29 Quoted by Robert Speaight in *Georges Bernanos: A Study of the Man and the Writer*. New York, Liveright, 1974, p. 267.
30 *Dialogues des Carmélites*. Paris, Editions du Seuil, 1949, p. 128.
31 'Our Friends the Saints' in *Last Essays of Georges Bernanos*, translated by Joan and Barry Ulanov. New York, Greenwood Press, 1968, pp. 236–41.
32 Preface to *Le Coup de grâce*. In *Oeuvres complètes*. Paris, Gallimard, Editions de la Pléiade, 1982, p. 79.
33 Janet Flanner, *Paris Was Yesterday*. New York, Viking Press, 1972, p. 124.
34 Jacques Lacan, 'Motifs du Crime Paranoïaque' in *Obliques* no. 2, 1972, pp. 99–103.
35 Jean Genet, 'Lettre à Pauvert' in *Twentieth Century French Drama*, edited by Germaine Brée and Alexander Y. Kroff. Toronto, Macmillan, 1969, p. 592.
36 Genet, *Les Bonnes*. In *Oeuvres complètes*, vol. IV. Paris, Gallimard, 1968, p. 176.

CONCLUSION

1 Michelet, *Histoire de la Révolution française*, vol. I, pp. 1081–2.
2 René Girard, *Le Bouc émissaire*. Paris, Grasset, 1982, p. 74.
3 See Dr Roger Goulard, *Les Sanson: 1688–1847: Une lignée d'executeurs des jugements criminels*. Melun, Archambault, 1968.
4 See Thomas Szasz, *The Manufacture of Madness*. New York, Harper and Row, 1970.
5 Michael Kroll, 'The Room with No Exit'. *California Living Magazine* in the *San Francisco Chronicle*, 4 March 1984, pp. 25 ff.

BIBLIOGRAPHY

Anchel, Roger. *Crimes et châtiments au XVIIIe siècle*. Paris: Perrin, 1933.
Anderson, Bonnie S. and Judith P. Zinsser. *A History of Their Own*, vol. II. New York: Harper and Row, 1988.
Anouilh, Jean. *L'Alouette*. Paris: La Table Ronde, 1957.
——*Antigone*. In *Nouvelles Pièces noires*. Paris: La Table Ronde, 1967.
The Arabian Nights Entertainment. New York: A.L. Burt, no date.
Arasse, Daniel. *La Guillotine et l'imaginaire de la Terreur*. Paris: Flammarion, 1978.
Archives Nationales de France.
Bataille, Georges. *La Littérature et le mal*. Paris: Gallimard, 1957.
Bates, William Nickerson. *Sophocles, Poet and Dramatist*. New York: Russell and Russell, 1940.
Beaumarchais, Pierre-Augustin Caron de. *Théâtre. Lettres*. Paris: Gallimard, Editions de la Pléiade, 1957.
Beccaria, Cesare. *Traité des délits et des peines*, translated by André Morellet, ed. Roederer. Paris: Imprimerie du Journal de l'économie publique de morale et de politique, 1797.
Bédier, Joseph. *Le Roman de Tristan et Iseut*. Paris: Piazza, 1946.
Bernanos, Georges. *The Last Essays of Georges Bernanos*, translated by Joan and Barry Ulanov. New York: Greenwood Press, 1968.
——*Dialogues des Carmélites*. Paris: Editions du Seuil, 1984.
Beroul. *The Romance of Tristan*, ed. Alfred Ewert. Oxford: Blackwell, 1967.
Belloc, Hilaire. *Marie Antoinette*. New York: G.P. Putnam, 1909.
Bellini, Vincenzo and Carlo Peppoli, librettist. *I Puritani*. Callas, Di Stefano, Rossi-Lemeni, Serafin. Angel CDC 747308 8, 1987.
Berriat-Saint-Prix, Charles. *Des Tribunaux et de la procédure du grand criminel au XVIIIe siècle jusqu'en 1789*. Paris: Aubry, 1859.
Biré, Edmond. *Journal d'un bourgeois de Paris pendant la Terreur*. Paris, 1884.
Blanc, Olivier. *La Dernière Lettre*. Paris: Robert Laffont, 1984.
——*Olympe de Gouges*. Paris: Syros, 1981.
Boccaccio, Giovanni. *Concerning Famous Women*, translated, with an introduction and notes, by Guido A. Guarino. New Brunswick: Rutgers University Press, 1963.
——*The Decameron*, translated by G.H. McWilliam. Baltimore: Penguin Books, 1972.
Brecht, Bertolt. *Die Antigone des Sophokles*. In *Gesammelte Werke*, vol. 6. Frankfurt: Suhrkamp Verlag, 1967.
——*Collected Plays*, ed. Ralph Manheim and John Willett, vols. 1–9. New York: Pantheon Books, 1972.

—— *Die Heilige Johanna des Schlachthöfe*. Frankfurt: Surhkamp Verlag, 1960.
Cameron, K.C. *Shelley, The Golden Years*. Cambridge, Mass. Harvard University Press, 1968.
Campan, Mme Jeanne Louise Henriette. *Mémoires sur la vie de Marie-Antoinette*. Paris: Firmin-Didot, 1866.
Campbell, Joseph. *The Power of Myth*. With Bill Moyers. New York: Doubleday, 1988.
—— *The Masks of God: Primitive Mythology*. New York: Penguin Books, 1984.
Cantarella, Eva. 'Dangling Virgins: Myth, Ritual and the Place of Women in Ancient Greece.' In *Poetics Today*, vol. 6 nos. 1–2, *The Female Body in Western Culture. Semiotic Perspectives*, p. 91.
Castries, Duc de. *Julie de Lespinasse*. Paris: Albin Michel, 1985.
Carlyle, Thomas. *The French Revolution*. London: Chapman and Hall, 1891.
Cerati, Marie. *Le Club des Citoyennes Républicaines Révolutionnaires*. Paris, 1966.
Chateaubriand, François René de. *Mémoires d'outre-tombe*. Paris: Gallimard, Editions de la Pléiade, 1962–4.
Christophe, Roger. *Les Sanson*. Paris, 1956.
Caliborne, Robert. *The Roots of English*. New York: Random House, 1989.
Clarétie, Jules. *Camille Desmoulins, Lucile Desmoulins*. Paris: Plon, 1875.
Clemenceau-Jacquemaire, Madeleine. *The Life of Madame Roland*. Translated by Laurence Vail. London and New York: Longmans, Green and Co., 1930.
Clément, Catherine. *Opera, Or the Undoing of Women*. Minneapolis: University of Minnesota Press, 1988.
Davies, Nigel. *Human Sacrifice in History and Today*. New York: Dorset, 1988.
Delarue, Jacques. *Le Métier de bourreau*. Paris: Fayard, 1979.
Desmazes, Charles Adrien. *Le Châtelet de Paris*. Paris, 1934.
Dickens, Charles. *A Tale of Two Cities*. New York: Signet, 1980.
Dispot, Laurent. *La Machine à Terreur*. Paris: Grasset, 1978.
Donaldson, Gordon. *The First Trial of Mary, Queen of Scots*. Westport: Greenwood Press, 1969.
Donizetti, Gaetano and Felice Romani, librettist. *Anna Bolena*. Angel Records AVC 34031, 1972.
Douglas, Alfred. *The Tarot*. New York: Penguin, 1972.
Duhet, Paule-Marie. *Les Femmes et la Révolution, 1789–1794*. Paris: Gallimard, Collection Archives, 1977.
Duras, Duchesse de (Louise Henriette Charlotte de Durfort). *Journal des prisons de mon père*. Paris: Plon, 1889.
Ehrenreich, Barbara and Deirdre English. *Witches, Midwives and Nurses: A History of Women Healers*. Oyster Bay, New York: Glass Mountain Pamphlets, 1973.
Eliot, George. *Adam Bede*. London: William Blackwood, c. 1875.
Elliot, Grace Dalrymple. *During the Reign of Terror. Journal of my Life during the French Revolution*. London, 1910.
Esmein, Adhémar. *Histoire de la procédure criminelle en France*. Paris: Larose and Forcel, 1916.
Eusebius Pamphili. *The Ecclesiastical History*. Cambridge, Mass.: Harvard University Press, 1959.
Ewen, Frederic. *Bertolt Brecht: His Life, His Art and His Times*. New York: Citadel Press, 1967.
Flanner, Janet. *Paris Was Yesterday*. New York: Viking Press, 1972.
—— *Paris Journal 1944–1965*. New York: Harcourt, Brace, Jovanovich, 1977.
Fleischmann, Hector. *La Guillotine en 1793*. Paris, 1908.
—— *Les Prisons de la Révolution d'après les mémoires du temps*. Paris, 1908.

BIBLIOGRAPHY

——*Les Femmes et la Terreur*. Paris, 1909.
——*L'Histoire licencieuse*. Paris, 1910.
——*Marie-Antoinette Libertine*. Paris, 1911.
Foucault, Michel. *Punir et surveiller*. Paris: Gallimard, 1975.
Fournier, Edouard. *Histoire du Pont Neuf*. 2 vols. Paris, 1862.
Fox, James. 'Madame Claude.' Interview-portrait in *The Sunday Times* Magazine section, 26 July 1987, p. 27.
Foxe, John. *The Acts and Monuments*. London, 1837–41.
France, Anatole. *Les Dieux ont soif*. Paris: Calmann-Lévy, no date.
Fraser, Antonia. *Mary Queen of Scots*. New York: Delacorte Press, 1970.
——*The Warrior Queens*. London: Mandarin, 1989.
Frye, Northrop. *Anatomy of Criticism*. New York: Atheneum, 1968.
Furet, François. *Penser la Révolution française*. Paris: Gallimard, 1978.
Furet, François and Denis Richet. *La Révolution française*. Paris: Fayard, 1973.
Genet, Jean. *Oeuvres complètes*, vols. I–IV. Paris: Gallimard, 1967–8.
——*Les Bonnes* and *Lettre à Pauvert*. In *Twentieth Century French Drama*, ed. Germaine Brée and Alexander Y. Kroff. Toronto: Macmillan, 1969.
Giordano, Umberto and Luigi Illica, librettist. *Andrea Chénier*. Recorded in London, 1976: Domingo, Scotto, Milnes, Levine. RCA Compact Disc 2046–2RG.
Girard, René. *Le Bouc émissaire*. Paris: Grasset, 1982.
——*La Violence et le sacré*. Paris: Grasset, 1972.
Gouges, Olympe de. *Déclaration des droits de la femme et de la citoyenne*. Photocopy, Bibliothèque Nationale.
Goulard, Dr Roger. *Les Sanson: 1688–1847: une lignée d'exécuteurs des jugements criminels*. Melun: Archambault, 1968.
Greer, Germaine. *The Obstacle Race. The Fortunes of Women Painters and Their Work*. New York: Farrar, Straus and Giroux, 1979.
Hansen, Chadwick. *Witchcraft in Salem*. New York: Brazilier, 1969.
Hardy, Thomas. *Tess of the d'Urbervilles*. New York: Harper and Bros, 1950.
Harrison, G.B., editor. *The Letters of Queen Elizabeth I*. London: Cassell, 1935.
Harvey, John. *Anouilh. A Study in Theatrics*. New Haven and London: Yale University Press, 1964.
Heilbrunn, Carolyn G. *Writing a Woman's Life*. New York: W.W. Norton, 1988.
Hibbert, Christopher. *The Days of the French Revolution*. New York: Morrow Quill, 1981.
Hole, Christina. *Mirror of Witchcraft*. London: Chatto and Windus, 1957.
Hughes, Muriel Joy. *Women Healers in Medieval Life and Literature*. New York: Columbia University Press (King's Crown), 1943.
Hunt, Lynn. *Politics, Culture and Class in the French Revolution*. Berkeley: University of California Press, 1984.
Jones, Ann. *Women Who Kill*. New York: Ballantine Books, 1980.
Joufrois. Altfranzösisches Rittergedicht, ed. Konrad Hofman and Fritz Muncker. Halle: Niemeyer, 1880.
Kamerbeek, J.C. *The Plays of Sophocles: Commentaries. III: The Antigone*. Leiden: E.J. Brill, 1978.
Karlsen, Carol F. *The Devil in the Shape of a Woman*. New York and London: Norton and Company, 1987.
Kershaw, Alistair. *A History of the Guillotine*. London: Calder, 1965.
Lasserre, Adrien. *La Participation collective des femmes à la Révolution française*. Paris: Alcan, 1906.
Lea, Henry Charles. *Superstition and Force. Essays on the Wager of Law*. Philadelphia: H.C. Lea, 1866.

―――*Materials towards a History of Witchcraft*, ed. Arthur C. Howland. Philadelphia: University of Pennsylvania Press, 1929.

Le Brun, Annie. *Petits et Grands Théâtres du Marquis de Sade*. Exhibition catalogue, Paris Art Centre, 1989.

―――*Soudain un bloc d'abîme, Sade*. Paris: Pauvert, 1985. (Translated by Camille Naish as *Sade: A Sudden Abyss*. San Francisco: City Lights Press, 1991.)

Lefèbvre, Georges. *The Coming of the French Revolution*, translated from *Quatre-vingt-neuf* by R.R. Palmer. Princeton: Princeton University Press, 1967.

Le Fort, Gertrud von. *La Dernière à l'échafaud*, translated from the German by Blaise Briod. Paris: Desclée, de Brouwer and Compagnie, 1937.

Lely, Gilbert. *Vie de Sade*. Paris: Gallimard, 1967.

Lenôtre, G. (pseudonym for Louis Léon Théodore Gosselin). *La Captivité et la mort de Marie-Antoinette*. Paris: Perrin, 1902.

―――*La Guillotine et les exécuteurs des arrêts criminels pendant la Révolution*. Paris: Perrin, 1903.

―――*Les Noyades de Nantes*. Paris: Perrin, 1912.

―――*Paris révolutionnaire*. Paris: Perrin, 1904.

―――*Le Tribunal révolutionnaire*. Paris: Flammarion, 1937.

―――*Vieilles maisons, vieux papiers*. 2 vols. Paris: Perrin, 1905.

Levy, Barbara. *Legacy of Death*. Farnborough, Hants: D. C. Heath, 1973.

Lofts, Nora. *Anne Boleyn*. New York: Coward, McCann and Geoghegan, 1979.

Loiseleur, Jules. *Les Crimes et les peines dans l'antiquité et dans les temps modernes*. Paris: Hachette, 1863.

Lombroso, Cesare. *The Female Offender*. London, 1895. (Translation of *La Donna Deliquente*. Milan, 1915.)

Loomis, Stanley. *Du Barry: A Biography*. New York and Philadelphia: J.B. Lippincott, 1959.

―――*Paris in the Terror*. New York and Philadelphia: J.B. Lippincott, 1964.

Luke, Mary. *The Nine Days Queen. A Portrait of Lady Jane Grey*. New York: William Morrow, 1986.

Maestro, Marcello. *Voltaire and Beccaria as Reformers of Criminal Law*. New York: Columbia University Press, 1942.

Maistre, Joseph de. *Les Soirées de St. Pétersbourg* followed by a *Traité sur le sacrifice*. Paris, 1821.

Malory, Sir Thomas. *Tales of King Arthur*, ed. and abridged by Michael Senior. New York: Schocken, 1980.

Mandrou, Robert. *Magistrats et sorciers*. Paris: Plon, 1968.

Mather, Cotton. *On Witchcraft. Being: Wonders of the Invisible World*. First printed in Boston in October 1692. Reprinted, with additional matter and old wood-cuts. Mount Vernon and New York: Peter Pauper Press, no date.

Maton de la Varenne. *Mémoire pour les exécuteurs des jugements criminels de toutes les villes du royaume où l'on prouve la légitimité de leur état*. Paris: Froullé, 1790.

Melchior-Bonnet, Bernardine. *Charlotte Corday*. Paris: Perrin, 1972.

Mercier, Sebastien. *Le Nouveau Paris*, vol. I. Paris, 1798.

Michelet, Jules. *La Sorcière*. Paris: Garnier-Flammarion, 1966.

―――*Histoire de la Révolution française*. Paris: Gallimard, Edition de la Pléiade, 1952.

―――*Les Guerres de religion*. In *Oeuvres complètes*, vol. VIII. Paris: Flammarion, 1980.

―――*Les Femmes de la Révolution*. In *Oeuvres complètes*, vol. XVI. Paris: Flammarion, 1980.

―――*Jeanne d'Arc*. Paris, 1853.

BIBLIOGRAPHY

Morrison, N. Bryson. *Mary Queen of Scots*. New York: Vanguard Press, 1960.
Murray, Margaret A. *The Witch Cult in Western Europe*. Oxford: Clarendon Press, 1921.
——*The God of the Witches*. London: S. Low, Marston and Co., 1933.
Neale, John Ernest. *Queen Elizabeth*. New York: Harcourt, Brace and Co., 1934.
Obliques no.2. Special issue on Genet. Paris: Librairie Mandragore, 1972.
Pichon, Ludovic. *Code de la Guillotine*. Paris, 1910.
Poole, W.F. *The Mather Papers. Cotton Mather and Salem Witchcraft*. Boston, 1868.
Poulenc, Francis and Georges Bernanos, librettist. *Dialogues des Carmélites*. Recorded in Paris, 1958: Duval, Crespin, Scharley, Dervaux. Reissued as EMI Compact Disc 7493312.
Pritchard, John Laurence. *A History of Capital Punishment*. New York: Citadel Press, 1960.
Pronko, Leonard Cabell. *The World of Jean Anouilh*. Berkeley and Los Angeles: University of Los Angeles Press, 1968.
Ricci, Corrado. *Beatrice Cenci*. 2 vols. New York: Boni and Livernight, 1925.
Riedel, Frederick Carl. *Crime and Punishment in the Old French Romances*. New York: Columbia University Press, 1938.
Roland, Manon. *Mémoires de Madame Roland*. Edition présentée par Paul de Roux. Paris: Mercure de France, 1966.
Romans de Claris et Laris, ed. Dr Johann Alton. Tübingen: Bibliothek des literarischen Vereins in Stuttgart, 1884.
Rosen, George. *Madness in Society*. London: Routledge and Kegan Paul, 1968.
Rousseau, Jean-Jacques. *The Social Contract*, translated by Maurice Cranston. Harmondsworth: Penguin Classics, 1968.
Rudé, George. *The Crowd in History, 1730–1848: A Study of Popular Disturbances in France and England*. New York: Viking, 1973.
Russell, Geoffrey Burton. *Witchcraft in the Middle Ages*. Ithaca and London: Cornell University Press, 1972.
Sackville-West, Vita. *Saint Joan of Arc*. Boston: G.K. Hall, 1984.
Sanson, Henri. *Sept générations d'exécuteurs 1688–1847. Mémoires des Sanson*. Paris: Dupray de la Maherie, 1862.
Schama, Simon. *Citizens*. New York: Alfred Knopf, 1989.
Schiller, Friedrich von. *Mary Stuart. The Maid of Orleans. Two Historical Plays*, translated by Charles E. Passage. New York: Frederick Ungar, 1967.
Seilhac, Comte V. de. *Scènes et portraits de la Révolution en Bas-Limousin*. Paris, 1878.
Shaw, G.B. *Saint Joan*. In *Complete Plays with Prefaces*, New York: Dodd, Mead and Co., 1963.
Shelley, Percy Bysshe. *The Poetical Works of Percy Bysshe Shelley*. London: Frederick Warne and Co., c. 1909.
Shirer, William L. *The Rise and Fall of the Third Reich*. New York: Simon and Schuster, 1960.
Simon, Rita James. *Women and Crime*. Lexington: D.C.Heath and Co., 1975.
Sitwell, Edith. *Fanfare for Elizabeth*. New York: Macmillan, 1962.
Slavin, Arthur J., editor. *Henry VIII and the English Reformation*. Lexington, Mass.: C. Heath, 1968.
Sophocles. *Antigone*. In *The Complete Plays of Sophocles*, translated by Sir Richard Claverhouse Jebb, ed. Moses Hadas. New York: Bantam, 1967.
——*Antigone*, translated by F. Storr, Loeb Classical Library. Cambridge, Mass: Harvard University Press, 1981.
——*The Theban Plays*, translated by E.F. Watling. London: Penguin, 1978.

Speaight, Robert. *Georges Bernanos: A Study of the Man and of the Writer*. New York: Liveright, 1974.
Sprenger, James and Henry Kramer, Institutoris. *Malleus Maleficarum*, translated and ed. by Montague Summers. London, 1928.
Stanton, Elizabeth Cady, editor, with Susan B. Anthony and Matilda Joslyn Gage. *A History of Women's Suffrage*. New York: Arno, 1969.
Starkey, Marion L. *The Devil in Massachusetts*. New York: Doubleday, 1949.
Steegmuller, Francis. *Cocteau: A Biography*. New York: Little Brown, 1970.
Stendhal. *Romans et nouvelles*. Paris: Gallimard, Editions de la Pléiade, 1952.
Stokes, Hugh. *Mme de Brinvilliers and Her Times, 1630–1676*. London and New York, 1912.
Stone, Merlin. *When God was a Woman*. New York: Dorset Books, 1976.
Summers, Montague. *The Geography of Witchcraft*. New York: Alfred A. Knopf, 1927.
——*The History of Witchcraft and Demonology*. New York: Alfred A. Knopf, 1926.
Szasz, Thomas. *The Manufacture of Madness*. New York: Harper and Row, 1970.
Tomalin, Claire. *The Life and Death of Mary Wollstonecraft*. New York: Meridian, 1983.
Travitsky, Betty. *The Paradise of Women. Writings by Englishwomen of the Renaissance*. New York: Columbia University Press, 1989.
Vassiltchikov, Marie. *Berlin Diaries 1940–1945*. New York: Alfred Knopf, 1987.
Verdi, Giuseppe and Temistocle Solera, librettist. *Giovanna d'Arco*. Live recording, Milan, 26 March 1951: Tebaldi, Bergonzi, Panerai, Simonetto. Foyer Compact Disc 2-CF 2019, 1989.
Villiers, Marc de. *Histoire des clubs de femmes et des légions d'amazones 1793–1848–1871*. Paris: Plon, 1910.
Voltaire, François-Marie Arouet de. *The Maid of Orleans*. In *The Works of Voltaire. A Contemporary Version*, vols. 40–1, translated by William F. Fleming. New York: The St Hubert Guild, 1901.
——*Mélanges*. Paris: Gallimard, Editions de la Pléiade, 1961.
Warnicke, Retha M., *The Rise and Fall of Anne Boleyn*. Cambridge: Cambridge University Press, 1989.
Weaver, William. *Verdi*. New York: Thames and Hudson, 1977.
White, Helen C. *The Tudor Book of Saints and Martyrs*. Madison: University of Wisconsin Press, 1963.
Willett, John. *The Theatre of Bertolt Brecht*. New York: New Directions, 1959.
Williams, Charles. *Witchcraft*. London: Faber and Faber, 1941.
Williams, Neville. *Henry VIII and his Court*. London: Macmillan, 1971.
Yourcenar, Marguerite. *Le Coup de grâce*. In *Oeuvres complètes*. Paris: Gallimard, Editions de la Pléiade, 1982.
——*Un Homme obscur*. In *Oeuvres complètes*. Paris: Gallimard, 1982.
Zweig, Stefan. *Marie Antoinette. The Portrait of an Average Woman*, translated by Eden and Cedar Paul. New York: Garden City, 1933.
——*Mary Queen of Scotland and the Isles*, translated by Eden and Cedar Paul. New York: Viking Press, 1935.

INDEX

abortion as capital crime 93
Académie Française 232
accusatorial Law 10
Adler, Freda 248–9
adultery as capital crime 2–3, 10, 41, 45, 49, 61, 195, 213
Ady, Thomas 33
Agnes, Saint 37, 38
Aguesseau, Henriette-Alexandrine d', Duchesse d'Ayen 180
Aigrepont, Geneviève and Madeleine d' 167
Aiguillon, Duc d' 161, 162
Aiguillon, Duchesse d' 161
Albigensian heresy 11
Alembert, Jean d' 145
Alençon, Duc d' 17
Allerac, Mme d' 121
Almachius, Roman prefect 39
Anchel, Roger 92–3
Anderson, Maxwell 219
Anges, Jeanne des 34
Anne of Cleves 50
Anouilh, Jean 191–3, 209–11, 241; *Antigone*: 191–3, 209; adolescent choices of heroes 192; political effectiveness of 193; theatricality of 191–2; *L'Alouette (The Lark)*: 209–11; humanism of 210; theatricality of 209
Antigone: *see* Anouilh, Brecht, Gluck, Sophocles
Arasse, Daniel 107, 108, 118, 167–8
Arc, Jacques d' 15, 17
Arc, Jeanne d' or Joan of 8, 12–22, 26, 35, 115, 120, 185, 195, 197–211, 227, 230, 241; androgyny and 14; armour of 16; burning of 8, 20, 21, 22; canonisation of 204; declared heretic and sorceress 20; examined by theologians 16, 18; examined for virginity 16, 18; knightly qualities of 16, 17, 22; literary treatments of 13, 21, 185, 197–203, 204–11; male attire and 14, 15, 18, 19, 20; mother and rehabilitation trial 15; operatic treatments of 2, 185, 203–4; portraits of 13, 14; puberty and 34; recantation of 20; trial of 19; Voices and 15, 19, 21; witchcraft and 13, 26
Arc, Pierre d' 16, 17
Ariosto 59
Artois, Comte d' 114, 125, 126, 145
Askew, Anne 52, 86
Atanasiou, Genica 191
Aubin, Guillaume 83
Aubry, Louis-Yves 133
Aubry, Pierre 133, 141
Augustus Caesar 170
Aulon, Jean d' 17
Austen, Ann 87
Aylmer, John 53

Babington, Sir Anthony 62–3, 72
Bade, Margrave of 104
Bailly, Jean-Sylvain, mayor of Paris 128, 135
Balmarino, Lord 78
Barbaroux 112, 114, 115, 120
Bardari, Giuseppe 217
Barker, Janet 28
Barnave 132

INDEX

Barre, Chevalier de la 40, 117
Barry, Chon du 163
Barry, Comte Guillaume du 159
Barry, Comte Jean du 159
Barry, Jeanne Bécu Vaubernier, Comtesse du 77, 109, 157–66, 168, 179; afraid of execution 166; becomes royal mistress 159; exiled from court 162–3; illegitimate birth and convent education of 158; imprisoned and tried 165; kindness of 162–3; presented at court 160; royalist activities of 164; snubbed by Marie Antoinette 161
Barthes, Roland 106
Bartholomew, John and Mary 97
Bas, Laurent 114
bastardy 96
Bastille, storming of 6, 104, 147, 169
Bataille, Georges 246
Baudricourt, Robert de 15
Bayard, Chevalier 22
Bayard, Dr 174
Béarn, Comtesse de 160
Beaufort, Margaret 45, 53
Beaumarchais, Pierre Caron de 125
Beccaria, Cesare 94, 102, 104, 251
Bécu, Anne 158
Bedford, Duchess of 18
beheading 37–41, 115, *see also* decapitation, guillotine; aristocratic self-control and 40; efficiency of 37; in Germany 78–9; last beheadings in England 78; martyrdom and 38, 243; nobility and 39, 243; saints and 39
Bellay, Joachim du 58
Bellini Vincenzo 213–14; *Beatrice di Tenda* 213; *Il Pirata* 213; *I Puritani* 213–14, 241
Belzunce, Henri de 119
Bentham, Jeremy 250
Berliner Ensemble 208
Bernanos, Georges 109, 226–30, 242, 245; *Dialogues des Carmélites* 226–30, 242
Bernardin de Saint-Pierre 137
Beroul 196–7 (*Tristan* of)
Bertin, Rose 131
bestiality and paganism 11
Biétrix de Rozières 133
Billet, Louise 93
Blackstone, William 90
Blamont, Mme de 184

Blanc, Olivier 133, 135–8, 141, 182
Blandina, early martyr 39
Boccaccio 82, 92; *Concerning Famous Women* 82; *Decameron* 92
Bodin, Jean 32
Boleyn, Anne 41–9, 50, 64, 212, 243; character of 43, 47; courtly attributes of 42, 46; ennobled 44; executed 48–9; married to Henry VIII 44; miscarries of son 46; produces daughter 44; sentenced 48; tried for adultery 46–7; witchcraft and 43, 46, 47
Boleyn, Mary 48
Bonaparte, Marie 119
Bonaparte, Napoleon 17, 183–4
Bonaparte, Prince Roland 119
Borgia 219
Bosc, Louis 145, 154, 156
Bothwell, Earl of (James Hepburn) 60–1,
Bouchard, Nicole 178–9
Boullé, Thomas 33–4
bougrerie 11–12
Brandon, Charles, Duke of Suffolk 42, 52
Brantôme 58, 61
breaking on wheel 1
Brecht, Bertolt 21, 193–5, 207–9, 211, 241; *Antigone des Sophokles, Die*: 193–4; humanism of 194; jazz rythmns and 194; *Caucasian Chalk Circle, The*: 207; *Gesichte der Simone Machard, Die* (*The Visions of Simone Machard*): 208; *Heilige Johanna des Schlachthöfe, Die* (*Saint Joan of the Stockyards*): 204, 206–7; economic war and 207; parody of Goethe and Schiller 207; *Trial of Joan of Arc at Rouen in 1431, The*: 208
Brée, Germaine 193
Brereton, William 47
Breton, André 191
Bretteville, Mme de 111
Bridges, Sir John 56
Brienne, Loménie de 133
Brière, Marie-Thérèse 91
Brinvilliers, Marie-Madeleine, née d'Aubray, Marquise de 72–6, 77, 244; arrested and tortured 74; as female criminal type 75; birth of 73; executed 75; experiments with poison 73–4;

INDEX

marriage and adultery of 73; murders father and brothers 74
Brinvilliers, Marquis de 72–4
Brissac, Duc de 163–4
Brissot (de Warville) 104, 112, 137, 147, 148, 153
Brossier, Marthe 32
Browne, Sir Anthony 56
Browne, Elizabeth 99
Brune, General 170
Brutus 118, 181
Buddha 248
Buffon 145
Buisset, Matthinette du 8
Bull, executioner 63–4
Burgundy, Duke of 17
burial alive 7, 9; modesty and 9; symbolism of 7
burning of women 8, 22–3
Burroughs, George 88
Burton, Mr 9
Busne, Lieutenant de 129
Buzot 112, 142, 152, 154, 155

Caesar, Julius 10
Calcraft, executioner 99
Callas, Maria 213–14
Calvin, Jean 85
Cameron, K.N. 69
Campan, Mme 126
Campbell, Joseph 197, 246–7
Campeggio, Cardinal 43
Camus, Albert 1
Cannet sisters 145, 146
Cantarella, Eva 81–2, 189
Capecelatro 219
Carafa 218
Carlemigelli, Marie-Françoise 183
Carlier, executioner 76–7
Carlyer, Vauldrue 8
Carlyle, Thomas 109, 113, 121, 155, 177
Carmelites 109
Carrichon, Abbé 180
Carrier, Martha Allen 90
Carrier, Thomas 90
Carthusian martyrs 44
Castiglione, Baldassare 219
Catalano, Marzio 69–70
Catherine of Aragon 41, 42, 44, 45
Catherine of Russia 104
Cauchon, Pierre, Bishop of Beauvais 18–20
Cecilia, Saint 39

Cenci, Beatrice 66–72, 219, 244; affair with father's overseer 69–71; arrested, charged and tortured 70–1; beaten by father 68; beheaded 71–2; birth of 67; helps murder father 70; raped by father 69; sequestred by father 69; treated as martyr 71
Cenci, Bernardo 67, 71, 72
Cenci, Cristoforo 67, 68
Cenci, Count Francesco 67–71, 219; children of 67; murdered 70; sodomy and 68, 71; violent childhood of 67
Cenci, Giacomo, 67–9, 71–2
Cenci, Lucrezia Petroni, 67–72; arrested and tortured 70–1; executed 72; marries Francesco 67; sequestred by Francesco 69
Cenci, Rocco 67, 68
Cenci, the 77
Chabillon 133
Chabot 114, 115
Chamfort 135
Chanel, Coco 191
Chapuys, Eustace 46
Charlemagne 107
Charles of Spain 45
Charles I of England 138
Charles V of Spain 8
Charles VII, Dauphin of France 15, 20,
Charles VIII 23
Chartres, Duc de 160
Chastelard 59, 63, 66
Chateaubriand, Alphonse-René de 170
Châtelet, Duc de 167
Chaumette 142, 166, 171, 173
Chauveau-Lagarde 116–17, 129, 155, 165
Chénier, André 118, 135
chivalrous allegory 41
Chivalry 6, 11, 12, 21, 22, 49, 59, 195, 197–9, 234, 243, 251; chivalric romance 195–7, 241; female execution and 6; parodied by Voltaire 198–9
Choiseul, Duc de 122, 160, 161
Choiseul-Stainville, Béatrix de 160, 175
Christ 37, 248
Christina, Queen of Sweden 73
Chrysostom, St John 26
Cicero 26
Cixous, Hélène 214
Claiborne, Robert 40
Clarétie, Jules 170
Claris et Laris 9, 92

INDEX

Claude, Queen of France 42, 46
Claude, Mme 159
Claudel, Paul 204
Clavière 149
Clemenceau-Jacquemaire, Madeleine 146, 148, 151, 152, 154
Clément, Catherine 214–15
Clement, Pope 43
Clement IV, Pope 12
Clement VII, Pope 66, 71
Clère, Catherine 121
Cleves, Duke William of 32
Clifton, Alice 97
Coccia, Carlo 218
Cocteau, Jean 190–2, 195
Colbert 33
Cole, Ann 87
Comédie Française 132, 134
Comforters of St John the Beheaded 71–2
concealment of pregnancy as crime 93–4
Condorcet, Marquis de 135, 143, 148
Condorcet, Mme Sophie de 147
Constantine 94
Constituent Assembly 103, 136
Corday d'Armont, Jacques de 110
Corday d'Armont, Marie Charlotte de ix, 5, 109, 110–20, 122, 125, 129–31, 132, 138, 141, 143, 153, 156, 157, 162, 167, 168, 172, 173, 176, 177, 181, 183, 223, 244; childhood and education of 110–11; examined for virginity 119, 131; executed 117–18; imprisoned and tried 115–17; journey to Paris 112–13; judged by posterity 120; 130–1; murders Marat 114; reaction to September massacres 112; republicanism of 111–12
Corey, Giles 89
Corey, Martha 88–9
Corneille, Pierre 110, 111, 130
Corneille, (Thomas) 115
Cousin, Henry, executioner 8
Couthon 176–7, 178, 180, 181
Cranmer, Thomas 48, 51, 57
Cromwell, Thomas 46, 50
Culpeper, Thomas 51
Curie, Marie 13

Dada 191
Danton 112, 113, 118, 119, 121, 132, 142, 150, 151, 170, 171, 180, 183
Darnley, Lord Henry 60–1

Daubenton 134
David, J.-L. 115–16, 119, 128, 131, 177
Davison, secretary to Elizabeth I 64
decapitation 1, 166; in Germany 78–9; whether death coincides with 118
Declaration of the Rights of Man 4, 103, 115
Declaration of the Rights of Woman 4, 136–7, 142
Delavacquerie, Mme 115
Dello Joio, Norman *The Trial at Rouen* 204
Demougeot, Jean-Louis 95
Dereham, Francis 50–1
Desgrez 74–5
Desmoulins, Camille 115, 118, 168, 169–72, 173, 180, 183; arrested and executed 171; as revolutionary 169; criticises Robespierre 170; marries Lucile 169
Desmoulins, Horace 171, 172
Desmoulins, Lucile, née Duplessis 109, 168, 169–72, 173, 174, 183; arrested and tried 171; childhood and marriage of 169–70; courageous death of 172; support for husband 170
Desmoulins, père 169, 172
Dickens, Charles, *A Tale of Two Cities* 224, 241
Diderot, Denis 114, 145
Dillon, General Arthur 171–2
Diogenes Laertius 81
Diogenes the Cynic 81
Dionysus 80
Dispot, Laurent 120
Donaldson, Sam 250
Donizetti, Gaetano 2, 211–13, 217, 218, 223; *Anna Bolena* 211–13, 215, 223, 241; *Lucia di Lammermoor* 213, 217; *Maria Stuarda* 215, 217–18
Douglas, George and Willy 62
Dreux d'Aubray 73–4
Drouais 157
Dualism 12
Ducis 135
Dudley, Guildford 54–7
Dudley, John, Earl of Northumerland and Lord Protector 54–5, 58
Dudley, Robert, Earl of Leicester 60, 215–16
Dufriche-Valazé 104, 155
Duhet, Paule-Marie 184
Dullin, Charles 191

INDEX

Dumouriez, General 139, 149, 155
Dunois, Jacques 16
Duplessis, father of Lucile 169, 172
Duplessis, Mme, 'Daronne' 169, 172
Duras, Duc de 134
Durfort-Duras, Duchesse de 179
Dyer, Mary 86

Edgeworth, Abbé 245
Edward IV of England 50, 51–5
Eggidi or Exili 73
Ehrenreich, Barbara and Deirdre English 23–4, 29, 31, 35
electrocution 249
Eliot, George 99–100
Elisabeth, Mme, sister to Louis XVI 127, 128–9, 172, 175
Elizabeth I, Queen of England 41, 44, 46, 48, 49, 51, 53, 57, 58–9, 61–5, 84, 217; birth of 44; celibacy of 57, 65; contrast with Mary Stuart 65; illegitimacy of 48; in Schiller's *Maria Stuart* 216–17; reaction to death of Mary 64; signs death warrant of Scottish Queen 63; witchcraft laws and 84
Ellen, Mrs 55–6
Encyclopédie, l' 32
Enlightenment, the 103, 244
Entführung aus dem Serail, Die 37
Equal Rights Amendment 6, 248
Erasmus 59
Establishments of Saint-Louis 8, 91, 93
Estates General 136, 169
Eulogius, Roman prefect 38
Euphemia, Saint 37, 39
Eusebius Pamphili 39
Evrard, Simone 113–15,
Ewen, Frederick 194
execution, female: literary treatment of 185–203, 204–11; modern American methods of 249–50; Nazis and 78; operatic treatment of 190, 203–4, 211–19; sexual crimes and 95–6; subversion of the guillotine and 168; symbolism of 7–8, 81
executioners 8, 39, 56, 63–4, 76–7, 99, 105, 130, 172, 250; dislike of executing women 5–6, 77, 83; executioner of Paris on hanging 82; expertise of Germans in beheading women 78, 105

Fabre d'Eglantine 142
Feckenham 56
federalism 137
Ferdinand of Naples 218
Ferretti, a prison guard 251
Fersen, Count Axel 125
Ficino, Marsilio 219
Fisher, Bishop 44
Fisher, Mary 87
Flanner, Janet (Genêt) 234–6, 237
Fleischmann, Hector 106
Fleur, Charles-François 83
Fleury 134
Florian 135
Foch, Marshall 16
Forbin, Mlle de 113, 120
Foucault, Michel 101, 106, 250
Fouchais, Mme de la 121
Fouquier-Tinville, Antoine-Quentin 115–17, 121, 128, 139–41, 165, 171, 172, 175, 176, 178, 181–3
Foxe, John 22
Francis I of France 42,
Fraser, Antonia 58, 60–1, 63, 65, 131
fratricide 177, 186–9
Frederick of Prussia 138, 174
French Revolution x, 1, 4, 5, 79, 103–11, 124, 127, 130, 136, 145, 160, 173, 244
Fréron 169, 170
Freud 247
Frobenius, Leo 247
Frye, Northrop 195

Galmyn de Montgeorges, Count Gilbert de 76–7
Garde, Mme de la 158
Gardiner, Bishop 51, 55
Gaufridy, Louis 33, 34
Gaule, John 85
Gaunt, Elizabeth 9
Gauthier des Anthieux, Mlle 110
Gavars, Philippe 32
Genet, Jean 1, 2, 13, 233, 237–40, 242; *Bonnes, Les (The Maids)*: 233, 237–40, 241, 242; and revolution 240; as tragedy 239–40; structure and aesthetics of 237; *Letter to Pauvert* 237–8, 240; *Miracle de la Rose* 237; *Notre-Dame-des-Fleurs* 1, 237
Genlis, Mme de 160
Gentille, Citizeness 173
George III 223
Gide, André 191, 230

INDEX

Giordano, *Andrea Chénier* 224–6
Girard, René 131–2, 244–6; *Le bouc émissaire* 246
Girondins 112, 115, 121, 138, 147–8, 150, 151, 152, 154, 170, 183; execution of 155; ministry of 148–9
Gluck, Christoph Willibald von 122, 124, 190
Gnosticism 12
Godwin, William 220
Goering, Hermann 78
Goethe 123, 200, 207
Gomard, Brother 158
Gommery, Elizabeth 91
Goncourt brothers 126
Good, Sarah 88
Gouges, Olympe de x, 4, 6, 109, 132–41, 143, 145, 156, 157, 244; begins writing 133; *Declaration of the Rights of Woman* 135–6; early years and gallantry of 132; executed 141; federalism of 4; 139; imprisoned and tried 139–40; opposition to violence 139; patriotic and feminist texts 135; women's clubs and 141–2
Gourdan, Mme 158
Graham, Barbara 250–1
Grammont, an actor 130, 171–2, 173
Grandchamp, Sophie 150, 155
Grandier, Urbain 33, 34
Grandmaison, Maria 178
Gredeler, Marie 150
Greer, Germaine 131
Greive, Citizen 165
Grey, Frances Brandon, Duchess of Suffolk 52–4
Grey, Lord Henry, later Duke of Suffolk 52–3, 55
Grey, Lady Jane 41, 52–6, 58, 218; ambition of John Dudley through Jane 54–6; ambition of parents 53; ambition of Thomas Seymour through Jane 53; beheading of 56; marriage to Guildford Dudley 54; Protestantism and 54, 57; reluctance to be Queen 55
Grimm 7
Groison, Marie 83
Guellard, Commissioner 114
Guerra, Monsignore 72
Guillotin, Dr Louis 1, 104–5, 107–8
guillotine 1, 79, 103, 105–9, 174, 184; female epithets for 106–9; female victims of 109; invention of 103–5
Guise, Mary of 57–8

Halbourg, Catherine, 'Eglé' 167
hanging 1, 7, 78–102; as woman's death 81–2; crimes punishable by 91–4; in England 83; literary treatment of 84, 92, 99–101; symbolism of 78–9; technique of 82
Hanriot 181–2
Hansen, Chadwick 87–9,
Hansen's *Zauberwahn* 24, 29
Hardy, Thomas 99–100
Hari, Mata 234
Harrison, G.B. 61
Harvey, John 193
Hauer, a painter 117
Hawkins, Jane 86
Hébert, le Père Duchesne 115, 128–9, 130, 142, 156, 173–4, 183
Hébert, Françoise-Marie, *née* Goupil 142, 171, 173–4
Hébert, Scipion-Virginie 173, 174
Helen of Troy 81
Helvétius 145
Henri II 58
Henri III 32
Henri IV 223
Henry, Barbe 175
Henry VI 15
Henry VII 58
Henry VIII 41–7, 50, 52, 53, 54, 58, 64
Hercules 177
heresy 12; and sorcery 28
Herman, judge 128–9
Herries, Lord 62
Hibbens, Anne 86
Hibbert, Christopher 172, 181
Himmler 249
Hippel, Theodore von 136
Hitler 207
Holbach, Baron d' 145
Hölderlin 194–5
Holy Inquisition 18, 23, 27, 29, 33; burning and 23; confession and 29; trial of Jeanne d'Arc and 18; witchcraft and 27
Homer 162
Honegger, Artur 190, 191, 204
Hooper, Bishop 22
Hopkins, Matthew 85
Houillon, Marie-Jeanne 91

INDEX

Howard, Catherine 50–2, 57, 64; accused of adultery and executed 51; lewd infancy of 50
Hughes, Muriel Joy 31
Hugo, Victor 103, 104
Hume 153
Hunt, Lynn 106, 177
Hutchinson, Anne 86

Innocent VIII, Pope 24
Inquisitorial procedure 11
Isabella of Portugal 45
Ives, Professor E.W. 46

Jacobins 112, 114, 118, 141, 147, 148, 164, 168, 170, 178, 180, 184
Jacobs, George 88
Jacobs, Margaret 91
Jacobus de Varagine 37, 39, 40
James I of Scotland 57, 58
James II 85
Jarry, Alfred 134
Jefferson, Thomas 137
Jones, Ann 34, 97–9, 248
Joseph II, Emperor 123, 163
Juliana, St 37, 38
Jung, C.G. 247
Jungian psychology and Tarot 80–1

Kamerbeek, Professor F.C. 190
Kant, Immanuel 9
Karlsen, Carol F. 85–8, 90, 99
Kaunitz, Prince 122, 127
Kean, Edmund 219
Kilmarnock, Lord 78
Kincaid, a pricker 28
Knights Templar 12
Knox, John 58–9, 85
Kolly, Mme de 140
Kremer, Henry 24–5
Kubatza, Marie 78

Lacan, Jacques 214, 234, 236–7
La Harpe 135
La Hire 16
Ladvenu, Brother 21
Lafayette 103, 127, 137, 149, 155
Lafleurtrie 165
Lally-Tollendal, Marshall 40
Lamarche, a forger 155
Lamballe, Princesse de 125, 127–8, 132, 150, 164, 244
Lameth, Mme de 126

Lancelin family 234–7
Lang, Andrew 21, 35
Lanthenas 152
Lassois, Durand 15, 17
Laurent, Jean 93
Lavallery, Citizen 164
Lazarus 40
Le Fort, Gertrud von 227, 230
Le Franc de Pompignan, J.-J. 133
Le Paistour, Marguerite 5
Lea, Henry Charles 24, 27, 28, 29
Lebrun, Pons-Denis-Ecouchard 126
Leczinska, Queen Marie 159
Lefèbvre, Georges 124, 143
Legenda Aurea 37–40
Lenôtre, G. 140
Léon, Pauline 142
Leopold of Tuscany 104
Lescombat, Marie-Catherine 83–4, 95, 98
lethal injection 249
lettres de cachet 73, 76, 103, 161
Literary Gazette, The 219
Lofts, Nora 42–3, 45–6, 48
Logre, Professor 235–6
Lohengrin 10
Loiseleur, Jules 8,
Lombroso, Cesare 75, 119
Loomis, Stanley 111, 146, 148–9, 151, 158–60, 163, 165, 179, 180
Lorre, Peter 207
Lothringer, Abbé 117, 130
Louis XII 42
Louis XV 122, 123, 124, 159–60, 161–3
Louis XVI 73, 103, 123–4, 125, 127–8, 138, 148–50, 245, 247
Louis XVII, son of Marie Antoinette 128, 130, 167, 181
Louis, Dr Antoine 105
Louvet 114, 120
Lovat, Lord 78
Lubomirska, Princesse 175
Lucretia 81
Lucy, Saint 37
Luke, Mary 54, 57
Luther, Martin 21, 89
Lux, Adam 118, 130, 221
Luxembourg, Jean de 18

McClary, Susan 215
MacLaine, Shirley 21
Maclaurin, C. 35
madness and execution 213–23, 241

INDEX

Maffei 217
Magdalene, Saint Mary 40
Maiden, Scottish 1, 106
Maillié, Mme de 182
Maistre, Joseph de 245
Malesherbes, Guillaume Lamoignon de 73
Malleus Maleficarum 24–7, 243
Malraux, André 120
Mandrou, Robert 33, 36, 89
Manox, Henry 50
Marat, Jean-Pierre 104, 106, 111–15, 120, 132, 136, 138, 177
Marescot, Dr 32
Margaret of the Netherlands 45
Margaret, Saint 37, 38, 39
Maria Theresa, Empress of Austria 122, 123, 130, 161
Marie Antoinette de Lorraine et d'Autriche ix, 5, 13, 109, 121–32, 137, 140, 141, 148, 150, 152, 155, 156, 157, 158, 160, 161, 166, 167, 168, 172, 173, 180, 174, 175, 190, 244, 245; amateur theatricals and 124–5; charged with incest 128–9; childhood and education of 122; constitutional monarchy and 126–7; defies court etiquette 124; executed 129–30; imprisoned 127; provokes gender anxiety 131; scandalous attacks on 125–6; tried by Revolutionary Tribunal 127–9; uncomsummated marriage of 123
Marie of the Incarnation, Mother 226
Mark Antony 170
Marion, a barber's wife 8
Marion, a tailor's wife 8
Martin, Mary 97
Martyrdom 39–40, 79
Massieu, Brother 21
Masson, Jean 83
Mather, Cotton 87
Mather, Increase 87, 89
Mather, Mrs Increase 89
Mauger, Perrette 8
Maupeou, Chancellor 162
Maxwell, Lord 62
Mayet, Mme 182
Medici, Catherine de' 58
Mercadante 219
Mercier, Sébastien 135
Méricourt, Théroigne de 142–3
Messalina 122, 165

Metastasio 190
Meunier, Marie-Geneviève 227
Michelet, Jules 7, 9, 30, 110, 112, 119–20, 128, 133, 138, 141, 146, 148, 152, 156, 166, 168, 169, 170, 171, 172, 173, 178, 179, 181, 183
Migenes-Johnson, Julia 7
Mirabeau 127, 130, 132, 135, 137, 138, 183
Mitchell, Aaron 249
Monaco, Princesse de 182
Moniteur, Le 106, 135, 157, 244
Montaigne, Michel de 32, 162
Montané 115, 117
Montané, Mme 154
Montesquieu 110
Moray, Earl of 60, 62
More, Sir Thomas 44, 49
Morellet, Abbé 94
Mortemart, Pauline de 164
Motte-Valois, Comtesse de la 125
Mouchy, M. and Mme de 179–80
Mountain, the 113, 138, 139, 143, 153
Moura, a servant 76–7
Murray, Margaret 13, 29, 30
Musgrave, Thea, *Mary Queen of Scots* 219
Muzio, Emmanuele 204

National Assembly 4, 135, 143
National Convention 136, 184
Navarre, Marguerite de 42, 46
Nazareth, Joseph of 180
Necker 169
Neher, Carola 207
New Yorker, The 234
Nicholson, Margaret 223
Noailles, Charlotte-Françoise-Caroline de, née de Cossé-Brissac, 'Mme Etiquette' 122, 124, 161, 180
Noailles, François de 57
Noailles, Louise de 180
Norfolk, Dowager Duchess of 50
Norfolk, Duke of 45, 50, 55, 62
Norris, Sir Henry 47, 49,
Nottingham, Sheriff of 63
Nurse, Rebecca 91

Occard de Corberon, Mme 179
Olimpio, Cenci's overseer 68–71
Olybius, Roman prefect 38, 39
Orff, Carl 195
d'Orléans, Duchesse 180

INDEX

Orphic cults 80
Osborne, Sarah 88
Ovid 162

Pacetus 81
Page, Sir Richard 47
Palm d'Aelders, Etta 142
Palmer, R.R. 103
Palumbo 218
Papin, Christine and Léa 2, 233–7
Papinian 92
Paris Commune 112, 142, 150, 153, 166
Paris Parliament 33, 105
Paris, University of 18, 20
Parr, Catherine 51–3
parricide 177–8, 186
Parris, Samuel 88
Pascal, Blaise 150, 162
Paschasius, Roman consul 37
patricide 72, 74
Paul, Saint 19, 21
Pausanias 81
Pé de Louësmes, Comte and Comtesse 77, 162
Peete, Louise 250
Percy, Lord Harry 42, 43, 48
Perkins, William 30
Pétain, Marshall 6
Peter, Saint 40
Pétion 114, 120, 147, 148, 154, 170
Phillip II of France 12
Phillips, Wendell 6
Phipps, Margaret 89
Phlipon, Gatien 145, 146, 151
Phlipon, Marguerite, *née* Bimont 144, 145
Picard, Mathurin 33
Picasso, Pablo 191
Pidansat de Mairobert 158
Pigray, Pierre 32
Pirot, Abbé 75
Pisan, Christine de 209
Pius X, Pope 221
Plutarch 110, 111, 145, 153, 230
Poe, Edgar Allan 185
Poitou, women of 179
Pole, Margaret, Countess of Salisbury 54
Polignac, Mme de 125, 126
Pompadour, Marquise de 160, 162
Poole, W.F. 24
Poulenc, Georges 2, 109, 229; *Dialogues des Carmélites* 2, 215, 229

pregnancy and execution 8, 95–6, 98, 118, 140, 167, 174, 182, 251
Pritchard, John Laurence 23, 78, 99, 250
Proctor, Elizabeth 88
Proctor, John 88
prostitutes and execution 166–7
Protestantism 23, 59, 84, 89
Provence, Comtesse de 131
Puritanism 85–6, 89

Quakers 86–7
quartering (penalty of) 1, 9, 47, 71–2
Quérhoënt, Mme de 181

Rabelais 59
Racine 222
Rais, Gilles de 13, 16
Ravaillac, François 223
Raynal, Abbé 111, 120
Reagan, Ronald 122
Reformation 23, 45
Regnart, a painter 117
Renaissance 12, 36, 41, 57, 109, 185, 219, 243
Renault, Cécile 176–7, 178, 181
Restif de la Bretonne, Nicolas 133
Revolutionary Tribunal 109, 118–19, 121–2, 130, 140, 141, 145, 157, 171, 176, 181, 183
Ricci, Corrado 66, 67–72
Riccio, David 60
Richard, Mme 117, 175
Richelieu, Duc de 160–1
Riedel, Carl 10, 80
Robert-Kéralio, Mme 142
Robespierre, Augustin 178, 181
Robespierre, Maximilien 104, 112, 113, 118, 129, 135, 138, 147, 151, 170, 171, 173, 174, 176, 178, 180–1, 182, 183, 221, 247
Rochford, Lady 50
Rochford, Lord George 47
Roederer, *procureur-syndic* 78, 142
Rohan, Cardinal de 125
Rohan-Chabot, Duc de 164
Roland, Chevalier 22
Roland, Eudora 146, 153, 156
Roland, Marie-Jeanne, *née* Phlipon 2, 109, 120, 132, 133, 138, 144–57, 158, 166, 167–8, 172, 173, 183, 244, 245; childhood and education of 144; disillusioned with religion and sex 145; disillusioned with revolution

271

152; executed 155–6; federalism and 148–9; Girondin ministry and 148–9; imprisoned 153–4; married to Roland 146; revolution and 147; September massacres and 150–1
Roland de la Platière 144–53, 156
Roman Law 7, 10, 11
Romance 9–10, 22, 41, 45, 92, 185, 202–3, 215, 241
Romani, Felice 211–13, 217
Romanticism 201–4, 211–23, 241
Ronsard, Pierre de 58, 59, 61
Ronzi di Begnis, Giuseppina 218
Rosalie, a maid 129
Rossini 218
Rouget de l'Isle 139
Rousseau, Jean-Jacques x, 110, 111, 114, 124, 137, 145, 171, 200, 201
Rousseau de Lacombe, Guy du 91
Roux, Paul de 149, 151
Russian Revolution 230

Sachs, Maurice 191
Sackville-West, Vita 12, 14–16, 18, 21
sacrifice 101, 245–7; Druids and 91; scapegoat theory and 244–7
Sade, Marquis de 13, 245, 246; *Aline et Valcour* 245
Saint-Amaranthe, Mme de 178
Saint-Just 136, 178, 180, 183
Saint-Louis 8,
Saint-Pern, Mme, 182
Saint-Saëns 190
Sainte-Beuve 145, 152
Sainte-Croix, Captain Gaudin de 73–4
Sainte-Sévère 16
saints, Christian 37–41, 57; beheading and 37, 38, 39; Bernanos and 227, 230; chastity and 37–41, 57; guillotining of statues 7; nobility of 39–40; pagan lust and 37–8; Roman prefects and 37–9
saints in Genet 242
Sanson, Charles-Henri 5, 40, 41, 83–4, 95, 104–6, 110, 117, 118, 130, 141, 155, 156, 166, 168, 174–6
Sanson, Henry 245
Sanson family ix, 5,
Sanson *Memoirs* 83, 179
Santacroce, Cardinal 67
Santacroce, Ersilia 67
Sartre, J.-P. 120
Sauceron, Perrine 32

Schama, Simon 103, 116, 120, 126, 131, 149, 150, 166–7
Scheherazade 3–4
Schiller, Friedrich 2, 200–3, 204, 207, 215–17, 219, 223, 241; *Maid of Orleans, The (Die Jungfrau von Orleans)* 200–3; *Maria Stuart* 215–17, 223, 241
Schlöndorff, Volker 230
Schmidt, Tobias 105
Schopenhauer 245
Scober, James 28
Scott, Sir Walter 213
Scottish Maiden (execution machine) 1
seduction 92; as crime 92; literary treatment of 99–101
Seghers, Anna 208–9, 211
Seneca 26
September massacres 112, 121, 138, 139, 150, 170, 172, 244
Sere, Anna del 218
Sérilly, Mme 182
Servan 104, 149, 152
Sévigné, Mme de 74–5
Sévin, Claire 167
Sextus Tarquinius 81
sexual crimes 247
Seymour, Edward, Lord Protector 53, 54, 57
Seymour, Jane 44, 45, 49, 50, 52, 64
Seymour, Lord Thomas 54–5
Shakespeare, *Henry VI Part One* 13, 162, 200
Shaw, George Bernard 12–15, 202, 204–6, 208, 209, 211, 241; ironic treatment of canonisation 206; *Saint Joan* 204–6; superbity as tragic flaw 205
Shelley, Mary 69, 219
Shelley, Percy Bysshe 66, 69, 219–23, 224; *Cenci, The* 66, 219–23, 241; feminism of 220
Shirer, William 78
Sicily, Queen of 16
Simon, a gaoler 128, 173
Simon, Rita James 251
Sitwell, Edith 41–2, 47, 50, 64–5, 212
Sixtus V, Pope 67
Smeaton, Mark 47
sodomy 1, 12; as buggery 46, 47
Sogner 218
Solera, Temistocle 203
Sophocles 81, 185–90, 191, 195, 241;

INDEX

Ajax 81; *Antigone* 185–90, 191, 241; clash of individual and state 186; Fascist distortions of 194–5; punishment and structure 187–8; Sophocles' female heroine 189–90; *Oedipus at Colonus* 185, 190; *Oedipus Rex* 185
Spee, Friedrich von 33
Spoleto, Maria di 67–8
Spooner, Bathsheba 98
Spooner, Joshua 98
Sprenger, James 24–6
Staël, Mme de 135, 184
Stanton, Elizabeth Cady 6
Starkey, Marion 85, 89–91
Steane, J.B. 214
Steegmuller, Francis 190–1
Stendhal 1, 2, 66
Storr, F.A. 189
Stuart, Mary, Queen of Scotland 41, 57–66, 217, 218, 219, 243, 244; authenticity of Casket letters 61; betrothal to Dauphin Francis 58; birth and coronation of 57; birth of son 60; chivalry and 59; claims English throne 58; contrast with Elizabeth 65; education in France 58; escapes from Lochleven 61; executed 62–4, 66; focus of plots 62–3; imprisoned in England 62–3; literary treatment of 215–17; marriage to Darnley 60; martyrdom and 63; operatic treatment of 217–19; possible complicity in murder 60–1; raped by Bothwell 60; returns to Scotland 59; tried 62
Summers, Montague 23, 24, 27, 36, 41, 84–5, 87
Swedenborg 21
Swinburne, A.C. 219
Szasz, Thomas 21, 35, 36, 87, 245–6, 248

Tabouillot, Claire 175
Talbert d'Arc, Jeanne 227
Talbot, Sir John 17
Talleyrand 111
Tarot cards 80–1, 83
Tasso 145
Tchaikovsky, *The Maid of Orleans* 204
Teresa of Avila, St 13
Terror, the 109, 118, 151, 165, 170, 181, 184, 243, 244, 245
Tertullian 93

Thérèse of Lisieux, St 227, 230
Thery, Dr 174
Third Estate 135
Thorndike, Sybil 219
Thousand and One Nights, The 2–4, 247
Tifero, Jesse Joseph 249
Tiquet, Angélique 76–7
Tiquet, Claude 76
Tisset, Citizen 108
Tituba, a slave 88
Tomalin, Claire 143
Tour du Pin, Mme de la 123
Tour du Pin, M. de la 128
tragedy 185–95, 200–203, 242
Travitzky, Betty 52, 57, 61
Tronçon-Ducoudray 140
Troyes, Chrétien de, *Perceval* 10
Tudor, Mary, Queen, daughter of Henry VIII 45, 46, 53, 55, 56, 58
Tudor, Mary, sister to Henry VIII, later Duchess of Suffolk 42, 52
Turgot 106

Valentinian I 94
Vallin, Pierre 24
Vandenyvers, bankers 164–5
Vassiltchikov, Princess Marie 78
Vatrin, Hélène 175
Verdi, Giuseppe 2, 203–4, 218; *Giovanna d'Arco* 203–4 as *Orietta di Lesbo* 204
Vergniaud, Pierre 112, 147, 148
Vesta, goddess 37
Vestal Virgins 7
Vigée-Le Brun, Elisabeth 131, 163
Villiers, Marc de 141–3
Villon, François 162
Virel, Mme de 121
Virgin Mary 180
Voltaire, François-Marie Arouet de 32, 94, 104, 114, 140, 145, 162, 171, 197–203, 241; assaults on Joan's virginity 198; attacked by church 200; *Maid of Orleans, The* (*La Pucelle d'Orléans*) 198–200, 241; satire of Holy Inquisition 199

Wagner, Richard 10, 80,
Walsingham, Sir Francis 62–3
Walter, Gérard 141, 156, 169
Walting, E.F. 187–9
Warhol, Andy 249
Warnicke, Retha M. 45–8, 65, 212

INDEX

Webster, Mary 87–8
Weidmann, Eugene 234
Weigel, Helen 207
Weston, Sir Francis 47
Weyer, Johann 32
White, Helen C. 40
Willett, John 194
Williams, Charles 13–14, 25–6, 28
Williams, Helen 179
Williams, Neville 42
Winthrop, John 86, 97
witchcraft 13, 14, 21, 24, 23–31, 34–6, 85–91, 203; copulation with devils and 25–6; female hysteria and 34; healing arts and 29–31; in New England 85–91; Inquisition and 26; medical profession and 30–1; midwifery and 29; pricking and 28; sabbath and 29; sorcery or heresy and 28; torture and 27; troubadours and 197

Wollstonecraft, Mary 136, 143, 145, 179, 220
Wolsey, Cardinal 42–4
Wotan 80
Wriothesley, Chancellor 51–2
Wyatt rebellion 56

Xaintrailles 16

Yourcenar, Marguerite 84, 230–3, 241, 242; *Coup de Grâce, Le* 230–3; *Memoirs of Hadrian* 232; *Oeuvre au noir, L'* 232; *homme obscur, Un* 84

Zillman, Frau 78
Zimmer, Pauline 78
Zweig, Stefan 2, 59–61, 63, 65, 121–4, 129, 161
Zwingli, Ulrich 54